Global
Intellectual
History

Columbia Studies in International and Global History

Columbia Studies in International and Global History

Matthew Connelly and Adam McKeown, Series Editors

The idea of "globalization" has become a commonplace, but we lack good histories that can explain the transnational and global processes that have shaped the contemporary world. Columbia Studies in International and Global History will encourage serious scholarship on international and global history with an eye to explaining the origins of the contemporary era. Grounded in empirical research, the titles in the series will also transcend the usual area boundaries and will address questions of how history can help us understand contemporary problems, including poverty, inequality, power, political violence, and accountability beyond the nation-state.

Cemil Aydin, *The Politics of Anti-Westernism in Asia: Visions of World Order in Pan-Islamic and Pan-Asian Thought*

Adam M. McKeown, *Melancholy Order: Asian Migration and the Globalization of Borders*

Patrick Manning, *The African Diaspora: A History Through Culture*

James Rodger Fleming, *Fixing the Sky: The Checkered History of Weather and Climate Control*

Steven Bryan, *The Gold Standard at the Turn of the Twentieth Century: Rising Powers, Global Money, and the Age of Empire*

Heonik Kwon, *The Other Cold War*

Global

Intellectual

History

EDITED BY

Samuel Moyn & Andrew Sartori

COLUMBIA UNIVERSITY PRESS *NEW YORK*

Columbia University Press
Publishers Since 1893
New York   Chichester, West Sussex
cup.columbia.edu
Copyright © 2013 Columbia University Press
Paperback edition, 2015

Library of Congress Cataloging-in-Publication Data
Global intellectual history / edited by Samuel Moyn and Andrew Sartori.
pages cm. — (Columbia studies in international and global history)
Includes bibliographical references and index.
ISBN 978-0-231-16048-3 (cloth : alk. paper)—ISBN 978-0-231-16049-0
(pbk. : alk. paper)—ISBN 978-0-231-53459-8 (e-book)
1. Intellectual life—Philosophy. 2.   Civilization, Modern—Philosophy.
I. Moyn, Samuel, author, editor of compilation. II. Sartori, Andrew,
1969– author, editor of compilation.
CB358.G56 2013
306.4'2—dc23
2012042114

Cover design: Catherine Casalino
Cover image: © haveseen – Fotolia.com

References to Web sites (URLs) were accurate at the time of writing.
Neither the editors nor Columbia University Press is responsible for URLs
that may have expired or changed since the manuscript was prepared.

Contents

Part III. Concluding Reflections

Preface

This volume began with a conference with the same title, which took place on April 9 and 10, 2010. The conference was held under the auspices of the New York area's Consortium for Intellectual and Cultural History, with generous funding and logistical assistance from New York University's Erich Maria Remarque Institute. For making the event possible, the editors thank Katherine Fleming, Tony Judt, and Jennifer Ren.

For the participation in this enterprise at the conference, or later, of Thomas Bender, Manu Bhagavan, Federico Finchelstein, Suzanne Marchand, Walter Mignolo, Timothy Roberts, Dominic Sachsenmaier, Jerrold Seigel, and Gary Wilder, the editors also are grateful.

In between the conference and the volume, the Columbia University Press editorial staff smoothed the way, with special thanks to our acquiring editor Anne Routon, her assistant Alison Alexanian, and the four anonymous readers they commissioned for their astute guidance.

Having much more pressing local business than the exploration of global intellectual history promised, our families—Amy, Alisa, Lily, Izzie, and Madeleine—did not help with this book but deserve our thanks anyway, with love and affection.

Global
Intellectual
History

Part I

A Framework for Debate

1

Approaches to
Global Intellectual History

SAMUEL MOYN AND ANDREW SARTORI

Among the last decade's most notable developments in the historians' guild has been a turn toward "global history." The roots
of global history are older, in different tendencies in international history to strain beyond its usual diplomatic agents or in world history
to make into approved topics the transnational flows of populations,
diseases, and goods. But the citizens of the post–Cold War world,
at least in some places, conceived of themselves as living in an age
of "globalization" and pushed this trend to impressive heights.[1] The
field of intellectual history, however, has lagged behind, although its
objects of study—thinkers and concepts—were presumably some of
those most amenable to spread across vast geographical spaces.

There are a few reasons for this lag. In the North Atlantic academy,
intellectual history has been, and to some extent remains, marginal
to the historical discipline. But it also may have had good reason to
avoid the trend. Scholars working on the classic areas of this field,
western Europe from antiquity to the present, may have felt that this
turn beyond the nation hardly affected the practice of a field that had
stayed relatively free of the lures of national history in the first place.
Early modernists had long been aware of a transnational "republic
of letters," and modernists were often most interested in what Karl
Mannheim called the "free-floating" intellectual, among whose other

traits was to address larger communities or even travel between them. Meanwhile, with the exception of historians of the early modern Atlantic world, the smaller group of scholars focusing on the intellectual history of the United States maintained a sense of their enterprise as beleaguered in an era of ascendant social history, leading them to stick to the defense of intellectual and cultural history framed in terms of conventional spatial boundaries. If they remained wary of the usual study of American national history, it was not because it was too culturally or geographically parochial. In fact, when one intellectual historian, Thomas Bender, tried to take U.S. history past the global turn, his own home subfield was not given much prominence.[2]

More recent signs, however, suggest that there will be a "global intellectual history" just as transformative for this part of the discipline.[3] When a new journal for the field emerged in 2004, entitled *Modern Intellectual History* without any geographical designator, its main mission was still to unify practitioners of the European and U.S. intellectual fields. This same journal, however, likewise shows that the turn to "global history" has now begun to influence intellectual history quite significantly.[4] In a parallel development, historians of science have woken up to the global percolations of the theories they once studied in drastically restricted geographical locales.[5] More important, as pioneering examples of a global concept history begin to be published, the question now is not whether such ventures will take place but what models they will feature and what is at stake in choosing among them. The problem is far more one of theory than one of practice, for posing the difficulty (evidentiary, linguistic, professional, and so forth) of enacting a global history depends, first, on developing plausible models of what the subject matter of such a historiography ought to be.

A Gallery of Alternative Models

Global Intellectual History is intended to showcase the available choices at a threshold moment in the possible formation of an intellectual history extending across geographical parameters far larger than usual. This chapter offers an analytical orientation to the different possible approaches, versions of most of which are then defended by the individual contributors. This orientation then moves to the issue of chronology and the definition of the global itself. Is a premodern global history possible? Even today are there not spaces on the earth that fall outside the networks of social life and intellectual circulation but whose inclusion is required for a truly global framework? Whatever model of global intellectual history is adopted must be tailored to the spaces across which, from era to era, concepts could appear. But it may even be that the expansive space that is today called "the global" has never really existed.

The answer to these kinds of questions depends substantially on how the global is conceptualized as a scale, and there are several nascent approaches that need to be distinguished, for purposes of analytical clarity even if in practice they might overlap. We might begin by distinguishing among, first, the global as a meta-analytical category of the historian; second, the global as a substantive scale of historical process, and hence a property of the historian's subject matter; and third, the global as a subjective category used by historical agents who are themselves the objects of the historian's inquiry. With this in mind, we might then identify different versions of these three modes of the "global" in global intellectual history. Consider, first, universal history and comparative history. Then there are the various approaches that emphasize intermediating agents or modes of circulation, or else theories of larger structural transformations (Marxism, notably) that allow for new conceptual movement or networking practices. Each of these approaches has its own lineage, either in older forms of what were, in effect, global intellectual histories or in other historiographies. Finally, and for this reason, it is sometimes thought to be fruitful to take a second-order approach that, without directly addressing how to study global intellectual history now, insists on historical perspective as a first step to gain purchase on that problem. After all, far-flung spaces have long been subject to theorization and interpretation in different times and places, notably as an outcome of the colonization of the world.

Universal and Comparative History

In the early modern period, Europeans moved to craft a "universal history." Ethnographic encounters, comparative philology, and archaeological discovery made this step unavoidable, challenging and ultimately overturning biblical models that were seen to be too constricted in their geographical and chronological parameters. Of course, early modern Europeans did this in ways that frequently left them "in the grip of sacred history," with the terms of biblical salvation history barely transformed to accommodate threatening data. The most famous figure to emerge from these traditions, G. W. F. Hegel, produced a version of universal history that placed an extraordinary premium on the role of thought in organizing and driving forward the unfolding of a world history.[6]

Hegel himself might have ended the narrative of the self-realization of "reason in history" with the European state, but others carried the project forward to examine the implications for other parts of the world of the claims of European modernity to universality. An example is Joseph Levenson's *Confucian China and Its Modern Fate*, which examines the crisis of China's classical claims to civilizational universality in the face of modern Europe's higher universalism. For Levenson, the Hegelian supersession of Chinese by Western universalism forced Chinese intellectuals into choosing between the radical embrace of modern universalism or a new traditionalism, in which tradition was valued for its particularity rather than its universality. A global history was already implicit here: Confucian China's fate would be the fate of the nonmodern non-West everywhere as institutionally or culturally contingent rationality was forced to come to terms with the better reason of the modern West. Such an approach was also implicit in much of the area studies and developmentalist work of the postwar period in the United States, and it still has adherents today. This tradition of idealist universal history is alive and well and not just in the controversial propositions of Francis Fukuyama. Extremely sophisticated philosophers like Robert Pippin have proposed reconstructing Hegel's claim about the specificity of modern society as a unique realization of freedom.[7] It also forms the central reference point in "Casting the Badge of Inferiority Beneath Black Peoples' Feet," by Mamadou Diouf and Jinny Prais, chapter 9 in this volume. They explore the ways in which black intellectuals have challenged the parochialisms of Hegelian universal history to find a place for both Africa and black people in a reconstituted and cosmopolitan universal history.

Alternatively, a global intellectual history might compare intellectuals or intellectual practices or ideas and concepts geographically or chronologically. In such an enterprise, the point might be to elaborate on processes or tendencies that developed on a global scale or to use comparison to elaborate on the different processes or tendencies that developed in different parts of the world or in different eras. Indeed, in a minimal conception the idea of a "global intellectual history" might be seen as merely a call to create a more inclusive intellectual history that respects the diversity of intellectual traditions and broadens the parameters of thought beyond the narrow limits defined by the traditions institutionalized in the Western or Eurocentric academy. In other words, this would be a call to attend to non-Western intellectual histories with a rigor commensurate with the scholarship on Western intellectual histories.[8]

If the project of a "total history" could divide the world according to the dominant cereal staple, or the frontier between sedentary and nomadic societies, parallel historical analyses organized around repeating themes or transitions could similarly be developed around the intellectual world, as in Siep Stuurman's "Common Humanity and Cultural Difference on the Sedentary–Nomadic Frontier," a comparative study of Herodotus, Sima Qian, and Ibn Khaldun, chapter 2 in this volume. In this approach, "the global" is first and foremost an analytical category in the space of the analysis itself; that is, a comparison treats particular cases as distinct and separate in order to establish them as commensurable and hence comparable. What makes the approach global is not the geographical spread of the concept or thematic but the fact that a comparison between geographically constrained spaces is possible even without a connection between them. Stuurman, for example, does not suggest that the three figures in his study were influenced by or otherwise connected to one another. Indeed, a direct influence or connection between them might even muddy the terms of comparison.

Put differently, the global scale of the enterprise is established by the intention of the investigator and the terms of the investigation. It is not an actor's or native category, nor does it depend on specific historical conditions of interconnectedness on which many of the other approaches focus. This does not mean that we could not make a case that historically specific forms of connectedness provide an epistemo-logical foundation for specific kinds of comparison. For example, we could conceive of "uneven development" as a historically specific basis for the comparison of nationalist discourses in different parts of the world and, indeed, for the emergence of comparative consciousness within nationalist discourses in different parts of the world.[9] Indeed, in order to set the terms of comparability, some meta-analytical cat-egories are required, and they will almost certainly be historical, such as "civilization," "nation," "urban culture," and "literary tradition." Yet the comparison, as in Stuurman's chapter, could also proceed from such general categories without much notice of their historical condi-tions of possibility and could certainly be used as a basis for investiga-tion without regard to more specific arguments about the development of global space as a practical reality. Any loss to the enterprise from not historicizing the possibility of comparison could perhaps be offset by gains in the revelation of striking parallels and distinctive points between compared locales.

For example, one popular topic for comparative intellectual history both old and recent is the development of "science." In the aftermath of Joseph Needham's famous and controversial attempt to determine why ancient China never developed modern science—with Confucian-ism once against taking the blame, together with other factors like the nature of the alphabet—G. E. R. Lloyd more recently compared ancient Greek and Chinese natural thinking.[10] Even though he is a historian of science, Lloyd develops a more general notion of "sys-tematic inquiry" that allows the comparison of drastically different systems of knowledge without judgment as to the relative success or failure of either side to anticipate or lay the groundwork for modern approaches. Lloyd's comparative study—which supposes no historical connection between his geographical scenes—offers an example of a history in which the historian provides the global forum after the fact in order to clearly distinguish the unique characteristics of its different sectors. Offering his own term of art for the object of comparison, pre-sumably in order to skirt the whole problem of how two disparate and disconnected intellectual cultures could develop a comparable intel-lectual practice, Lloyd suggests that a global juxtaposition offers many opportunities for new interpretations.

Intermediaries, Translations, and Networks

A global intellectual history might be less concerned about establishing the parameters of a global scale of inquiry—in either a Hegelian or a comparative sense—than about insisting on an implicit holism according to which cultural, social, linguistic, civilizational, or geographical boundaries are always occupied by mediators and go-betweens who establish connections and traces that defy any preordained closure. Contrary to claims of the incommensurability of cultures, this approach could be used to show how individuals crossing seemingly insurmountable borders learned how to make intellectual cultures mutually intelligible.

Such intermediation might even undermine the assumption that these cultures could be conceptualized as discrete in the first place.[11] In one version, the story of intermediating travelers could focus on their inability to transcend culturally the borders they cross physically; Edward Said's *Orientalism* (1978) is the classic example of this approach. But far from seeing a global forum created or lived through travel, this version of intermediation actually reinstates the notion of a parceled system with noncommunicating domains. In the more generous approach, linked to either assumptions about the conditions of hermeneutic intelligibility or the deconstructive impulse to undo oppositions between cultures, intermediation is singled out for its more positive ramifications.

Typically, of course, such studies never use the global as a direct object of analysis. In the most noteworthy accounts of "intellectual migration" in earlier generations, cultural divergence did not need to be thematized beyond the difficulties of language and manners that a European forced to live in America might expect.[12] Today, stories about overcoming conceptual boundaries in the past could be taken as a refusal of spatial closure. They focus the historical investigation on mediators (linguistic, practical, institutional, or material) and go-betweens at the boundaries of conventional units of study—between, say, East and West, or North and South. In the large literature on go-betweens from one culture to another, friendship has taken pride of place as a trope through which to conceptualize intellectual transfer that might otherwise remain too abstract.[13] Such an approach relies on a historically general holism to suggest that intermediaries have always occupied boundaries but would then typically go on to investigate specific practices of mediation in particular times and places. It might even show that particular achievements are possible by acquiring through travel a sharper understanding of what at first seemed distant and strange.

At this point, the literature on travel and migration is sufficiently well developed that new frontiers for exploration have come into view beyond whether their histories illustrate global misunderstandings or intelligibility.[14] In this volume, besides outlining how the historiography of traveling and encountering has developed, chapter 4, "Joseph Banks's Intermediaries," by Vanessa Smith, shows how a tendency to narrate encounter and exchange against the background of literacy and the circulation of printed materials has made theorizing global intellectual history as travel apply to some realms of interaction but not others. Given the pride of place accorded to the early modern period in the historiography of travel, further innovations in the field should be inflected by new histories of transport, which in the nineteenth century, along with technologies of transmission like the mail and telegraph, took a quantum leap.

Smith's critique of the bias toward print does not imply that literacy will become irrelevant to approaches based on travel, encounter, and exchange; language certainly mattered. A somewhat related approach concentrates not on individual mediators but on the linguistic means through which mediation might occur, however distorted in content. A newly popular construction of the global centers on the translation that must occur in personal travel or the disembodied circulation of knowledge. The theoretical presumption in such a move from individuals to their languages is both obvious and forceful: understanding, and therefore conceptual mediation, always takes place in linguistically embodied media that even the most creative and intrepid individuals have not created for themselves. The contact between languages, whether or not geographically contiguous in their usage, is always the contact of two particular languages, each with their own historical trajectories, semiotic ecologies, and hence specific possibilities of mutual translatability. Thus it might be thought that the best way to explore conceptual transmission across wide spaces is to explore translations of key terms or key books from one language to another. On the basis of older forms of reception theory, which had a marked impact on literary study a generation ago, the study of how words and texts from one place were received somewhere else offers one model for forging a global concept history.[15]

Perhaps in part because of the specific challenges of translating from a phonetically written to an ideographically written language (making the older elements from which a neologism was constructed literally visible on the page), and perhaps in part because of the centrality of diplomatic exchange in a region marked by a more ambiguous Western presence than in classical colonial contexts, scholars of East Asia have recently taken the lead in this endeavor. They have helped create illuminating case studies of the creation of what has been called a "global lexicon." As with intermediation, in Said's picture, one premise centering global intellectual history on translation might be incommensurability. In another collection, edited by Lydia Liu, the leader in this approach, the possibility that words and concepts are necessarily "lost in translation" is examined first. The inevitable failure of translation is a crucial element, but even if every translation were in some sense a failure, emphasizing only this ignores that translation still occurs. As Liu argues, while the difficulty or even impossibility of translation is by now a classic philosophical theme, it has not stopped attempts at translation. Nor do historians need a perfect translation of local terms and concepts to examine the renderings that past actors have proposed and their consequences. In practice, the historical study of translations shows how complex and differentiated the continuum has been between the two extremes of the absolute incommensurability of tongues and the perfect achievement of universal communicability.[16]

The global appears in the model of translation in a somewhat different way than in the study of individual travelers and intermediaries. Studies focusing on enactments of crossing borders are typically empirical in emphasis, involving studies of the lives and times of travelers themselves. Yet as a study by Maya Jasanoff of British collectors in the age of empire suggests, the multiplication of vivid examples may lead mainly to the important but simple conclusion that people can be interested in other cultures and other people.[17] The translation model, at least in its recent versions, is less interested in the success of attempts at understanding than in the historical and often power-laden settings of enacted translations. More important, given its focus on collective language use and the generalization of individual coinages or renderings through broad usage, the translation model frequently concludes with visions of language zones, or even the globalization of specific concepts or words across such zones. In this endeavor, as with intermediaries, the global—in Liu's phrase, "world making"—is engaged indirectly on the basis of specific acts of translation. But it also emerges as a space for the percolation of concepts via geographically expansive areas, including the very idea of an "international" arena.[18]

Liu's own studies concentrate on how Chinese intellectuals created equivalences between the Chinese "host language" and European "guest languages." These processes, she proposes, cannot be reduced to the axis of fidelity and infidelity without obscuring the many contextual considerations and political investments that conditioned the formation of specific translative neologisms. The history of "individualism" in Chinese (geren zhuyi), for example, is not marked by consistent antithesis to conceptions of collective life, community, nation, and state. Instead, its lexical history is one of disjunctures and shifts that are more interesting than interrogating the fidelity of the rendering into Chinese may suggest but that are nevertheless central to the process of producing translated equivalents.[19]

For others, however, an emphasis on translation as a practical site of mediation is still too narrow, requiring a conflation of word and concept and thereby reinstating the closure of linguistic systems. Instead, it is the circulation of concepts and their material vehicles across a space defined by a multiplicity of translations, each circumscribed by a preceding history of translations, that makes up the unified conceptual field of a global intellectual history. Christopher Hill's "Conceptual Universalization in the Transnational Nineteenth Century," chapter 6 in this volume, argues that the work of translating the concept of, say, "rights" from English into Japanese cannot be adequately grasped without first recognizing that the concept of rights had itself been elaborated through a long history of earlier translations that rendered it irreducible to the lexical specificity of one language or the contextual contingencies of one national or regional history. The

moment of translation between English and Japanese cannot be iso-
lated from the larger circulation in which it is located. This means that
the emphasis on moments of translation, along with its assumptions
about discrete linguistic and cultural domains, begins to give way to a
more comprehensive emphasis on a wider process of the universalization of concepts across linguistic boundaries.

Investigating the circulation of intellectual concepts or their bear-
ers in global space is related to emphasizing the role of intermediaries
or the media of translated languages through which they typically
work.[20] In a general sense, we might say that the interest in intermediation and translation is merely a variation on the interest in
circulation (or perhaps vice versa) but that circulation insists on the
necessity of a wider investigation than any single point of interface.
Networks promise such a broader approach.

A basic and empiricist version of the network model concentrates
on recovering the topography of the network and tracing its construction, spread, and functionaries. As with the famous cases of historical commodity networks, from cotton to ostrich feathers, the norm
for network histories of ideas are studies that use far-flung knowledge
brokers—in a sense, a plurality of intermediaries—to understand the
development of a single concept, tradition, or ideology. A comparison
of different monotheisms demonstrates the importance of establishing the details of a model of networking circulation in each case. In
rabbinic Judaism and (especially Sunni) Islam, the authority of a single text around which very loosely integrated local groups coalesced
manifested the modalities of geographical expansion from Near Eastern origins, while in Christianity, newly converted groups and Chris-
tianized territories were inducted into a more integrated ecclesiastical
hierarchy.[21] Politics (including war) certainly played a role in determining the size, shape, and structure of the religious network across
vast spaces, but intraintellectual factors also counted for much. In
fact, this example suggests some limits to translation as a generally
applicable model, for until the Reformation and its vernacularization
of the Bible allowed "Christendom" to mean something other than the
expanse of the universal church, all three monotheisms grew and traveled in part through the preservation of a higher, "sacred" language
that often was barred from translation into local media.[22] The general

point is that a series of intellectual, institutional, and political factors conditioned the features of the proprietary networks through which particular traditions of thought traveled. To skip ahead to contemporary times for another example, scholarship has recently been devoted to reconstructing transnational networks propagating theories from existentialism to neoliberal economics.[23] Perhaps it is not too much of a stretch to classify ambitious and high-profile recent histories of specific literary genres—the novel, most prominently—with all the geographical unevenness and temporal staggering they reveal, as part of this style of global intellectual history.[24]

At a slightly higher level of ambition are works that aim to reconstruct the topography of general networks through which sets of ideas (on the analogy of the creation of markets for goods in general) could travel. A classic site of investigation here—though rarely framed in terms of global intellectual history—is the early modern European "republic of letters."[25] No doubt future historians will approach the creation of the Internet in similar terms. But investigations of circulation typically turn on stronger claims about the historical constitution of patterns of interconnectedness: "webs," "networks," and so on. If studies of intermediaries tend to center on established spatial or cultural boundaries to look at their points of contact, studies of circulation tend to look at the specific connections that constitute spatial continua in disjunctive cultural, linguistic, or geographical spaces. Within those chains of interconnectedness, historians might show how ideas or texts travel through the book market or through expansive intellectual networks. They might emphasize the connectedness of disparate sites or emphasize the disjunctures that interrupt the continuity between disparate sites. A text like Adam Smith's *Wealth of Nations* might have had a different significance in the many places to which it traveled, so a global intellectual history might try to disaggregate a history of that text's multiple receptions in the face of its apparent unity.[26]

In the end, for this kind of investigation to count as a specifically global intellectual history, a much stronger sense of the practical significance of interconnectedness must be assumed. The strongest claims to such an approach thus have hinged on the category of "globalization." Unlike intermediation or even local forms of translation, which need to focus only on the crossing of a localized border, conceptions

of circulation frequently set up large-scale structures of multidirec-
tional and delocalized cultural transfer. Of course, interconnectedness
itself might be conceptualized in quite different ways: as a result of a
European colonialism with world ambitions; or of the construction of
an international system; or of the intertwining of multiple networks
of trade, communication, transportation, military engagement, and
diplomacy; or of the historical development of capitalist society.

Two examples dramatize the conceptions of global interconnection
that scholars have been willing to entertain (and they also illustrate the
problem of the chronological specificity of such webs of intellectual connection, a topic discussed later in this chapter). Sanjay Subrahmanyam
has written extensively on the "connected histories" of the sixteenth
and seventeenth centuries: a world composed of a patchwork of extensive, competing empires mutually engaged with one another politically,
economically, and (of greatest interest to him in his more recent work)
intellectually, as, for example, in his essay on the sixteenth-century
circulation of millenarian themes from Europe to Southeast Asia.[27] For
Subrahmanyam, the period from the mid-fourteenth through the mid-
eighteenth century was an age of travel and discovery and represented
a crucial moment in which a global imagination and a nascent "modernity" (i.e., "early modernity") emerged, not as the continued unfolding of a privileged European trajectory spreading out in ever widening
concentric circles from the Mediterranean to the Atlantic and thence to
the Indian Ocean and the rest of the world, but as "a more or less global
shift, with many different sources and roots, and—inevitably—many
different forms and meanings depending on which society we look at it
from." The dynamic between the "local and regional" and "the supraregional, even the global," in which the circulation of cultural forms was
generated from several sites neither systemically integrated nor culturally insulated, was already a key characteristic of this era.[28] From this
perspective, Subrahmanyam has been as interested in the connections
between South Asia and Central Asia as in exchanges between the non-
West and the West. His interest in the latter axis is in the non-Eurocentric organization of an early modern world that resists the conventional
scholarly impulse to universalize the parochial insights of European
traditions of modern social theory and most existing macrohistorical
paradigms.[29]

Subrahmanyam's work notwithstanding, the most seductive cases for a "global intellectual history" conceived as transmission across a worldwide scale tend to unfold in modern circumstances. (Indeed, "global" approaches to circulation skew toward modern histories, that is, toward a period in which patterns of interconnectedness have deepened enough to be deemed global.) In his work on the American Declaration of Independence, David Armitage offers an impressive version of the conventional diffusion from European (or Atlantic) metropoles to other places infected by the "contagion of sovereignty."[30] Armitage does not spell out his theoretical assumptions or lay out the principles of this diffusion. Although he collaborated with Subrahmanyam in examining the global trajectories of ideas in the revolutionary ferment at the close of the early modern period, Armitage's "global history" of the Declaration operates—at least with respect to the idea of state sovereignty and the international order of which it became the chief building block—in a frankly modernist key and according to a trickle-down model.

In Armitage's approach, a "global history" involves noting the appearances of an idea starting from its American ground zero to its invocation later and elsewhere. Armitage's study lacks the empirical specifics of establishing a network of cultural interconnections, and it also does not discuss whether later invocations garbled the original message. But the case history of sovereignty provides a striking example of global diffusion that illustrates the need for an account of how otherwise very different groups of intellectuals across the globe opt in modern times to organize their politics in terms of an idea that had previously been absent from the world. While we might doubt its modernist presumptions and inquire about the means by which circulation occurs, Armitage's account seems to leave no doubt that some sort of explanation is needed for the mobility of concepts, one that neither the activities of personal intermediaries nor even the specific processes of linguistic translation can fully illuminate on their own.

The Global in Intellectual History

A global intellectual history might study the emergence of a consciousness of and conceptions of the global scale as itself a problem of intellectual history, or at least as a precondition for developing a sophisticated theory of the global against the backdrop of prior theorizations. Such an approach might look into the history of spatial imaginations, mapping, world pictures and representations of the globe, or the history of cosmopolitanisms. In one sense, such an approach represents the far extreme from comparison in that it treats the global as a native or actor's category—a concept that belongs to the archive and is itself the object of investigation, rather than as a meta-analytical category belonging to the investigator. But from another view, since even the briefest reflection makes clear that the global scale has been imagined historically in many different ways, the intellectual history of conceptions of the global is nevertheless fully commensurable with comparative inquiry, so that we might undertake comparative analyses of spatial concepts. Duncan Bell's "Making and Taking Worlds," chapter 11 in this book, considers the ways in which conceptions of "the global" were "world making" insofar as they reconstituted the horizons of universality.

As Sheldon Pollock demonstrated, there is no need to presume modernity in order to begin comparing the universalistic—and, in a sense, global—worldviews of various traditions.[31] The point is not so much that cosmopolitanism has ancient roots (as the history of the term itself implies) as that different cultural and textual traditions have linked the premise of common humanity to wildly different institutional bases and schemes of power. Once again, however, stories about intellectual "globalization" as the rise of *consciousness of* the globe overwhelmingly favor modern circumstances, as Armitage's account of internationalization through the rise of a mature system of linked states suggests.

That one commits to studying the globe as an actor's category does not preempt decisions about whether then to study that category in terms of intermediaries, translation, or networks. In Pollock's approach, which compares Sanskrit with Latin cosmopolitanism and emphasizes the different politics to which each led, the linguistic embodiment afforded by vernacularism counts for much, whereas for Armitage the creation of "the international" is more a story of the intellectual breakthroughs that led to today's vision of an order composed of states as building blocks (though allowing for debates about their transcendence in regard to core norms). The success of Pollock's brand of global intellectual history founded on comparison, however, makes it difficult to imagine the evolutionary stories of the rise of global consciousness favored in certain traditions of liberal political philosophy that celebrate the rise of universalism or by pundits for whom the world is finally flat.[32] Instead of a tale of asymptotic progress toward closer and closer approximation with the geographical earth, studies of actor's categories center on deciphering how contextual factors predominate. In a sense, this historiography recovers the eternal localism of globalism. In this volume, Bell's case of the later nineteenth century's "Anglobalization" is an example of global intellectual history as the study of evolving and historically situated conceptions of the global as actors entertained them, and the effects of such transformations on the imagined limits of political feasibility.

An emphasis on the intellectual history of conceptions of the global might serve as a supplement or complement to substantive investigations of the global processes of the various kinds we have been discussing. But—especially given the understandable emphasis on local ideological conditioning of delocalizing visions—the investigation of global consciousness as a native category (i.e., as a category used by people in the time and place of study) can also assume a critical relation to such histories, most notably when it takes the form of a critique of the global as a colonial category.[33] The postcolonial scholarship that flourished in the past three decades proceeded from a deep suspicion of (classically, Hegelian) metanarratives that enfold global history into the history of the modern West. Here, the native category "global" is treated as an artifact of the history of European colonial violence, and the invocation of the globe is unveiled as a discourse of domination that produces commensurability and homogeneity by excluding other (subaltern) voices. As Dipesh Chakrabarty put it, "'Europe' remains the sovereign theoretical subject of all histories, including the ones we call 'Indian,' 'Chinese,' 'Kenyan,' etc."[34] From this perspective a threefold problematic is implied for any global intellectual history: a refusal to allow the global scope of particular colonial claims to obscure the local scope of their enunciation; a rigorous interrogation of the conception of the "global" as a category of colonial exclusion; and the opening of historical investigation to forms of "otherness" that exceed and disrupt the parameters of the uniformity, commensurability, and coherence of global space and time. In this volume, Janaki Bakhle's "Putting Global Intellectual History in Its Place," chapter 10, voices this line of critique.

For Chakrabarty and others, the discipline of history is bound to the theoretical sovereignty of a hyperreal "Europe." This is not the real Europe with all its complexities but the imaginary Europe of the social sciences and humanities that has so often figured as the model and vehicle of progress, development, reason, and modernity and has thus served as the measure of the relative successes and failures of all other peoples' histories. As a consequence, to unveil the violence implicit in conceptions of the global requires an investigation of the theoretical foundations of historical discourse and the recovery of nonhistorical forms of temporality. But the same broad postcolonialist impulse might also tend toward an insistence, in the context of the surging interest in global histories in many parts of the world, on the need to pluralize the voices producing intellectual history. In this way, a global intellectual history would be realized not at the level of the object of study but at the level of the profession itself, in which the inequitable distribution of institutional power and authority stands as the single biggest obstacle to overcoming Eurocentrism.[35]

Even as they challenge the notion of the global as, in the first instance, an artifact of imperial domination, postcolonial approaches have also broached the possibility of what we might call subaltern internationalisms or globalisms. If the globe has been an actor's category, it has not only been one for the colonizers—as Cemil Aydin, Bakhle, and Diouf and Prais all emphasize in their chapters. Indeed, it might be thought most constructive to respond to the colonialist lineages of the global by recovering resistance to the concept that reincorporated it. In a sense, this approach would extend Subrahmanyam's insistence that global intellectual history is not simply the study of dissemination from the West to the rest, but across spaces that do not match current maps of power. In another sense, it proceeds from a recognition of the unequal distribution of power characteristic of the modern world of capitalism and colonialism to seek out transversal attempts by subaltern intellectuals to gain momentum for its unsettling from below.[36] In one form, this approach points toward alternative forms of universalism. While often labeled as a "derivative discourse" with origins in ill-conceived mimicry, anticolonial nationalism did not involve simply the modular reproduction of a Western model (as in Armitage's work on sovereignty, at least apparently). It also created rival visions of the globe with which to displace colonial and neocolonial ones. In this volume in chapter 7, "Globalizing the Intellectual History of the Idea of the "Muslim World," Cemil Aydin develops an account of pan-Islamism as an alternative internationalism and a counteruniversalism that challenges the privileging of itineraries of conceptual movement that have Western origins.[37]

Chronology and the Problem of Modernity

As important as the what of global intellectual history is the when. Broadly speaking, we might say that there are three approaches: always, sometimes, and never. And crucially, it turns out that the model of studying ideas across large geographical spaces is always inflected by assumptions about the appropriate chronology for doing so.

The claim that no global space has ever existed is best to start with, for it follows from the postcolonialist worry about the historical entanglements of the notion of global space. The postcolonialist approach, after all, sows suspicion about whether the scale of the global has ever been a practical reality in any sense that warrants treating the category of the global as anything other than a native category. "Behind the globalization fad," Frederick Cooper argued,

> is an important quest for understanding the interconnectedness of different parts of the world, for explaining new mechanisms shaping the movement of capital, people, and culture, and for exploring institutions capable of regulating such transnational movement. . . . It is salutary to get away from whatever tendencies there may have been to analyze social, economic, political, and cultural processes as if they took place in national and continental containers; but to adopt a language that implies there is no container at all, except the planetary one, risks defining problems in misleading ways. The world has long been—and still is—a space where economic and political relations are very uneven.[38]

Here we have a more empiricist iteration of the postcolonialist suspicion of claims about the global, and what this suspicion implies above all is that there is no global intellectual history to be written except at the polar extremes of comparison and native categories, because a truly global level of integration has never taken place.

By itself, this suspicion leaves unexplained the proliferation of the global as a native category and attempts to see it operative in any era. But it does provide a bulwark against confusing the subjective appeal of the concept of the global (to historical subjects and to ourselves as historians) with the actuality of a global intellectual history, a conflation that can distract from the specific vectors of movements and connection that organize the world unevenly and discontinuously. From this perspective, there is only a history of how people, including historians, have imagined the global, but no history of the global as such.

How radical a claim the opponent of global inquiry wants to make is unclear, however. Students of large-scale intellectual phenomena should be aware of the lumps and gaps that disrupt any assumption they might make about space as an even medium of transmission (whether through intermediation, translation, or networks). Samuel Moyn's "On the Nonglobalization of Ideas," chapter 8 in this volume, makes a related point in insisting that various historically specific episodes of globalization of concepts will inevitably be selective, favoring some notions and traditions with success even as others fail. But caution about how comprehensive "globalization" ever was is not incompatible—as Cooper himself acknowledges—with the transformations of intellectual history that the contributors to this volume describe. Is there a better term than "global" for this collection of disparate enterprises? After all, we might take "global" as denoting not the achievement at any time of a fully global space for concepts or thinkers but simply the methodological concern with experimenting beyond familiar geographical boundaries (and without, at the same time, imposing some other boundaries, like regional, continental, or intra-imperial). If the Scylla to be avoided is the fiction of a space for historical practice that is not itself constituted in some way, then the Charybdis is unreflectively incorporating, as a matter of methodology, geographical constraints that are both historically contingent and descriptively false. For now, anyway, the first error seems much less pervasive than the second, and so the designation "global" is a good reminder that no one knows, without investigating, the geography of any idea in historical practice, even if its geography will never be "everywhere."

At the other extreme from the denial of the reality of global space at any point are universal history, comparative history, and some kinds of histories of intermediaries. For Hegel, world history is the product of the self-realization of reason in history, meaning that world history is the end product of history rather than its presupposition. But all of human history has been leading up to the realization of history on a global scale, that is, the history of human freedom in modern circumstances. In this case, the whole historical process always stands as an object of inquiry *retrospectively*, even if not for past historical agents. In comparative history, to the extent that the global is understood to be a meta-analytical category for the investigator, the global is a transhistorical category insofar as it can be applied to any historical epoch, regardless of whether that epoch imagined the global or lived it in any practical sense. This commitment to a transhistorical notion of the global—at least for retrospective analytical purposes—might be qualified with the recognition that the form of inquiry is itself historically conditioned, whether by the dialectical development of reason in the philosophy of history or, as Manu Goswami contends, by the structures of uneven development that make comparison unavoidable in the age of developed capitalism. But even if it is available only for an investigation beginning in a specific era, global intellectual history singles out a domain that could be investigated in any epoch, regardless of whether its own actors were aware of global space. Finally, an emphasis on intermediaries can certainly be applied indiscriminately across time and space, since there can be little doubt that intermediaries have always straddled the boundaries of social spaces through history. But this idea does leave open the question of whether such intermediation is quantitatively and qualitatively constant or variable and whether such intermediaries always constitute an open-ended web whose traces are exhaustive enough to imply a default holism.

In between the never and the always are many possibilities. Whether it is Alexander in India, Egypt in Greece, Buddhists on missions, the Mediterranean world, the Silk Road, the transcontinental extension of the Mongol Empire, or the Islamic trading world, it is easy to imagine a version of global intellectual history that looks to the histories of interconnectedness for an object of investigation. Such a history might follow a kind of Smithian logic of the extension of the market, in this case, the market of ideas. But such a *longue durée* approach need not assume the smooth contours of Adam Smith's developmentalism; instead, it might be episodic or disjunctive. But such a history would presumably try to complement the renewed interest in the histories of transcivilizational and transcontinental networks with the intellectual historian's specialist inquiries. Subrahmanyam is exemplary here.

But any *longue durée* history will ultimately have to confront the intensification of interconnectedness (global or otherwise) in the early modern and modern period. For this reason, most intellectual history inclining toward a global scale of inquiry, but not specifically comparative in approach, tends to lean toward the early modern and modern period. In this volume, Sheldon Pollock's approach in chapter 3, "Cosmopolitanism, Vernacularism, and Premodernity," resists a modernism that otherwise dominates global intellectual history (including perhaps in this volume). Likewise, Subrahmanyam's insistence on the early existence of the fully global does, too, but there are obvious reasons why global intellectual history so far has made the deepest inroads in modern studies. Implicit in this modernist bias is the sense that the global is a more plausible and significant scale of historical process in the modern period than in earlier times, whether starting in the "age of discovery" and the "age of commerce" in the sixteenth century, as in Subrahmanyam's explorations of "connected histories"; in the era of colonialism, imperialism, and developed capitalism in the eighteenth or nineteenth centuries; in the anticolonialism and global nation-state formation in the late nineteenth and twentieth centuries; or even, as in Arjun Appadurai's account of recent cultural globalization, in the globalized multilateral cultural flows that began only in the 1980s.[39] In a series of provocative recent works exemplifying this last and narrowest chronological frame, Faisal Devji offers close readings of Al-Qaeda as a movement that, unlike its Islamist forebears like the Egyptian Muslim Brotherhood, selectively draws on abstracted elements of Islamic tradition to articulate an essentially ethical protest. This, in combination with its decentralized organization and its lack of commitment to any determinate state-form or political vision, draws it close to environmentalism, antiglobalization activism, and human rights movements, that is, to the globalized "landscapes" of the post–Cold War world in which it operates as an agent of globalization whose partisans work hard to give their practices planetary significance.[40]

Some scholars would argue that the interconnectedness that makes possible a global intellectual history focused on the scale and velocity of circulation has been not only intensified in the modern period but also qualitatively transformed. Approaches to global interconnectedness that turn on the category of capitalism, however, need to be further disaggregated from general approaches to networked circulation, in part because they insist on the chronologically modern circumstances of the subject matter. A Marxian approach to global intellectual history, for example, would be inclined to consider phenomena of circulation as part of, or symptomatic of, wider processes of social transformation operating beyond practices of circulation.

Andrew Sartori's recent book and chapter 5 in this volume, "Global Intellectual History and the History of Political Economy," outline this perspective.[41] In this Marxian global intellectual history, circulation as a general historical phenomenon must be distinguished from circulation specifically in a capitalist society, to the extent that in a capitalist society, circulation is bound to practices of generalized commodity production. In the same way, the sorts of premodern universalism that Pollock and others emphasize need to be distinguished from the modern, emancipatory cosmopolitanism on which both liberalism and Marxism center. As such, Marxian global intellectual history might be expected to be concerned with the material and practical conditions for the mobility and transposability of concepts theoretically identified with the historically specific practices of a capitalist society. The question for such an approach is not merely the channels that make mobility possible but also the social transformations that make specific intellectual practices and concepts plausible and meaningful across large spatial extensions.

Conclusion

Following a trajectory from Hegel to Marx, these introductory thoughts are intended to highlight what sorts of alternative models come into view when we think beyond either the idealistic ambience of older stories of "reason in history" or the more recent fashion of globalization in order to insist on the necessary union of theoretical preconception and empirical detail. On the one hand, despite the ventures sketched here, it is a moment of early planning and primitive construction for the field of "global intellectual history." Yet on the other hand, the alternatives that historians might use in framing projects and organizing data already have begun to come into view. No presentation of theoretical choices structuring a nascent field now can obviate the necessary research or anticipate what theoretical modifications will be needed as that research suggests new ways of conceptualizing the field. But debates about rival models, and contending presumptions about chronology, are already clear enough to allow us to reflect on which paths into the global seem most promising—if the trip makes sense at all.

One understandable response to an emphasis on theoretical alternatives is that different ones suit different problems. Choose your historical topic, the assumption goes, and the theory and method will follow, although we could also say that the choice of historical topic follows from the historian's theoretical presuppositions. Historians interested in fascinating individuals may have a defensible bias in the direction of intermediaries. Given their proclivities and expertise, literary scholars may gravitate toward translation. And the rare historians with a soft spot for social theory may worry about whether the autonomy of the intellectual realm across borders can be defended if it is not linked to social practices generally.

Our reason for presenting a gallery of different approaches is not to insist that readers pledge allegiance to a single one while smashing the others. It is likely to be the proliferation of models for global intellectual history, as applied to new sources, that drives the field forward. But this attitude conceals its own moment of complacency, insofar as the different models are based on different and mutually exclusive assumptions about the nature of ideas, the conditions of their geographical spread, the distinctive character of modernity, and, ultimately, how scholarship can transcend description in the service of explanation. Conceptual rigor is a necessary prerequisite to more forceful, and sharply conceived, research agendas—and it cannot be expected to arise from the practice of empirical research itself. For this reason, at a moment when basic choices lie before the field (including whether to construct such a field at all), it seems wise to pause in order to identify, compare, and contrast basic options so as to make clear both the possible paths forward and the presuppositions underlying each of them.

Notes

1. See, for example, C. A. Bayly et al., "*AHR* Conversation: On Transnational History," *American Historical Review* 111, no. 5 (2006): 1440–64; and the *Journal of Global History*, started in 2006.

2. Even though he has no chapters on intellectual history in his landmark collection (Thomas Bender, ed., *Rethinking American History in a Global Age* [Berkeley: University of California Press, 2002]), intellectual notions do figure in recent syntheses that offer global perspectives, including Bender's own *A Nation Among Nations: America's Place in World History* (New York: Hill & Wang, 2006).

3. For some early tentative thoughts, see the forum in the *Journal of the History of Ideas* 66, no. 2 (2005), entitled "Intellectual History in a Global Age." Sociologists and political scientists (notably in the recent literature on so-called global norm-diffusion) have thematized these issues for some time. But as might be expected, their penchant for modeling without regard for reconstituting the intricacies of the past has made no impact on the historical enterprise. In sociology, see Pierre Bourdieu, "On the Social Conditions of the International Circulation of Ideas," in *Bourdieu: A Critical Reader*, ed. Richard Shusterman (Malden: Blackwell, 1999), 220–28; and Randall Collins, *The Sociology of Philosophies: A Global Theory of Intellectual Change* (Cambridge, Mass.: Belknap Press, 1998).

4. On South Asian intellectual history, see the following forums: Shruti Kapila, ed., "An Intellectual History for India," *Modern Intellectual History* 4, no. 1 (2007): 1–171; and Faisal Devji and Shruti Kapila, eds., "The Bhagavad Gita and Modern Thought," *Modern Intellectual History* 7, no. 2 (2010): 269–457.

5. James A. Secord, "Knowledge in Transit," *Isis* 95, no. 4 (2004): 654–72; and the landmark forum in *Isis* 101, no. 1 (2010), notably Sujit Sivasundaram, "Sciences and the Global: On Methods, Questions, and Theory," 146–58; as well as Marwa Elshakry, *Reading Darwin in the Middle East* (Chicago: University of Chicago Press, forthcoming).

6. For some orientation on universal history and its transformations, see Adalbert Klempt, *Die Säkularisierung der universalhistorischen Auffassung: Zum Wandel des Geschichtsdenkens im 16. und 17. Jahrhunderts* (Göttingen:

Musterschmidt, 1960); and Tamara Griggs, "Universal History from the Counter-Reformation to the Enlightenment," *Modern Intellectual History* 4, no. 2 (2007): 219–47. On Hegel's historicism, see Michael N. Forster, *Hegel's Idea of a "Phenomenology of Spirit"* (Chicago: University of Chicago Press, 1996), part III; and Terry Pinkard, *Hegel's Phenomenology: The Sociality of Reason* (Cambridge: Cambridge University Press, 1994). On the claim about the persistence of biblical scripts, see Karl Löwith, *Meaning in History: The Theological Implications of the Philosophy of History* (Chicago: University of Chicago Press, 1949); Daniel Smail, "In the Grip of Sacred History," *American Historical Review* 110, no. 5 (2005): 1337–61; and Robert Pippin, *Modernism as a Philosophical Problem: On the Dissatisfactions of European High Culture* (Malden: Blackwell, 1999), 25–28.

7. Joseph R. Levenson, *Confucian China and Its Modern Fate: A Trilogy* (Berkeley: University of California Press, 1969); Carl E. Pletsch, "The Three Worlds, or the Division of Social Scientific Labor, circa 1950–1975," *Comparative Studies in Society and History* 23, no. 4 (1981): 565–90; Francis Fukuyama, *The End of History and the Last Man* (New York: Free Press, 1992); Pippin, *Modernism as a Philosophical Problem*.

8. John Dunn, "Why We Need a Global History of Political Thought" (unpublished manuscript). Compare the *Thesaurus Linguae Sericae*, a massive online project of *Begriffsgeschichte* focused on classical Chinese, available at http://tls.uni-hd.de/ (accessed October 2011).

9. See notably Harry D. Harootunian, *Overcome by Modernity: History, Culture and Community in Interwar Japan* (Princeton, N.J.: Princeton University Press, 2000); Rebecca E. Karl, *Staging the World: Chinese Nationalism at the Turn of the Twentieth Century* (Durham, N.C.: Duke University Press, 2002); Manu Goswami, *Producing India: From Colonial Economy to National Space* (Chicago: University of Chicago Press, 2004); and the collection of essays in *boundary 2*, 32, no. 2 (2005), a special issue on comparability edited by Harry Harootunian and Hyun Ok Park.

10. G. E. R. Lloyd, *The Ambitions of Curiosity: Understanding the World in Ancient Greece and China* (Cambridge: Cambridge University Press, 2002). In an earlier study along the same lines, Lloyd more boldly compared the two as scenes of science. See G. E. R. Lloyd, *Adversaries and Authorities: Investigations into Ancient Greek and Chinese Science* (Cambridge: Cambridge University Press, 1996).

11. See Homi Bhabha, *The Location of Culture* (New York: Routledge, 1994).

12. Laura Fermi, *Illustrious Immigrants: The Intellectual Migration from Europe, 1930–1941* (Chicago: University of Chicago Press, 1968); Donald Fleming and Bernard Bailyn, eds., *The Intellectual Migration: Europe and America, 1930–1960* (Cambridge, Mass.: Belknap Press, 1969); and Martin Jay, *Permanent Exiles: Essays on the Intellectual Migration from Europe to America* (New York: Columbia University Press, 1986).

13. Leela Gandhi, *Affective Communities: Anticolonial Thought, Fin-de-Siècle Radicalism, and the Politics of Friendship* (Durham, N.C.: Duke University Press, 2006); and Vanessa Smith, *Intimate Strangers: Friendship, Exchange and Pacific Encounters* (Cambridge: Cambridge University Press, 2010).

14. See, for example, Kumkum Chatterjee and Clement Hawes, *Europe Observed: Multiple Gazes in Early Modern Encounters* (Lewisburg, Pa.: Bucknell University Press, 2008); Harry Liebersohn, *The Traveler's World: Europe to the Pacific* (Cambridge, Mass.: Harvard University Press, 2006); Simon Schaffer et al., eds., *The Brokered World: Go-Betweens and Global Intelligence, 1770–1820* (Sagamore Beach, Mass.: Science History Publications, 2009).

15. The key text was Hans-Robert Jauss, *Towards an Aesthetic of Reception*, trans. Timothy Bahti (Minneapolis: University of Minnesota Press, 1982).

16. See Lydia H. Liu, ed., *Tokens of Exchange: The Problem of Translation in Global Circulations* (Durham, N.C.: Duke University Press, 1999), part I, "Early Encounters: The Question of (In)commensurability"; and Lydia H. Liu, *The Clash of Empires: The Invention of China in Modern World Making* (Cambridge, Mass.: Harvard University Press, 2004). The more recent collection, Carol Gluck and Anna Lowenhaupt Tsing, eds., *Words in Motion: Towards a Global Lexicon* (Durham, N.C.: Duke University Press, 2009), focuses more on the distinctive local meanings of words that would presumably interfere with their filtration into a context-transcendent "global lexicon."

17. Maya Jasanoff, *Edge of Empire: Lives, Culture, and Conquest in the East, 1750–1850* (New York: Knopf, 2005).

18. Liu, *Clash of Empires*.

19. Lydia H. Liu, *Translingual Practice: Literature, National Culture, and Translated Modernity. China, 1900–1937* (Stanford, Calif.: Stanford University Press, 1995). See also Douglas R. Howland, *Translating the West: Language and Political Reason in Nineteenth Century Japan* (Honolulu: University of Hawai'i Press, 2002).

20. See, for example, Mark Gamsa, "Cultural Translation and the Transnational Circulation of Books," *Journal of World History* 22, no. 3 (2011): 553–75.

21. See, for example, F. E. Peters's various comparative histories, such as *Judaism, Christianity, and Islam: The Classical Texts and Their Interpretation*, 3 vols. (Princeton, N.J.: Princeton University Press, 1990).

22. Compare the complicated status of written classical Chinese as a medium of intellectual exchange between literate Chinese and Japanese down to the nineteenth century: Douglas R. Howland, *The Borders of Chinese Civilization: Geography and History at Empire's End* (Durham, N.C.: Duke University Press, 1996).

23. See Jennifer Ratner-Rosenhagen, *American Nietzsche: A History of an Icon and His Idea* (Chicago: University of Chicago Press, 2011); Martin Woessner, *Heidegger in America* (Cambridge: Cambridge University Press, 2010);

Angus Burgin, *The Great Persuasion: Reinventing Free Markets Since the Depression* (Cambridge, Mass.: Harvard University Press, 2012); and Philip Mirowski and Dieter Plehwe, eds., *The Road from Mont Pèlerin: The Making of the Neoliberal Thought Collective* (Cambridge, Mass.: Harvard University Press, 2009).

24. The project developed as Franco Moretti hoped to place his own story of the European genre in global perspective by lengthening the chronology and calling on international research teams to fill out the story of the novel's imitators and propagators. Compare Franco Moretti, *Atlas of the European Novel, 1800–1900* (New York: Verso, 1999); and Franco Moretti, ed., *The Novel*, 2 vols. (Princeton, N.J.: Princeton University Press, 2007). Stanford University, where Moretti taught, even founded the Center for the Study of the Novel to trace transnational percolation. See also Christie McDonald and Susan Rubin Suleiman, eds., *French Global: A New Approach to Literary History* (New York: Columbia University Press, 2010).

25. Recently an entire online journal, *Republics of Letters*, was begun for the early modern topic, including Anthony T. Grafton's "A Sketch Map of a Lost Continent: The Republic of Letters," *Republics of Letters* 1, no. 1 (2009), available at http://rofl.stanford.edu/node/34 (accessed March 2012). See also such works as Peter N. Miller, *Peiresc's Europe: Learning and Virtue in the Seventeenth Century* (New Haven, Conn.: Yale University Press, 2000); and Pamela H. Smith, "The Movement of Knowledge in the Early Modern World," in *Cultures in Motion*, ed. Daniel Rodgers et al. (Princeton, N.J.: Princeton University Press, forthcoming).

26. Emma Rothschild, "Arcs of Ideas: International History and Intellectual History," in *Transnationale Geschichte: Themen, Tendenzen, Theorien*, ed. Gunilla-Friederike Budde, Sebastian Conrad, and Oliver Janz (Göttingen: Vandenhoeck & Ruprecht, 2006), 217–26.

27. Sanjay Subrahmanyam, "Connected Histories: Notes Towards a Reconfiguration of Early Modern Eurasia," *Modern Asian Studies* 31, no. 3 (1997): 735–62.

28. Ibid., 737, 745.

29. Sanjay Subrahmanyam, "Historicizing the Global, or Labouring for Invention," *History Workshop Journal* 64, no. 1 (2007): 329–34.

30. David Armitage and Sanjay Subrahmanyam, *The Age of Revolutions in Global Contexts, ca. 1760–1840* (New York: Palgrave Macmillan, 2009); David Armitage, "'The Contagion of Sovereignty': Declarations of Independence Since 1776," *South African Historical Journal* 52, no. 1 (2005): 1–18; and, for the claim about American priority, David Armitage, *The Declaration of Independence: A Global History* (Cambridge, Mass.: Harvard University Press, 2006), 103. See also C. A. Bayly and Eugene Biagini, eds., *Giuseppe Mazzini and the Globalisation of Democratic Nationalism, 1830–1920* (Oxford: Oxford University Press, 2008); and C. A. Bayly, *Recovering*

Liberties: Indian Thought in the Age of Liberalism and Empire (Cambridge: Cambridge University Press, 2012).

31. Sheldon Pollock, *The Language of the Gods in the World of Men: Sanskrit, Culture, and Power in Premodern India* (Berkeley: University of California Press, 2006).

32. For an account that begins with comparative cartographical practices and then argues for an early modern breakthrough to authentic human universalism, see John H. Headley, *The Europeanization of the World: On the Origins of Human Rights and Democracy* (Princeton, N.J.: Princeton University Press, 2007).

33. Harry Liebersohn's recent study of the Europe's "rediscovery" of gift exchange of its (colonial) periphery does not make clear whether this is a global history because gifting practices were imported from abroad or because the colonial situation allowed exotic cultures to become a screen for fantasmatic projection. See Harry Liebersohn, *The Return of the Gift: European History of a Global Idea* (Cambridge: Cambridge University Press, 2011).

34. Dipesh Chakrabarty, *Provincializing Europe: Postcolonial Thought and Historical Difference* (Princeton, N.J.: Princeton University Press, 2001), 27.

35. See Dominic Sachsenmeier, *Global Perspectives on Global History: Theories and Approaches in a Connected World* (Cambridge: Cambridge University Press, 2011).

36. See, for example, Sugata Bose and Kris Manjapra, eds., *Cosmopolitan Thought Zones: South Asia and the Global Circulation of Ideas* (Houndsmills: Palgrave Macmillan, 2010); Kris Manjapra, *M .N. Roy: Marxism and Colonial Cosmopolitanism* (Delhi: Routledge India, 2010); Nico Slate, *Colored Cosmopolitanism: The Shared Struggle for Freedom in India and the United States* (Cambridge, Mass.: Harvard University Press, 2012).

37. Compare Cemil Aydin, *The Politics of Anti-Westernism in Asia: Visions of World Order in Pan-Islamic and Pan-Asian Thought* (New York: Columbia University Press, 2007).

38. Frederick Cooper, *Colonialism in Question: Theory, Knowledge, History* (Berkeley: University of California Press, 2005), 91–92.

39. Arjun Appadurai, *Modernity at Large: Cultural Dimensions of Globalization* (Minneapolis: University of Minnesota Press, 1996).

40. Faisal Devji, *Landscapes of the Jihad: Militancy, Morality, Modernity* (Ithaca, N.Y.: Cornell University Press, 2005); Faisal Devji, *The Terrorist in Search of Humanity: Militant Islam and Global Politics* (New York: Columbia University Press, 2008).

41. Andrew Sartori, *Bengal in Global Concept History: Culturalism in the Age of Capital* (Chicago: University of Chicago Press, 2008).

Part II

Alternative Options

2

Common Humanity and Cultural Difference on the Sedentary–Nomadic Frontier

Herodotus, Sima Qian, and Ibn Khaldun

SIEP STUURMAN

This chapter examines concepts and discourses about common humanity and cultural difference in the writings of Herodotus (Greek world, fifth century B.C.E.), Sima Qian (Han China, around 100 B.C.E.), and Ibn Khaldun (Islamic North Africa, fourteenth century C.E.), focusing on their discussion of the interactions among the sedentary civilizations, to which they themselves belonged, and the nomadic peoples in the steppe and the desert.[1] This is not a random choice. The steppe peoples inhabited the great band of grasslands extending across Eurasia from the Ukraine to Manchuria. Another frontier traversed North Africa where the desert nomads confronted the sedentary civilization of the Mediterranean littoral. For two thousand years, from the Scythian incursion in Persia in the sixth century B.C.E. to the "partition" of central Eurasia by Qing China and czarist Russia in the Treaty of Nerchinsk (1689), the sedentary–nomadic divide was the great ecological and cultural frontier of the Old World[2] and thus was a major structural feature of world history.

In world history, civilizations are frequently identified as the major indicators of cultural boundaries. From Arnold Toynbee to William McNeill's *Rise of the West* (1963) and beyond, it has been customary to see civilizations as the building blocks of world history. McNeill, however, offered a revisionist view. Although civilizations remained the main units of his narrative, he contended that the endogenous development of civilizations was not sufficient to explain the dynamics of world history. Instead, he posited "that the principal factor promoting historically significant social change is contact with strangers possessing new and unfamiliar skills."[3] Not civilizations per se but the interfaces between them were the linchpin of his explanatory framework. Consequently, frontiers were the engine of history. In his later review of his own work, McNeill questions his initial assumption "that discernibly separate civilizations were the autonomous social entities whose interactions defined history on a global scale."[4] His solution is to make more room for ecumenical processes and transcivilizational flows of people, goods, skills, and ideas.

This raises the question if, and in what terms, we are still justified in speaking of civilizations as world-historical units. Here, McNeill moves from sociopolitical to intellectual history: "A shared literary canon, and expectations about human behavior framed by that canon, are probably central to what we mean by a civilization."[5] This leads me to a related question, not raised by McNeill but crucial to any global intellectual history: How does contact with strangers affect the evolution of a civilization's canon? A cross-cultural encounter implies the acknowledgment of other cultures and other "self-evident" worldviews. Such encounters saddle the guardians of the canon with a novel problematic that can be summarized in just five words: How to conceive of cultural difference?

The canons of civilizations generally originate in religious teachings, mythical stories, didactic and epic poetry, books of wisdom, and philosophy. When encounters with strangers gain greater importance, they lead to the new intellectual disciplines of history, geography, and ethnography. This chapter focuses on these novel trends, with a comparative reading of the sedentary–nomadic frontier by three canonical historians who are far apart in space and time. These historians have been well researched, but almost exclusively in the intellectual contexts of their own civilizations.[6] I will show that beyond their rootedness in their native political and intellectual milieus, they share the problematic of sedentary–nomadic interactions. A reading of Herodotus, Sima Qian, and Ibn Khaldun along these lines enables us to reinterpret and recontextualize their writings, discovering similarities where others have perceived mostly differences.

Thinking Across Frontiers

Basically, there are two ways to think across cultural and ethnic frontiers, which I call *common humanity* and the *anthropological turn.*

By appealing to universal values and human commonalities, notions of common humanity bracket cultural differences. A discourse of common humanity transforms a stranger into a fellow human being. While common humanity seeks to transcend cultural difference by abstracting from it, the anthropological turn concentrates on difference. Whereas common humanity is expressed mainly in the languages of religion and philosophy, the privileged languages of the anthropological turn are history, geography, and ethnography. The anthropological turn becomes thinkable when people discern an intelligible pattern in the ways of strangers, when they seek to understand the customs of strangers as an interlocking and functioning whole instead of a random series of outlandish oddities, and when they begin to imagine how strangers might see them. Whereas common humanity turns a foreigner into a fellow human being, the anthropological turn deconstructs the semantics of "we" versus "them."

In the long run of world history, thinking across cultural boundaries has been far from self-evident. The German Egyptologist Jan Assmann stated that despite their diplomatic exchanges with neighboring peoples, the Egyptians of the Old and Middle Kingdoms could not conceive of an intelligible social order beyond their frontier. Egypt was equated with the ordered world, beyond whose borders lived "absolute aliens with whom any relations would be unthinkable."[7] Against that background, even the portrayal of strangers as "others" with "deviant" customs and ideas is an accomplishment. The emergence of the anthropological turn in histories and ethnographies enables us to see frontiers and borderlands as zones of creative interaction and not only as sites of hostility and prejudice. The widespread adoption of "Othering" and "Orientalism" (or "Occidentalism") as a framework for intellectual history in the past decades makes it easy to overlook the significance of the anthropological turn and has led to an underestimation of the critical and universalistic impulses in "frontier texts."

That people focus on difference and depict the culture of others in a series of contrasts with their own way of life is not in itself very significant. The human mind always seeks to understand the unknown by comparing it with the known.[8] The anthropological turn enables people to make comparisons systematically and self-reflexively. Even those ethnographies that contain negative judgments and stereotypical representations are a first step toward appraising the rationality of foreign cultures. Encounters with strangers can take many forms, from war to cooperation. In this sense, the frontier is the real or imagined locus of rejection and acceptance, incomprehension and mutual understanding. We should bear in mind that this is not an all-or-nothing game. The denial of other peoples' humanity and the recognition of their equality represent two extreme cases, whereas most history is played out on the continuum between the two extremes.

As a rule, common humanity and the anthropological turn coexist in a civilization's discourse on foreigners. Civilizational canons typically appeal to everlasting truths, usually by linking social norms and collective stories and memories to the loftier realms of the cosmic and the divine. In the process, local ideals are transformed into universal concepts and standards of humanity. Virtually all discourses of common humanity include the assumption or the conclusion that all human beings share one or more attributes, origins, faculties, potentialities, or obligations. This assumption enables me to offer a working definition of common humanity that indicates the kind of discourses I am looking for. Accordingly, I define common humanity as *culturally significant similarity*. This definition has the advantage that the qualifier "culturally significant" includes the representational nature of common humanity. Taking the argument further, we can conceive of equal dignity and equality as progressive intensifications of common humanity.

Notions of common humanity usually emerge from a canon's internal logic. As a canon aspires to higher levels of authority and truth and its discourse becomes more abstract and general, it becomes harder to demarcate it geographically. To say that certain ideas and moral imperatives are absolutely true sits ill with the admission that they lose their validity on the other shore of the Black Sea or beyond the Great Wall. The inner logic of philosophical and religious truths pushes them beyond the perimeter of the civilization in which they originated. From "our ways," they are transformed into delocalized truths underpinning an emergent notion of common humanity.

In remote antiquity, when no one was able to draw up an ethnographic map of the entire planet, sages and philosophers sought true knowledge about the human condition that transcended their local communities. When Homer has his storytellers declare that all men must die and that all men need the gods, he is not just telling us how things were among the Greeks and the Trojans. Assertions about the attributes of all humans are always made in local contexts, but their generalizing semantics enable, and frequently push, authors and readers alike to think beyond the confines of their local horizon. Consequently, "imagined humanities" became discursively available long before they could be empirically verified, and even longer before modern globalization.

As a rule, such imagined humanities blended factual and normative discourses. We can illustrate this with an argument about common humanity in the writings of the fourth-century B.C.E. Chinese sage Mencius, one of the founding fathers of the Confucian tradition. Mencius seeks to make a case for empathy as a constituent part of human nature: "My reason for saying that no man is devoid of a heart sensitive to the suffering of others is this. Suppose a man were, all of a sudden, to see a young child on the verge of falling into a well. He would certainly be moved to compassion." According to Mencius, the man's compassion is spontaneous and not based on considerations of self-interest or reputation. "From this it can be seen," he concludes, "that whoever is devoid of the heart of compassion is not human."[9] Here, Mencius appears to be making two claims wrapped up in one. The first one is factual. Empathy with a helpless child in distress is an intuitive and involuntary feeling. No one fails to be moved by a child on the brink of a fatal accident. But Mencius's conclusion shifts to a normative plane, saying that people lacking empathy are not truly human.

The first part of the argument grounds empathy in an ontology of the human. The propensity to compassion is lodged in everyone's heart.[10] But in the second part, Mencius assumes that some people are morally deaf to the cries of an endangered child. Such people, he concludes, are not fully human. Displaying symptoms of moral illiteracy, they are unable to realize their human potential. It follows that Mencius's argument for common humanity is predicated on a dialectic of the factual and the normative. By doing the right thing, people feeling empathy for others realize their humanity. However, the very fact that Mencius makes the case for common humanity in this particular way shows his awareness that, in real life, many people do not do the right thing. He thus tries to convince such people to mend their ways, pointing out that otherwise they will deviate from the *telos* of their real nature.

The Confucian tradition presents a model case of the invention of common humanity. It belongs to the intellectual traditions of the Axial Age, when the privileged languages of common humanity were religion, wisdom, and philosophy. Such languages were abstract and universalizing and thus well suited to express commonalities "beyond" or "behind" cultural difference. What they could not do was supply a language for dealing with contingent historical and geographical differences. The alternatives faced by those who cross frontiers are seldom philosophically straightforward. Instead, travelers in foreign lands have to navigate the dangerous waters of historical contingency. To accomplish that, they need other, more empirically and temporally sensitive, modes of knowledge. It was the frontier experience that gave rise to geography and ethnography. Even so, the religious and philosophical languages of common humanity retained their importance, albeit at one remove. Without any notion of common humanity, the humanity of the stranger would be unthinkable. And yet common humanity is not sufficient to come to terms with the stark reality of cultural difference.

History, Contingency, and the Plurality of Cultures

At one point, Mencius observes that he has heard "of the Chinese converting barbarians to their ways, but not of their being converted to barbarian ways."[11] He thus is aware of the problem of the foreign "other," but he does not pursue it in any detail, and he seems to take

Sino-centrism for granted. It fell to the inventors of the new discourse of history to flesh out the accounts of the "barbarians" beyond the frontier. What is called "history," we should add, usually included a fair amount of geography and ethnography. While the great religions and philosophies of the Axial Age expounded perennial truths, history dealt with the contingencies of time and place.

Next I examine how Herodotus, Sima Qian, and Ibn Khaldun, themselves urban men of letters in sedentary societies, discussed nomadic peoples. The nomads were seen as "other" and were routinely classified as "barbarians," sometimes even as "savages," but they also were redoubtable warriors and indispensible partners on the "Silk Road," the grand highway of Eurasian travel and trade. Contrary to sedentary stereotypes, towns and agriculture also were present in the nomadic orbit.[12] Likewise, the desert nomads discussed by Ibn Khaldun were valiant warriors who protected and guided merchants and other travelers across the Sahara to the thriving Islamic civilizations of West Africa. Both as economic middlemen and in their role as raiders and conquerors, the nomads were appreciated and respected but also feared and despised. Until the eighteenth century C.E., they were major autonomous players in world history. We shall now see how the three historians discussed the nomads and their dealings with the sedentary civilizations.

Herodotus on the Scythians

The Scythians are discussed in the *tour d'horizon* of the known world that Herodotus presents in the first four books of his *Histories*, before he turns to the story of the Persian wars. The tenor of his approach to non-Greeks is set in the opening lines of book I, in which he announces that he wrote his history to record for posterity the "great and marvelous deeds" performed by Greeks and barbarians alike.[13] Herodotus gives equal space and voice to Persians and Greeks, and his portrayal of the Persians, who after all are the enemy in the great war that is the main subject of the book, is remarkably fair.[14] Herodotus deploys the anthropological turn in his lapidary observation that the Egyptians are wont to label as barbarians all peoples who do not speak

Egyptian, and, in a more theoretical mode, in his famous maxim that when asked to select the best customs and laws, all humans choose their own *nomoi* over all others.[15] Ethnocentrism thus comes naturally, but as Herodotus's metatext shows, it is not an iron cage from which there is no escape.[16]

To the Greeks, the nomadic culture of the Scythians inhabiting the steppe north of the Black Sea certainly was more "strange" than Egyptian or Persian customs. In contrast to the Egyptians, the Persians, and the Greeks themselves, the Scythians had few large cities and no writing. We should not, however, overstate Scythian otherness in Greek eyes. Herodotus's Scythian ethnography is serious and open-minded. He observes that most of the peoples of the North are slow-witted but at once makes an exception for the Scythians.[17] In the opening section of the Scythian ethnography, he recounts how they used psychological warfare, displaying an accurate understanding of the role of the imagination in power relations.[18] Herodotus displays a fairly detailed knowledge of Scythian culture, which is not surprising, as there had been Greek colonies on the northern coast of the Black Sea for more than two centuries. The Greeks imported slaves, cattle, wheat, honey, wax, hides, and gold from Scythia and exported wine, olive oil, textiles, and handicrafts.[19] The Scythians admired Greek art and sometimes manufactured copies of it. Greek traders traveled widely in the Scythian interior, marketing art tailored to Scythian tastes. In his classic study of Greco-Scythian contacts, Ellis Minns praises "the energy of the Greek trader who studied the necessities of his barbarian customer and . . . what would be a delight to his eyes."[20] The presence of a police force of Scythian public slaves in fifth-century Athens, where Herodotus lived for several years, is also worth mentioning.[21] Against this background, the issue of the reliability of Herodotus's claim to have visited Scythia himself is of secondary importance.

The second reason for Herodotus's interest in the Scythians is that they were enemies of the Greeks' enemies. Much of book IV is a gleeful account of the Persians' failure to conquer Scythia. This is perhaps the earliest extant analysis of how a regular army can be defeated by guerrilla tactics. The Scythians wisely avoid a direct confrontation with the heavily armed and numerically superior Persian infantry. But the Persians are lured into Scythia, in search of an enemy they cannot find in a land from which they cannot draw sustenance. Herodotus diagnoses their plight as a consequence of the inability of the Persian king, Darius, to understand the functioning of Scythian society. When the Persian army is exhausted by the inconclusive campaign, the Scythians finally dispatch a herald, who brings Darius a gift, consisting of a bird, a mouse, a frog, and five arrows. The king naively interprets these offerings as a surrender of earth, water, and arms, indicating the Scythians' submission. But according to his councillor Gobryas, the Scythian message is not auspicious at all. Instead of an easy victory, it spells Persian doom: "Unless you become birds, Persians, and fly up into the sky, or mice and hide in the earth, or frogs and leap into the water, you will be shot by these arrows and never return home."[22] After further misadventures, Darius is forced to admit that Gobryas is right, and the Persians abandon the campaign, happy to get out alive.

At that juncture, with the Persian army exhausted and vulnerable, the Scythians propose an alliance with the Greek cities of Asia Minor. Now is the time to cripple Persian power once and for good, they argue, but the petty despots of the Greek cities, afraid of the democrats in their midst, refuse the offer. Herodotus gives the Scythians the last word, and the episode concludes with their critique of the Greeks' servile mentality.[23]

By using their nimble and dexterous tactics, relying on mobile homes and fast-moving mounted archers, the Scythians managed to evade and harass the huge Persian war machine. Herodotus sincerely admires their technology of military nomadism, observing that

> the Scythian race [genos, sometimes rendered as "nation"] has in that matter which of all human affairs is of greatest import made the cleverest discovery that we know; I praise not the Scythians in all respects, but in this greatest matter they have so devised that none who attacks them can escape, and none can catch them if they desire not to be found.[24]

Besides military strategy, Herodotus displays a detailed knowledge of Scythian food, clothing, dwellings, animal husbandry, and funeral rites. His acquaintance with Scythian culture is further evidenced by his discussion of their language, mentioning, for example, the Scythian words for snow, for Zeus and the other gods, and their name for the Amazons ("man killers").[25]

Interestingly, Herodotus's only critical observations concern Scythian ethnocentrism. He relates two stories of Scythians, Anacharsis and Skyles, who visited Greece and "went native" there. Back home, when their adoption of Greek religious rites was discovered, both were killed. But ethnocentrism is not presented as a specifically Scythian defect. "They too," Herodotus concludes, are "terribly averse to practice the customs of foreigners."[26] In the final analysis, Scythian parochialism is just another example of Herodotus's maxim about the ubiquity of ethnocentrism.

Herodotus's Scythian ethnography is generally written in an appreciative and respectful manner. He analyzes Scythian society as a functionally interlocking set of customs and techniques, well adapted to military defense and survival in the steppe environment. Admittedly, Herodotus does depict the Scythians as "others," whose way of life is in many respects the opposite of what Greeks would consider normal. Although he is well aware of this, there is no patronizing condescension in his discussion of Scythian culture. In the narrative structure of the *Histories,* an entire book is devoted to the Scythians, placing them on a par with the Persians and the Egyptians. (Herodotus also has fairly accurate information on the caravan trails through the nomadic desert lands of the Sahara.)[27] The Persians, who once assisted in marrying an Assyrian princess to a Scythian king to underwrite a treaty (a gesture that might be read as submissive), likewise regarded the Scythians as greatly different, but probably not as utter savages.[28] Thus, we may conclude, Herodotus depicts the Scythians as starkly different, but he does not theorize the sedentary and the nomadic as higher and lower rungs in a universal cultural hierarchy.

Sima Qian on the Xiongnu

Herodotus was critical of all empires, but Sima Qian regarded the empire as his natural habitat. Unlike Herodotus, the Chinese historian assumed that one central empire should, and perhaps would, dominate "All Under Heaven" in the future. Even so, imperial rule was precarious and fragile. The unification of China by the short-lived Qin dynasty in 221 B.C.E. lay less than a century in the past when Sima Qian was born. The fall of the Qin (210–206) was generally attributed to its Draconian governing methods. The adoption of Confucianism as an authoritative creed by the Han dynasty indicated the search for a style of governance that would penetrate the hearts and minds of the people. Although severe punishments did not disappear, the essence of Confucian political culture is best summarized as "government by means of civilization."

Following in the footsteps of his father, Sima Tan, Sima Qian served as Grand Astrologer under the severe Emperor Wu (r. 141–87). Sima Qian was not, however, a servile court chronicler. Indeed, in 99 B.C.E., he suffered the disgrace and humiliating punishment of castration for questioning the emperor's judgment. Even so, his lifelong vindication of the critical role of historical inquiry cannot be explained by personal resentment. Sima Qian himself justified it with the interpretation of Confucius's *Spring and Autumn Annals* by his older contemporary, Dong Zhongshu. According to Dong, Confucius had "criticized the emperor, reprimanded the feudal lords and condemned the high officials." Sima Qian approvingly cites Dong in the final autobiographical chapter of his history of China.[29] But unlike Herodotus, his claim is expressed in indirect speech.

Against the background of the fall of the Qin, an expansionist policy was fraught with danger. An important faction at the imperial court, to which Sima Qian belonged, feared that the militaristic ethos of imperial expansion, coupled with onerous taxes and conscription, might bring back the Qin's despotic politics. Emperor Wu, however, did not heed such warnings. Instead, he launched major expeditions against the powerful confederation of the Xiongnu, which challenged the Chinese along the Great Wall frontier. For the Chinese, long used to a feeling of cultural superiority, the military resilience of the nomadic federation was hard to swallow. How could those "barbarians," who had neither great cities nor the mastery of writing, wield so much power?

Like Herodotus's *Histories*, Sima Qian's *Shiji* (*Records of the Historian*, written circa 100–90) contains a fair amount of geography and ethnography, culled from official documents and travelers' reports.

Sima Qian himself participated in several expeditions to the Great Wall frontier. Given the strategic issues of the day, it is no wonder that his chapter on the Xiongnu is one of the longest of a very long text. It opens with the observation that the Xiongnu have been "a source of constant worry and harm" to the Han. Accordingly, Sima Qian explains, the empire "has attempted to determine the Xiongnu's periods of strength and weakness." "Thus," he declares, "I made the account of the Xiongnu."[30] On the face of it, this looks like instrumental research in the service of the empire. There follows a concise narrative of Xiongnu history, replete with the negative statements ("they have not . . .") found in so many travelogues about nomadic culture drafted by observers from sedentary societies. At one point, Sima Qian observes that marauding and plundering appear to "come naturally" to the Xiongnu.

Sima Qian's realistic appreciation of the nomads' military strategy and skills is remarkably similar to Herodotus's discussion of the Scythians. Although he does not go quite as far as Herodotus's encomium of military nomadism as the cleverest invention he knew of, Sima Qian also does not revert to the standard "civilized" underestimation of it. Also like Herodotus, he emphasizes that nomadic customs, food, clothing, animals, weapons, and tactics are well suited to the steppe environment. And like Herodotus, Sima Qian is aware of the strategic importance of trade across the frontier. The Xiongnu needed agricultural and artisanal products, while the Chinese were dependent on the steppe for their horses. Sima Qian's Xiongnu ethnography wavers between a censure of their "un-Chinese" ways and an open-minded appraisal, often bordering on grudging admiration of their military aptitude and efficient style of governance. His description of the political organization of the Xiongnu confederation conveys an impression of efficient statecraft rather than primitive bloodthirsty despotism. The confederation's sophisticated combination of central control and decentralized administration was likely to call to mind a contrast with the unwieldy bureaucracy of the Han empire. Admittedly, Sima Qian gives numerous examples of Xiongnu ruthlessness and cruelty, but elsewhere he relates even more instances of similar behavior among the Han.

Sima Qian's critical distance from a naive Sino-centrism is exemplified by the story of Zhonghang Yue, a eunuch sent to the north by

Emperor Wen not long after 174 B.C.E. to accompany a Han princess who was given in marriage to the Xiongnu ruler under the prevailing peace treaty. The court had forced this mission on Zhonghang, and when he arrived, he promptly went over to the Xiongnu side, where he was received with great favor and made a councillor of the ruler. Sima Qian quotes him extensively, first when Zhonghang warns the Xiongnu not to adopt Chinese consumption patterns and second when he refutes a Han envoy's criticism of nomadic customs.

Zhonghang begins by pointing out that the Chinese vastly outnumber the nomads (the ratio was something like fifty to one). Nonetheless, the Xiongnu can withstand and sometimes prevail against Han power because their way of life is well adapted to warfare and the steppe environment. He also warns the nomads not to adopt Chinese tastes and luxuries, using as an example the utter uselessness of Han silk robes when riding on horseback "through the brush and brambles." In the long run, Chinese luxuries would sap the military virtues underpinning Xiongnu power. The eunuch highlights the dangers of luxury to a militarized society, an argument showing some affinity with later European explanations of the fall of the Roman Empire.

Thus far, the eunuch has stressed mainly the perils of Sinification. In his refutation of the Han envoy, however, he offers a critique of Han society from a Xiongnu perspective. The envoy had condemned the nomadic custom of giving the best food and clothing to their young men, thus showing insufficient respect for the aged. Zhonghang retorted that the Han did the same in wartime, and the envoy had to admit that such was indeed the case. Well, Zhonghang argued, since warfare is the main business of the Xiongnu, the allotment of the best nourishment and clothing to the young, who bear the brunt of the war effort, is appropriate: "The young men are willing to fight for the defense of the nation, and both fathers and sons are able to live out their lives in security. How can you say that the Xiongnu despise the aged?"[31]

The eunuch goes on to explain that the nomads are well provided with everything they need and actually have more leisure time than the common people among the Han, who toil unceasingly in hardship and poverty. In answer to the envoy's objections to the Xiongnu "un-Chinese" marriage code, Zhonghang explains that its purpose is to guarantee the growth of the population and to safeguard the preservation of the clans, so that the ruling families will stand firm and stay together in turmoil and war. He follows this with a searing critique of Han society:

> In China, on the other hand, though a man would never dream of marrying his stepmother or his brother's widow, yet the members of the same family drift so far apart that they end up murdering each other! This is precisely why so many changes of dynasty have come about in China! Moreover, among the Chinese . . . enmity arises between the rulers and the ruled . . . although danger threatens, the Chinese people are given no training in aggressive warfare, while in times of stability they must still wear themselves out trying to make a living. Pooh! You people in your mud huts—you talk too much!
> . . . Just because you wear hats, what does that make you?[32]

In this fascinating passage, Sima Qian seems to be telling his readers that if an intelligent and unprejudiced Chinese man were to familiarize himself with the "barbarian outlook" on the world, this is how he might judge it.

Elsewhere, he remarks that the lifestyle of other nomads resembles that of the Xiongnu and that the Wusun, who live in the western part of Inner Asia, fear and respect the Xiongnu but hardly think about distant China.[33] Such a "global" perspective, showing that not everyone believes that China is the center of the world, might teach the Han some modesty. Zhonghang Yue's cultural self-transformation is in itself a highly significant psychological argument, and it literally punctures Mencius's assertion that he has never heard of Chinese adopting barbarian ways. In Sima Qian's narrative, the eunuch is the most striking, but by no means the only, instance of such border crossing. Sima Qian has Zhonghang Yue invert the standard Han discourse in a similar way that Herodotus attributes to "the Egyptians" when he reports that they called all people who did not speak Egyptian "barbarians." The historian's empathetic treatment of the Xiongnu is all the more striking considering that they were China's greatest enemies. Nicola di Cosmo thinks it likely that Sima Qian (like Herodotus) "might have been regarded as a 'barbarophile' by contemporaries."[34]

The point of this story is that there are no good reasons for the Xiongnu to become "civilized" along Chinese lines, and very good reasons not to do so. Consequently, cultural pluralism is an enduring feature of history. For Sima Qian, this is perhaps regrettable, and elsewhere he muses about a future when all peoples in the world will long for China, but even so he understands quite well that the barbarians are there to stay.

Ibn Khaldun and the Sedentary–Nomadic Dialectic

In Ibn Khaldun's time, the mid- and late fourteenth century C.E., Berber dynasties ruled the Maghrib. It is noteworthy that the word Berber is derived from the Latin *barbarus*.[35] In the eleventh century, Arabian geographers described the Berbers, using time-worn stereotypes of nomadic life, as people "who do not know of ploughing . . . their property consists only of camels and they live on flesh and milk."[36] Ibn Khaldun uses the term *badw* (sometimes translated as "Bedouin"; a thirteenth-century Arabic-Latin dictionary published in el-Andalus translates the adjective *badawi* as *rusticus*, i.e., "belonging to the countryside").[37] The similarity to ancient sources on the steppe nomads is apparent, but we shall see that Ibn Khaldun's understanding of the "Bedouin" is less stereotypical than the ancient view. His concept of *badiya*, often translated as "desert," refers to the "open country outside of towns" and the various modes of social organization, a "continuum of rural and nomad ways of living."[38]

Like the Scythians and the Xiongnu, the Berbers managed to form powerful tribal federations. Some of them became military commanders in the service of the dynastic states of the Mediterranean littoral, while others gathered commercial wealth and finally adopted urban culture. Moreover, they converted to Islam, making them equal partners in the *ummah* with the descendants of the Arab invaders. The Berbers' military power was crucial to the rise of the Fatimid caliphate in the tenth century, and the first real Berber dynasty was the Almoravids in the twelfth century. Henceforth, Berber dynasties, often involved in bloody internecine struggles, ruled the Maghrib. This was the setting of Ibn Khaldun's political career in the mid-fourteenth century.

Before he started writing his history, Ibn Khaldun was employed as adviser, minister, and military recruiter for various Berber princes. While raising troops among the desert tribes, he gained firsthand experience of nomadic life. He learned the lessons of politics the hard way: his autobiography tells a grim story of political infighting, treason, conspiracies, coups d'état, disgrace, imprisonment, participation in hopeless battles, and a nearly hopeless fight for survival in the desert.[39] Not unlike Machiavelli, Ibn Khaldun felt the need to retire and reflect on the deeper historical patterns beneath the incessant alternation of prosperity and misfortune that he had experienced over the years. Living under the protection of a Bedouin clan in the desert stronghold of Qal'at Ibn Salamah, he wrote the first draft of his *Muqaddimah*, an analysis of history that sought to unravel and understand the underlying forces determining the rise and fall of dynasties and states.

Like Herodotus and Sima Qian, Ibn Khaldun was an urban man of letters with a keen interest in nomadic culture, but with considerably more firsthand experience. Unlike them, moreover, he could draw on a rich corpus of previous historiography. "History," he declares in the opening lines of the *Muqaddimah*, "is a discipline widely cultivated among nations and races."[40] During the previous two centuries, several prominent Arabic historians came to privilege the art of secular government (*siyasa*) as the proper subject of historiography, leaving *shari'a* to the theologians.[41] A generation before Ibn Khaldun, al-Nuwayri rejected the annalistic organization of historical narratives, replacing it with narratives of the origin, rise, and decline of particular states. History now focused on explaining the staying power and eventual decline of secular state-power. These matters likewise occupied pride of place in Ibn Khaldun's historical writings.[42]

Elaborating on *siyasa* historiography, Ibn Khaldun advances a cyclical theory of the rise and fall of dynastic states to which the dialectic of sedentary and nomadic culture provided the crucial dynamic. His new explanatory concept was *asabiya*, derived from the Arab root *asab* (to tie together) and variously translated as "group feeling," "solidarity," and "social cohesion." The power and vitality of the Bedouin depend on their strong *asabiya*, first emerging from the blood ties of extended families and subsequently extended to clans and tribes. When the desert tribes form federations, solidarity must sustain ever larger political units. Later on, when residing in Cairo, Ibn Khaldun used *asabiya* to explain the historical success of the Turks and the Mongols.[43] Generally, he posits that ancient genealogies and distant memories are not sufficient to maintain a body politic unless clan ties and common experiences are involved. In the final analysis, he conceives of *asabiya* as a social force that cannot be summoned at will by a ruler, however magnificent his status and lineage might be.

In Ibn Khaldun's explanatory framework, sedentary and nomadic culture are far more closely intermeshed than Herodotus and Sima Qian believed. This is partly explained by the growing economic role of the desert. The introduction of the camel from the Arabian peninsula into Egypt led to the first networks of trans-Saharan trade.[44] The later spread of Islam to west Africa resulted in an intensification of the commercial and cultural exchanges across the Sahara.[45] The Berbers' conversion to Islam thus corresponded to basic economic trends. Nomads, merchants, and the urban populations north and south of the Sahara were now linked in a vast commercial and religious commonwealth.

According to Ibn Khaldun, the countryside is the primary element, "the basis and reservoir of civilization and cities."[46] The countryside comprises the agricultural lands in the hinterland of the cities, but also the desert in the strict sense of the term. Accordingly, "Bedouin" can refer to the camel riders of the Saharan interior as well as to the peasants dwelling in villages and hamlets. When the nomadic Bedouin prosper, some of them adopt a more sophisticated lifestyle, engage in trade and crafts, and finally assimilate to sedentary urban culture. The *asabiya* of sedentary culture thus derives from its origins in the countryside. This social transition is historically recurrent and inevitable. That is what Ibn Khaldun means by his thesis that Bedouins as well as sedentary peoples are "natural groups which exist by necessity."[47] Considering the cultures of the countryside and the towns to be equally "natural" and underscoring the demographic primacy of the former, he differs from Aristotle, who maintained that the *polis* was primary "by nature" because it alone enabled human beings to realize their full potential. Ibn Khaldun was familiar with the "philosophers" who used the term *polis* (town) to stand for "human social organization," but he probably did not believe that the city was indispensable to human life.[48] Even so, the pattern of interaction is not wholly symmetrical. The nomads "naturally" aspire to the wealth and comfort of urban life, but the urban population has no desire to return to a rural lifestyle.[49]

The basic political dynamic inevitably unfolds. The nomadic tribes are hardy and militarily resilient but also "wild" and unruly. Examples of such peoples are the Arabs and the Berbers, as well as the Slavonic peoples, the Kurds, the Mongols, and the Turkic peoples, showing that Ibn Khaldun is thinking not only of the Maghrib but also has in mind an African-Eurasian historical nexus.[50] He depicts the "natural" transition from nomadic to sedentary culture as a contradictory historical dialectic in which the nomads are civilized but also progressively divested of their primordial *asabiya*. Once a dynasty is founded, luxury and urban comfort induce corruption, bodily weakness, and effeminacy. The founder of the dynasty is energetic and knows how to keep the polity together; his son learns the trade under his guidance; the next ruler thrives on imitation and "tradition"; but the fourth-generation ruler is a weak leader, who fancies that political power is his birthright. Ibn Khaldun calls him "the destroyer" because his inept leadership usually brings about the collapse of the dynasty. Meanwhile, luxury has sapped the fighting spirit of his followers. Rather than defending the state themselves, they hire mercenaries. These hired warriors come from the desert tribes, and sooner or later one of their leaders takes over the reins of the tottering dynasty. New blood and fresh *asabiya* restore the vitality of the state, and the next dynastic cycle embarks on its fateful course.

Ibn Khaldun's historical analysis distinguishes between the underlying social structure and the political phenomena. The structural divide between sedentary and nomadic culture is environmentally and climatologically determined and remains in place over the centuries. Dynasties and states rise and fall, but agriculture, roads, and towns there will always be, just as the desert perpetually endures. Ibn Khaldun's use of al-Idrisi's world map also serves to highlight the division between the densely populated sedentary lands and the thinly populated or even "empty" spaces of the steppe and the desert.[51]

Although Ibn Khaldun himself was an urban, learned man who spent the last decades of his life in Cairo, "the mother of the world . . . and the mainspring of the sciences,"[52] his nomadic-sedentary dialectic destabilizes any fixed hierarchy of the two cultures. The Bedouin are depicted as physically robust, beautiful, resourceful, and virtuous but also as unkempt, "wild," and "almost like animals." The sedentary people are represented as civilized, ingenious, learned, and industrious but also as unhealthy, ugly, effeminate, and lacking solidarity and virtue. In both cases, religion may help restore the balance, taming the wildness of the desert people and imparting a common purpose to the sedentary (but the religious factor is not well integrated in Ibn Khaldun's theoretical framework).

For Ibn Khaldun, as for Herodotus and Sima Qian, the plurality of cultures is a permanent feature of history. While his Greek and Chinese predecessors were well-traveled and well-informed men, Ibn Khaldun's knowledge of nomadic life was tied up with his own political career and went deeper. He had seen enough to understand the strengths and weaknesses of both cultures. Whereas the cities were the seats of large-scale social organization, learning, and high civilization, the desert was the wellspring of *asabiya*, social resilience, and warrior culture. Both cultures were thus "natural" and "necessary." According to Ibn Khaldun, history is the ongoing story of their interaction.

Conclusion: Frontier Discourses in Historical Time

I have discussed Herodotus's, Sima Qian's, and Ibn Khaldun's treatment of nomadic culture in the languages available to them in their respective intellectual settings. Herodotus's discussion of the Scythians and his maxim regarding the "natural" ethnocentrism of all peoples are couched in a language indebted to the Greek Sophists' philosophical polemics contrasting the relativity of *nomoi* (customs and laws) with the immutability of *phusis* (nature). But Herodotus's rich ethnographic knowledge enables him to go beyond the Sophists' philosophical arguments and to invent a new historical-ethnological language. His version of the anthropological turn is part of that language. Herodotus's captivating historical examples are better suited than a purely philosophical argument to explain the relativity of customs and laws.

Like Herodotus, Sima Qian was educated in a world of philosophical pluralism. His father, Sima Tan, was probably the first thinker to distinguish between the Chinese philosophical schools according to their key ideas rather than the names of their founding masters.[53] Sima Qian himself was an eclectic Confucian. As noted earlier, he justified his critical approach to history with an indirect reference to Confucius's *Spring and Autumn Annals*. But in his discussion of the Xiongnu and other remote peoples, he had to go beyond these intellectual sources, forging a new language that enabled him to make sense of contingent historical change and cultural difference and, finally, to imagine how China might look to people beyond the Great Wall.

Ibn Khaldun was obviously indebted to the Arabic geographers and historians, who in turn had taken many ideas from their Greek predecessors. He had heard about the voyages of Ibn Battutah, the greatest traveler of his century, but he did not know if all his information was reliable.[54] Ibn Khaldun took from the geographers his division of the world into climate zones, with the North African littoral as the "temperate zone." Herodotus's maxim on the ubiquity of ethnocentrism can also be found in Arabic thought. In the opening section of his famous description of India, the eleventh-century polymath al-Biruni observes that the "depreciation of foreigners . . . is common to all nations towards each other."[55] Ibn Khaldun was familiar with the philosophical ideas of the Aristotelian school of Ibn Rushd (Averroes) and his followers, but his insistence that both the sedentary and the nomadic peoples exist through natural necessity does not quite fit into the standard Aristotelian model.[56] Geography and philosophy gave Ibn Khaldun concepts to analyze cultural difference. To arrive at a satisfactory explanation of the varying fortunes of history, however, he had to move beyond his intellectual sources. He did so by inventing the new concept of *asabiya*. Finally, he sought to combine his secular, *asabiya*-based explanation with the operation of divine guidance, but the combination did not add up to a consistent overall theory.

All three cases contain a further significant element: contact with travelers and personal experience. These three historians were well-traveled men who were eager to talk with travelers. All three had personally witnessed dramatic political events. Sima Qian and Ibn Khaldun were in touch with the main decision-making centers in their part of the world, and Herodotus finished his history when Greeks were fighting Greeks in the terrible war between Athens and Sparta. Their historical inquiries are unthinkable without those political cataclysms and passions. Indeed, it may well have been the fire and thunder of political upheaval that pushed them beyond their intellectual sources to the invention of these new discourses on cultural difference.

Another common element concerns temporality. All three histories discuss major and irreversible events, such as wars and conquests, but the temporal rhythm underpinning these linear narratives is cyclical. The inglorious end of Darius's Scythian campaign is an exemplary case of Herodotus's vision of the rise and decline of empires. On the eve of the wars with the Greeks, the Persian Empire extended from Egypt to the Indus. Nothing like it had ever been seen. However, the empire's failure to conquer Ethiopia, Scythia, and, finally, Greece, reaffirmed the limits set on all human exploits. For Herodotus, empires fail sooner or later, brought down by reckless rulers blinded by their excessive power, but also, on a deeper level, by the gods who strike down the hubristic arrogance of mortal men.[57] Herodotus's exemplary bad Persian king, Cambyses, came to grief through his own lack of prudence, but his death was caused by an "accidental" self-inflicted wound, in the same spot on the thigh where he himself had stabbed the holy calf Apis in Egypt. Cambyses's demise fits the political dynamic of Herodotus's narrative, but he was also, in a way understandable to a Greek audience, felled by the revenge of an Egyptian deity.

More than Herodotus, Sima Qian recounts history as an ongoing, long-term process. In line with his Confucian outlook, he theorizes the growth of order and civilization as the unfolding of the immanent logic of human and cosmic nature. But this natural-cosmic order must be realized by fallible human beings. There is no divine providence in Sima Qian's worldview. The history of China moves on, its basic rhythm found in the rise and fall of the imperial dynasties. Sima Qian refers to "the law of change, that when things reach their period of greatest flourishing, they must begin to decay."[58] The lessons of history show the need for "correction" and "reform," but its temporality is expressed in the language of a "return" to the Way of the ancient sage-rulers.[59]

Ibn Khaldun's history likewise displays a combination of linear and cyclical temporality. The rapid rise and subsequent political trajectory of Islam, to which he often refers, represents a momentous and irreversible trend in world history. The same is true of the rise of scientific and literary culture. But the sedentary–nomadic dialectic, the linchpin of his theory of history, can result only in a cyclical pattern of the rise and decline of states. The division of the world in urban and nomadic zones is a permanent structural feature of history. Urban civilization cannot, and will not, conquer or civilize the nomadic world. In the final analysis, the nomadic world, theorized by Ibn Khaldun as the basis and reservoir of civilization, is a necessary condition for the continuation and renewal of the urban zone.

In all three histories, the nomads are there to stay. There is no prospect of a civilizing mission by the sedentary peoples, let alone a temporality of civilizational progression. In the Chinese case, we may discern a cosmic dream of the dissemination of a universal Sinic culture, but the dream is punctured by the harsh reality of Xiongnu autonomy and resilience. Nowhere in the writings of these three historians is there any trace of the developmental temporality and the civilizing mission of the later European Enlightenment.

My notion of the anthropological turn is not found in the writings of Herodotus, Sima Qian, or Ibn Khaldun. Instead, it is a metaconcept that enables me to conceive of their nomadic ethnographies as instances of a world-historical problematic. The intellectual analogies and affinities that make this type of intellectual history thinkable are connected to an enduring world-historical setting, comprising recurrent frontier experiences. The Great Frontier of the Old World exhibits some sociopolitical features that recur over the centuries and thereby makes it plausible to decode the writings of Herodotus, Sima Qian, and Ibn Khaldun as contextually determined, inventive variations on a common theme. Consequently, we can read them as intellectual episodes in a global history of urban-agrarian "civilizations," nomadic "barbarians," and frontier experiences. In the end, any global intellectual history is connected to definite long-term sociopolitical patterns and frontier experiences. New ideas are inventions that alter the balance of social and political power, but these inventions can be understood only as they are "read off" against the patterns of moving peoples and the politics of empire.

Notes

1. Extensive references, not possible in the restricted space of this chapter, can be found in Siep Stuurman, "Herodotus and Sima Qian: History and the Anthropological Turn in Ancient Greece and Han China," *Journal of World History* 19 (2008): 1–40; as well as in Siep Stuurman, *De Uitvinding van de Mensheid: Korte Wereldgeschiedenis van het Denken over Gelijkheid en Cultuurverschil* (Amsterdam: Bert Bakker, 2009), 147–97.

2. Jerry H. Bentley, *Old World Encounters: Cross-Cultural Contacts and Exchanges in Pre-Modern Times* (New York: Oxford University Press, 1993), 23–28; Christopher I. Beckwith, *Empires of the Silk Road: A History of Central Eurasia from the Bronze Age to the Present* (Princeton, N.J.: Princeton University Press, 2009), 235. The long waves of political and cultural interaction across the Eurasia "steppe highway" were first discussed in Frederick J. Teggart, *Rome and China: A Study in Correlations in Historical Events* (1939; repr., Berkeley: University of California Press, 1969); see also Owen Lattimore, *Inner Asian Frontiers of China* (1940; repr., Boston: Beacon Press, 1962); William H. McNeill, *The Great Frontier* (Princeton, N.J.: Princeton University Press, 1983), 11–15; and, more recently, Clive Ponting, *World History: A New Perspective* (London: Pimlico, 2001), 146–54; James A. Milward, *Eurasian Crossroads: A History of Xinjiang* (New York: Columbia University Press, 2007), 17–30.

3. William H. McNeill, *The Rise of the West: A History of the Human Community* (Chicago: University of Chicago Press, 1991), xvi.

4. Ibid., xx.

5. Ibid., xxi.

6. But see David Schaberg, "Travel, Geography, and the Imperial Imagination in Fifth-Century Athens and Han China," *Comparative Literature* 51 (1999): 152–91; Stuurman, "Herodotus and Sima Qian"; Hyun Jin Kim, *Ethnicity and Foreigners in Ancient Greece and China* (London: Duckworth, 2009).

7. Jan Assmann, *The Mind of Egypt: History and Meaning in the Time of the Pharaohs* (New York: Metropolitan Books, 2002), 151.

8. See Muzhou Poo, *Enemies of Civilization: Attitudes to Foreigners in Ancient Mesopotamia, Egypt, and China* (Albany: State University of New York Press, 2005), 37.

9. *Mencius*, translated and introduced by D. C. Lau (London: Penguin Classics, 1970), 82 (II, A, 6).

10. See Hao Chang, "Some Reflections on the Problems of the Axial Age Breakthrough in Relation to Classical Confucianism," in *Ideas Across Cultures: Essays on Chinese Thought in Honor of Benjamin I. Schwartz*, ed. Paul A. Cohen and Merle Goldman (Harvard East Asian Monographs 150, 1990), 24–25.

11. *Mencius*, 103 (III, A, 4).
12. See Beckwith, *Empires of the Silk Road*, 325; Nicola di Cosmo, *Ancient China and Its Enemies: The Rise of Nomadic Power in East Asian History* (Cambridge: Cambridge University Press, 2002), 169–70.
13. Herodotus, I, 1. References are to book and chapter; translated by A. D. Godley, Loeb Classical Library (Cambridge Mass.: Harvard University Press, 1999).
14. See Michael Flower, "Herodotus and Persia," in *The Cambridge Companion to Herodotus*, ed. Carolyn Dewald and John Marincola (Cambridge: Cambridge University Press, 2006), 274–89.
15. Herodotus, II, 158; III, 38.
16. In the historiography, Herodotus's cross-cultural pluralism has been downplayed by François Hartog, *Le miroir d'Hérodote: Essai sur la representation de l'autre* (Paris: Gallimard, 1991); James Redfield, "Herodotus the Tourist," in *Greeks and Barbarians*, ed. Thomas Harrison (Edinburgh: Edinburgh University Press, 2002), 24–49; Vivienne Gray, "Herodotus and the Rhetoric of Otherness," *American Journal of Philology* 116 (1995): 185–211. Such assessments have been convincingly challenged by Rosalind Thomas, *Herodotus in Context* (Cambridge: Cambridge University Press, 2000); Rosaria Vignolo Munson, *Telling Wonders: Ethnographic and Political Discourse in the Work of Herodotus* (Ann Arbor: University of Michigan Press, 2001); Rosaria Vignolo Munson, *Black Doves Speak: Herodotus and the Languages of Barbarians* (Cambridge Mass.: Harvard University Press, 2005); and Tim Rood, "Herodotus and Foreign Lands," in *The Cambridge Companion to Herodotus*, ed. Carolyn Dewald and John Marincola (Cambridge: Cambridge University Press, 2006), 290–305.
17. Herodotus, IV, 46.
18. Ibid., 3–4.
19. See Ellis H. Minns, *Scythians and Greeks* (1913; repr., New York: Biblo and Tannen, 1971), 37, 283–91, 438–41; see also A. A. Maslennikov, "The Development of Graeco-Barbarian Contacts in the Chora of the European Bosporus," in *Scythians and Greeks,* ed. David Braund (Exeter: University of Exeter Press, 2005), 153–66.
20. Minns, *Scythians and Greeks*, 283.
21. See Balbina Bäbler, "Bobbies or Boobies? The Scythian Police Force in Classical Athens," in *Scythians and Greeks,* ed. David Braund (Exeter: University of Exeter Press, 2005), 114–122.
22. Herodotus, IV, 132.
23. Ibid., 142.
24. Ibid., 46. On the race-nation ambiguity, see C. P. Jones, "Ethnos and Genos in Herodotus," *Classical Quarterly* 46 (1996): 315–20.
25. Herodotus, IV, 31, 59, 110; see also Munson, *Black Doves Speak.*
26. Herodotus, IV, 76; I have changed the translation slightly.

27. See Rhys Carpenter, "A Trans-Saharan Caravan Route in Herodotus," *American Journal of Archaeology* 60 (1956): 231–42; Mario Liverani, "The Libyan Caravan Road in Herodotus IV. 181–185," *Journal of the Economic and Social History of the Orient* 43 (2000): 496–520.

28. See Amélie Kuhrt, *The Persian Empire: A Corpus of Sources from the Achaemenid Period* (London: Routledge, 2010), 33. The Bisitun inscription contains claims of Darius to authority over the Scythians, and it mentions his campaign against the Scythians in Central Asia, but not his forays into western Scythia (see Kuhrt, *The Persian Empire*, 141–50).

29. Sima Qian, *Records of the Historian*, 130, cited in Burton Watson, *Ssu-ma Ch'ien: Grand Historian of China* (New York: Columbia University Press, 1958), 50; see also Sarah A. Queen, *From Chronicle to Canon: The Hermeneutics of the Spring and Autumn Annals According to Tung Chung-shu* (Cambridge: Cambridge University Press, 1996); David Schaberg, *A Patterned Past: Form and Thought in Early Chinese Historiography* (Cambridge, Mass.: Harvard University Press, 2001), 308–12, 317.

30. Sima Qian, *Records of the Grand Historian*, trans. Burton Watson, vol. 2, *Han II* (New York: Columbia University Press, 1993), 129.

31. Ibid., 143–44.

32. Ibid., 144.

33. Ibid., 239–40.

34. Di Cosmo, *Ancient China and Its Enemies*, 271.

35. See Michael Brett and Elizabeth Fentress, *The Berbers* (Oxford: Blackwell, 2001), 83; Aziz al-Azmeh, "Barbarians in Arab Eyes," *Past and Present* 134 (1992): 3–18.

36. See Richard L. Smith, "What Happened to the Ancient Libyans? Chasing Sources Across the Sahara from Herodotus to Ibn Khaldun," *Journal of World History* 14 (2003): 493–94.

37. Guliana Turroni, *Il mondo della storia secondo Ibn Khaldun* (Rome: Jouvence, 2002), 116.

38. See Stefan Leder, "Bedouin Arabs—Origin [and] Signification of a Khaldunian Concept," in *Ibn Khaldun: Aux sources de la modernité* (Carthage: Académie tunisienne des sciences, des letters et des arts, 2008), 184, 187.

39. Ibn Khaldun, *Autobiographie*, trans. Abdesselam Cheddadi (Casablanca: Maison des arts, des sciences et des lettres, 2006), 61–145.

40. Ibn Khaldun, *The Muqaddimah*, trans. Franz Rosenthal, 3 vols. (New York: Pantheon Books, 1958), 1:6.

41. See Tarif Khalidi, *Arabic Historical Thought in the Classical Period* (Cambridge: Cambridge University Press, 1996), 193–200.

42. Ibid., 216–17, 222–31; for a heavier emphasis on Ibn Khaldun's rupture with previous Arabic historiography, see Allen James Fromherz, *Ibn Khaldun, Life and Times* (Edinburgh: Edinburgh University Press, 2010), 114–25.

43. See Walter J. Fischel, "Ibn Khaldun's Sources for the History of Jengiz Khan and the Tatars," *Journal of the American Oriental Society* 76 (1956): 91–99.

44. See Michael Ripinsky, "The Camel in Dynastic Egypt," *Journal of Egyptian Archaeology* 71 (1985): 134–14; and the references in note 27.

45. See Philip D. Curtin, *Cross-Cultural Trade in World History* (Cambridge: Cambridge University Press, 1998), 21–26.

46. Ibn Khaldun, *Muqaddimah*, 1:252.

47. Ibid., 1:250.

48. Ibid., 2:235, 417; on Ibn Khaldun's reception of Aristotelian thought, see Musin Mahdi, *Ibn Khaldun's Philosophy of History* (Chicago: University of Chicago Press, 1971).

49. Ibn Khaldun, *Muqaddimah*, 1:252–53.

50. Ibid., 1:251.

51. See Tarek Kahlaoui, "Towards Reconstructing the *Muqaddimah* Following Ibn Khaldun's Reading of the Idrisian Text and Maps," *Journal of North African Studies* 13 (2008): 300.

52. See Walter J. Fischel, *Ibn Khaldun in Egypt: His Public Functions and His Historical Research* (Berkeley: University of California Press, 1967), 18.

53. See Kidder Smith, "Sima Tan and the Invention of Daoism, 'Legalism' etc.," *Journal of Asian Studies* 62 (2003): 129–56.

54. Ibn Khaldun, *Muqaddimah*, 1:369–71.

55. Al-Biruni, *Alberuni's India, an Account of the Religion, Philosophy, Literature, Geography, Chronology, Astronomy, Customs, Laws and Astrology of India about A.D. 1030*, ed. and trans. Edward C. Sachau, 2 vols. (1888; repr., New Delhi: Asian Educational Services, 2004), 1:20.

56. See Fromherz, *Ibn Khaldun*, 138.

57. See Thomas Harrison, *Divinity and History: The Religion of Herodotus* (Oxford: Oxford University Press, 2000), 31–63.

58. *Han II*, 63.

59. See Schaberg, *A Patterned Past*, 276; Grant Hardy, *Worlds of Bronze and Bamboo: Sima Qian's Conquest of History* (New York: Columbia University Press, 1999), 120–35.

3

Cosmopolitanism, Vernacularism, and Premodernity

SHELDON POLLOCK

T he intensifying interactions today between local and translocal forms of culture and ways of political being, which have become truly global for the first time, have generated renewed scholarly interest in the idea of the "cosmopolitan."[1] As many historians have recognized, the processes at work in contemporary globalization are not altogether unprecedented. But our understanding of what exactly is new and different about them, beyond the fact of their temporal speed and spatial reach, depends on our capacity to grasp the character of the earlier processes of globalization—of a smaller globe, to be sure— and the cosmopolitan identities that have characterized other historical epochs.[2]

The labels by which we typically refer to these earlier processes— Hellenization, Indianization, Romanization, Sinicization, Christianization, Islamization, Russification, and the like—are often used crudely and imprecisely. Yet they do serve to signal the historically significant ways in the past of being translocal, of participating—and knowing one was participating—in political and cultural networks that transcended the immediate community. These ways varied widely. In Hellenization, the dominant commitment was to a language, a culture, and even an aesthetic. In Christianization, by contrast, to a certain set of beliefs; in Islamization, to a certain set of practices; and in Romanization, to a particular political order. Or this is how one might speculate, and speculation is all one can do for the moment. The comparative study of premodern processes of cosmopolitan transculturation—of how and why people may be induced to adopt languages or life ways or modes of political belonging that affiliate them with the distant rather than the near, the unfamiliar rather than the customary—is very much in its infancy, even for a phenomenon as significant in the creation, or construction, of the West as Romanization. And when these earlier processes do come under scholarly scrutiny, they are typically not seen as processes at all, through whose dialectical interaction the global and the local are brought into being simultaneously and continuously. Rather, they tend to be thought of as pregiven, stable, and sharply defined: the global or cosmopolitan as the exogenous, great tradition against the local or vernacular as the indigenous, little tradition. They have taken on the character of stable entities that interact in thinglike ways rather than being seen as constantly changing repertories of practices.

A number of factors account for the neglect of the quasi-global formation that characterized early southern Asia, one that came into being around the start of the Common Era and, at its height a thousand years later, extended across all of South Asia and much of Southeast Asia. The temporal and spatial magnitude of the Sanskrit cultural and political order; the conceptual otherness of the subject matter; the apparent anomalousness vis-à-vis peer formations such as Confucian China or Latinate Europe, which has served to make the South Asia case almost invisible; the difficulty of the languages involved; the risk of provoking specialists of the particular regions where such study has always been parceled out; the almost immediate discovery of countercases to any tendency one believes to have discerned—all these obstacles have combined to induce a powerful resistance to generalization and large-scale interpretation.[3] In addition, Sanskrit studies, heir to a brilliant and imperious intellectual tradition that had set its own agenda in the important issues of the human sciences, has had grounds to rest content with addressing the questions predefined by this tradition, and the historical expansion of the realm of Sanskrit culture was not one of them.

Symptomatic of the many problems of understanding this realm and its history is the question of how even to refer to it. The phrase adopted here, "Sanskrit cosmopolis," is not without its drawbacks. Besides being hybrid and ahistorical, it is actually uncosmopolitan in the cultural specificity of the form of citizenship implicit in it: membership in the *polis,* or the community of free males. But the very need for such a coinage reveals a social fact of some theoretical importance. Other great globalizing processes of the past found emic formulation and conceptualization, whether in terms of a cultural particularity (Hellenismos or Arabīya or Fārsīyat) or a political form (*imperium romanum* or *guo,* the Sinitic "fatherland"). But for neither the political nor the cultural sphere that Sanskrit created and inhabited was there an adequate self-generated descriptor. Even the word *saṃskṛti,* the classicizing term adopted for translating "culture" in many modern South Asian languages, is itself unattested in premodern Sanskrit in this sense. We find Indian theory distinguishing the great Way, *mārga,* from Place, *deśī,* but both terms refer, significantly, only to cultural practices and never to communities of sentiment. If we are therefore obliged to invent our own expression for the transregional power-culture sphere of Sanskrit, the fact that Sanskrit never sought to theorize its own universality should not be seen as a lack or failure. On the contrary, it points to something central about the character and existence of the Sanskrit cosmopolis itself: a universalism that never objectified, let alone enforced, its universalism.

The phrase "Sanskrit cosmopolis" carries three additional implications that make it especially useful here. The first is its supraregional dimension (cosmo-), which directs attention toward the expansive nature of the formation. The second is the prominence given to the political dimension (-polis), which was of particular importance to this form of global identification. Last, the qualification provided by "Sanskrit" affirms the role of this language in producing the forms of political and cultural expression that underwrote this cosmopolitan order.

The history of the Sanskrit language and its social sphere has long been an object of interest to Sanskritists, for its curious history holds considerable theoretical interest. The Sanskrit cosmopolis did not come into being simultaneously with the appearance of the Sanskrit language. Its development was slow and tentative, and for it to come about at all, the very self-understanding of the nature and function of the "language of the gods," as Sanskrit was known, had to be transformed. Ritualization (the restriction of Sanskrit to liturgical and related scholastic practices) and monopolization (the restriction of the language community, by and large, to the ritual community) gave way to a new sociology and politicization of the language just around the time that western Asian and central Asian peoples were entering into the ambit of Sanskrit culture. Whether these newcomers, the Śakas (Indo-Scythians) in particular, initiated these processes or simply reinforced those already under way cannot be determined from the available evidence. What is not in doubt is that then a new era—a cosmopolitan era—began.

Two key inventions, the second a subspecies of the first, marked the commencement of the cosmopolitan era in the literary-cultural domain and continued to mark its expansion: first, *kāvya,* or written literature, and, second, *praśasti,* or inscriptional royal panegyric. Sanskrit *kāvya,* a category that was clear and distinct in premodern South Asia, was a new phenomenon in Indian cultural history when it first appeared a little before the beginning of the Common Era. From the first, *kāvya* was almost certainly composed and circulated (though not typically experienced) in writing. It was this-worldly (*laukika*) in its themes, even when these concerned the divine (no *kāvya* was incorporated into temple liturgy until the waning centuries of the cosmopolitan order); it was directed above all toward investigating the elementary forms of human emotional experience; and at the same time (and for the same reason), it was centrally concerned with the nature of language itself, with its primary phonic and semantic capacities. In all these features, *kāvya* was new in the historical record, startlingly new to the participants in Sanskrit culture. Its novelty was thematized in the Sanskrit tradition itself with the story of the invention of *kāvya* told in the prelude to what came to be called the "first poem," the Vālmīki Rāmāyaṇa. In reflexively framing its own orality in a way that would be impossible in a preliterate world and in doing so around the narrative of human response to problems of a human scale, the Rāmāyaṇa account captures some of the central features of the new expressive form, *kāvya.*

Crucial to the theorization of *kāvya* in the cosmopolitan epoch was the restriction on the languages capable of producing it. The literary conquest of cosmopolitan space by Sanskrit produced a conception of literature as something able to be embodied only in language that was itself cosmopolitan. This was, of course, preeminently Sanskrit, though two other closely related idioms—Prakrit, the "natural" or informal language, and Apabhramsha, the dialectal (literally, decayed)—were counted as legitimate vehicles for *kāvya* from the first appearance of literary-theoretical reflection in the seventh century. Both Prakrit and Apabhramsha were in fact constituted as transregional koines through the production of literary texts and grammatical descriptions, and they were used for literary production (almost exclusively so) across the subcontinent, the former from about the second or third century and the latter from about the fifth or sixth. (Since neither was spatially circumscribed, or reflexively understood to be so circumscribed, in the production of literary and political texts, neither qualifies as an instance of vernacularization.) But both languages occupy a much more subordinate position in literary history than Sanskrit, having never achieved anything like Sanskrit's density of textual production or its spatial spread, and neither was ever used for the production of literary texts outside the subcontinent. Sanskrit was the transregional code that filled the domain of the literary. The closed set of literary languages meant in principle that *kāvya* could not be made in other, localized languages. In this thought world, the very idea of *deśi kāvya,* "vernacular literature," would have been a contradiction in terms. In practice it never was produced until the vernacular moment came, when it was. These propositions, along with others that define the literary as distinct from all other language use, will be explored through the comprehensive analysis of literature offered by King Bhoja of Mālava in the first quarter of the eleventh century.

Once Sanskrit emerged from the sacerdotal environment to which it was originally confined, it spread with breathtaking rapidity across southern Asia. Within three centuries, Sanskrit became the sole medium by which ruling elites expressed their power from as far west as Puruṣapura in Gandhāra (Peshawar, in today's northwest Pakistan) to Pāṇḍurāṅga in Champa (central Vietnam) and Prambanan on the plains of Java. Sanskrit probably never functioned as an everyday medium of communication anywhere in the cosmopolis—not in South Asia itself, let alone Southeast Asia—nor was it ever used (except among the literati) as a bridge- or link- or trade-language as were other cosmopolitan codes such as Greek, Latin, Arabic, and Chinese. Moreover, aside from the inscriptions, which had larger purposes, there is little evidence that it was ever used as the language of practical rule. Tasks such as chancery communication or revenue accounting seem to have been carried out through informal uses of local language. The work that Sanskrit did do was beyond the quotidian and the instrumental; it was directed above all toward articulating a form of political consciousness and culture, politics not as a transaction of material power—the power of recording deeds, contracts, tax records, and the like—but as a celebration of aesthetic power. This it did in large part through the new cultural-political practices that came to expression in the *prasasti,* which not only arose coevally with Sanskrit *kāvya* but, from the first, exploited the full range of resources of the language-centered aesthetic of literature. Inscribed on rock faces or copperplates or, at a later date, temple walls, and thus to varying degrees publicly available, the *prasasti* was the literary expression of political selfhood. To a large extent, the Sanskrit cosmopolis consisted of precisely this common aesthetics of political culture, a kind of poetry of polity in the service of what was in some measure an aesthetic state. To foreground aesthetics, however, is not to argue with Weber (or Clifford Geertz) that culture is all that constituted polity in the nonmodern non-West and that other core issues of power were never addressed. A case study of the pragmatics of inscriptional discourse among the Kalyāṇa Cāḷukya dynasty is meant to show how seriously matters of real power were taken and how carefully memory was manufactured in its interests.

Sanskrit philology was a social form as well as a conceptual form, and it was inextricably tied to the practices of power. Overlords were keen to ensure the cultivation of the language through patronage awarded to grammarians, lexicographers, metricians, and other custodians of purity, and through endowments to schools for the purpose of grammatical studies. They were also responsible for commissioning many of the most important grammars. For a polity to possess a grammar of its own was to ensure its proper functioning and even completeness, so much so that a competitive grammaticality, even grammar envy, can be perceived among kings in the Sanskrit cosmopolis, as the narrative of Jayasiṃha Siddharāja of Gujarat illustrates. Kings also evinced a consuming interest in demonstrating their Sanskrit virtuosity in literary matters. An encyclopedia of royal conduct from early-twelfth-century Karnataka, the *Mānasollāsa,* demonstrates how literary-theoretical competence (*śāstravinoda*) was as central to kingliness as military competence (*śastravinoda*). Episodes of grammatical and literary correctness such as these are not idiosyncratic tendencies of the persons or places in question. They point toward an ideal of proper rule and proper culture being complementary, an ideal in evidence throughout the cosmopolitan age, from the earliest recorded evidence in the second century and beyond into the vernacular epoch when so many cosmopolitan values of culture and power came to find local habitations and names.

Space and Comparison

Even if the transregional formation for which Sanskrit was the communicative medium was never named in the language, the transregionality of both power and culture was decisively manifested in shaping Sanskrit discourse. The analytical matrices employed in much Sanskrit systematic thought, from the typology of females in the *scientia sexualis* to instrumental and vocal music and dance, are effectively geocultural maps of this vast space. The basic geographical template by which culture was conceptualized was, for its part, established only in the early centuries of the cosmopolitan era, reaching its final form in a mid-sixth-century work on astral science, and was transmitted more or less invariantly for the next ten centuries. Of particular interest is the spatialization of Sanskrit literature itself, through the discourse on the "Ways" of literature, modes of literariness conceived of as regional styles within a cosmopolitan space. The regionality of the cosmopolitan language was qualified, however. It was the same Sanskrit everywhere—an elementary aspect of the language ideology of Sanskrit is its invariability across time and space— though differently realized in phonological, semantic, or syntactic registers. But these regional differences were in fact part of the repertoire of a global Sanskrit, with writers everywhere using them to achieve different aesthetic ends (the southern style for erotic verse, for example, or the northern for martial), and thus they constituted a sign precisely of Sanskrit's ubiquity. This idea is beautifully captured in a tenth-century tale of the origins of literary culture: Poetry Man is pursued by his wife-to-be, Poetics Woman, and in the process creates literature across South Asia—and only there. Literature is decidedly transregional if not quite universal.

But where was this "South Asia"? As represented in such treatises, the Sanskrit cosmopolitan order appears smaller than the cosmopolis was in actuality, for aside from the very occasional mention in Sanskrit texts of Suvarṇabhūmi (Malaysia), Yavadvīpa (probably Java), Śrīvijaya (Palembang), and the like, Southeast Asia never formed part of the representation (the same holds true of Tibet and parts of central Asia, which participated in a more limited fashion in the Sanskrit cosmopolitan order). The conceptual space of Sanskrit texts was slow to adjust, or so one might think, to the new and larger circulatory spaces through which people had increasingly begun to move. Indeed, these actual spaces were vast and so was the spread of Sanskrit culture, enabled by the diffusion of *kāvya* and *praśasti* on the part of peripatetic literati and the cultivation everywhere of a literarily uniform Sanskrit. Accordingly, in the first millennium it makes hardly more sense to distinguish between South and Southeast Asia than between north India and south India, despite what present-day area studies may tell us. Everywhere similar processes of cosmopolitan transculturation were under way, with the source and target of change always shifting, since there was no single point of production for cosmopolitan culture. Yet just as Southeast Asia was included in the circulatory space of the cosmopolitan order, so it came to be included in its conceptual space, thanks to the transportability, so to speak, of that space. In their own geographical imagination, the imperial polities of Southeast Asia—Angkor around 1000 is exemplary here—made themselves part of the cosmopolitan order by a wholesale appropriation of its toponymy. With Mount Meru and the Gaṅgā River able to be located everywhere, there was no spatial center from which one could be excluded; the Sanskrit cosmopolis was wherever home was. There is nothing in the least mystical about this replicability; it is a function of a different, plural, premodern logic of space.

While modern-day equivalents of the places mentioned in these spatializations are often provided here so that some geographical image will form in the mind's eye of the reader, establishing positive concordances is not the objective. The goal, instead, is learning to understand how people conceptualized macrospaces in the past and what work in the spheres of power and culture such conceptualization was meant, or not meant, to do. To explore this topic is not to presuppose a seamless continuity from the sixth century to today's representations of Akhaṇḍ Bhārat, "Undivided India," that have produced the "cartographic anxiety" behind so much of contemporary Indian political action.[4] The very appropriation and concretization of a sometimes imaginary and often vague geographical past in a precise and factual present is one of the deadly weapons of nationalism and a source of the misery of modernity. Premodern space, whether cosmopolitan or vernacular, is not the nation-space, and yet it was no less filled with political content than it was with cultural content. The attempt to recover knowledge of this space is not fatally distorted by the discourse of nationalism. Far from disabling a history of the premodern politics of space, the distortion of national narratives is precisely the condition that makes it necessary. Such a history need not be crippled by teleology; it can instead be seen as a history of the teleological. The national narrative is a second-generation representation made possible only by the existence of a first-generation representation, though one informed by a very different logic that nationalism often seeks to elide.

That the space promulgated by Sanskrit analytical matrices was conceived of not just as a culture-space but also as a power-space is demonstrated by the Sanskrit Mahābhārata. In this *itihāsa* (narrative of "the way it once was"), or "epic" in Western parlance (genre identity is no trivial matter, given the modern discourse on "nation," "epic," and "novel"), the transregional frame of reference structures the entire work. Moreover, the dissemination of its manuscripts and the distribution of royal endowments for its continual recitation actualized literary spatiality, turning representations into components of popular consciousness: people recited and listened to the Mahābhārata's story of a macrospace of power even while they inhabited that very space. The evidence assembled to demonstrate this claim aims to correct errors old and new, for instance, that it was only on mountaintops that the language of the gods touched the earth or that it was nationalist modernity that invented the political-cultural salience of Indian epic discourse.[5]

Whatever else the Mahābhārata may be, it is also and preeminently a work of political theory: the single most important literary reflection on the problem of the political in southern Asian history and, in some ways, the deepest meditation in all antiquity on the desperate realities of political life. Thus to mention it in reference to the ecumenical culture of the Sanskrit cosmopolis naturally raises the question of how the cultural order articulated with political practice. As noted earlier, understanding the character of polity in premodern South Asia is far more difficult than describing its cosmopolitan culture, and scholars have generated wildly discrepant accounts of what polity meant. While some of these are examined briefly, more attention is given to the modes and character of political imagination. This is not, however, a *pis aller*. Almost as important as what polities did—and just as real—is what they aspired to do. In its aspirations, the imperial polity of the Sanskrit cosmopolis was marked by several consistent, if elusive, features. It was territorially expansive, though territoriality in premodern South Asia remains an underdefined concept. It was politically universalistic, though what political governance actually meant is hard to pin down. It was ethnically nonparticularized, if the term "ethnic" may be used when it is not even certain that "ethnies" in the political-science sense actually existed. The fact that these aspirations were embedded in a set of cultural practices like *kāvya* and *praśasti* suggests that the practice of polity was, to some degree, also an aesthetic practice. *Kāvya* and *rājya* were mutually constitutive; every man who came to rule sought the distinction of self-presentation in Sanskrit literature, typically in the permanent public form of the *praśasti*. This constitutive relationship, however, presents interpretive challenges. The single available explanation of the social function of Sanskrit cosmopolitan culture is legitimation theory and its logic of instrumental reason: elites in command of new forms of social power are understood to have deployed the mystifying symbols and codes of Sanskrit to secure popular consent. Absolute dogma though this explanatory framework may be, it is not only anachronistic but also intellectually mechanical, culturally homogenizing, theoretically naive, empirically false, and tediously predictable.

The peculiar character of the Sanskrit cosmopolis as a cultural and political order becomes clear only through comparative analysis. "Beware of arriving at conclusions without comparisons," said George Eliot. I agree, though perhaps not for her reasons. Comparison always implicitly informs historical analysis, given that the individual subjectivity of the historian inevitably shapes his research questions. And these questions can be more sharply formulated and better answered if the comparison behind them is explicit.[6] Moreover, there is a natural proclivity to generalize familiar forms of life as universal tendencies and common sense, and comparison serves to point up the actual particularity, even peculiarity, of such supposed universalisms.

If some similarities link the Roman and the Sanskrit political-cultural orders, the differences are such that the one presents itself as a kind of countercosmopolis to the other. In both worlds, literature, after making a more or less sudden irruption into history, became a fundamental instrument for the creation of a cosmopolitan culture, with literati across an immense space being trained according to comparable standards and producing literature that circulated across this space. But Latin interacted with local idioms in a way radically different from that of Sanskrit. Radically different, too, were the origin and character of the empire form, as well as the modalities of affiliation to Roman culture, or Romanization.

The Sanskrit cosmopolis was characterized by a largely homogeneous language of political poetry along with a range of comparable political-cultural practices. Constituted by no imperial state or church and consisting to a large degree in the communicative system itself and its political aesthetic, this order was characterized by a transregional consensus on the presuppositions, nature, and practices of a common culture, as well as a shared set of assumptions about the elements of power—or at least on the ways in which power is reproduced at the level of representation in language. For a millennium or more, the Sanskrit cosmopolis was the most compelling model of power-culture for a quarter or more of the inhabitants of the globe. It ended, at various times and places in the course of the first five centuries of the second millennium, only under pressure from a new model. If the Sanskrit cosmopolis raises hard questions for political and cultural theory, so do the forms of life that superseded it. The fact that this later transformation occurred at all, however, has been of scarcely more interest to historical research than to the Sanskrit cosmopolis itself.

Premodern Cosmpolitanism

What, in fact, is modernity? The concept is notoriously unclear even in social theory, the science of modernity; so, too, then, must its periodization be. For some scholars, modernity began with capitalism, for others, with industrialization or colonialism or nationalism (whenever each of these may have begun). For still others, it has yet to begin, since they do not believe there has been any great rupture at all, only "small extensions of practices, slight accelerations in the circulation of knowledge, a tiny extension of societies, minuscule increases in the number of actors, small modifications of old beliefs."[7]

Modernity is a contrastive historical concept and therefore implies some understanding of what is counted as premodern. But much of the work on modernity (from Karl Marx to present-day scholars such as Anthony Giddens, Jürgen Habermas, Niklas Luhmann, and so down the alphabet) offers little in the way of a convincing account of the nature of the "premodern," at least in the case of South Asia. The actual modernity of a number of phenomena included on lists of things considered modern remains uncertain. Some are probably modern beyond dispute: commodities that incorporate abstract labor as a unit of value, the sovereign state, and the abstract individual. But consider the following criteria: the preponderance of formal over substantive rationality (in, say, the organization of work or systems of accounting), the division of manual and mental labor, the abstraction of the social as a totality that can be acted on, the economy conceivable as an independent domain, "embedded affinity to place," a reflexive appropriation of knowledge, the rise of expert systems that remove social relations from particular contexts, the questioning of moral frameworks that had once been accepted unhesitatingly, a new worry about the meaninglessness of life, and loneliness. All these have been posited as elements of modernity, but none has been shown to be unequivocally so, or to be entirely unknown to premodernity. By the same token, many of the properties ascribed to premodernity (e.g., "a just sense of security in an independently given world") seem to have been identified not through empirical historical work but by simply imputing counterpositive features required by the very narrative of modernity (with its "calculation of risk in circumstances where expert knowledge creates the world of action through the continual reflexive implementation of knowledge").[8] Just as we often conceive of the premodern by uncritically accepting the discourse of modernity, so we sometimes transfer to the past ideas or practices originating in modernity itself and so produce a premodernity that is not premodern. Moreover, European modernity and South Asian premodernity are obviously uneven and not absolute categories; the former displays premodern features, the latter modern ones, no matter what definitions we invoke.

There are, as a consequence, entirely legitimate issues in cultural and political history to be raised through notions of "early modernities," "multiple modernities," "alternative modernities"; I have raised some myself. If one of the defining or enabling features of European modernity was the vernacularization of the cultural and political spheres, the same occurred in South Asia independently of European influence.[9] Not only did Indian "premodernity" contain elements of European modernity, but in some key areas of culture, such as the analysis of language, it might even have stimulated the development of that modernity.

But there is no reason to set such received ideas on their head and find an Indian modernity (or nationalism or capitalism or whatever) *avant la lettre*. My concerns lie elsewhere. First, I want to understand the differences, if any, between the power-culture practices and their associated theories—legitimation, ideology, nationalism, civilizationalism, and the like—that came into being in modern Europe and the world of South Asia before the arrival of these practices and theories on the heels of European expansion. These are what I have in mind when identifying what I contrastively and commonsensically call "premodern" South Asian materials, without fretting too much over how "premodern" or "modern" is to be defined or who has the right to define them. Second, I want to determine whether it is possible to work conceptually around such theories of power-culture and to understand what alternative practices may once have been available.

From the Cosmopolitan to the Vernacular

Without the contrastive category of the vernacular, and the contrastive reality of both political and cultural self-understanding toward which it points, the cosmopolitan has no conceptual purchase. Like "cosmopolitan," "vernacular" is not something that goes without saying, and not only because of its own scalar ambiguities (how small qualifies as vernacular?). A range of conceptual and historical problems have combined to effectively conceal the very process of people knowledgeably becoming vernacular—what is termed here "vernacularization"—leaving it largely unhistoricized and even unconceptualized in scholarship. Until these problems are clarified and some reasonable working hypotheses framed, vernacularization itself cannot even be perceived, to say nothing of its political and cultural ramifications. The problems here are in fact not all that different from those presented by cosmopolitanism, though they are perhaps denser. Besides considering the pertinent relational boundaries, we need to be clear about what the process of vernacularization entails, in particular what role to assign to writing and to the creation of expressive texts. Only when we gain some clarity about the intelligibility and reality of the object of analysis, and how this object exists in time, can we begin to ask why it has the particular history it does.

Simply to define the vernacular over against the cosmopolitan and leave it at that—even to make unqualified use of any of the kindred terms or phrases adopted here, like "regional" and "transregional"—elides some important aspects of their relativity. An obvious one is the potential of a local language to become translocal, and the consequences of this for codes that are yet more local. The extreme case is offered by the cosmopolitan languages themselves. All of them began their careers as vernaculars: Latin in the third century B.C.E. was firmly rooted in Latium (central Italy) before setting out on its world conquest in lockstep with the advance of Roman arms. Sanskrit is the great anomaly here, since long before the onset of the cosmopolitan era it had become transregional—though not yet cosmopolitan—through the spread of Vedic culture.[10]

The vernaculars in the postcosmopolitan era expanded, too, but on a different order of magnitude. If a certain transregionality thus characterized the vernaculars that attained political-cultural salience, this was on a different scale from that of the cosmopolitan codes they displaced. This difference can be plotted along both the axis of material practice and that of subjective understanding. Sanskrit literary texts circulated from Sri Lanka to Sorcuq in central Asia, and from Afghanistan to Annam in Southeast Asia (just as Latin literary texts circulated from Iberia to Romania and Britain to Tunisia). They filled all the available cultural space, their expansion as literary-political media limited only by other cosmopolitan cultural formations. In northern Vietnam, for example, from the fifth century on, Sanskrit's advance was arrested by Chinese, just as that of Latin had been arrested by Greek in the eastern Mediterranean a few centuries earlier. The vernaculars inhabited much smaller zones. The limits they confronted, or, rather, helped produce, were certain political-cultural isoglosses, so to speak, whose history and character are probed in the course of the second part of this work.

The objective dimensions of vernacular place over against those of cosmopolitan space also were registered in the subjective universes of the vernacular intellectuals. To participate in Sanskrit literary culture was to participate in a vast world; to produce a regional alternative to it was to effect a profound break, one that the agents themselves understood to be a break, in cultural communication and self-understanding. It was in conscious opposition to this larger sphere that these intellectuals defined their regional worlds. They chose to write in a language that did not travel—and that they knew did not travel—as easily and as far as the well-traveled language of the older cosmopolitan order. The new power-culture places they projected, which were the conceptual correlates of the isoglosses just mentioned, fully testify to this sense of limit and contrast sharply with the spatial matrices at work in Sanskrit culture.

The localization in question is reflected in the South Asian term for the vernacular. If "Sanskrit cosmopolis" is a phrase hobbled by its hybridity, its adoption is an adversity that cannot be avoided and that anyway has uses in foregrounding the quasi-global, the political, and the cultural. "Vernacular" has similar liabilities and benefits. To be sure, a pejorative connotation haunts the Latin etymon—it refers to the language of the *verna,* or house-born slave, of Republican Rome—which has little political-cultural relevance to premodern South Asia. However, in a more common, indeed classical, sense the Latin *vernacularis* is "local," "native," "inborn," and even "Roman" (in contrast to *peregrinus,* "foreign"). Apart from the fact that the cosmopolitan culture of Rome could be conceived of as native (another of its radical differences from the Sanskrit order, deriving from Latin's very different history), the sense of local does map well against the South Asian idiom. In many South Asian languages, the conceptual counterpart to the cosmopolitan is *deśī,* the "placed," or "[a practice] of Place." Yet it is crucial to register at once the paradox that what was *deśī* was not often thought of as native, inborn, or sometimes even local. Not only was the creation of local places a cultural process consequent on literary vernacularization, but the very ubiquity of the self-same term *deśī* across South Asia also is a sign of the *cosmopolitan* origins of the literary vernacular itself.

Vernacularization is here understood—not a priori or stipulatively but from tendencies visible in the empirical record—as the historical process of choosing to create a written literature, along with its complement, a political discourse, in local languages according to models supplied by a superordinate, usually cosmopolitan, literary culture. The process can thus be broken down into three connected components: literization (writing, the symbolic elevation of what is written, and the internal transformations the literary text undergoes by the very fact of being written down); literarization (the production of boundary between the purely oral and *kāvya* on the basis of a relatively stable paradigm of literary properties that in addition to lexical, metrical, and thematic features included writing as a fundamental component); and superposition (the presence of a dominant language and literary formation).

If nationalists and other indigenists are predisposed to discover an ever deeper history for the literature of the Folk, reaching back to a golden moment of pure autochthony, historical analysis shows that literatures typically arise in response to other literature *superposed* on them in a relation of unequal cultural power. In premodern India, this other literature was preeminently Sanskrit but also, to some degree, Prakrit and Apabhramsha (which were particularly rich sources of metrical forms for the vernaculars to appropriate), Tamil in some areas of south India, and, much later, Persian in some areas of the north. Conformity with the superposed matrix and its norms was the goal of those vernacular textbooks meant to "ornament" the language. Indeed, they were part of a literary apparatus that was adopted whole-sale during the crystallizing moments of many vernacular literary cultures and formed a core component in the creation of what is here named the "cosmopolitan vernacular," that register of the emergent vernacular that aims to localize the full spectrum of literary qualities of the superposed cosmopolitan code.[11]

To speak of a cosmopolitan vernacular is not just to acknowledge that "different languages are penetrated by each other, thus revealing every language's intimate discord with itself, the bilingualism implicit in all human speech"; nor even to try to update the idea of "vernacular humanism," of "using the ancient languages as models and so making the vernacular languages into worthy vehicles for literature and culture."[12] Instead, it is to point to the historical creation of a medium of culture that was not only new in itself but appropriate to a new vision of power. It was a medium of Place for a political vision of Place but fashioned according to the time-honored model of *kāvya* and *rājya* of the great Way, which had been tied to no one place but was inclusive of them all.

Whatever else it may be, the vernacularization of literature and political discourse is a social act, and one that typically bears crucial geocultural and political entailments. While it is no easier to understand the practices of power in the second millennium than in the first, it is clear that during the period from 1000 to 1500, these practices took on far more distinctively regionalized traits than ever before. Whether crystallizing culture spheres were the cause or the consequence of crystallizing power spheres, or whether the two arose through a kind of dialectical dynamic, a new symmetry between the domains was manifestly being created. Functional regions began to coincide with formal regions — those new and coherent representations of place in vernacular literature that superseded the vast geocultural spaces prevalent during the preceding millennium. Understanding the nature of the new political order that arose with vernacularization is as difficult as understanding the nature of "empire" in the cosmopolitan epoch, and it has seemed preferable, therefore, to name this new political form neutrally as the "vernacular polity" rather than try to shoehorn it into some given European conceptual category (such as "protonation"). But one thing is certain: however much the fact may conflict with dominant social-science theory, especially of nationalism, power and culture had indeed a very considerable, if sometimes obscure, inclination for each other in premodern South Asia.

That the context of power fundamentally shaped the process of vernacularization in South Asia sits awkwardly with the unchallenged scholarly consensus regarding its origins as essentially religious, a kind of Indian Reformation. This view is as erroneous as is the one that locates the origins of European vernacularization in the real Reformation (sometimes Protestant presuppositions do not work even for Europe). Virtually all the reasons adduced for explaining vernacularization in South Asia as originating in a socioreligious rebellion are dubious. The presumed concomitance between Sanskrit and Brahmanism, on the one hand, and vernacularity and non-Brahmanism, on the other, does not hold for much of the period under discussion. The vision of Sanskrit as a sacred language "jealously preserved by the Brahmans in their schools" may not be the pure illusion of the colonial officer who gave it expression. Yet it is undoubtedly something that developed late in this history of the language, when, for reasons very likely having to do with vernacularization itself, language options shrank for many communities, and Brahmanical society reasserted its archaic monopolization over the language (the Catholic Church's eventual monopolization of Latin is an instructive parallel both historically and structurally).[13] In most cases, vernacular beginnings occurred independently of religious stimuli strictly construed, and the greater portion of the literature thereby created was produced not at the monastery but at the court. Only after vernacularization had been consolidated, and in reaction to an already existing courtly literary and political culture, did a more demotic and often more religiously insurgent *second* vernacular revolution take place (as in twelfth-century Karnataka, fifteenth-century Gujarat, sixteenth-century Assam, and elsewhere). Here the cosmopolitan vernacular was challenged and, in some cases, displaced by a regional vernacular, a register far more localized in everything from lexicon to metrics to themes. By foregrounding the role of power in creating both the Sanskrit cosmopolis and the various regional worlds that succeeded it, my account aims to redress an interpretive balance that for too long has been skewed toward the religious.

In the nexus of poetry and polity, we also encounter what is most salient and most neglected for a cross-cultural historical analysis of vernacularization. Between India and Europe, temporal, spatial, and other synchronies and symmetries abound. The tempo and structure of Dravidian and Germanic vernacularization, for example, form a striking contrast with those of north Indian and Romance languages. Many of the textual components in European vernacularization are comparable to those found in South Asia, such as the localization of superposed literary forms, genres, and themes. The social milieus are similar, too. The European vernaculars achieved literary expressivity—and often did so with astonishing abruptness—through the agency of courtly elites. Whereas vernacular culture was undoubtedly in some sense popular culture in its origins, the process of full vernacularization was decidedly not. Yet there are important differences, too. In Europe the vernacular's admission to literacy was more contested, both linguistically and ideologically. Vernacular distinction was slower in coming and was attended with greater anxiety; the cosmopolitan formation was more resistant in its claim to primacy. A far more significant divergence is found in the development of polity. In both areas, the political order that emerged in conjunction with vernacularization offered a regional alternative to the transregional imperial formation. But the specific character of the European form and its end point, the nation-state, was unlike anything found in South Asia. The cultural and political theory designed to make sense of the European nation-state is often, and too facilely, applied to the premodern world outside Europe, distorting thinking about language and identity, and identity and polity, and thereby occluding the specificity of the Indian case and its misfit with models designed to explain the

European. The comparative turn is therefore imperative for a history and theory of vernacularity in southern Asia.

The transformations in culture and power that began concurrently in India and Europe around the start of the second millennium were consolidated by its midway point. The rules of the new vernacular game of polity and poetry had largely been drawn up; the cosmopolitan power-culture order in both worlds was almost completely supplanted by the seventeenth century. If it is becoming possible to recognize vernacularization as a key historical problem only now that it is ending, the recognition is the easy part. Far more difficult is understanding the hard history of its origins, why across much of Eurasia the world abandoned cosmopolitanism and empire in favor of vernacularity and regional polities, and why this happened when it did. Whereas we can identify some factors that clearly contributed— reinvigorated trading networks in the early second millennium concentrated wealth in local power centers, and the expansion of Islam on its western and eastern frontiers offered new cultural stimuli—a unified explanation of the historical origins of vernacularism is as improbable as a unified explanation of the cosmopolitanism that preceded it. Yet the lack does not preclude us from learning lessons from these events, both for the theory of power and culture and for their practice.

To study the history of vernacularization is to study not the history of the emergence of primeval and natural communities of peoples and cultures but the historical inauguration of the naturalization of peoples and cultures through new conceptual and discursive practices. This naturalization took place by a double procedure of reduction and differentiation. As unmarked dialect was turned into unifying standard, heterogeneous practice into culture, and undifferentiated space into place, new regional worlds were created. What was inside these worlds would eventually be seen as the indigenous and natural; what was outside, as the exogenous and artificial. This did not happen everywhere in a similar manner. Not all ways of the cultural production of vernacular sameness and difference have been the same, any more than all cosmopolitanisms have been the same. Figuring out what may have been distinctive about these vernacular and cosmopolitan practices is a precious, if elusive, prize.

Notes

This chapter is adapted and reorganized from Sheldon Pollock, *The Language of the Gods in the World of Men: Sanskrit, Culture, and Power in Premodern India*. Copyright © 2006 by The Regents of the University of California. Reprinted by permission of University of California Press.

1. See, for example, Sheldon Pollock, "Introduction: Cosmopolitanisms," in *Cosmpolitanism*, ed. Carol Breckenridge et al. (Durham, N.C.: Duke University Press, 2002), 1–14.

2. Arjun Appadurai has rightly cautioned against a "rush to history" meant to neutralize the "special anxiety about its own not-newness" that contemporary globalization seems to provoke. Arjun Appadurai, "Globalization and the Rush to History," Sawyer Seminar lecture, Columbia University, 1999. An example is A. G. Hopkins, ed., *Globalization in World History* (New York: Norton, 2002).

3. Heine had a sense of this resistance 150 years ago: "Es ist zu wünschen, daß sich das Genie des Sanskritstudiums bemächtige; tut es der Notizengelehrte, so bekommen wir bloss—ein gutes Kompendium." Heinrich Heine, "Aphorismen und Fragmente," in *Sämtliche Werke* (Munich: Carl Hanser, 1964), 14:113.

4. The phrase is that of Sankaran Krishna, "Cartographic Anxiety: Mapping the Body Politic in India," *Alternatives* 19, no. 4 (1994): 507–21.

5. The first is Sylvain Lévi's assessment, cited in Jules Bloch, *Indo-Aryan from the Vedas to Modern Times* (Paris: Adrien-Maisonneuve, 1965), 14–15; the second is standard-issue postcolonial theory.

6. Curiously, little good theoretical work seems to be available on cultural and political comparison. See, for now, John Bowen and Roger Petersen, eds., *Critical Comparison in Politics and Culture* (Cambridge: Cambridge University Press, 1999), 1–19, and especially the chapter by Greg Urban, "The Role of Comparison in the Light of the Theory of Culture."

7. Bruno Latour, *We Have Never Been Modern* (Cambridge, Mass.: Harvard University Press, 1993), 47–48.

8. For most of these properties, see Anthony Giddens, *The Consequences of Modernity* (Stanford, Calif.: Stanford University Press, 1990), 84.

9. See Sheldon Pollock, "India in the Vernacular Millennium: Literary Culture and Polity, 1000–1500," *Daedalus* 127, no. 3 (1998): 41–74.

10. On the early history of the transregionality of this culture, which is not addressed in this book, the work of Michael Witzel is central. See, for example, Michael Witzel, "On the Localisation of Vedic Texts and Schools," in *India and the Ancient World: History, Trade, and Culture Before A.D. 650*, ed. G. Pollet (Leuven: Peeters, 1987), 173–213.

11. Texts that "adorn" the South Asian vernaculars by framing grammatical and rhetorical norms (the *Siyabaslakar* of ninth-century Sri Lanka,

the *Kannaḍabhāṣābhūṣaṇam* of eleventh-century Karnataka, the *[Braj] Bhāṣābhūṣaṇ* of seventeenth-century Jodhpur) are precisely equivalent to those meant to "illustrate" the European vernaculars.

12. Giorgio Agamben, *The End of the Poem* (Stanford, Calif.: Stanford University Press, 1999), 59; Erich Auerbach, *Literary Language and Its Public in Latin Antiquity and in the Middle Ages* (Princeton, N.J.: Princeton University Press, 1965), 319.

13. For the citations, see George Abraham Grierson, *Linguistic Survey of India*, vol. 1, pt. 1, *Introductory* (Calcutta: Supt. Government Printing, 1927), 1129. I mention the gradual decrease in language options in early modern South Asia in my "Sanskrit Literary Culture from the Inside Out," in *Literary Cultures in History: Reconstructions from South Asia*, ed. Sheldon Pollock (Berkeley: University of California Press, 2003), 39–130.

4

Joseph Banks's Intermediaries

Rethinking Global Cultural Exchange

VANESSA SMITH

This morn Tupia came on board, he had renewed his resolves of going with us to England, a circumstance which gives me much satis-
faction. He is certainly a most proper man, well born, cheif *Tahowa*
or preist of this Island, consequently skilld in the mysteries of their
religion; but what makes him more than any thing else desireable is
his experience in the navigation of these people and knowledge of
the Islands in these seas; he has told us the names of above 70, the
most of which he has himself been at. The Captn refuses to take him
on his own account, in my opinion sensibly enough, the government
will never in all human probability take any notice of him; I therefore have resolvd to take him. Thank heaven I have a sufficiency
and I do not know why I may not keep him as a curiosity, as well as
some of my neighbours do lions and tygers at a larger expence than
he will probably ever put me to; the amusement I shall have in his
future conversation and the benefit he will be to this ship, as well as
what he may be if another should be sent to these seas, will I think
fully repay me.[1]

This citation comes from an entry in the journal of Joseph Banks, written from Tahiti on July 12, 1769. It records Banks's pleasure in learning
that Tupaia, the Raiatean priest who had been a valuable guide and

interlocutor during his sojourn on the island, has resolved to travel to England on the *Endeavour*. His delight is easy to comprehend. Tupaia, as Banks indicates, was an authority on Society Islands religion, history, and culture; a linguist and a traveler; a navigator and an ethnographer. But as he imagines Tupaia sailing beyond the Oceanic world and back to England, Banks finds himself unable to maintain his respectful recognition of Tupaia's intellectual authority. Instead, he foresees a world in which Tupaia will be regarded as curiosity rather than curious. Matching his rhetoric to his anticipations, he frames a now notorious comparison of the eminent Tahitian with an exotic animal.

Banks's diary entry, to which I will return later in more detail, sets out the problematic that I will examine in this chapter. From the earliest contacts, the expansion of European knowledge has depended on cultural intermediaries willing to act as local informants, translators, and guides, as well as in more profound capacities such as Tupiaia's, as intellectual interlocutors able to negotiate between not just languages but also epistemologies, methodologies, genres, and practices. The retrieval of these intermediating subjects from the archive is a fraught process precisely because of the shift we see played out in slow motion in the passage from Banks's journal. As they become embedded in writing, cultural intermediaries become subject to rhetorical and discursive imperatives that occlude or diminish their agency, subtly transforming them from subjects into objects of knowledge. This is a particular problem when considering the role of such intermediaries in intellectual history, whose relationship to writing is one of special privilege.

Intellectual History and the Cultural Intermediary

This volume's goal of extending the "global turn" to intellectual history begs the question of the cultural intermediary. Bearing in mind the global frame of reference, however, also enables us to question assumptions that inform the dominant construal of both intellectual history and cultural intermediarism. The concept of the cultural intermediary is still, in historical and sociological circles, frequently derived from the work of Pierre Bourdieu and his critique of cultural capital.

In his *Distinction*, cultural intermediaries (equated with "the new petite bourgeoisie" and comprising "all the occupations involving presentation and representation [sales, marketing, advertising, public relations, fashion, decoration, and so forth] and all the institutions providing symbolic goods and services") figure precisely as those who blur distinctions, between high and popular culture, facilitating a new cultural accessibility. In class terms, they represent a transitional status between the middle and the newly educated working classes, because "the indeterminacy of the new or renovated occupations means that the heterogeneity of the agents' trajectories is particularly marked."[2] Although Bourdieu's broader recognition of indeterminate status as critical to the role of the cultural intermediary is widely applicable, his specific critique of class relations is endogenous. In contrast, the notion of intermediarism that I am exploring here is, in keeping with the theme of the volume, exogenous. "Cross" is a silent qualifier in my use of "cultural intermediaries," and my primary emphasis in considering the concept of "culture" is on horizontal relations rather than Bourdieu's vertical axis of cultural authorization.

Either explicitly or implicitly, intellectual history is understood as textual history.[3] Given the intensity and acute reflexivity with which intellectual historians engaged and debated the pressures of a "linguistic turn" in the late 1980s, the conflation of intellectual with written history may be more a product of slippage than polemics.[4] The turn to a global intellectual history highlights the problems of equating the intellectual with the written, and it invites a new emphasis on the contributions of participants from cultures in which writing is a belated mode of communication (a move that, in turn, foregrounds the politicized dimensions of written production). It is in confronting the implicit bias toward written contributions in the production of knowledge that the work of postcolonial theorists becomes particularly useful to a globalized intellectual history. The analysis of cross-cultural encounter has engaged with increasing subtlety with the problem of imbalance in the written record. Edward Said's landmark *Orientalism* defined the discipline and discourse he examined in three increasingly nuanced ways, all archival and textually generative. Traditionally, he noted, "Anyone who teaches, writes about or researches the Orient — and this applies whether the person is an anthropologist, sociologist, historian, or philologist—either in its specific or general aspects is an Orientalist, and what he or she does is Orientalism." Said extended this academic definition to incorporate

> a very large mass of writers, among whom are poets, novelists, philosophers, political theorists, economists and imperial administrators, [who] have accepted the basic distinction between East and West as a starting point for elaborate theories, epics, novels, social descriptions, and political accounts concerning the Orient, its people, customs, "mind," destiny, and so on.

Finally, he drew on the discourse theory of Michel Foucault to politicize Orientalism as "the enormously systematic discipline by which European culture was able to manage—and even produce—the Orient politically, sociologically, militarily, ideologically, scientifically, and imaginatively during the post-Enlightenment period."[5] As many scholars have since noticed, Said's critique ironically repeated the gesture of consigning the Oriental subject to the status of object of European representation, by allowing no space for the emergence of Oriental agency. This paradox was seen to be intensified in the more virtuoso deconstructive theory that emerged in Said's wake: Gayatri Spivak's fine-grained analyses of the inevitable imprisonment of subaltern women within Western discourse, or Homi Bhabha's recognition that "native subjects" might destabilize Western documentary regimes from within by practicing an unsettling replication of Western law and its practices of inscription that was at once identical and different.[6]

In expanding the purview of Said's analysis from the discipline of anthropology to the practice of ethnography, whose methodologies had, since the fieldwork manifesto of Bronislaw Malinowski, been predicated on the primarily oral intermediating work of local informants, a first wave of scholarship remained focused on the textual trace.[7] The *Writing Culture* project of James Clifford and George Marcus inaugurated a new emphasis on writing as the "occulted" dimension of an anthropological fieldwork that claimed a kind of transparency in conveying the knowledge of indigenous informants to Western audiences. Clifford and Marcus turned from the dialogues of participant-observation foregrounded by Malinowski "to high-light the constructed, artificial nature of cultural accounts," and they promoted a radical self-consciousness in ethnographic writing.[8] The *Writing Culture* project highlighted the degree to which oral and writ-ten cultural practices combined to produce ethnographic knowledge. As Felix Driver and Lowri Jones show, there is a reciprocal require-ment to exhume intermediating bodies and voices from the archive of ethnographic exchange. Driver and Jones's work focuses on the collections of the Royal Geographical Society, founded in 1830, now comprising an archive of more than a million maps, half a million pho-tographs, and thousands of books, articles, manuscripts, artifacts, and artworks. Their project, representing the collection to a public audi-ence via both text and exhibition, reevaluates imperial exploration as "a joint project of work, undertaken for different reasons and with different results for the parties concerned, but a joint project none-theless." Their description of the "work" of imperialism necessarily extends to the archive that enshrines its traces. As Driver and Jones concluded, "We can think of the resulting contributions to geographi-cal knowledge as co-productions."[9]

For situations in which intermediaries are the representatives of oral cultures, doing justice to their role in the historical record requires the development of reading practices sensitized to both rhetorical imbalances and obfuscations in the sources. In simple quantitative terms, the entire literary archive of oral societies reifies the uneven-ness between Western recordation and indigenous objectification that postcolonialists have long critiqued. The most influential monograph to have grown out of the *Writing Culture* project, Mary Louise Pratt's *Imperial Eyes: Travel Writing and Transculturation*, describes the dis-crimination inherent in archival evidence:

> The more I studied the huge corpus of travel literature written by Europeans over two hundred and fifty years, the more aware I became of the participants whose voices I wasn't hearing. There was a huge gap in the archive. What had the people who received these visitors thought of them and the imperial designs they brought with them? How and in what forms of expression had they interpreted the historical processes they were living?[10]

The process of reading against the grain of the imperial record is potentially circular: evidence of local knowledge with which to counter European representations must often be extracted from the same sources that enshrine those representations. Moreover, when indigenous voices captured in recorded versions of chants, songs, and oral histories appear to offer the promise of a counterarchive to the European one, these too cannot be regarded as pure or original sources, since they also bear, however discreetly, the traces of the imperial, missionary, or administrative contexts in which they were produced. Another anthropological response has sought in modern indigenous versions of cultural practice a key to the cultural references in historical documents. This, however, risks reinforcing a long-standing separation between so-called modern, historied societies and so-called primitive societies that are regarded as locked in a perpetual present, able to comment with a timeless continuity on customs untouched by the politics of historical change.[11]

A number of strategies developed in relation to contact scenarios between European and nonliterate cultures may continue to help recast a globalized intellectual history. Mary Louise Pratt further remarked on a persistent indigenous presence in the archive: "From time to time as I read, I glimpsed the ongoing ways empire was coded by those in whose lives it intervened—coded in ceremony, sculpture and painting, in dance, parody, philosophy and history; in expressions unwitnessed, suppressed, lost, or simply overlaid with repetition and unreality." Her response to this recognition was to develop dialectical ways of reading designed to extrapolate the indigenous perspective veiled or silenced in historical accounts. Pratt coins the term "contact zone" for the notion of encounter that her analysis emphasizes. "Contact zone" evokes the copresence of imperial and indigenous subjects and "foregrounds the interactive, improvisational dimensions of imperial encounters so easily ignored or suppressed by accounts from the invader's perspective."[12] Pratt's theorization of the contact zone is comparable to Greg Dening's compelling metaphorization of "the beach" as a liminal space that stages the ambiguous power relationships of early contact, before territorial claims, and in which the two sides of encounter may be viewed as more evenly pitched and mutually inquiring.[13] Bronwen Douglas's

critical practice stresses the need, through a process of actively con-
testatory reading against the grain of imperial texts and images, to
unearth "countersigns" of indigenous agency. In a series of essays
and books, she applies her method to all the texts identified by Driver
and Jones: written accounts, images, cultural practices, maps, and
artifacts.[14] Greg Dening's reenvisioning of contact in theatrical rather
than essentialized terms exemplifies a turn to the performative in
ethnohistorical and ethnographic analysis of intercultural exchange,
which seeks to enable oral cultural practices to dictate the terms of
analysis. Dening disrupts his historical narrative with first-person
interpolations to remind his readers of the relativized and performative aspects of historical knowledge.[15] More radically, in his book
Shamanism, Colonialism and the Wild Man, Michael Taussig uses a
dialogic mode of writing to perform the shamanistic ritual that he
describes to his readers, thereby attempting to "heal" ingrained perceptions. He aims to enable the subject of writing to dictate the mode
of communication of cultural knowledge and to produce ontological transformations in his Western readership. The imbalances of the
written record have prompted others to depreciate texts in favor of
studying artifacts. Nicholas Thomas's redirection of anthropological
attention toward the object, both functional and artistic, recognizes
the "entanglement" of local and European practices and agendas in
colonial cross-cultural exchange, deprivileging the written archive
as the primary site of historical traces of encounter.[16]

The work of historians of science has reprised these evolving critiques of archival history by moving toward a greater recognition of
the intellectual contribution of non-European subjects to the development of global scientific knowledge. Bruno Latour's identification
of metropolitan "centers of calculation," epicenters at which knowledge was gradually gathered and archived in the service of projects
of empire, has proved hugely influential in the Orientalism mode.
Latour's analysis, equally indebted to Foucault's theories of discourse
and discipline, exposed the operations of an imperial will to know that
sought to render alterity portable, abstractable, and translatable for
accumulation at imperial centers.[17] More recent historians of science,
in turn, have highlighted the ways in which such Eurocentric formulations continue to occlude indigenous voices in the archive, instead

emphasizing the coproduction of scientific knowledge across global and imperial boundaries. Dhruv Raina and S. Irfan Habib, in their *Domesticating Modern Science: A Social History of Science and Culture in Colonial India* (2004), and Kapil Raj, in *Relocating Modern Science: Circulation and the Construction of Scientific Knowledge in South Asia and Europe,* focus on the South Asian appropriation of European scientific ideas and the reciprocal contribution of South Asian cultural intermediaries to the shaping of European scientific developments during the long nineteenth century. Raj rehearses a broader movement in his discipline from a "big-picture," grand-narrative account of Western scientific development to one through which "scientific knowledge turns out . . . to be local everywhere." Attendant on this disciplinary turn, he points out, is an emphasis on the intercultural *constitution* of knowledge:

> In particular, [the recent history of science] looks at the role of intercultural encounter in the circulation of the specialized knowledges that constituted science in this period. It addresses the following questions: What was the nature of the vectors of knowledge transmission? Who were the agents involved in the transmission and appropriation of knowledge and skills in the spaces of intercultural encounter? Was this a simple process of diffusion and acceptance or was there an active process of reception and reconfiguration of the circulating knowledges and skills? If the latter, where—outside of European metropolitan centres—was knowledge being reconstructed and certified? What was the relationship of this knowledge with its metropolitan sibling? Were these knowledges transportable? If so, what happened in the process of displacement?[18]

The kinds of intellectual historical investigation with which Raj affiliates himself do not reaffirm that "colonial science" or "colonial knowledge" constitute classifying discourses that exclude or forcibly appropriate indigenous or local knowledges from an imperial center. Rather, they "advance an alternative vision of the construction and spread of scientific knowledge through reciprocal, albeit asymmetric, processes of circulation and negotiation, a vision at odds with current post-colonial thinking." Raj sets out to demonstrate that South Asia was not a space for the simple application of European knowledge, nor a vast site for the collection of diverse information to be processed in the metropolis, nor indeed "of complicated and complex knowledge created by Indians, but codified and transmitted by Europeans." On the contrary, South Asia was an active, although unequal, participant in an emerging world order of knowledge. . . . The contact zone was a site for the production of certified knowledges which would not have come into being but for the intercultural encounter between South Asian and European intellectual and material practices that took place here. In other words, although these knowledges had different trajectories in specialist communities in South Asia and Europe and were appropriated and integrated differently in the two regions (not least because of colonial domination), they partook of, and were constructed through, the same circulatory processes.[19]

Although Raj rejects a conventional postcolonial analysis here, his adoption of Mary Louise Pratt's term "contact zone" indicates the influence that certain second-wave postcolonial theories have had in rethinking the history of science. Whereas the work of South Asian historians of science has promoted the reconsideration of the role of cultural intermediaries in shaping both European science and its peripheral redactions, in a final revisionist twist Alix Cooper argued that the opening up of contact with foreign cultures during the early modern period, including the global circulation of indigenous knowledge, technologies, and practices, led to a reconceptualization of the "indigenous" in Europe—to a valuing, recording, and archiving of European local knowledge. Her work complicates the polarization of European and "exotic," demonstrating instead that in the realm of nature and its attendant cultural practices, the exotic gradually began to be perceived as a prerogative of home.[20]

Banks's Networks of Knowledge

The variety and texture of recent thinking about the intercultural production of knowledge offer new lenses for reexamining key figures in intellectual history, as well as the debts and entanglements of the facts they employed and the methodologies and epistemologies of their investigations. In the rest of this chapter, I consider one such figure: Joseph Banks, botanist on the *Endeavour*, long-term president of the Royal Society, and object of veneration and scandal.[21] I contend that what might be said to link these disparate and, at times, apparently contradictory aspects of Banks's career is in fact an engagement with and a gradual reconceptualization of the role of the cultural intermediary. This is not to dispute influential and compelling alternative conceptions of Banks's role as a "servant of empire" or as an exemplary recipient and dispenser of patronage, occupying a Latourian "center of calculation."[22] Each of these models, however, in seeking to do justice to the unequal power relations of empire, continues to privilege the metropole in conceptualizing the development of botanical knowledge. By foregrounding the significance of Banks's early travels and encounters in inaugurating a model of dialogue that was put into practice with later informants and interlocutors across the globe, I hope to show the fundamental role of indigenous cultural intermediaries in one branch of Enlightenment intellectual investigation. I should stress here that my concern in the ensuing discussion is not, as with much of the history of science scholarship I have discussed, with reclaiming particular, purportedly European, objects or inventions as cultural coproductions. Rather, my focus is on a reconceptualization of cultural intermediation itself that, I argue, followed on Banks's experience of indigenous interlocution.

Studies of Banks's legacy have recognized the fundamental role of knowledge networks in both the development of the Royal Society under his presidency and the shaping of colonial agriculture under his remote direction. Building on the precedent offered by Carl Linnaeus, the inaugurator of the classificatory method, who corresponded with travelers, collectors, and gardeners across the globe in applying his classificatory system to botanical and biological specimens, Banks built up a wide network of correspondents among travelers, administrators, and agriculturalists across the world of late-eighteenth- and nineteenth-century European empire. David Philip Miller early and influentially recuperated Banks's modus operandi to the Latourian paradigm of knowledge accumulation, arguing that "there is little doubt that Joseph Banks, more than any other individual of his times, did . . . make himself a centre of accumulation."[23] John Gascoigne provided the definitive account of the ways in which Banks's presidency of the Royal Society built on the seventeenth-century tradition of a Republic of Letters: a virtual scientific community that communicated across national boundaries and in spite of national conflicts, using Latin as its shared language, in a quest to extend European scientific knowledge. Gascoigne argues that

> Banks was more than an ex officio citizen of the Republic of Letters, for it became part of his programme for the betterment of the Royal Society and of science more generally to establish an international network of correspondence and exchange. He did so on a scale which foreigners recognized as exceptional and as betokening a real commitment to European rather than British science.[24]

Harry Liebersohn develops Gascoigne's notion of networks of knowledge into a detailed account of the ways in which European naturalists, artists, and philosophes—French, German, Russian, and Spanish as well as British—became involved in voyaging projects, coimplicating their different national politics, disciplines, knowledges, and texts in early encounters. Liebersohn is particularly attentive to the operations of patronage in the eighteenth century, offering an engrossing analysis of its role in establishing and consolidating Banks's scientific empire. Indeed he asserts that "one can almost write a history of voyage patronage in late-eighteenth and early-nineteenth-century England through the career of [this] one individual." Liebersohn, like Gascoigne, links Banks's objectives to those of the Republic of Letters but emphasizes the importance of his class status in mobilizing networks and discourses of patronage.[25]

Yet although the plurality of Banks's Royal Society projects is increasingly recognized, this expanded vision remains Eurocentric. An emphasis on the Republic of Letters as the main context for the development of correspondence networks has the potential to relegate the contributions of nonliterate indigenous subjects, who are understood to occupy, always and only, a highly mediated position in European letters, journals, and documents. In the texts of European intermediaries, European subjects play the role of "local" informant, dispensing local knowledge gathered from indigenous intermediaries, who typically remain unnamed and frequently unmentioned. In rethinking the role of the cultural intermediary in the Banksian archive, I want to retrieve the contribution of individual local informants to Banks's knowledge and also to suggest an alternative lineage for Banks's developing practice as president of the Royal Society. Rather than linking this to the textual tradition of the Republic of Letters or to British and European networks of patronage, I propose that Banks's taste for interlocution and intermediation was formed from, and his practice modeled on, conversations he had with Tupaia aboard the *Endeavour*. Moreover, I argue that his relationship with Tupaia was equally significant for his later negotiations of systems of patronage and publicity in the metropole.

"A Most Proper Man"

Although Tupaia came from Raiatea, where he was a high priest of the dominant war god Oro, when Banks encountered him he was an exile in Tahiti, deposed after the Boraboran invasion of Raiatea. For some time he had been an influential religious adviser to Purea, the most powerful chief in Tahiti.[26] By the time of James Cook's visit in 1769, Purea, and hence Tupaia, had lost local political favor.[27] Nonetheless, his huge repository of ritual and cultural knowledge and, indeed, his very in-between status, neither inside nor outside the culture under scrutiny, made Tupaia an important and acknowledged authority for both Banks and Cook. An appreciation of his value was reflected in both men's responses to his decision to sail with the *Endeavour*. Banks's reference to Tupaia as "a most proper man" in the journal entry quoted at the beginning of this chapter is affirmative in an unbounded sense: referencing both his eminent suitability as a cultural intermediary and his propriety in performing that role. Yet when Banks returned to England, it was in regard to issues of propriety that his and Tupaia's interlocutory relationship and the knowledge it brought to light came under scrutiny. In contrast, Cook's comments are those of a captain required to justify the presence of a new body on shipboard in terms of its usefulness to the expedition:

For some time before we left this Island several of the natives were daily offering themselves to go away with us, and as it was thought that they must be of use to us in our future discoveries, we resolved to bring away with us one whose name is *Tupia*, a Cheif and a Priest: This man had been with us the most part of the time we had been upon the Island which gave us an oppertunity to know some thing of him: we found him to be a very intelligent person and to know more of the Geography of the Islands situated in these seas, their produce and the religion laws and customs of the inhabitants then any one we had met with and was the likeliest person to answer our purpose.[28]

The intellect and knowledge Tupaia demonstrated at a local level in Tahiti are understood to be applicable to a broader scene: his personal intelligence and acquired knowledge combine to make him a worthwhile addition to the *Endeavour* community. However, Cook also hints at local values and agendas of advancement that his own set of criteria does not encompass. Like most of the European explorers of the Pacific at this time, he acknowledges a context of wider importuning, in which not one but "several" natives offer themselves to accompany the voyage and which is accorded different motivations: personal connection, desire for status, and interest in the customs of elsewhere.

A number of critics have distinguished between Cook's and Banks's interactions with cultural intermediaries by addressing Banks's affectively engaged enthusiasm for cross-cultural exchanges of knowledge. In *Sexual Encounters: Pacific Texts, Modern Sexualities*, Lee Wallace summed up a tendency in previous scholarship to "map . . . the outer limits of disciplinary and affective masculinity" onto the figures of James Cook and Joseph Banks, commenting that "the figures of Cook and Banks have routinely been used as markers for opposing poles of masculine definition with regard to British adventure in the South Seas." She noted the contrast between positive depictions of Banks's willing self-immersion in Tahitian cultural practice and ritual and those of Cook's imperialist detachment. Wallace's own contribution was to recognize that these two, apparently oppositional, modes of encounter might be read as "flip sides of the same coin." This was not merely a version of the more commonplace understanding that the

Royal Academy's protoscientific explorations functioned "in the service of empire," just as the Admiralty's territorial explorations did. Wallace further probed the sentimentalism that framed Banks's, and more significantly, John Hawkesworth's, construction of his encounters as affectively and sexually engaged: "Representationally shackled to Cook, Banks's masculine affect, his sympathy for and susceptibility to Polynesian femininity, rhetorically mitigates the aggression of encounter and so legitimates British presence in the Pacific."[29] In his comparison of Cook and Banks, David Turnbull fixes on Cook and Tupaia as the parallel authorities of the *Endeavour* voyage, close in age (they both were in their mid-forties at the time they met) and status, and sharing projects of knowledge centered on mapping and voyaging.[30] Yet Cook and Tupaia emerge in Cook's writings more as epistemological competitors than coexplorers. Banks, in contrast, who at twenty-five was at the time of the *Endeavour*'s visit to Tahiti just young enough to have been Tupaia's, or indeed Cook's, son, seems to have had a relationship with Tupaia that included aspects of mentoring. Banks was able to acknowledge the Raiatean as senior in both age and knowledge. His exchanges with Tupaia are characterized by an enabling perception of similarities; each appears to recognize the other as an informant and a cothinker.

Once the *Endeavour* set sail from Tahiti, Tupaia's authority emerged as both immediate and comprehensive. He had, as Banks mentions in his journal entry, mapped numerous Polynesian islands on paper. Although these do not appear in cartographic perspective, the voyage accounts acknowledge that he accurately calculated the number of days required to sail between different islands.[31] Since only minor consonantal shifts distinguish Oceanian dialects, Tupaia was well equipped to communicate with other Polynesians, and this in turn led to a wide perception of his authority among the islanders that the ship encountered. William Monkhouse, the *Endeavour*'s surgeon, recorded in his journal at Poverty Bay in New Zealand that "Topia's name was now ecchoed incessantly—he talked with them—."[32] As interpreter he was also, of course, free to translate British information on his own terms, as he was the sole conduit for European knowledge in these early exchanges. Here postcolonial theory's acknowledgment of the power of the medium finds its indigenous equivalent. It is clear that

Tupaia was not simply a transparent translator. Instead, he figures in Banks's journal as a conscious cultural comparativist who registered similarities and subtle distinctions between Society Islands practices and those farther afield. Moreover, Banks represents Tupaia's ability to extrapolate and relativize as he translates. Reporting an occasion on which relations with local inhabitants began to sour, he tells of how

> Tupia who I beleive guessd that they were coming to attack us immediately went upon the poop and talkd to them a good deal, telling them what if they provokd us we should do. . . . They answerd him in their usual cant "come ashore only and we will kill you all." Well, said Tupia, but while we are at sea you have no manner of Business with us, the Sea is our property as much as yours. Such reasoning from an Indian who had not had the smallest hint from any of us surprizd me much and the more as these sentiments I never had before heard him give a hint about in his own case.[33]

Both Cook and Banks were equally aware of Tupaia's value to the expedition, but their sense of this value is linked to alternative perceptions of the role of the intermediary. Whereas Banks figures this as dialogic in the proper sense—reciprocal and interlocutory—Cook stresses Tupaia's role as functionary, focusing on the ways in which his capacities as translator, navigator, and informant served the greater purpose of the British expedition. As I noted, while his journal entry mentioning Tupaia's decision to accompany the voyage acknowledges Tupaia's superior qualifications, Banks also links them to his own project of exploration. As the account of the voyage progresses, Cook, while recording Tupaia's initiatives in directing the ship's course and parleying with the local people, continues to stress his supplementary and functional role: "Tupia always accompanies us in every excursion we make and proves of infinate service." His attitude is encapsulated in a recurring phrase in his journal, "by means of Tupia." On January 31, at Queen Charlotte's Sound, he writes: "I next, by means of Tupia, explained to the old man and several others that we were come to set up a mark upon the Island in order to shew to any ship that might put into this place that we had been here before."[34] On leaving New Zealand, projecting further voyages of Pacific exploration, he refers to the advantage that Tupaia would give the British, primarily in his ability to serve as an ambassador in promoting friendly relations:

> But, should it be thought proper to send a ship out upon this service while *Tupia* lieves and he to come out in her, in that case she would have a prodigious advantage over every ship that have been upon discoveries in those seas before; for by means of Tupia, supposeing he did not accompany you himself, you would always get people to direct you from Island to Island and would be sure of meeting with a friendly reseption and refreshments at every Island you came to.[35]

Banks, by contrast, always acknowledges Tupaia's initiative. There is no sense that orders are issued that Tupaia carries out effectively: rather, Banks records Tupaia's practices and strategies of cross-cultural interaction, which appear, in the absence of any other source of command, to be self-motivated. Thus, in New Zealand, interchange with the Maori is represented not as an act of translation via Tupaia as the interpreter but as a conversation between Maori and Tupaia that is later translated to include the British: "They came tolerably near and answerd all the questions *Tupia askd them* very civily"; "After they had done this for some time they came nearer and *Tupia talkd with them* from the stern; they came into better temper and answerd *his* questions"; "Just then Tupia came upon deck, they ran *to him immediately, he assurd them* that their freind would not be killd."[36] Instead of asking what the British would achieve "by means of Tupia," he asks what Tupaia seems to manage by way of the British. This impression is augmented by Banks's tendency to figure Tupaia as in every way capable: he alone was equipped to "comfort" and "make easy" two Maori boys taken on board the *Endeavour*, able to cure himself of scurvy or to find a way of roasting coconuts that "made them lose intirely their acridity." He embraces the spectrum of useful skills: nurturer, surgeon, cook, preacher ("he however seemd to be much better vers'd in such legends than any of them, for whenever he began to preach as we calld it he was sure of a numerous audience who attended with most profound silence to his doctrines").[37] Tupaia appears to encompass traditionally masculine and feminine spheres of knowledge with a self-sufficient expertise of which Banks is clearly in awe.

Tupaia's illustration of longhouses and canoes in Tahiti. (Add. 15508, f.12
© The British Library Board. All Rights Reserved 2012)

One of the things that Banks and Tupaia seem to have shared was
an interest in specific forms of local manufacture and in individual
botanical specimens. Among a series of pictures that have recently
been identified as drafted by Tupaia while he was aboard the *Endeavour* is one illustrating a view toward the shore, showing two different types of canoe, a longhouse, and different varieties of trees and
plants with reticulated branches and leaves and carefully rendered
fruits. These include coconut and banana palms, taro, breadfruit, and
pandanus. Jennifer Newell claims that the drawing "provides unique
insights into the conceptions and priorities of a Polynesian man of the
late eighteenth century," noting that "he has drawn each plant as a
specific type."[38] Tupaia's typology, as evidenced in the image, comes
close to the Linnean system favored by Banks, in appearing to cat-
egorize according to edibility and usefulness. The image appears to
have been drawn while the *Endeavour* was still in the Society Islands.
Another shows Banks trading a handkerchief for a lobster during the
ship's visit to New Zealand. Here Tupaia appears to have shifted his

interest from use to exchange value and to be thinking about natural productions as both subsistence and trade, much as Banks did on his return to Britain. The first image is framed from the vantage point of the ship, and the second records an exchange between a representative of the land and one who has come across the sea. Tupaia appears to be using the perspective of the traveler to elaborate from a local to a global perspective.

Tupaia himself never reached England, so Banks was unable to host him, to continue their exchanges, and to see what kinds of knowledge the Raiatean was interested in gathering in Britain for dissemination in the Society Islands. He died in Batavia and is mourned in the pages of Banks's journal. Throughout this text, Banks's ethnographer's accreditation of Tupaia's learning, his recognition of his sensibility and reason, and his noninstrumentalism in comparison with Cook all speak to an understanding that they were coparticipants both in the discovery of facts and in the establishment of modes of interpretation. But Banks and Tupaia also were linked by a form of Tahitian patronage. Tupaia was Purea's erstwhile lover as well as her chief adviser. Banks subsequently became Purea's lover while in Tahiti, a relationship that, once it was intimated in Hawkesworth's *Voyages*, scandalized British society. In Tupaia's case, the role of consort had been one of personal advancement and power. In turn, he appears to have encouraged the union between Banks and his own former lover, while the preeminent woman implicitly ratified the bond between the two men. When Banks returned to England, however, he and Tupaia became scandalously identified in the British public imagination, through the figure of Purea ("Oberea"), as exchangers of sexual, not cultural, knowledge. The legacy of Purea's Tahitian patronage threatened to destabilize those metropolitan patronage networks that Banks was trying to consolidate in the period between the *Endeavour* voyage and his presidency of the Royal Society. Botanical and sexual knowledge become figures for each other in the cycle of Banks satires that followed the publication of Hawkesworth's *Account of the Voyages* in 1773. In John Scott's *Epistle from Oberea, Queen of Tahiti, to Joseph Banks* (1773), Purea is portrayed in "wise debate" with her "faithful senate," formulating policy regarding the arrival of British ships. By opting for gift exchange over war, she is said to have "sooth'd the terrors of Tupia's mind." A footnote suggests that Tupaia himself represents the greatest token of her intimacy with Banks: "Tupia was Prime Minister to Oberea. She consented that he should come to England with Mr. Banks, and thereby gave the strongest proof of her attachment to that gentleman. Unfortunately this great politician and philosopher died on the voyage."[39] The rest of the poem unfolds as a catalog of the sexual highlights of Banks's voyage, cribbed from Hawkesworth. In this context Tupaia's death implicitly represents both the death of the possibility of authorization through cultural exchange and its substitution with the scandalous figure of an excessively libidinized Banks.

"Not a Proper Sample"

Although keen to return to the Pacific, Banks eventually disengaged from Cook's second expedition after his attempts to redesign the *Resolution* to accommodate "all kind of curious things, for use, amusement and pleasure," modifications for which he "had put himself to very great expence," led to the ship's being declared top heavy and restored to its original form.[40] There were other ways in which Banks was considered inappropriate as a representative of science for the second voyage. Not just luxury but libido played a role: the scandal of his relations with Tahitian women had begun to surface, and it later transpired that a disguised female companion was awaiting him at the Cape of Good Hope, intending to join him as a transvestite assistant. If Banks hoped for further exchanges of knowledge in the mode he had enjoyed with Tupaia, it was not until July 1774, when the *Adventure* returned from Cook's second circumnavigation, that Banks got his proxy "Tahitian" friend: Mai. Like Tupaia, Mai was a Raiatean refugee who had been living in Tahiti since the early 1760s. Unlike Tupaia, he reached Britain and later returned to Tahiti. Anne Salmond's assessment of the relationship between Banks and Mai foregrounds the latter's role as a replacement exotic: "Mai's arrival in London was reported by the British press, who delighted in this exotic visitor. For Banks, who had hoped to bring Tupaia to Britain, his advent was a godsend. He carried Mai off and lodged him in his townhouse."[41] Mai is represented here as both substitute and trophy. But like Banks at this stage of his career, Mai figures in the literature of his visit as a less than ideal scientific interlocutor: much more specimen than authority.[42]

Cook's comments on Mai exemplify the skepticism with which he was greeted:

> I at first rather wondered that Captain Furneaux would encumber himself with this man, who, in my opinion, was not a proper sample of the inhabitants of these happy islands, not having any advantage of birth, or acquired rank; not being eminent in shape, figure or complexion. For their people of the first rank are much fairer, and usually better behaved, and more intelligent than the middling class of people, among whom Omai is to be ranked.[43]

As "improper sample" rather than acknowledged authority, Mai is regarded as unfit to mediate Tahitian culture. Cook's comments make clear the ways in which issues of "rank" were interwoven with perceptions of intelligence. Mai is understood to belong to the second level of Tahitian status hierarchy (the *ra'atira* class, who were tenant farmers rather than rulers), a distinction made primarily in terms of physical description. Bougainville, who had brought a Tahitian, Ahutoru, back to Paris some years earlier, had been forced to defend his visitor against similar hierarchies:

> The inhabitants of Taiti consist of two races of men, very different from each other, but speaking the same language, having the same customs, and seemingly mixing without distinction. The first, which is the most numerous one, produces men of the greatest size; it is very common to see them measure six (Paris) feet and upwards in height. I never saw men better made, and whose limbs were more proportionate: in order to paint a Hercules or a Mars, one could no where find such beautiful models. Nothing distinguishes their features from those of Europeans: and if they were cloathed; if they lived less in the open air, and were less exposed to the sun at noon, they would be as white as ourselves: their hair in general is black. The second race are a middle size, have frizzled hair as hard as bristles, and both in colour and features they differ but little from mulattoes. The Taiti man who embarked with us, is of this second race, though his father is chief of a district: but he possesses in understanding what he wants in beauty.[44]

Like Mai, Ahutoru is perceived to be a member of the "second race" in Tahiti and becomes the subject of an anxiety that second-rate ("second race") products may be veritable cultural imposters, misrepresenting themselves at the metropole.

The notion of a hierarchy, ostensibly intellectual but implicitly in rank, between Banks's two friends Tupaia and Mai, is rehearsed throughout the archive of Mai's visit to London. In the preface to his *A Voyage Round the World*, George Forster figured Mai as the sensual child to Tupaia's self-regulating adult:

> He was not able to form a general comprehensive view of our whole civilized system, and to abstract from thence what appeared most strikingly useful and applicable to the improvement of his country. His senses were charmed by beauty, symmetry, harmony, and magnificence; they called aloud for gratification, and he was accustomed to obey their voice. The continued round of enjoyments left him no time to think of his future life; and being destitute of the genius of Tupaïa, whose superior abilities would have enabled him to form a plan for his own conduct, his understanding remained unimproved.

The comparison between Mai's concupiscence and Tupaia's austere authority is sustained implicitly in Forster's discussion of the complicity between Mai's avidity for British objects and a British desire to load him with what would prove, once decontextualized, to be useless gifts:

> He carried with him an infinite variety of dresses, ornaments, and other trifles, which are daily invented in order to supply our artificial wants. His judgment was in its infant state, and therefore, like a child, he coveted almost every thing he saw, and particularly that which had amused him by some unexpected effect. To gratify his childish inclinations, as it should seem, rather than from any other motive, he was indulged with a portable organ, and electrical machine, a coat of mail, and a suit of armour. Perhaps my readers expect to be told of his taking on board some articles of real use to his country; I expected it likewise, but was disappointed.[45]

Figured repeatedly as greedy child, Mai is regarded as ill equipped to reciprocate British generosity with authentic gifts of Society Islands cultural knowledge: he is consistently represented as recipient rather than donor.

Between the death of Tupaia and the forging of his fortuitous allegiance with Mai, Banks, as we have seen, had achieved a two-sided public identity: his scientific reputation became coimplicated with sexual notoriety. A related phenomenon was manifest in relation to Mai, whose metropolitan explorations were reported as double entendre. Thus, as earlier with Tupaia, Banks and Mai also seem to have become interchangeable, being paired in the public imagination by perceived resemblance. The satirical verse written after Mai's arrival in Britain teases out the meaning of the association between two men understood to be united by a dubious similarity rather than enduring contact. In *An Heroic Epistle, from Omiah to the Queen of Otaheite* (1775), London is depicted as a city

> Where Macaronies, *Sçavoir vivres* rife,
> And varied whims of puppyhood surprise:
> Whose only care is in ambiguous dress
> To veil their sex, that wiser folks may guess.

Banks, famously caricatured in 1772 as both the "fly-catching" and "botanic macaroni" and depicted in variously "ambiguous" states of cross-cultural dress and undress during his time in Tahiti, is a shadow presence in the epistle. Meanwhile, Mai, as commentator, stands aloof from a declining metropolitan civilization, criticizing its arts and sciences, including the transactions of the Royal Society. William Preston's *Seventeen Hundred and Seventy-Seven* concludes with a call for sexual exchange (a concept rendered synonymous, by means of the popular image of Banks, with scientific exchange) between London and Tahiti:

> In pleasure's sources, what a gainful trade!
> Of mutual science, what exchanges made![46]

In this compromised context of exchange, Mai and Banks are depicted as both passive and active: swapping roles of overweening carnality and curious effeminacy, their associated authority undermined even as it is acknowledged.

Conclusion: Taking Notice

It is this co-identification of the nascent figure of the scientist with the exotic figure of the cultural intermediary that, it seems to me, was anticipated by Banks in the journal entry I cited at the beginning of this chapter. Banks's skeptical anticipation that "the government will never in all human probability take any notice of" Tupaia anticipates a lack of official curiosity about indigenous cultures that must be compensated for by the compromised curiosity of the privately wealthy. Indeed, Banks intimates that a figure like Tupaia, despite the wealth of cultural and navigational knowledge he conveys, can be understood in British terms *only* as something collected on the whim of a wealthy gentleman. But such a perception constrains Banks as well as Tupaia. Caught between the identities of serious scientist and wealthy dilettante, Banks is relegated, in a society that can see the curious exotic only as exotic curiosity, to the role of undiscriminating aristocratic collector. Tupaia's and Banks's authority as voyaging subjects are, in other words, codependent. If Tupaia is to be disregarded, Banks knows he will find himself equally reduced, from man of science to showman. Banks's turn at the end of the passage to the prospect of improving and interesting conversation, mutual respect and admiration, and real amusement clearly frames the notorious tiger comparison as a false perception, effectively a joke between engaged interlocutors at the expense of British society and, belatedly, of some of the more humorless versions of postcolonial reparative reading.

Once Banks was confined to the metropole, his notion of the cultural intermediary also became confined to European interlocutors: travelers and settlers, gardeners and collectors, who could engage in detailed correspondence first and foremost on the climate, soil, and botanical productions of new territories. As Banks's interests centered more on the acquisition of botanical specimens and on colonial agriculture, his interest in local manners and customs beyond the realm of cultivation was undoubtedly increasingly sidelined. Even by the time he drafted his instructions for Archibald Menzies, botanist on the Vancouver expedition (1791–1795), Banks's curiosity regarding local practice seems largely confined to a preoccupation with determining the existence of cannibalism:

> In all instances where you can procure a friendly intercourse with the natives you are to make careful enquiry into their manners, customs ceremonies Religion Language manufactures and every other thing in your opinion likely to interest mankind & if you find the Abominable Custom of Eating human Flesh which they are said to Practice to be really in use among them you are if you can do it with safety & propriety to be present at some of their fam'd repasts in order to bear witness to the existence of a Practice all but incredible to the inhabitants of Civilis'd Countries and discern if you can the original motives for a custom for which it seems impossible to suggest any probably Cause.[47]

Again, a classic transition appears to have been effected, with interest in mediated cultural knowledge reduced to observation ("bear witness") and prejudiced by exoticizing speculation. Yet the influence of Banks's first and, I would argue, formative cultural intermediary, Tupaia, can be sensed even in an archive in which more immediate indigenous presence dwindles. I earlier suggested that Tupaia's drawings from the *Endeavour* voyage reflect an interest both in the typological observation and recordation of botanical productions and in their incorporation within cross-cultural exchange. Whether these emphases reflected Tupaia's own priorities or his exchanges with Banks, it remains notable that Banks was to continue to promulgate these principles in his instructions to his botanical informants across the globe. The illustrations of George Tobin from William Bligh's *Providence* voyage to transport breadfruit specimens to the Caribbean, a key Banksian project, were, as Jenny Newell points out, distinguished by their attention to "illustrating the resources in the landscape": they testify to natural use value as seen from the perspective of the ship and of exchange. Tupaia's illustration of the Polynesian shoreline is prototypical of the kinds of detailing and focus that Banks later required of European cultural intermediaries like Tobin. Moreover, each of the types of Europeans that Banks later found qualified to act as his intermediaries belongs to one or two of the range of categories encompassed by Tuapai's exemplary expertise. As David Mackay summarizes, "Occupationally the Banksian collectors fell predominantly into four groups: horticulturalists, gardeners, and botanists; physicians, surgeons, and apothecaries; civil servants, officials and army officers; and naval and merchant officers, navigators and explorers."[48] Earlier I drew attention to Banks's expressions of awe in detailing the range of accomplishments demonstrated by Tupaia, Purea's chief "official," who is represented as combining the skills of the physician and apothecary, navigator, and explorer with those of a mediator of botanical and religious expertise. As a traveling local informant, with an interloper's authority, Tupaia modeled the qualifications for informed cultural observation and analysis. Perhaps, then, it was his subsequent European intermediaries who constituted the "repetition of *partial presences*," the mimic versions, of Banks's first and greatest interlocutor, Tupaia.[49] Certainly Tupaia continues to interrogate a globalized intellectual historical project, critiquing its assumptions and expanding its frame.

Notes

Many thanks to Felix Driver for his timely and insightful contributions to my thinking on this topic.

1. Joseph Banks, *The* Endeavour *Journal of Joseph Banks 1768–1771*, ed. J. C. Beaglehole, 2 vols. (Sydney: Public Library of New South Wales / Angus & Robertson, 1962), 1:312–13.

2. Pierre Bourdieu, *Distinction: A Social Critique of the Judgment of Taste*, trans. Richard Nice (Cambridge, Mass: Harvard University Press, 1984), 359.

3. The Wikipedia entry on intellectual history is in the explicit mode, defining it as "the history of human thoughts in written form. . . . It studies ideas as they are expressed in texts, and as such is different from other forms of cultural history which deal also with visual and other non-verbal forms of evidence. Any written trace from the past can be the object of intellectual history. . . . anyone who has put pen to paper to explore her thoughts can be the object of intellectual history." Available at http://en.wikipedia.org/wiki/Intellectual_history (accessed July 19, 2011). The implicit mode is represented most famously by the work of Hayden White, whose approach, in Russell Jacoby's formulation, can be expressed in two ways: "either he

classifies history as a literary endeavour or he considers all the humanities essentially literary." Russell Jacoby, "A New Intellectual History?" *American Historical Review* 97, no. 2 (1992): 408.

4. Exemplary here are Dominick LaCapra, *Rethinking Intellectual History: Texts, Contexts, Language* (Ithaca, N.Y.: Cornell University Press, 1983); and the essays collected in Dominick LaCapra and Steven L. Kaplan, eds., *Modern European Intellectual History: Reappraisals and New Perspectives* (Ithaca, N.Y.: Cornell University Press, 1982).

5. Edward Said, *Orientalism* (New York: Vintage Books, 1978), 2–3.

6. Gayatri Spivak, *In Other Worlds: Essays in Cultural Politics* (London: Routledge, 1987); Gayatri Spivak, "Can the Subaltern Speak?" in *Marxism and the Interpretation of Culture*, ed. Cary Nelson and Lawrence Grossberg (London: Macmillan, 1988); and Homi Bhabha, *The Location of Culture* (London: Routledge, 1994). For the foundational critique of Said's theory, see Aijaz Ahmad, *In Theory: Classes, Nations, Literatures* (London: Verso, 1992).

7. Bronislaw Malinowski, *Argonauts of the Western Pacific* (1921; repr., New York: Dutton, 1961).

8. James Clifford and George E. Marcus, eds., *Writing Culture: The Poetics and Politics of Ethnography* (Berkeley: University of California Press, 1986), 2.

9. Felix Driver and Lowri Jones, *Hidden Histories of Exploration: Researching the RGS-IBG Collections*, published for the exhibition Hidden Histories of Exploration held at the Royal Geographical Society (with IBG) from October 15 to December 10, 2009 (London: Royal Holloway, 2009), 7, 11.

10. Mary Louise Pratt, *Imperial Eyes: Literature and Transculturation* (London: Routledge, 1992), 5.

11. Joannes Fabian, *Time and the Other: How Anthropology Makes Its Object* (New York: Columbia University Press, 2002); Claude Lévi-Strauss, *The Savage Mind* (London: Weidenfeld & Nicholson, 1989), 233–42.

12. Pratt, *Imperial Eyes*, 5, 8.

13. Greg Dening, *Islands and Beaches: Discourse on a Silent Land, Marquesas 1774–1880* (Honolulu: University of Hawai'i Press, 1980).

14. Exemplary among these are Bronwen Douglas, "Art as Ethno-historical Text: Science, Representation and Indigenous Presence in Eighteenth and Nineteenth Century Oceanic Voyage Literature," in *Double Vision: Art Histories and Colonial Histories in the Pacific*, ed. Nicholas Thomas and Diane Losche (Cambridge: Cambridge University Press, 1999), 65–99; Bronwen Douglas, "Seaborne Ethnography and the Natural History of Man," *Journal of Pacific History* 38, no. 1 (2003): 3–27; and Bronwen Douglas, "In the Event: Indigenous Countersigns and the Ethnohistory of Voyaging," in *Oceanic Encounters: Exchange, Desire and Violence*, ed. Margaret Jolly, Serge Tcherkezoff, and Darrell Tryon (Canberra: Australian National University ePress, 2009), 175–97.

15. The approach is theorized by Greg Dening in "The Theatricality of History Making and the Paradoxes of Acting," in *Performances* (Chicago: University of Chicago Press, 1996), 103–27; and is exemplified most thoroughly in his *Beach Crossings: Voyagings Across Time, Cultures, and Self* (Philadelphia: University of Pennsylvania Press, 2004).

16. Michael T. Taussig, *Shamanism, Colonialism, and the Wild Man: A Study in Terror and Healing* (Chicago: University of Chicago Press, 1987); Nicholas Thomas, *Entangled Objects: Exchange, Material Culture and Colonialism in the Pacific* (Cambridge, Mass: Harvard University Press, 1991); Nicholas Thomas, *Oceanic Art* (London: Thames & Hudson, 1995); Nicholas Thomas, with John Pule, *Hiapo: Past and Present in Niuean Barkcloth* (Dunedin: University of Otago Press, 2005).

17. Bruno Latour, *Science in Action: How to Follow Scientists and Engineers Through Society* (Cambridge, Mass.: Harvard University Press, 1987), esp. 215–57.

18. Kapil Raj, *Relocating Modern Science: Circulation and the Construction of Scientific Knowledge in South Asia and Europe* (New York: Palgrave Macmillan, 2007), 10–11.

19. Ibid., 13.

20. Alix Cooper, *Inventing the Indigenous: Local Knowledge and Natural History in Early Modern Europe* (Cambridge: Cambridge University Press, 2007).

21. Or as Gillian Russell puts it, "variously the libertine dilettante motivated by licentious curiosity, the man of science and agent of empire, and the macaroni man of fashion." Gillian Russell, "An 'Entertainment of Oddities': Fashionable Sociability and the Pacific in the 1770s," in *A New Imperial History: Culture, Identity, and Modernity in Britain and the Empire, 1660–1840*, ed. Kathleen Wilson (Cambridge: Cambridge University Press, 2004), 53.

22. These approaches are represented by Gascoigne, Liebersohn, and Miller, respectively, and each is discussed later.

23. David Philip Miller, "Joseph Banks, Empire, and 'Centres of Accumulation' in Late Hanoverian London," in *Visions of Empire: Voyages, Botany, and Representations of Nature*, ed. David Philip Miller and Peter Hanns Reill (Cambridge: Cambridge University Press, 1996), 33.

24. John Gascoigne, *Science in the Service of Empire: Joseph Banks, the British State and the Uses of Science in the Age of Revolution* (Cambridge: Cambridge University Press, 1998), 148. See also John Gascoigne, *Joseph Banks and the English Enlightenment: Useful Knowledge and Polite Culture* (Cambridge: Cambridge University Press, 1994).

25. Harry Liebersohn, *The Traveler's World: Europe to the Pacific* (Cambridge, Mass.: Harvard University Press, 2006), 98, 103.

26. Teuira Henry, *Ancient Tahiti* (Honolulu: Bernice P. Bishop Museum, 1928), 190–95; John Davies, *The History of the Tahitian Mission, 1799–1830*, ed. C. W. Newbury (Cambridge: Hakluyt, 1961), xxvi.

27. James Cook, *The Journals of Captain James Cook on His Voyages of Discovery I: The Voyage of the* Endeavour, *1768-1771*, ed. J. C. Beaglehole (Cambridge, Hakluyt and Cambridge University Press: 1955), 563; David Turnbull, "Cook and Tupaia, a Tale of Cartographic *Méconnaissance?*" in *Science and Exploration in the Pacific: European Voyages to the Southern Oceans in the Eighteenth Century*, ed. Margarette Lincoln (London: Boydell, 1998), 127; Glyndwr Williams, "Tupaia: Polynesian Warrior, Navigator, High Priest— and Artist," in *The Global Eighteenth Century*, ed. Felicity Nussbaum (Baltimore: Johns Hopkins University Press, 2003), 40–41.

28. Cook, *Journals*, 117.

29. Lee Wallace, *Sexual Encounters: Pacific Texts, Modern Sexualities* (Ithaca, N.Y.: Cornell University Press, 2003), 9, 11, 12.

30. Turnbull, "Cook and Tupaia," 117.

31. Gordon R. Lewthwaite, "The Puzzle of Tupaia's Map," *New Zealand Geographer* 26 (1970): 1–19.

32. Cook, *Journals*, 570.

33. Banks, Endeavour *Journal*, 1:434–35; compare 447.

34. Cook, *Journals*, 240, 242.

35. Ibid., 291. Glyn Williams takes the first section of this quotation as an indication that "Cook left readers of his journal in no doubt about Tupaia's importance." Williams, "Tupaia," 43. However, in my reading, the second part of Cook's comment aligns it rhetorically with a tendency to figure Tupaia's role as instrumental rather than authoritative.

36. Banks, Endeavour *Journal*, 1410, 411, 437; my italics.

37. Ibid., 1:403–4; 2:85; 2:34.

38. Jennifer Newell, *Trading Nature: Tahitians, Europeans and Ecological Exchange* (Honolulu: University of Hawai'i Press, 2010), 72–73.

39. [Major John Scott], *An Epistle from Oberea, Queen of Otaheite, to Joseph Banks, Esq. Translated by T. Q. Z. Esq. Professor of the Otaheite Language in Dublin, and of All the Languages of the Undiscovered Islands in the South Sea; and Enriched with Historical and Explanatory Notes*, 2nd ed. (London: J. Almon, 1774), 7.

40. John Elliot and Richard Pickersgill, *Captain Cook's Second Voyage: The Journals of Lieutenants Elliott and Pickersgill*, ed. Christine Holmes (London: Caliban, 1984), 7.

41. Anne Salmond, *The Trial of the Cannibal Dog: The Remarkable Story of Captain Cook's Encounters in the South Seas* (New Haven, Conn.: Yale University Press, 2003), 296.

42. Rüdiger Joppien refers to Mai as "a curiosity, a visually striking personality, and a living experiment." Rüdiger Joppien, "Philippe Jacques de Loutherbourg's Pantomime 'Omai, or, a Trip Round the World' and the Artists of Captain Cook's Voyages," in *The British Museum Yearbook: Captain Cook*

and the South Pacific, ed. T. C. Mitchell (London: British Museum Publications, 1979), 3:82.

43. James Cook, *A Voyage Towards the South Pole, and Round the World; Performed in his Majesty's Ships the* Resolution *and* Adventure *in the Years 1772, 3, 4, and 5. Written by James Cook, Commander of the* Resolution, *in Which Is Included Captain Furneaux's Narrative of His Proceedings in the* Adventure *During the Separation of the Ships,* 2 vols. (London: W. Strahan and T. Cadell, 1777), 1:169–70.

44. Louis de Bougainville, *A Voyage Round the World, Performed by Order of His Most Christian Majesty, in the Years 1766, 1767, 1768, and 1769*, trans. J. R. Forster (1772; repr., Amsterdam: N. Israel, 1969), 214. For a discussion of Ahutoru's visit to Paris, see Vanessa Smith, "Costume Changes: Passing at Sea and on the Beach," in *Sea Changes: Historicizing the Ocean*, ed. Bernhard Klein and Gesa Mackenthun (New York: Routledge, 2004), 37–53.

45. George Forster, *A Voyage Round the World*, ed. Nicholas Tomas and Oliver Berghof, 2 vols. (Honolulu: University of Hawai'i Press, 2000), 11–12.

46. William Preston, *Seventeen Hundred and Seventy-Seven; or a Picture of the Manners and Character of the Age, in a Poetic Epistle from a Lady of Quality* (London: T. Evans, 1777), 25.

47. Draught of Instructions for Mr. Menzies, series 61.04, CY 3011/198, 199 (February 20, 1791), Papers of Sir Joseph Banks, State Library of New South Wales.

48. David McKay, "Agents of Empire: The Banksian Collectors and Evaluation of New Lands," in *Visions of Empire: Voyages, Botany, and Representations of Nature*, ed. David Philip Miller and Peter Hanns Reill (Cambridge: Cambridge University Press, 1996), 40.

49. Homi Bhabha, "Of Mimicry and Man," in *The Location of Culture* (New York: Routledge, 1994), 88.

5

Global Intellectual History and the History of Political Economy

ANDREW SARTORI

A s Ann Stoler has observed, abstractions have been understood primarily as intrusions into the flux of the life-world:

> A convention in the study of colonial governance is to treat state bureaucracies as information-hungry machines, ambitiously taxonomic, bent on categorical claims about those social differences that mattered and those that did not. Scholars of the colonial have become deft at identifying the distance between these normative, imposed categories of social difference that so contrast with the more mobile social and intimate relations in which people lived.[1]

The critique of colonial knowledge and epistemic violence has turned on the suspicion of abstraction as bound intrinsically to the operation of power. The form of abstraction that is the object of critique in colonial studies is, however, taxonomic in nature. It is a conceptual abstraction that is essentially a generalization, an abstraction from the richness of the empiricities of social life that is the result of reducing the number of qualities that characterize empirical reality to arrive at broader categories that are also correlatively less rich (possibly to the point of travesty). Power enters this process by determining the sets to be formed out of such reductions, an analysis based on the nominalist contention that such abstractions serve to render populations more governable.

Stoler's own interest in destabilizing what she (correctly, I think) identifies as a conventional alignment in colonial studies of colonizer with structure and colonized with human agency has led her to emphasize the contingencies of intimacy and affect that underwrote the appearance of epistemic certitude and institutional stability that colonialism produced.[2] In this chapter, I pursue an intellectual move in the opposite direction. Rather than dissolving the colonial state into the local contingencies of thick life-worlds, I question how adequately the domain of the subaltern-social that is the ostensible object of colonial knowledge can be characterized in the ethnographic and subjectivistic terms of "the more mobile social and intimate relations in which people lived." The core of this argument is a concern with a mode of abstraction that differs from the taxonomic forms that have been at the heart of critiques of colonial knowledge: namely, the abstractions of political economy.

Modes of Abstraction

In a Marxian reading, "political economy" is understood as a science of social abstraction. It is an attempt to grasp, in the form of economic categories, the structures of objective interdependence that both constrain and enable individual agency in capitalist society and yet are the unintended consequences of individual projects undertaken under the constraining and enabling circumstances so reconstituted. The abstractions with which political economy deals (concepts like value, labor, and capital) are not "abstractions" in the sense of being generalizations, that is, abstractions whose referents are merely aggregations of concrete particularities. Rather, they seek to grasp real abstractions—social practices that are, in some sense, themselves abstract.

To take Marx's own example, it might seem that a category like "value" is grounded in the generalization of "human labor," away from particular forms of laboring activity and toward an undifferentiated "productive expenditure of human brains, muscles, nerves, hands, etc."[3] But Marx in fact argued that "abstract labor" was the peculiar characteristic of a society in which labor is generally undertaken as a means to acquire the products of others, with value serving as an impersonal and abstract mechanism for the distribution and coordination of particular laboring activities.[4] The abstractness of abstract labor is posited practically in the fact that the function of labor is entirely separate from, and, at a certain level, indifferent to, the specific product that a particular form of labor actually produces. The function of labor in a capitalist society is thus to produce simultaneously "use values" through specific kinds of labor and "value" as a means of acquiring use values. The latter, social aspect of the labor cannot be derived from or reduced to the former through any process of generalization from the physical nature of diverse human activities or the material specificity of its products. As such, the abstractions of political economy, while necessarily "conceptual" in nature, nonetheless do not turn on a "thinning" of the empirical in the same sense as generalizing abstractions do. Since categories like "value" or "capital" name structured and structuring forms of relationship that turn on essentially abstract structures of interdependence, the object of political-economic abstraction is already abstract.

Far from assuming that labor was a metaphysical foundation of analysis, Marx contended that the abstractness of even so basic an analytic category as "labour as such" can be transhistorical only in the limited sense that the proposition that all specific forms of labor are instances of labor in general can be formulated in every society. "Labour as such" is always a potentially valid conceptual generalization. Only in capitalist society, however, does the concept "labour as such" become "not merely the mental product of a concrete totality of labours" but "true in practice." So only in capitalist society do specific forms of labor serve as manifestations of "labour as such," rather than "labour as such" serving as a conceptual generalization derived from specific forms of labor:[5]

> Men do not therefore bring the products of their labour into relation with each other as values because they see these objects merely as the material integuments of homogeneous human labour. The reverse is true: by equating their different products to each other in exchange as values, they equate their different kinds of labour as human labour. They do this without being aware of it.[6]

In Marx's critical evaluation, the power of political-economic discourse lay in its capacity to grasp real abstractions (abstractions posited at the level of practical activity itself) and, whether or not adequately, to connect the objective force of these abstractions to the structure of social organization as a whole. In the process, Marx was trying to show how concepts with very long histories—money, capital, profit, commodity—might at the same time be historically specific in their purchase on capitalist society. Thus Marx saw two different kinds of concept at work here: the first is a kind of positive concept, an abstraction that groups positivities into sets; and the second is a kind of relational concept, a concept whose meaning is determined by its relationship to a whole constellation of social practices.

Seen in this light, it seems to me a profound misunderstanding of Marx's critical social theory to suggest, as Timothy Mitchell did, that "while critical theory has interrogated almost every category of modern social science, it has left perhaps the most central one untouched . . . the idea of the economy."[7] The commodity does not merely *represent* social or economic relationships in Marx; it *constitutes* them. Far from being an economistic explanation of history, Marx's critical theory sought to grasp the historicity of the economic as a peculiarly capitalist form of social interdependence. No recourse to particular institutions, local and concrete ecologies of practice (in a Heideggerean or Foucauldian sense), and/or the networks that interlink them ("marketplaces" rather than "markets," in Michel Callon's terms) is sufficient to explain the emergence of the peculiar forms of abstraction that characterize modern social interdependence. Such explanations must always assume the abstractness of the social forms instantiated, reproduced, or enforced in such contingent institutions and networks in a manner that precludes the possibility of their "explaining" them. This is why, in the end, every attempt to think of the history of political economy in terms of the sublime complexity of the empirical ends up treating economic discourse in conventionally constructivist ways, as a discourse emerging from an institutional space outside the thick relational network it takes as its object, which then "performs, shapes, and formats the economy, rather than [merely] observing it."[8]

The Social History of Subjectivity

The approach I have in mind here should not be conflated with the dogmatic affirmation of political economy from the standpoint of "hard" economistic approaches, as opposed to the "soft" tendencies of postcolonialist cultural studies.[9] Instead, political economy must be understood as a discourse whose intellectual history has been constitutively bound to the history of the modern emergence of "the social" as a realm of objective interdependence grounded in the mediating role of labor. Insofar as the question here concerns the status of political-economic concepts, it immediately becomes clear that the categories of social practice constitutive of such objective interdependence must also have a subjective dimension. The issue is not the assertion of materiality against ideation, for the primacy of the social turns on practices that are constitutive of both. Recognizing the primacy of the social in this sense is different from subordinating subjectivity or ideation to the determination of a prior level of the real called the social (e.g., as would be the case in Durkheimian sociology). Instead, the social stands for a set of practical relations in which subjectivity and ideation assume their significance and intelligibility. In this sense, the Marxian approach shares with the Heideggerean and Foucauldian traditions an emphasis on practical activity as the grounds for overcoming the subject–object dichotomy, but it differs from them in foregrounding the significance of practices of abstract mediation that render the emphasis on situational immediacy insufficient. As Herbert Marcuse put it, "Marxian theory rejects such a science of economics [as would make the economic dimension of human life a natural process], and sets in its place the interpretation that economic relations are existential relations between men."[10] In capitalist society, Marx himself argued, political-economic categories are *"Daseinsformen, Existenzbestimmungen"* (forms of being-in-the-world, determinations of existence) that constitute historically particular modes of subjectivity as well as historically particular experiences of objective circumstances, with absolutely no guarantee of commensurability or functional interdependence between the two.[11] Through its emphasis on commodity exchange in the sphere of circulation, political economy is a discourse intrinsically connected to concepts of individuality, equality, and freedom. And through its emphasis on commodity production through the division of labor, political economy is a discourse also intrinsically connected to concepts of hierarchical subordination, functional integration, disciplinary regulation, instrumental rationality, and technical mastery.

In this reading, the problematic status of political-economic abstractions also implies a rethinking of the status of modern political-theoretical abstractions, both liberal and illiberal.[12] The liberal subject, as Marx explained in a quintessentially Hegelian passage of his *Grundrisse*, is posited in the act of exchanging equivalents. It is in the act of exchanging commodities *as values* that subjects posit themselves as equal—insofar as the act of exchange posits a relationship of mutual recognition between two commodity-owning subjects whose differences are merely an occasion for the relations of mutual dependence that give rise to the practical positing of their equality (commodity-exchange) and whose products, the objectification of those exchanging subjects, are to be exchanged as equivalents expressing equal value, that is, equal quantities of abstract labor. Furthermore, the subject of commodity exchange also posits himself or herself as free, insofar as subjects who enter into exchange treat one another reciprocally as means to their own ends and hence understand themselves to be the free determining subjects of the exchanges that constitute social interdependence. The equivalence of the exchanging subjects is posited in the form of their products, leaving the subjects of the exchange indifferent to one another, without bringing about any further realization of the social relationship of mutual dependence objectively implied.[13] Indeed, such subjects experience themselves as individuals opposed to the domain of social interdependence as an objective, external relationship among the products of labor, so that "the various forms of social connectedness confront the individual as a mere means towards his private purposes, as external necessity."[14] "Equality and freedom are thus not only respected in exchange based on exchange values, but, also, the exchange of exchange values is the productive, real basis of all *equality* and *freedom*" in their modern liberal sense—as distinct from their classical-republican sense, in which "developed exchange value was not their basis, but where, rather, the development of that basis destroyed them."[15]

Seen in this light, the problem of the historical emergence of modern political theory, whether liberal or antiliberal, is bound to the problem of the historical emergence of political economy, to the extent that their conceptual frameworks were formed in relation to the same kinds of real abstraction. The transnational availability of liberal political-theoretical concepts is bound to the transnational purchase of political-economic concepts; and the postcolonial critique of the abstractness of liberal political theory is therefore subject to the same problems as the postcolonial critique of political-economic abstractions. For Uday Singh Mehta, for example, the conception of "reason" that forms the anthropological foundation of the universality of the liberal individual's rights in civil society is bound to "a thicker set of social credentials that constitute the real basis of political inclusion" as the implicit conditions for the "actualization" of universal capacities.[16] Because of the parochialism of this practical and affective substratum, when liberalism encountered forms of life that did not share the same norms of personhood and sociability, it was predisposed to regard such unfamiliarity as a sign of political disqualification, a difference that was to be erased as the immature unreason of an incomplete humanity. The abstractness of liberal individuality is thus understood as the result of an act of conceptual abstraction that obscures the actual social or affective densities that constitute its real conditions of possibility. If, however, liberal political concepts are grounded in the same kinds of abstraction as political economy is, then the abstractness of its conception of individuality cannot be reduced to an obfuscation of concrete cultural processes but must be understood as an expression (however mediated) of practical abstraction. That liberalism has at various times entailed hostility to particular forms of social connection is indisputable, but that this hostility stems from the prejudices of concrete life-worlds is more contestable. From this perspective, it matters a great deal that James Mill's infamous hostility to Indian society and culture was different only in degree, rather than in quality, from his hostility to forms of aristocracy, priest craft, custom, and superstition that he considered to be prevalent in Britain itself—a commensurability that was fundamental to the primarily metropolitan political aims of his *History of British India*.[17] Mill's was not, in other words, a hostility toward what Mehta terms the "unfamiliar" but a hostility toward what he took to be the familiar. It is this liberal capacity for hostility toward the familiar, hardly peculiar to Mill, that must first be explained.

The history of political-economic concepts that I am imagining here exceeds the limits of a more traditionally narrow "history of the human sciences" approach. The history of political-economic abstractions is part of a much wider terrain of intellectual history. It is an intellectual history whose epochal specificity is marked by the role of real abstractions in framing the formal logic of discourses that ostensibly have little to do with political economy. This in turn opens a space for the incorporation of political-economic concepts in such discourses. Indeed, some of these discourses are, at first glance, much further from political economy than liberal political theory is, as, for example, in the neo-Vedantism of later nineteenth- and twentieth-century Bengal, which transformed, I have argued elsewhere, a philosophical language elaborated long before the advent of capitalist society into a means for conceptualizing the role of labor in constituting social relations.[18]

Capitalism and Commercial Society

The kind of abstract interdependence characteristic of capitalist society must not be conflated with a more generalizable condition of transnational "connectedness." Large-scale interconnectedness and cosmopolitanisms are not new in history, nor did they require capitalism.[19] The emergence of political-economic discourse as a constellation of concepts calibrated to grasp capitalist social forms, however, was premised on the development of a new kind of social abstraction. The capacity of these concepts to travel both widely and deeply—in the circulation of political-economic discourse in multiple metropolitan and colonial contexts and in vernacularized forms of social and political discourse that exceeded the narrow parameters of elite disciplinary forms—was correlatively premised on the extension of the practical problematic of social abstraction to new social locations around the world after their emergence in early modern Europe.[20] I realize that in characterizing the birth of political economy in these terms, I open myself to criticism from exponents of an Afro-Eurasian "early modernity," who might see this as a lazy iteration of Eurocentric diffusionism.[21] I am persuaded that early modern European capitalism emerged in a context defined by a complex, non-Eurocentric network of commercialization that may have generated indeterminate "potentialities" for capitalist development.[22] But that in no way contradicts the theoretical claim that early modern capitalist society, in its specifically Marxian sense, was initially a Eurocentric development. That is, even if the conjuncture that initially produced modern capitalist social relations in parts of early modern Europe was conditioned by Europe's embeddedness in a transcontinental system of commercial interdependencies, there is little reason to think that modern capitalism was incubating across that entire transcontinental network.

"It is unfortunate but true," Sanjay Subrahmanyam noted, "that abstract thought on the relationship between trade, whether external or internal, and the material conditions in which they found themselves did not greatly exercise the inhabitants of southern India" in the years from 1500 to 1650, a period, as Subrahmanyam showed, of commercial dynamism in the region.[23] One must recognize the sheer force of the fact that there was no parallel development of political-economic discourse remotely commensurable with that in seventeenth- and eighteenth-century Europe, that is, no discourse capable of conceptualizing social interdependence in terms of political-economic forms and hence as a coherent object of inquiry. This was the case, to the best of my knowledge, in India, in the Islamic world, in China, and indeed anywhere else one might reasonably have expected such a discourse given the development of mercantile capital, the penetration of commercialized/monetized relations into both social reproduction and political organization, and the elaboration of an analytical vocabulary of commercial practices.

Writing as an exceptionally sophisticated theorist within the Marxist tradition itself, Jairus Banaji suggested that the massive accumulations of mercantile capital at work in the Islamic trading world intensified competition among capitals, which in turn generated an incentive for individual capitals to seek more control over production as a mechanism for regulating the costs of production. This was a crucial prehistory to the development of modern capitalist social relations, one that reached back centuries before the industrial era. Banaji observed that concepts of "profit, capital and accumulation of capital are all found in the Arabic sources of the ninth to fourteenth centuries." Furthermore, Arab writers had a self-conscious understanding of the elements of commerce and mercantile capital. Banaji is undoubtedly right, and we might speculate further that any society with developed mercantile capital will have a sophisticated conceptual apparatus around activities and forms that we might retrospectively describe as "political-economic" in nature.

Yet Banaji's further provocation that Ibn Khaldun's *Muqaddimah*, composed in the fourteenth century, contained "a clear resonance of the labour theory of value (or *a* labour theory of value)" cannot be understood to imply that the discourse of political economy had a substantial prehistory in the medieval Arab world any more than in the European one of Aquinas.[24] Banaji is correct that Ibn Khaldun saw "labor" as the source of "profit," but what he meant by "profit" was the wealth created by one's labor, either as a livelihood or as capital accumulation when that wealth exceeded one's needs of sustenance. This labor theory of *wealth*, however (and perhaps this is the point of the equivocation in Banaji's own formulation), did not lead him to a labor theory of *value*, a conception of labor as a socially mediating practice. Ibn Khaldun characterized the pursuit of mercantile profit as based not on the productive exploitation of labor but on the sale of merchandise "for a price higher than its purchasing price, either by waiting for market fluctuations or by transporting the merchandise to a country where that particular merchandise is more in demand and brings higher prices, or by selling it for a high price to be paid at a future date." Ibn Khaldun never implied that a labor theory of wealth, which he shared with John Locke, was connected to a labor theory of property, a connection that might have laid the foundation for a labor theory of value by characterizing labor as constitutive of extrapolitical forms of social relationship. Ibn Khaldun also characterized the extraction of unpaid labor as directly based on overt social relations (primarily on the political status of "rank") rather than as a function internal to economic exchange, thereby treating labor exclusively as socially mediat*ed* rather than socially mediat*ing*.[25] The point here is not to fetishize the "labor theory of value" but to stress that there is no basis for believing that Ibn Khaldun considered labor to be a social mediation in the sense that classical political economy took it to be.

Similarly, the extraordinarily sophisticated understanding of market-exchange and money that Abu Hamid al-Ghazali developed at the turn of the twelfth century led him to a critique of interest taking that opposed the legitimate function of money as a medium of commodity exchange to the illegitimate function of money as capital (i.e., as a means to more money). He denounced the charging of interest on the borrowing of money because gold and silver coins "are created to cir-culate from hand to hand, to govern and facilitate exchange," whereas "when someone is trading in dirhams and dinars themselves, he is mak-ing them his goal, which is contrary to their functions. Money is not cre-ated to earn money," for when it becomes its own goal, "money will be imprisoned and hoarded."[26] Such a critique never implies a connection among the functions of exchange, accumulation, and production but sees interest taking as a form of hoarding, that is, as a withdrawal from the commodity circuit that forms the metabolism of modern capital.[27]

Neither Ibn Khaldun nor al-Ghazali foreshadowed classical political economy.[28] This was not for want of extraordinary intellectual sophisti-cation. Nor was it a symptom of any incompleteness in the progressive unfolding of a conception of social science. Nor can it be adequately understood in terms of a discursive context motivated by different assumptions and different problematics, though this is doubtless the case and worthy of detailed investigation.[29] Fundamentally, this indif-ference to the problematics of political economy stemmed from the fact that the object for which political economy was developed—capitalist social relations—simply did not exist as a problematic call-ing for systematic conceptualization. This is not to fall back on the stereotypes of "natural" or "traditional" society propounded by Karl Polanyi or Robert L. Heilbroner. To speak of the absence of capital-ist social relations is to say almost nothing about the forms of social organization actually in operation.[30] Nor is this to suggest that there is nothing more interesting to say about Ibn Khaldun or al-Ghazali; on the contrary, it is to suggest the condition of possibility for asking more interesting questions about their "economic" thought.

Banaji's emphasis on the role of mercantile capital in the develop-ment of modern capitalist social relations represents an intriguing complication to Marx's characterization of the antagonism between older forms of merchant's capital and modern capitalist development. Nevertheless, nothing in premodern Arab political thought suggests the need for a revision of Marx's more basic conceptual distinction between mercantile and modern capital.[31] Yes, early modern South Asia was renowned for the scale of its textile-manufacturing activities; yes, it saw deepening monetization and improved communication infrastructures, accelerating from the sixteenth century; yes, it saw long-standing structures of exchange becoming attached to wider overseas markets; and yes, this no doubt led to transformations in indigenous production systems that "increased possibilities of accumulation and detached the ends of exchange from those of immediate subsistence" in ways that have seemed to signify the imminence of "a transition to capitalism."[32] But as David Washbrook pointed out, in an ecological context in which price was subject to violent fluctuation, in which extensive mercantile networks consequently tended to be geared toward managing high levels of risk, and in which the interlinking of commercial and political processes often made maximizing short-term gains through revenue farming more appealing than investing in longer-term economic growth, there are good reasons to think that even without colonialism's negative impact, the transition to capitalism

> may have always remained "immanent"—or at least, incapable of moving far beyond a mercantile capitalism. Before the onset of colonialism, there was very little by way of institutional change: to redefine the relations of "property" and to give capital a clearer dominance over labour. The rights to property, and to possession of goods, skills and labour, which were being bought and sold, were still lodged in institutional structures (and ideologies) informed by a logic in which the imperatives of subsistence and social reproduction continued to impose obligations and take precedence over those of profit.[33]

The continued social and political "embeddedness" of early modern India's economic life may have as much been an enabling condition of its vibrancy as a limit on its dynamism.[34] So it is not surprising that despite C. A. Bayly's ambitious attempts to find autonomous and more or less contemporaneous non-Western corollaries for the various forms associated with Western modernity, he was forced to accede, when confronted with liberalism and its conception of social organization on the basis of free exchange, to the narrative of Western diffusionism. His only consolation was the rapidity of that diffusion.[35] After all, Bayly himself noted long ago that the commercialization of Indian society between 1600 and 1800 did not represent any indigenous "sprouts of capitalism" and that, on the contrary, such "'commercialization' actually blocked out the possibility of 'capitalism'" through its dependence on political coercion, status norms, and its indifference to bringing "the producer's labour and tools more directly under the control of capital."[36] It is not clear that what we have learned since about "portfolio capitalists"—who played such a key role in the political organization of the post-Mughal successor states, combining revenue farming, the local agricultural trade, control of military resources, military and state financing, and Indian Ocean commerce—substantially tempers the acuity of Bayly's earlier judgment.[37]

A Global Intellectual History?

There is thus little basis for repudiating a modernist and ultimately Europe-centered account of the emergence of political-economic discourse. But it does not follow that the abstractions of political economy and liberal political theory are therefore susceptible to the conventional postcolonialist critiques of abstraction as either Western parochialism or modalities of colonial power. The question of whether the lived texture of people's lives involves a mobility and intimacy that political economy does not grasp is beside the point. The issue is not whether concrete social relations have such density and fluidity. Instead, the issue is whether the density and fluidity of life-worlds—the interweaving of psychical, symbolic, and institutional forms—*immediately* determine and sustain the fabric of social interdependencies. In the age of modern capital, I believe, it is more plausible to see the capacity of such thick life-worlds to reproduce themselves as conditioned by the kinds of abstract interdependencies that characterize modern capitalist society, so that such thick life-worlds become modes of concretely inhabiting a society based on abstract interdependence, and so that abstract interdependencies become necessary media for reproducing the broad contours of thick life-worlds.[38] This does not mean that life-worlds do not matter. It means that how they matter cannot be understood outside their relationship to the abstract forms of interdependence that the categories of political economy were developed to grasp.

An analysis of political economy's historical significance in any specific context must first consider the empirical-cum-theoretical question of the degree to which the real abstractions it names are operative as practices structuring social interdependence. This does not mean that colonial states, or violence in general, were not important to extending, imposing, or securing such practices in a history written "in letters of blood and fire."[39] On the contrary, any history of political economy's widening circulation will have to grapple with the role of empires in subordinating, transforming, marginalizing, or destroying preexisting commercial societies. I am not suggesting that we ignore the centrality of the colonial state or the capacity of political economy to serve as an instrument of colonial domination. But we cannot limit critical engagement to the role of colonial state agency in the constitution, regulation, and maintenance of economic relations as if the colonial story were only a perpetually arrested moment of "primitive accumulation." As political-economic concepts began to have real purchase, not just on directly political forms of coercion, but also on forms of social organization that exceeded and constrained political agencies, the relationship of political-economic abstractions to the social must have begun to exceed the more conventional problematic of the epistemic and institutional violence of colonial abstraction. If political economy has served state agents as a technology of governance, under what (various) conditions has it been able to perform this service (more or less) effectively? This is a problem of intellectual history that the many attempts to historicize political-economic discourse have not even begun to address. I am not suggesting that the concepts of political economy are identical with the social relations that they seek to grasp. I am suggesting that it is impossible to understand the epistemological status, and hence the history, of those concepts without recognizing the importance of their referential relation to a peculiar form of historical object, an object that itself is abstract.

The obvious and predictable objection to my argument is that it fails to take account of the many levels of practical mediation that separate the abstractions of political economy from the concrete reality of an empirically diverse world that can be understood only as "the concentration of many determinations."[40] This objection would be more convincing, however, if intellectual historians were more inclined to take account of the significance of the referential force that political-economic abstractions imply and the historicizing implications that they therefore carry.

At no point have I argued that the relevance of the categories of political economy to any particular social location is transparently given, that their purchase on every specific social location is the same, or that the relationship of every social location to "capitalist society" is identical. "Hitching much of the world to European ideas, European political institutions, and Europe's capitalist economies," Jane Burbank and Fred Cooper reminded us, "did not spin the world's peoples into a single web, as images of 'globalization' imply. European empires left fragmented societies and great disparities of economic condition in their wake."[41] We cannot afford to ignore their concern that the category of the "global" implies an actual saturation of the globe with homogeneous forms of multilateral interconnection, generalizing forms of interconnection that have specific vectors and contours while obliterating disconnections and exclusions that the contradictory dynamics of capitalism can as easily reinforce, reconstitute, or intensify as eradicate.[42]

"The rise of capital was not . . . a force in itself," according to Chris Bayly. "It spread in a social ecology which had already been created by wider aspirations to power, ownership, justice and sanctity."[43] But it also is true that the history of capitalism has tended to reshape such contingencies so that its structures and dynamics cannot be directly resolved into institutional and cultural structures of action and meaning. Likewise, while the intellectual history of the claims made through political economy has been rich and varied, there is also a history to be told about the very availability, plausibility, and purchase of political-economic concepts as modalities of claims making. The history of concept formation and dissemination therefore cannot be reduced to the history of the claims made through those concepts.[44] A global history of political-economic concepts might therefore be global insofar as it examines the presence in various histories of conceptual forms that exceed the limits of place and institutional location. At the same time, that history must remain alert to the many different ways that those global concepts have assumed purposive significance in different local, institutional, and political contexts.

Even the history of the dissemination of the canonical texts of political economy demonstrates the heterogeneity of their reception and meaning in different contexts.[45] Yet this important observation should not blind us to the more fundamental fact of the dissemination of those texts, their various arguments, and their key concepts throughout the world of intellectuals and state agents and forgers of political argument; or to the dissemination of political-economic arguments and concepts to the domain of popular politics. The fact that a specific locality might experience the social abstraction that political economy names through mediating institutions or practices or social conflicts that refract the practical implications of those abstractions should not blind us to the significance of the presence of such abstractions. The actual production of commodities is not always directly regulated by mechanisms of free exchange (the market), but this should not lead us to ignore the significance of the degree to which such production processes are geared to the production of commodities, to which the production of commodities is being organized and controlled by forms of capital (whether private, corporate, or state owned), and to which the conditions of human reproduction thereby come to depend on the capacity to buy and sell commodities.

What exactly, then, is the purchase of the concept of the "global" in the intellectual history of political economy? One thing is clear: it cannot turn on a conception of "globalization" as a unilinear trajectory toward deepening interconnections and integration, toward convergence and homogeneity under the umbrella of multinational and/or financial capital. Marx's account of capitalism's dynamism did not turn primarily on Adam Smith's emphasis on the extension of the market but, rather, on capital's intervention in the production process, which created the conditions for generalizing the commodity form of the product.[46] From this perspective, a Marxian approach to the intellectual history of abstractions must turn not on the development of the "world market" but on the generalization of capitalist social relations. It must turn on the degree to which labor assumes the role of a social mediation. Such a conception does not rest on the expansion of "global" multilateral trade or core-periphery relationships or international capital flows or even the disembedded circulation of cultural forms. The problem is not, as Jairus Banaji put it long ago, to identify the "general and abstract determination" of the integration of the colonial world to "the world reproduction process of capital" and thereby to dissolve the "concrete processes by which capitalist relations evolved in various parts of the world economy . . . into the abstract identity of world capitalism." Instead, the task is specifying the ways in which capitalist relations developed in particular historical contexts.[47]

Two examples point to the necessary disaggregation of the "global" invoked here from the "global" of "globalization."

1. Most historically minded accounts of globalization describe twentieth-century global integration as a parabolic curve, with one high point in 1913 and a second in the present. But to describe the intervening period of the twentieth century as one of declining levels of global political and commercial integration is different from arguing that it represented a period of lapse or retreat in the salience and power of capitalist social forms. If we consider the import substitution strategies that became central to many twentieth-century nationalist political-economic imaginations and policy programs of the less developed world, these strategies could figure in the globalization narrative only as instruments of *dis*integration. But a Marxian analysis would suggest that they served to deepen the penetration of capitalist social relations into the societies being *dis*integrated from the global-cum-imperial economy.[48] A Marxian account of the dissemination of capitalist forms of social interdependency must be distinguished from approaches that emphasize global networks of circulation and interdependence, that is, of convergence. For example, fundamental to India's experience of British colonial rule was the displacement of some regions from a position of centrality in transnational commercial

networks in the seventeenth and eighteenth centuries, to colonial and agrarian marginality in the nineteenth. For this region as a whole, traditionalization and peasantization could be commensurate with deepening subordination to capital.[49]

2. Since the 1970s, sub-Saharan Africa has seen the emergence of a juxtaposition between spatially circumscribed, privately secured sites of integration into contemporary circuits of capital alongside more characteristic, massive exclusion-zones.[50] But the term "exclusion" refers to a marginality that presumes a scale of incorporation to which it stands as an exception. The fact that for several decades, sub-Saharan Africa had been substantially expelled from international capital circuits should not be conflated with never having been subject to the impact of capital in the first place. With the exception of a large swath of southern Africa, subjection to capital rarely took the form of the radical dispossession associated with classic proletarianization, because peasant households could offset the costs of labor through self-exploitation.[51] But without assuming that colonialism substantially transformed some dimensions of social interdependence, making modern capital important to social reproduction, it would be difficult to understand why Africa's exclusion from the circuits of international capital was generally experienced as a loss of capacities and a loss of expectations for the future rather than as a release from the exploitative forces of Western colonialism and capitalism.[52] It would be difficult to understand why African nations crave capital investment or why disinvestment has led to a decline in living standards even in the absence of military conflict.[53] Smallholding agriculturalists in Africa might have had options available to them that were not available to proletarian workers in the copperbelt of Zambia. Nonetheless, the availability of those options shaped the politics of their interface with forms of capitalist social interdependency that such peasants could no longer have experienced as straightforward externalities to the reproduction of the peasant household.[54] From this perspective, the task for a global intellectual history is to remain alert to the different modes in which social abstraction might be experienced under different relationships to capitalist society (including marginalization and exclusion), without losing sight of the global significance of these abstractions.

Path dependency and structural convergence are thus far from mutually exclusive emphases. In this sense, a global intellectual history does not need to rely on claims about spatial exhaustiveness or the convergence of historical trajectories. Instead, it turns on the degree to which certain abstractions are necessary to investigating the historical elaboration of both similarities and differences. Global intellectual history is what intellectual history becomes once it begins to grapple with the problematic of real abstraction. As soon as we recognize that we *must* grasp the pathways of African divergence through the categories of political economy, the problem of a global intellectual history is posed. That recognition immediately leads to a further question: What concepts did the historical subjects themselves need in order to grapple with the new problematics of abstraction they were experiencing? This is how I approached the history of neo-Hindu thought, focusing on how old philosophical concepts were used to think about new forms of social abstraction in later nineteenth-century Bengal, making them commensurable with historically and geographically alien forms of discourse (Comteanism, Hegelianism).[55] We also could easily read the transformations in African occult belief and antioccult practice in relation to such categories of abstraction. For example, "witchcraft" might be considered to have entered global intellectual history without being part of the circulation of concepts beyond Africa, by reference to its object (the forms of social abstraction it is used to make sense of) and its comparability to other conspiratorial imaginaries.[56]

Global intellectual history will have to trace the history of the transformation and movement of concepts in relation to the extension of capitalist social forms while remaining alert to the empirical limits of that expansion and to the practical significance of the ebb and flow of capital's movements. But if we take seriously the relationship between political-economic discourse and capitalist social forms, we will have to insist on the conceptual integrity of another problem in intellectual history, namely, the horizontal and the vertical dissemination of political-economic concepts across conventionally defined cultural and social boundaries. From this perspective, the identification of social abstraction as the condition of possibility for a certain kind of global intellectual history does not depend on an undifferentiated conception of "the global" as a scale of inquiry. It does not even presume that the global is the relevant scale of intellectual-historical inquiry. Instead, the identification of social abstraction focuses on real abstraction that exceeds specific scalar limitations (even the vast scale of empires) in its capacity to act as a determination on them.

The point is that the practical significance of the global does not turn on directly networked global integration, which has never yet taken place on a planetary scale. Rather, it depends on the generalization of structures of social interdependency that make labor into a medium of social relationships rather than merely an activity governed by social relationships. At the level of empirical spatial exhaustiveness, such a "global intellectual history" may not really be "global" at all. It may be marginal in practical terms to some parts of the world at various periods of time; it may be more or less opaque to particular social actors, depending on the specific kinds of relationship that subordinate their capacity (or incapacity) for social and/or biological reproduction to capital; and it is relevant to many parts of the world only through complex and dense mediations. Yet because of the impossibility of grasping this problematic of abstraction at the level of the concrete institutional or spatial scales within which it is empirically manifested, I cautiously retain the concept of the "global," in the face of its dangers, as the banner under which such an intellectual history might, for the moment, ride.

Notes

Thanks to the participants at the Global Intellectual History workshop, especially Sam Moyn, and also to the Social Theory Workshop at the University of Chicago, especially Moishe Postone and Bill Sewell.
1. Ann Laura Stoler, *Along the Archival Grain: Epistemic Anxieties and Colonial Common Sense* (Princeton, N.J.: Princeton University Press, 2009), 32.
2. Ibid., 47, 101.
3. The following reading of Marx is deeply indebted to Moishe Postone, *Time, Labor and Social Domination: A Reinterpretation of Marx's Critical Theory* (Cambridge: Cambridge University Press, 1996), esp. chap. 4.
4. Karl Marx, *Capital: A Critique of Political Economy*, 3 vols. (New York: Vintage, 1977), 1:165–66.
5. See Karl Marx, *Grundrisse: Foundations of the Critique of Political Economy (Rough Draft)* (Harmondsworth: Penguin, 1973), 103–5. On the chronological

shallowness of the history of the concept of labor in China, see Rudolf G. Wagner, "The Concept of Work/Labor/Arbeit in the Chinese World," in *Die Rolle der Arbeit in verschiedenen Epochen und Kulturen,* ed. Manfred Bierwisch (Berlin: Akademie, 2003), 103–36.

6. Marx, *Capital,* 1:166.

7. Timothy Mitchell, *Rule of Experts: Egypt, Techno-Politics, Modernity* (Berkeley: University of California Press, 2002), 3.

8. See Michel Callon, "Introduction: The Embeddedness of Economic Markets in Economics," in *The Laws of the Markets,* ed. Michel Callon (Oxford: Blackwell, 1998), 2. To see how lazily "Actor Network Theory" dismisses Marx, see Bruno Latour, *Reassembling the Social: An Introduction to Actor-Network-Theory* (Oxford: Oxford University Press, 2007), 175, 178–79.

9. Contrast Dipesh Chakrabarty, *Provincializing Europe: Postcolonial Thought and Historical Difference* (Princeton, N.J.: Princeton University Press, 2000), 51–57, with Rajnarayan Chandavarkar, *Imperial Power and Popular Politics: Class, Resistance and the State in India, c. 1850–1950* (Cambridge: Cambridge University Press, 1998), 1.

10. Herbert Marcuse, *Reason and Revolution: Hegel and the Rise of Social Theory* (Boston: Beacon Press, 1960), 281.

11. Karl Marx and Friedrich Engels, *Werke* (Berlin: Dietz, 1971), 13:637.

12. Compare Andrew Sartori, *Bengal in Global Concept History: Culturalism in the Age of Capital* (Chicago: University of Chicago Press, 2008).

13. Marx, *Grundrisse,* 240–45.

14. Ibid., 84.

15. Ibid., 245, italics in original; and compare Steve Pincus, "Neither Machiavellian Moment nor Possessive Individualism: Commercial Society and the Defenders of the English Commonwealth," *American Historical Review* 103, no. 3 (1998): 705–36.

16. Uday Singh Mehta, *Liberalism and Empire: A Study in Nineteenth-Century British Liberal Thought* (Chicago: University of Chicago Press, 1999), 47, 49.

17. Javed Majeed, *Ungoverned Imaginings: James Mill's "History of British India" and Orientalism* (Oxford: Oxford University Press, 1992).

18. See Sartori, *Bengal in Global Concept History,* chaps. 4, 5.

19. See, for example, Sanjay Subrahmanyam, "Connected Histories: Notes Towards a Reconfiguration of Early Modern Eurasia," *Modern Asian Studies* 31, no. 3 (1997): 735–62; Charles H. Parker, *Global Interactions in the Early Modern World: 1400–1800* (Cambridge: Cambridge University Press, 2010); Andre Gunder Frank and Barry K. Gills, eds., *The World System: Five Hundred Years or Five Thousand?* (London: Routledge, 1996); Sheldon Pollock, *The Language of the Gods in the World of Men: Language, Culture and Power in Premodern India* (Berkeley: University of California Press, 2006).

20. Compare Joyce Appleby, "Locke, Liberalism and the Natural Law of Money," in *Liberalism and Republicanism in the Historical Imagination* (Cambridge,

Mass.: Harvard University Press, 1992), 58–89; and Pincus, "Neither Machiavellian Moment nor Possessive Individualism."

21. Sanjay Subrahmanyam, "Historicizing the Global, or Labouring for Invention?" *History Workshop Journal* 64, no. 1 (2007): 329–34.

22. See, for example, Frank Perlin, "Proto-Industrialization and Precolonial South Asia," *Past and Present* 98 (February 1983): 30–95. The often-quoted term "potentialities" is from Irfan Habib, "Potentialities of Capitalist Development in the Economy of Mughal India," *Journal of Economic History* 29, no. 1 (1969): 32–78. I should note that Habib himself argued emphatically against such potentialities.

23. Sanjay Subrahmanyam, *The Political Economy of Commerce: Southern India, 1500–1650* (Cambridge: Cambridge University Press, 2002), 343.

24. Jairus Banaji, "Islam, the Mediterranean and the Rise of Capitalism," *Historical Materialism* 15, no. 1 (2007): 58. See also Anthony Parel, "Aquinas' Theory of Property," in *Theories of Property: Aristotle to the Present*, ed. A. Parel and T. Flanagan (Waterloo: Wilfrid Laurier University Press, 1979), 89–111.

25. Ibn Khaldun, *The Muqaddimah, an Introduction to History*, trans. Franz Rosenthal and edited and abridged by N. J. Dawood (Princeton, N.J.: Princeton University Press, 1967), 297–98, 300, 304, 312.

26. S. M. Ghazanfar and A. Azim Islahi, "Economic Thought of an Arab Scholastic: Abu Hamid al-Ghazali (A.H. 450–505/A.D. 1058–1111)," *History of Political Economy* 22, no. 2 (1990): 391, 394–95.

27. S. M. Ghazanfar, "The Economic Thought of Abu Hamid Al-Ghazali and St. Thomas Aquinas: Some Comparative Parallels and Links," *History of Political Economy* 32, no. 4 (2000): 873–75.

28. For an argument that Islamic economic thought fills "the Great Gap" that Joseph Schumpeter identified as separating Aristotelian economic thought from the science of modern economics, see the essays in S. M. Ghazanfar, ed., *Medieval Islamic Economic Thought: Filling the Great Gap in European Economics* (London: Routledge, 2003). For an attempt to write a history of Indian "economic thought" from ancient times to the twentieth century, see Ajit K. Dasgupta, *A History of Indian Economic Thought* (London: Routledge, 1993).

29. Compare Quentin Skinner, "Meaning and Understanding in the History of Ideas," *Visions of Politics*, vol. 1, *Regarding Method* (Cambridge: Cambridge University Press, 2002), chap. 4.

30. Karl Polanyi, *The Great Transformation: The Political and Economic Origins of Our Time* (Boston: Beacon Press, 2001); Robert L. Heilbroner, *The Worldly Philosophers: The Lives, Times, and Ideas of the Great Economic Thinkers* (New York: Touchstone, 1999).

31. Marx, *Capital*, 3:440–55.

32. David Washbrook, "India in the Early Modern World Economy: Modes of Production, Reproduction and Exchange," *Journal of Global History* 2, no. 1 (2007): 97–98.

33. Ibid., 98, 106–8.
34. Ibid., 98–100; and compare Sudipta Sen, *Empire of Free Trade: The East India Company and the Making of the Colonial Marketplace* (Philadelphia: University of Pennsylvania Press, 1998), chap. 1; although this must be balanced against Tirthankar Roy, "Where Is Bengal? Situating an Indian Region in the Early Modern World Economy," *Past and Present* 213 (2011): 115–46.
35. C. A. Bayly, *The Birth of the Modern World, 1780–1914: Global Connections and Comparisons* (Oxford: Blackwell, 2004), chap. 8.
36. C. A. Bayly, *Rulers, Townsmen and Bazaars: North Indian Society in the Age of British Expansion, 1770–1870* (Oxford: Oxford University Press, 2002), 193–96.
37. Sanjay Subrahmanyam and C. A. Bayly, "Portfolio Capitalists and the Political Economy of Early Modern India," *Indian Economic and Social History Review* 25, no. 4 (1988): 401–24.
38. Sartori, *Bengal in Global Concept History*, chaps. 1, 2.
39. Marx, *Capital*, 1:875.
40. Marx, *Grundrisse*, 101.
41. Jane Burbank and Frederick Cooper, *Empires in World History: Power and the Politics of Difference* (Princeton, N.J.: Princeton University Press, 2010), 288–89.
42. Frederick Cooper, *Colonialism in Question: Theory, Knowledge, History* (Berkeley: University of California Press, 2005), chap. 4; and see also Michael Lang, "Globalization and Its History," *Journal of Modern History* 78, no. 4 (2006): 899–931.
43. Bayly, *Birth of the Modern World*, 7.
44. Compare Sartori, *Bengal in Global Concept History*.
45. Compare Emma Rothschild, "Arcs of Ideas: International History and Intellectual History," in *Transnationale Geschichte: Themen, Tendenzen und Theorien*, ed. Gunilla Budde, Sebastian Conrad, and Oliver Janz (Göttingen: Vandenhoeck & Ruprecht, 2006), 217–26.
46. Compare Robert Brenner, "The Origins of Capitalist Development: a Critique of Neo-Smithian Marxism," *New Left Review* 104 (1977): 25–94.
47. Jairus Banaji, "Capitalist Domination and the Small Peasantry: The Deccan Districts in the Late Nineteenth Century," *Economic and Political Weekly* 7, nos. 33–34 (1977): 1397, 1400.
48. For example, Manu Goswami, *Producing India: From Colonial Economy to National Space* (Chicago: University of Chicago Press, 2003).
49. See, for example, Perlin, "Proto-Industrialization"; Sugata Bose, *Peasant Labour and Colonial Capital: Rural Bengal Since 1770* (Cambridge: Cambridge University Press, 1993); Tirthankar Roy, *Traditional Industry in the Economy of Colonial India* (Cambridge: Cambridge University Press, 1999); James Vaughn, "The Politics of Empire: Metropolitan Socio-Political Development and the Imperial Transformation of the British East India

Company, 1675–1775" (Ph.D. diss., University of Chicago, 2008); Spencer Leonard, "A Fit of Absence of Mind? Illiberal Imperialism and the Founding of British India" (Ph.D. diss., University of Chicago, 2009); Ralph Austen, "Market Integration Through Peasantization: The Economic Transformation of Africa, the Caribbean and India Under Modern Colonialism" (unpublished manuscript).

50. James Ferguson, "Globalizing Africa: Observations from an Inconvenient Continent," in *Global Shadows: Africa in the Neoliberal World Order* (Durham, N.C.: Duke University Press, 2006), 25–49.

51. The work of Giovanni Arrighi, Martin Legassick, John Saul, and Harold Wolpe focuses on the political dynamics of dispossession in southern Africa.

52. See James Ferguson, *Expectations of Modernity: Myths and Meanings of Urban Life on the Zambian Copperbelt* (Berkeley: University of California Press, 1999).

53. Ferguson, "Globalizing Africa," 26, 28.

54. See, for example, Frederick Cooper, "Africa and the World Economy," in *Confronting Historical Paradigms: Peasants, Labor, and the Capitalist World System in Africa and Latin America*, ed. Frederick Cooper et al. (Madison: University of Wisconsin Press, 1993).

55. Sartori, *Bengal in Global Concept History*.

56. See Peter Gerschiere, *The Modernity of Witchcraft: Politics and the Occult in Postcolonial Africa* (Charlottesville: University of Virginia Press, 1997); Jean Comaroff and John Comaroff, "Alien-Nation: Zombies, Immigrants and Millennial Capitalism," *South Atlantic Quarterly* 101, no. 4 (2002): 779–805; Jean Comaroff and John Comaroff, "Occult Economies and the Violence of Abstraction: Notes from the South African Postcolony," *American Ethnologist* 26, no. 2 (1999): 279–303; and James Howard Smith, *Bewitching Development: Witchcraft and the Reinvention of Development in Neoliberal Kenya* (Chicago: University of Chicago Press, 2008). But for this rereading to work, the construct of "moral economy" that organizes much of this literature would have to be refigured in a way that makes visible the ways that local moral economies themselves have developed during the longer history of Africa's encounter with capitalism, rather than treating capitalism as an external force to which moral economies must respond. For essays on how this kind of investigation might proceed, see Ralph Austen, "The Moral Economy of Witchcraft: An Essay in Comparative History," in *Modernity and Its Malcontents: Ritual and Power in Postcolonial Africa*, ed. Jean Comaroff and John Comaroff (Chicago: University of Chicago Press, 1993), 89–110; and Hylton White, "Outside the Dwelling of Culture: Estrangement and Difference in Postcolonial Zululand," *Anthropological Quarterly* 83, no. 3 (2010): 497–518.

6

Conceptual Universalization in the Transnational Nineteenth Century

CHRISTOPHER L. HILL

T he nascent discipline of global intellectual history must confront a fundamental question: What makes the global? What defines the scale and shape of this history's globe, and is it dealing with one globe or several? Until it has resolved this problem of definition, global intellectual history is likely to remain a series of "big-frame" national histories—how intellectuals in one country grappled with ideas from elsewhere—or a collection of comparative studies that recapitulate national frames as they try to overcome them. We can begin to answer the question by investigating specific examples of concepts moving *in the world* (not between nations). By examining the patterns of their movement in a given period, the conditions that made their movement possible, and the consequences of the movement for the concepts themselves, we can begin to understand the scale and organization of intellectual fields that are "global" in historically specific terms, defined by and defining particular moments. With such a working understanding, we can start to develop methods of research. This chapter is meant to explore the shape of one transnational intellectual field in the nineteenth century and to propose methods that may apply to other parts of the enterprise of global intellectual history. My example is the intellectual field defined by the universalization of concepts from European social thought in the nineteenth century. We can see the outlines of the field by tracing the ways in which originally European ideas such as "civilization" and "society" reached Japan during the Meiji period (1868–1912).

My argument is that as concepts moved around the world, they experienced multiple mediations, including translation into other languages and mass reproduction in the form of textbooks and publications for popular audiences. The resulting process of abstraction attenuated the concepts' connection to their originators and to the European historical examples from which they were derived. Mediation and abstraction allowed the "universalization" of concepts in a specific sense: the *use* of a concept as if it were valid in all places at all times. To avoid confusion, I want to make clear that I am not talking about the *universality* of concepts, a quality presumed to inhere in their meaning. Rather, I am talking about a *universalization* that can be observed in a concept's use. (I will address universality later.) In the nineteenth century the movement, circulation, or "travel" of concepts was essential to their universalization. Travel thus created the transnational intellectual field that should be the proper object of a global intellectual history for the nineteenth century. The extent of intellectual circulation by the end of the century may show that the scale of this intellectual field finally became coextensive with the geographical globe, to the disadvantage of other intellectual "worlds" defined by distinct processes of universalization. Investigating this and other issues requires research into the technological, political, and economic conditions underlying the field's emergence; the processes of mediation through which concepts spread; and the socially situated uses to which they were put. In trying to define and study a *transnational* intellectual field, the project I propose differs from recent fruitful studies of conceptual transfer, translation, and "crossed history."[1] Each of these tends simply to multiply the frame of national history in positing departures and arrivals, source and target languages, or the distinct actors of intercrossings. As I will note along the way, "nation" was one idea universalized during the nineteenth century. The political consequences are part of the history of conceptual universalization. Allowing national frames to define the method of global intellectual history, however, would install an intellectual and political blind spot in the enterprise just as it is being founded.

The Era of Civilization and Enlightenment

The period in Japan beginning in the early 1870s, shortly after the establishment of a new state in 1868, and extending into the middle of the 1880s is frequently called the era of "civilization and enlightenment" (*bunmei kaika*). The period saw intensive study of the institutions, technology, and thought of European countries, primarily those of Britain, France, and Germany, and the United States. Following the example set in the 1850s and 1860s by the Tokugawa state and some of the individual domains of that period, the new government organized study missions to North America and Europe that investigated a host of aspects of life in these regions, from systems of government to newspapers and education. The Meiji government also sent students to study in European and U.S. universities. In addition, it enacted a series of reforms, many modeled on institutions and practices observed abroad, including the introduction of a military draft, public schools and institutes of higher learning, and new legal codes.

The era is remarkable for the number of new concepts that appeared. With the government promoting the study of foreign languages, a wide range of European and North American works on philosophy, law, and political economy were translated into Japanese, including Montesquieu's *L'esprit des lois* (1748, trans. 1874), the American Declaration of Independence (1776, trans. 1866), Johann Bluntschli's *Allgemeines Staatsrecht* (1851, trans. 1872), and John Stuart Mill's *On Liberty* (1859, trans. 1872). Translation produced a steady flow of neologisms, from names for technologies such as the telegraph (*denpō*) to designations for abstract concepts like "society" (ultimately translated as *shakai*), which posed a particular challenge that I will discuss later. The phrase *bunmei kaika* joined two such words, each a translation of the English *civilization* and its cognates in other European languages.[2] The duplication in the Japanese phrase, which is lost in the customary reverse translation as "civilization and enlightenment," alerts us that the meaning of civilization was in dispute. *Bunmei*, moreover, is written with characters signifying "letter(s)" and "brightness" (文明), and *kaika* with characters signifying "opening" and "change" (開化). The two translations recall an ambiguity in the concept of civilization as it emerged in France and Britain, as to whether civilization was a condition or a process.[3] Translation, then, was a part of debates in the 1870s and 1880s over the nature of civilization and how to accomplish it.

Fukuzawa Yukichi, one of the era's most important intellectuals, defined civilization in his book *Outline of a Theory of Civilization* (*Bunmeiron no gairyaku*, 1875) as not a state of material comfort but a process that included the moderation of human sentiment, the increase of knowledge, and "the tendency toward successive improvement of human intercourse for the better."[4] Described in this way, the value of civilization would seem self-evident, but Fukuzawa and other reformers inside and outside the government commonly distinguished between civilization as end and means. In *Outline of a Theory of Civilization*, Fukuzawa disparages Japan in comparison to Europe but argues that European civilization is merely the most advanced example of civilization at present and thus a model to follow rather than an end in itself.[5] "The independence of the country is the goal," he declared, "and the civilization of the nation [*kokumin*] is the means to reach that goal."[6] Remarks like these reveal the instrumental orientation of much civilization and enlightenment thought. The orientation supported a tutelary attitude toward the inhabitants of the Japanese islands: for Japan to survive, the argument went, the people had to be civilized. There were disputes over how to reach this end, with some, like Fukuzawa, stressing the transformation of mentalities and others focusing on material changes, but all agreeing that the people would be civilized whether or not they desired it. Many of the reforms that resulted, from changes in diet and hairstyles to changes in religiosity and the organization of labor and leisure, were carried out with such disregard for existing patterns of life that Takashi Fujitani likens them to a "cultural terror."[7]

Fukuzawa's view of civilization as the means to achieve independence was not up-by-the-bootstraps idealism. The treaties that the Tokugawa government signed with the United States and the European empires in the 1850s and 1860s limited Japanese sovereignty so long as standards of civilization did not prevail within its borders. Revising the treaties, with their much resented privileges of extraterritoriality, depended on demonstrating that Japan had become a civilized country as defined by European international law. The Meiji government's domestic policy of civilizing the people and its diplomatic policy of treaty revision thus operated with the same logic and goal.[8] The conjoint strategy reflected the prescriptive force of the late-nineteenth-century system of states and empires: the only way out of semicolonial domination was to establish a sovereign state ruling a civilized nation. Even having come this far, however, we can recognize that concepts like state and nation gained their normative power through a transnational intellectual field that grew, among other ways, through the work of translation. The history of this field cannot be grasped if we confuse historical phenomena like the nation-form with analytical categories.

Many of the new institutions and social practices that appeared in this period endured. It therefore has a privileged place in historical writing on nineteenth- and twentieth-century Japan. To sketch out the most common tendencies in historiography since the end of the Asia Pacific War: In the 1950s and 1960s, modernists in Japan and modernization theorists abroad treated the era of civilization and enlightenment as the political, economic, and intellectual beginning of the modern in Japan. English-speaking historians presented the period as Japan's Enlightenment, analogous to a period in Atlantic intellectual history that they associated with the establishment of democratic capitalism. By this account, the example of civilization and enlightenment could provide the foundation for a similar transformation of Japan and its realignment as an ally in the Cold War.[9] Historians in Japan during the same period did not take as optimistic a view of the early Meiji period. Liberals such as Maruyama Masao, a scholar of political thought, turned to the era to ask what had gone wrong in Japan. Scholars like Maruyama, often referred to as postwar modernists, used the Enlightenment in Atlantic history as the basis for negative comparisons of Japan with Europe. That is, the era of civilization and enlightenment was the origin of a distorted intellectual and political modernity in Japan that led to fascism and a disastrous war. In more hopeful moments, modernists wondered whether it might also offer the foundation for a true, European-style modernity, but they did not think that establishing it in Japan would be as simple as modernization historiography suggested.[10]

Modernization and modernist historiography, each tending to focus on the state and its allied reformers, were challenged in the 1960s and 1970s by a variety of social history known as *minshūshi*, "people's history," which examined the consequences of Meiji-era reforms for farmers, laborers, and other non-elite groups. Irokawa Daikichi and other scholars of people's history also searched the era for precedents for a progressive Japanese democracy.[11] In the late 1980s and 1990s, the relatively simple view of the "people" in people's history came under scrutiny in Japan and the United States as historians reevaluated the era of civilization and enlightenment as the period in which a Japanese national identity was solidified and bound to the state. This historiographical turn was a critical revision of people's history among Japanese historians, and it finally put an end to histories of modernization in English-language scholarship, which had staggered on for many years.[12] Because such reevaluations of the period required a resolute historicization of ideas of nation and nationality, they eventually reinvigorated the study of the era's intellectual history. Some of the most interesting recent work on the period focuses on the history of translation and the adoption of such concepts as state, sovereignty, and rights, so that it now is common to speak of the "translation culture" (*hon'yaku bunka*) of the early Meiji period.[13]

A few observations on these trends in historiography, thinking particularly about intellectual history: First, the idea of the early Meiji period as the inception of the modern remains strong. Even historians who argue that some of the practices and institutions that appeared in the Meiji period have pre-Meiji roots view the 1870s and 1880s as a decisive transformation. Second, the paradigm of influence and reception seems almost unmovable. The historiography of the 1950s and 1960s presented the intellectual history of early Meiji as the adoption of "Western" ideas. The more recent work on translation and conceptual history takes a more sophisticated view of the process, but the focus on transfer into Japan is basically unchanged. Both the paradigm of reception and the emphasis on the Meiji period as a beginning, however, tend to obscure the histories *outside* Japan of the concepts in question. Many of the key concepts dated only to the seventeenth and eighteenth century in Europe. As concepts they were thoroughly historical, not "Western." The stress on reception, moreover, often overlooks the politics behind the use of concepts such as civilization and rights. Recent work on the intellectual history of civilization and enlightenment notably tends more toward Reinhart Koselleck–style conceptual history than a Quentin Skinner– or a J. G. A. Pocock–style history that accounts for the political usage of the new concepts.[14] Even the forthrightly political people's history focused on popular struggle against ideas imposed from above without inquiring deeply into the source of their authority.

Worldly Paths

We can account for the normative force of the concepts that appeared in the early Meiji period, while avoiding the reductive emphasis on use over meaning in Skinner's work, by asking how concepts such as civilization were universalized.[15] These concepts could legitimate the new government's efforts to reorganize Japanese society because they were alleged to be true anywhere, anytime. To understand the process of universalization, however, we have to reconsider the era of civilization and enlightenment in Japan in terms of a longer and broader history, which is essentially the transnational history of liberalism. Doing so requires setting aside the paradigm of reception and relinquishing the national border that it draws around the beginning of the Japanese modern. With this in mind, I offer several examples of ideas of society and social change that traveled from Europe to Japan during the nineteenth century in ways that illustrate how social thought developed through transnational circulation.[16]

The concept of civilization that appeared in eighteenth-century France and Britain was twinned from its beginning with the idea of progress. Forms of governance figured prominently in definitions of both.[17] The Scottish philosopher Adam Ferguson notably attached an evolutionary history to forms of political organization in *An Essay on the History of Civil Society* (1767). Ferguson's argument, which tied the historical development of civilization to the creation of republican government, was widely read on the European continent, where it appeared in the work of Benjamin Constant, Victor Cousin, and other French liberals during the Bourbon Restoration. (Ferguson's *Essay* appeared in French in 1783.) The idea that civilization developed in time was essential to the case that François Guizot made for a liberal

French monarchy in *Histoire générale de la civilisation en Europe* (1828). Guizot contended that a liberal monarchy that avoided the "excesses" of the Revolution but preserved its reforms was the *telos* of European history.[18] Guizot's arguments on the evolution of political institutions gained wide attention (Alexis de Tocqueville, Karl Marx, and John Stuart Mill read him with interest).[19] Four translations of Guizot's book appeared in Britain between 1837 and 1846. One of two translations from 1837 was published in the United States in 1840 and then rereleased with notes by Caleb Sprague Henry, a professor of philosophy and history in New York.[20] Fukuzawa drew on Guizot in *Outline of a Theory of Civilization* to establish that civilization was a historical stage that Japan could reach. Fukuzawa, however, read Henry's annotated edition of a British translation.[21] The path of ideas from Ferguson to Fukuzawa begins in Scotland and passes geographically through France, England, and the United States before reaching Japan, with successive translations, annotations, and "repurposings" along the way.

The European historical novel, another important means of describing society and its transformations, also had a far-flung career. Novels like Walter Scott's *Waverly* (1814), which led the rise of the genre, are commonly taken as the sign of changes in historical consciousness during the nineteenth century, including a growing opinion that social forms evolved in ways that could not be resisted.[22] Whereas Guizot gave a history to civilization, Scott made one for the nation—potentially any nation, once the genre was established. He won followers in Europe, such as Alexandre Dumas *père* in France, and around the world. In the United States, James Fenimore Cooper used Scott's methods to describe the evolution of colonies into a nation, and writers such as José de Alencar followed Cooper's example to create "foundational fictions" in South and Central America. Scott's descriptions of the relationship of the British periphery to England had a profound effect on fiction in Britain's overseas periphery, its settler colonies. The encounter of Bankim Chandra Chatterjee with the work of Scott and his contemporary Edward Bulwer-Lytton helped transform Indian fiction.[23] Scott and Bulwer-Lytton were translated into Japanese in the 1880s, as writers were looking for new techniques to describe a rapidly changing society. Another contribution came through translations via English of French historical novelists such as Dumas.[24]

The circulation of liberal political economy, whose theory and rhetoric contributed to new descriptions of society and its evolution, was similarly complex. The misnamed founder of liberal economics, Adam Smith, innovated through summary in *The Wealth of Nations* (1776), by drawing together currents of thought in England, Scotland, and the European continent, including those of the French Physiocrats.[25] Jean Baptiste Say, who considered himself an interpreter of Smith despite his own contributions to the field, helped reintroduce these ideas in France.[26] In turn, Say's *Traité d'économie politique* (1803) was translated in Britain in 1821. Along with editions of Smith and David Ricardo, the translation spurred the popularization of liberal theory in the United States and became a college standard.[27] The first course in liberal economics offered in Japan—incidentally taught by Fukuzawa Yukichi—used an American textbook marked by Say's work, Francis Wayland's *Elements of Political Economy* (1837).[28] The first works of liberal theory published in Japanese also were translations of books meant for nonspecialists: John Hill Burton's *Political Economy for Use in Schools and for Private Instruction* (1852), roughly half of which Fukuzawa included in *Conditions in the West* (*Seiyō jijō*, 1867), and William Ellis's *Outlines of Social Economy* (1846), translated by Kanda Takahira as *Elementary Economics* (*Keizai shōgaku*, 1867). The latter was a double translation from a Dutch edition by Simon Vissering, Kanda's teacher at Leiden University.[29]

Reproduction, Mediation, Abstraction

These examples offer rich material for studies of "translingual practice" in the manner of Lydia Liu and the collection *Words in Motion*. One case would be the translation of the English word "society" and related words in other European languages (*société*, *Sozietät*, etc.). Crafting a Japanese equivalent for "society" was difficult because no word existed to signify a group whose members were formally equal but whose scale extended beyond acquaintances. The lexicographer Saitō Tsuyoshi found that writers tried out more than forty words and phrases between the 1790s and 1880s. The compound *shakai*, which ultimately prevailed, was originally coined in Chinese (*shehui*) as a translation for the Dutch *klooster* ("cloister" or "monastery" in English). It entered Japanese in 1826 with this meaning and was not clearly used as a translation for "society" until 1875, finally becoming the generally accepted translation after 1877. Other translations continued to circulate until the late 1880s.[30] It would be possible, following Liu, to treat "society"/*shakai* and other negotiated translations as signifiers for heterolinguistic signs, that is, signs whose production requires more than one language. In light of its importance in treaty revision, "civilization"/*bunmei* could be seen as what Liu calls a "super-sign," a variety of heterolinguistic sign that articulates relations of imperial domination through a meaning established by treaty.[31] According to this approach, the history of civilization and enlightenment thought in Japan would be the history of heterolinguistic signs.

Translation-focused studies are troubled, however, by several problems. Most have difficulty deciding on the difference between a word and a concept. Clearly these are not identical, but the slippage means that Liu's recent work and many of the stimulating essays in *Words in Motion* are effectively conceptual history, despite the ostensible focus on words and translation.[32] More gravely, translation studies tend toward a binary logic exemplified by Liu's focus on linguistic transactions between English and Chinese to establish equivalents for terms such as the English "right."[33] Like "society," "right" was a heterolinguistic sign (or, better, a concept with signifiers in *several* languages) well before the British and Chinese empires clashed. Negotiations over a Chinese equivalent continued an already transnational history that constrained the potential meanings of both "right" and its eventual equivalent, *quanli*. Liu gestures toward the longer history, but the emphasis on creation of equivalents posits an essential difference between a concept's national history—starting with the struggle to find an equivalent—and what would be, from this perspective, its extranational prehistory.[34] Aside from resurrecting the national frames they hope to escape (a politically hazardous tendency when dealing with the age of nationalism), national or international histories of translation lose sight of the source of the normative power of concepts in circulation in the nineteenth century, which was not the creation of equivalents, or the concepts' "Western" origin, but the assertion that they applied in all places at all times. The key question for any history of concepts in circulation must be how they were universalized.

We cannot understand universalization simply by studying translation, reception, or appropriation. There are essential lessons to learn from how and why ideas traveled the world at specific moments. The histories of travel I offered earlier provide interesting examples. First, there *appears* to be a lot of serendipity, even chance, in how ideas traveled. If a certain book fell into the hands of someone with certain linguistic skills, it might be translated. The more ubiquitous the book was, the more likely this would happen. Thus Burton's *Political Economy* and Ellis's *Outlines of Social Economy*, which were in the domain of political economy but not especially important, were translated into Japanese and had an important influence. As the cases of Burton and Ellis also suggest, many of the works through which concepts such as civilization and society traveled belonged to the vulgate of ideas. They were textbooks or books written for popular audiences. Thus while the ideas of Smith, Ricardo, and other key figures in political economy eventually made it to Japan, they passed through one or several mediations involving other writers. Translation—another kind of mediation—also was part of the movement of ideas. But this was truly a matter of *movement*, not just the creation of equivalents, because works often circulated in languages other than the one in which they were first written. (Recall that Fukuzawa read Guizot in a British translation annotated by a professor in the United States.) For Japan as for many countries, English was the most important language of translation; anything translated into English was likely to get more attention. Finally, in the early Meiji period there seems to have been no sense that one should find the original source of an idea. More important was its usefulness in responding to the dire geopolitical situation.

These observations, all concerning how concepts arrived in Japan, have to be tempered by one more that turns the others on their heads (or puts them upright). The fact that concepts such as civilization traveled so widely, through so many different circuits, that they were repeatedly picked up, translated, and used by authors without acknowledgment of the source—if they knew the source—shows that the concepts were recognizable in places far from their country or region of origin. That writers treated signifiers from different languages as if they were equivalents, regardless of whether languages are ultimately incommensurable, is further proof. In light of the transnational currency of concepts like society, what *seems* to be a large degree of contingency in which works became influential simply indicates the concepts were available in *any number* of works by this time. The fact that many of the concepts arrived in mediated form—through the intellectual vulgate, through translation—means it was not necessary to go to the origin to get the concepts, which by this time may have been more recognizable in their popularized than in their original forms anyway. Such recognizability came from the *reproduction* of concepts, not their original *production*. And as much as geopolitics inflected the creation of equivalents—a key part of the circulation of ideas—the readiness with which equivalents were accepted shows that these concepts' lingering associations with particular parts of the globe did not leave them looking any less universal.

Several material factors underlay the patterns of circulation of European concepts in the nineteenth century. Changes in technologies of publishing and transportation, particularly the rotary press and steam navigation, made the circulation of printed matter cheaper and faster.[35] Increases in literacy in western and central Europe and North America supported the rise of publishers offering popularizing books in large print runs. (This was the specialty of one of Guizot's British publishers, the Edinburgh firm of William and Robert Chambers, which also published Burton's introduction to political economy.) The large runs may have been meant for domestic markets but nonetheless injected more physical volumes into international circuits. European imperialism also affected the movement of concepts outside Europe. The transportation channels established by the European empires facilitated the physical circulation of works, while the familiarity of imperial languages such as French and English made them accessible, in translation if not in the original languages. Students trained at European or North American universities, such as Kanda, or at missionary-founded local colleges, introduced concepts from European thought to non-European intellectual milieus. Colonial governance made some European ideas, such as those clustered around the concept of "population," a part of social practice.[36] Similar reorganizations of governmentality could be found in noncolonized areas, as the example of Meiji Japan shows. In both cases, intellectuals often regarded

European ideas as technologies to block further imperial incursion, even as they tried to distinguish the ideas from imperialism's ideological apparatus.[37]

These material factors distinguish the era when conceptual universalization as I have defined it could take place. The process of universalization that can be seen in the movement of ideas such as society and civilization from Europe to Japan was grounded in print mass-production and circuits of communication facilitated by imperialism. More broadly, it was grounded in capitalism and imperialism in their nineteenth-century forms. The shift from the free-trade imperialism of the middle of the century to the formal colonization of its end facilitated universalization by more tightly linking distant parts of the world to Europe and, in the 1890s, to the United States. (While my examples are limited to the nineteenth century, we can therefore extrapolate that this mode of universalization probably dominated until the era of decolonization.) I have stressed the importance of reproduction over original production, but it should be clear that this historically specific process of universalization included engagement and revision, not simple repetition, and did not take place without antagonists such as the Neo-Confucian social thought that had been hegemonic in Japan since the early seventeenth century.

The paradigm of "intercrossing" from the work of Michael Werner and Bénédicte Zimmermann allows us to describe the mode of engagement under these historical conditions with more precision. Werner and Zimmermann use intercrossing to describe the ways that two or more concepts or bodies of thought are modified through mutual contact. As opposed to the linear trajectories of influence posited by studies of conceptual transfer, Werner and Zimmermann stress that contact affects all "parties" in an exchange. Nonetheless, the resulting transformations may be asymmetrical: one side may be affected differently and to a greater extent than the other.[38] Outside the Atlantic world, asymmetrical interaction with Europe was the norm in the nineteenth century. When Neo-Confucian views of governance and post-Enlightenment social thought crossed in Meiji Japan, for example, Neo-Confucianism emerged greatly diminished, as an "Oriental" particularism, even though not long ago it had been the source of Enlightenment adulation.

It should now be possible to theorize, inductively, the process of conceptual universalization characteristic of the nineteenth century and the role that the travel of concepts played in it. As concepts like society and civilization circulated, their connection to their original source was attenuated. Scottish ideas of political economy, for example, reached Japan after many mediations along multiple paths. Smith's ideas (themselves a synthesis) moved through Say to Wayland and thereby to Japan, where Fukuzawa used Wayland's textbook in his course on economics. The same constellation of ideas reached Japan along different paths, such as Kanda's translation of Ellis (based on a Dutch translation of the English original) and Fukuzawa's translation of Burton. As concepts moved further away from their origin, along multiple paths, the first source may have become irrelevant because it was no longer the means through which people encountered the concepts. At the same time, propositions first derived from examples in European history, such as Guizot's view that liberal monarchies were the *telos* of the evolution of civilization in Europe, became increasingly disconnected from those examples as they were used to understand human communities in other parts of the world. The result was a process of abstraction through which a concept such as civilization, originally a description of human life in Europe, became "civilization in general." The process could be sped up by efforts to disengage the generality of concepts from the exemplarity of Europe, as when Fukuzawa argued in *Outline of a Theory of Civilization* that Europe was only the most advanced example of civilization, not civilization per se. Intercrossings with competing views of the order of human relations whose result was asymmetrical served the process of abstraction: the "disqualification" of competing ideas as regional particularisms compounded European ideas' appearance of generality. As a consequence, it became possible to use them as if they applied to all human communities in all places and all times. In a phrase, they were universalized.[39]

Universalization and Particularization

To understand conceptual universalization, we have to take what is likely an unpopular step back from the view of universality as an inherent quality and universalization as the recognition or Hegelian realization of such universality. By reconsidering what universalization consists of, whether it is *historically* possible for all concepts, and indeed whether the process is the same for all concepts that are universalized, it may be possible to put universality on firmer ground. In the transnational history of nineteenth-century social thought, the universality of concepts concerning human aggregations was an effect of how they were used, not of their "meaning." The quality of universality, moreover, emerged as concepts were used *outside* their point of origin. For a thinker in France to regard the history of European civilization as the model of the history of the world may have been just banal ethnocentrism. When an intellectual in Japan used a concept abstracted from European examples to appraise the history of Japan and propose social policy to suit, the concept had gained an entirely different breadth of application. For historians, the ultimate measure of the universality of an idea must be its incorporation into social practice in places far from its origin, including not only behavior in the world of ideas but also modes of governance and, potentially, resistance.

The role of abstraction in the process of universalization observable in the nineteenth century suggests an operative definition for distinguishing between concepts that are universalizable and those that are nonuniversalizable at a given moment: a nonuniversalizable concept is one that cannot be abstracted without a loss of meaning too great for the process of transformation I have described to take place. By this measure, however, nonuniversalizability would be a historically specific quality subject to the same contextual factors affecting universalization. Universality thus had a counterpart in particularity, understood not as an inherent quality but as an outcome: particularization. For several centuries the concept of "way" (Chinese *dao*, Japanese *dō*), important to many strands of thought in East Asia, including governance, has been particularized as a matter of "Eastern religion." One wonders, however, if its status may change in a new economic and political environment.

I should be clear: that such concepts were accepted as universal does not mean they were innocent. The more universal they seemed, the more politically potent they could be. As Fukuzawa's habit of comparing Japan negatively with Europe suggests, universality as I am defining it, as a consequence of use, is essentially normative. In the era of civilization and enlightenment, concepts such as civilization and society carried strong assertions about the form that human relations in Japan should take, in fact *had to* take. The force of such assertions depended on the putative universality of the concepts: if "civilization" could be used as if it were a stage in the development of all societies, then Fukuzawa could say that the populace of Japan must be civilized from above if it would not civilize itself. The normative quality of universality-in-use was not limited to policies meant to protect the Japanese state's sovereignty. Beginning in the 1870s the state exploited the universality of the corpus of international law to transform its relations with China and Korea and ultimately to legitimate its colonization and "reform" of the latter.[40] Domestically and internationally, the universalized concept of civilization was a means to protect and aggrandize the state.

The example of the Japanese state's actions in East Asia contradicts the view that the dissemination of concepts from European social thought was intellectual imperialism that directly benefited European and, by the 1890s, U.S. empires. The universalization of concepts such as civilization, right, and sovereignty strengthened these empires' claims that colonization was legal and beneficial. Yet the support did not arrive directly as proof of the superiority of European civilization, for example. Rather, it was mediated by the concepts' universality-in-use and ultimately by the transnational— not "Western"—intellectual field created by the circulation of works and ideas. The universalization of these concepts legitimated the organization of the globe as a system of sovereign states and colonial dependencies, strengthening the position of *any* empire in it. Theodore Roosevelt's endorsement of Japan's domination of Korea, on the grounds that Japan "played the game of civilized mankind," is an example. In the Taft-Katsura Agreement (1905), the United States pledged not to interfere in Korea in exchange for a free hand colonizing the Philippines. The agreement among imperial powers on the universality of civilized right (reprised later in 1905 in the Second Anglo-Japanese Alliance, concerning Korea, India, and Burma) simultaneously particularized colonial objections.[41]

From Generalizing to Relativizing Universalisms

It is now common to note that European universalism made antico-lonial movements possible. As before, we should recognize that the universalization of concepts through use, not an inherent universal-ity "turned against hypocrisy," allowed such resistance. Note also that often the concepts supporting anticolonialism were subtly different from those that legitimated colonization. As observed earlier, many key concepts from European social thought were used as if they were valid in any situation. Once universalized, "civilization" was a measure that could be applied to any human community. We could say that such concepts were used in a "generalizing" manner established dur-ing the Enlightenment.

Other concepts, however, were universalized in a different way. In these cases the concept was used as if it were universally valid *as a category* but described a phenomenon that was essentially different in every iteration. An example is "culture" (*Kultur*) as it was used from the nineteenth century onward, beginning in Germany: every place "had" a culture, but every culture was different. Moreover, every culture was the equal of any other in and because of its difference. In contrast to generalizing uses, we could say that such concepts were used in a "relativizing" fashion: the universality of the category was insepa-rable from the difference of all possible instances from one another. Concepts used in generalizing and relativizing ways often competed. As Brett Bowden shows, *Kultur* was an antagonistic response to "civi-lization."[42] In the 1890s a group of Japanese intellectuals known as the Seikyōsha used relativizing logic to defend the country's "national culture" (*kokumin bunka*) against generalizing uses of civilization by domestic reformers and Japan's treaty partners, who demanded that the country meet the standard of civilization to regain full sovereignty. The Seikyōsha writers likened Japan to Germany in its struggle for cultural independence from France after the Napoleonic wars, citing Johann Gottlieb Fichte and other champions of German culture.[43]

Nineteenth-century intellectual history is riddled with similar pairs of universalized concepts used in generalizing and relativizing man-ners. Among the most important examples is "state" versus "nation": in international law, each state was categorically identical; in nationalist thought all nations were the same in that each differed from all the others.[44] Both generalizing and relativizing universalistic concepts are normative, but the latter are paradoxically so, because they assert difference on normative grounds. Again, the distinction can be observed in use: state and right underwrote the "generalizing universalism" of international law; nation and culture, the "relativizing universalism" of movements for national self-determination and the protection of cultural difference. In the nineteenth century, the two types were universalized through the same mechanisms; they existed in the same historically specific intellectual field.

The spread of concepts universalized through relativizing uses in the nineteenth century and their special prominence in the twentieth, especially in the form of Wilsonian nationalism, was consequential. Relativizing universalisms enabled responses to economic and political domination that were both constrained and transforming. Anticolonial nationalism, an important example of a relativizing universalism assaulting a generalizing one, was constrained by the normative dimensions of the concept of nation (particularly the restriction that an individual may belong to only one) and therefore undertook to transform diverse populations into singular nations with rights.[45] The competition of generalizing and relativizing universalisms significantly affected the intellectual field: by the late twentieth century, generalizing uses of "civilization" were joined by relativizing uses meant to explain the rise of competitors to Europe and North America. (The title of Samuel Huntington's 1993 essay "The Clash of Civilizations?" exemplifies the change.)[46] Indeed, generalizing uses of universalized concepts now are often on the defensive against relativizing uses. Generalizing uses of the concepts of liberal economics—extensively universalized after the disappearance of large-scale alternatives to capitalism—face only disperse and fitful opposition, but generalizing uses of human rights discourse encounter persistent challenges on the basis of national particularity and cultural sensitivity.[47] The mid-twentieth-century shift in balance between the generalizing uses of universalized concepts that dominated in the nineteenth century and the relativizing uses that dominate today marks the beginning of a change in the structure of the transnational intellectual field. (Distinguishing between generalizing and relativizing universalisms thus helps us periodize the transnational intellectual field of social thought.) Such a change is not the topic of this chapter, but we may observe that several material factors are again involved, particularly the rise of electronic media, from radio to Internet-delivered text and video, and the emergence of a polycentric economic and political structure. Because these conditions will endure for the foreseeable future, political actors whose goals are best served by generalizing uses (such as environmental campaigns and programs to establish labor standards) must recognize that struggles over universalization will take place in a field dominated by relativizing uses.

The Shape of Global Fields

I began with the question of what makes the "global" of global intellectual history. I am now in a position to offer a definition for the nineteenth century. The circulation and universalization of concepts from European social thought show the formation of a transnational intellectual field that by the end of the century was coextensive with the physical globe. Material conditions such as the resumption of formal colonization and improvements in transportation supported the field's extension. Intellectually, the field was defined by the constellation of universalized concepts and the "particularisms" excluded from it through asymmetrical encounters. Geographically, if we account for both production and reproduction, the aggregate travels of the concepts in question would approximate the field's scale and shape. (Its edges would be indistinct.) The field as a whole reveals a historically specific process of universalization characterized by physical circulation, mediation, reproduction, and abstraction, in which many critical steps took place outside Europe. Generalizing uses of universalized concepts dominated the field, although competition from relativizing uses increased by the century's end.

Understanding the history and dynamics of the nineteenth-century intellectual field, and of global intellectual fields in general, requires a change in methods. As I have observed, many approaches to the study of supranational intellectual phenomena reproduce the national frameworks they set out to escape. Because global intellectual fields form through the transnational circulation of concepts (whether or not the fields reach the scale of the physical globe), we must approach such circulation in nonnational terms while treating the nation-state as one of several factors shaping it. For the same reason, we should resist "scaling up" national frameworks to the global level, approaching transnational intellectual fields as the composite of national histories. Because the circulation of ideas determines the shape of these fields, their scale must be defined by circulation alone.

Doubtless this approach poses challenges: in contrast to the spuriously self-evident boundaries of national history, the boundaries of a given topic in global intellectual history will not always be clear at the beginning of the project and will have to be refined during research.[48] The examples I have given from the nineteenth century suggest some strategies for research that can simultaneously illuminate the issue of scale. The importance of accounting for the material conditions that affect both the circulation of ideas and their relationship in the field, such as communication technologies and regional and global political orders, should be self-evident by now. Because reproduction is as important as production to the circulation of concepts, global intellectual histories may need to pay as much attention to popularizers and the intellectual vulgate as to the well-studied originators of ideas and their intellectual monuments. Practically, this may mean examining textbooks and the catalogs of publishers of books and magazines for popular audiences. In addition to studying translation and the establishment of equivalents, such histories will need to examine the role that languages of translation played in the travel of works and ideas. Whether these were imperial, sacred, or mercantile languages (*linguae francae*) would depend on the era and the concepts at stake. While the genesis of ideas will remain important, global intellectual histories will also profit from looking for the moments when ideas begin to lose their association with one part of the world and become common property. Attention to use, in addition to meaning, will maintain a focus on intellectual processes, such as the universalization of ideas rather than the dissemination of ideas treated as universal in themselves. The same focus on process will help reveal transformations in the structure of global fields, such as the shift from generalizing to relativizing uses between the nineteenth century and the present, in addition to changes in their geographical scope.

The intellectual geography that would follow from these methods would be lumpy, uneven, and heterogeneous. The position of "originating" countries or regions would change significantly. In the nineteenth century, Europe would remain the first site of many crucial ideas, but many of the important events would take place elsewhere. The terrain would be shifting—dynamic—rather than stable. Above all, it would be a complex landscape in which material conditions, transformations of intellectual practice, and political domination and resistance are intertwined.

Notes

Names of Japanese authors are given in the customary order of family name followed by personal name.

1. For examples, see Hans-Jürgen Lüsebrink, "Conceptual History and Conceptual Transfer: The Case of 'Nation' in Revolutionary France and Germany," in *History of Concepts: Comparative Perspectives*, ed. Iain Hampsher-Monk, Karin Tilmans, and Frank van Vree (Amsterdam: Amsterdam University Press, 1998), 115–28; Lydia H. Liu, *The Clash of Empires: The Invention of China in Modern World Making* (Cambridge, Mass.: Harvard University Press, 2004); and Michael Werner and Bénédicte Zimmermann, "Beyond Comparison: Histoire Croisée and the Challenge of Reflexivity," *History and Theory* 45, no. 1 (2006): 30–50.

2. Douglas R. Howland, *Translating the West: Language and Political Reason in Nineteenth-Century Japan* (Honolulu: University of Hawai'i Press, 2002), 33.

3. Brett Bowden, *The Empire of Civilization: The Evolution of an Imperial Idea* (Chicago: University of Chicago Press, 2009), 27, 32.

4. Fukuzawa Yukichi, *Bunmeiron no gairyaku* (Tokyo: Iwanami shoten, 1995), 57. An English translation is available as *An Outline of a Theory of Civilization*, trans. David A. Dilworth and Cameron G. Hurst (Tokyo: Sophia University, 1973); here, see 35.

5. For example, Fukuzawa, *Bunmeiron no gairyaku*, 27–29; *Outline of a Theory of Civilization*, 14–15.

6. Fukuzawa, *Bunmeiron no gairyaku*, 297; *Outline of a Theory of Civilization*, 193.

7. T. Fujitani, *Splendid Monarchy: Power and Pageantry in Modern Japan* (Berkeley: University of California Press, 1996), 19. The forced reorganization of

daily life in the Meiji period was supported by changing views of history. See Christopher L. Hill, *National History and the World of Nations: Capital, State, and the Rhetoric of History in Japan, France, and the United States* (Durham, N.C.: Duke University Press, 2008), chaps. 2, 5.

8. Alexis Dudden, *Japan's Colonization of Korea: Discourse and Power* (Honolulu: University of Hawai'i Press, 2005), 27–32, 45–46. On the standard of civilization in international law see Bowden, *Empire of Civilization*, chap. 5.

9. Carmen Blacker, *The Japanese Enlightenment: A Study of the Writings of Fukuzawa Yukichi* (Cambridge: Cambridge University Press, 1964); Albert Craig, *Civilization and Enlightenment: The Early Thought of Fukuzawa Yukichi* (Cambridge, Mass.: Harvard University Press, 2009). On the historiography of modernization, see John W. Dower, "E. H. Norman, Japan and the Uses of History," in *Origins of the Modern Japanese State: Selected Writings of E. H. Norman*, ed. John W. Dower (New York: Pantheon, 1975), 46–65.

10. Maruyama Masao, "Nihon fashizumu no shisō to undō," in *Maruyama Masao shū* (Tokyo: Iwanami shoten, 1995), 3:259–322; available in English as "The Ideology and Dynamics of Japanese Fascism," trans. Andrew Fraser, in *Thought and Behaviour in Modern Japanese Politics*, ed. Ivan Morris (Oxford: Oxford University Press, 1963), 25–83; J. Victor Koschmann, *Revolution and Subjectivity in Postwar Japan* (Chicago: University of Chicago Press, 1996), chap. 4.

11. Irokawa Daikichi, *Meiji no bunka* (Tokyo: Iwanami shoten, 1970), in *Nihon rekishi sōsho*, vol. 12; translation available as *The Culture of the Meiji Period*, ed. Marius B. Jansen (Princeton, N.J.: Princeton University Press, 1985); Carol Gluck, "The People in History: Recent Trends in Japanese Historiography," *Journal of Asian Studies* 38, no. 1 (1978): 25–50.

12. Fujitani, *Splendid Monarchy*; Oguma Eiji, *Tan'itsu minzoku shinwa no kigen—"Nihonjin" no jigazō no keifu* (Tokyo: Shin'yōsha, 1995), available in English as *The Genealogy of Japanese Self-Images*, trans. David Askew (Melbourne: Trans-Pacific Press, 2002).

13. Kamei Shunsuke, ed., *Kindai Nihon no hon'yaku bunka* (Tokyo: Chūōkōronsha, 1994); Howland, *Translating the West*.

14. Howland's thoroughly researched *Translating the West* is an example.

15. For Quentin Skinner's distinction between meaning and use, see "Meaning and Understanding in the History of Ideas," *History and Theory* 8, no. 1 (1969): 3–53.

16. The examples are drawn from Hill, *National History and the World of Nations*, 11–13. The book as a whole argues that the consolidation of the international state system and capitalist market in the late nineteenth century made these concepts credible and useful in areas where they had not been so before. For another compelling example, see Sheldon Garon,

"Savings-Promotion as Economic Knowledge: Transnational Insights from the Japanese Experience," in *Worlds of Political Economy: Knowledge and Power in the Nineteenth and Twentieth Centuries*, ed. Martin Daunton and Frank Trentmann (New York: Palgrave Macmillan, 2004), 163–88.

17. Bowden, *Empire of Civilization*, 30, 46, 51.
18. Fania Oz-Salzberger, "Civil Society in the Scottish Enlightenment," in *Civil Society: History and Possibilities*, ed. Sudipta Kaviraj and Sunil Khilani (Cambridge: Cambridge University Press, 2001), 58–65; Ceri Crossley, *French Historians and Romanticism: Thierry, Guizot, the Saint-Simonians, Quinet, Michelet* (London: Routledge, 1993), 39, 71, 76.
19. Larry Siedentop, introduction to *The History of Civilization in Europe*, by François Guizot (New York: Penguin, 1997), xxx–xxxvii.
20. Editions: *Lectures on European Civilization*, trans. Priscilla Maria Beckwith (London: John Macrone Whiting, 1837); *General History of Civilisation in Europe*, anonymous translator (Oxford: Talboys, 1837); *General History of Civilisation in Europe*, anonymous translator (Edinburgh: Chambers, 1839); *The History of Civilization in Europe*, trans. William Hazlitt the Younger (London: Bogue, 1846); *General History of Civilization in Europe*, anonymous translator (New York: Appleton, 1842), text identical to Oxford edition.
21. Matsuzawa Hiroaki, "Kaisetsu," in *Bunmeiron no gairyaku*, by Fukuzawa Yukichi (Tokyo: Iwanami shoten, 1995), 368.
22. Georg Lukács, *The Historical Novel*, trans. Hannah and Stanley Mitchell (Lincoln: University of Nebraska Press, 1983), 23.
23. Doris Sommer, *Foundational Fictions: The National Romances of Latin America* (Berkeley: University of California Press, 1991), 26–27, 52–56; Katie Trumpener, *Bardic Nationalism: The Romantic Novel and the British Empire* (Princeton, N.J.: Princeton University Press, 1997), 11–12; Priya Joshi, *In Another Country: Colonialism, Culture, and the English Novel in India* (New York: Columbia University Press, 2002), 152, 154–61.
24. Maeda Ai, "Meiji rekishi bungaku no genzō—Seiji shōsetsu no baai," *Kindai Nihon no bungaku kūkan* (Tokyo: Shin'yōsha, 1983), 3–4; Atsuko Ueda, "The Production of Literature and the Effaced Realm of the Political," *Journal of Japanese Studies* 31, no. 1 (2005): 67, 77.
25. Joseph A. Schumpeter, *History of Economic Analysis*, ed. Elizabeth Boody Schumpeter (New York: Oxford University Press, 1954), 182–85.
26. Eric Roll, *A History of Economic Thought*, 5th ed. (London: Faber & Faber, 1992), 290.
27. Ibid., 383; Schumpeter, *History of Economic Analysis*, 515.
28. Dorothy Ross, *The Origins of American Social Science* (Cambridge: Cambridge University Press, 1991), 43; Tessa Morris-Suzuki, *A History of Japanese Economic Thought* (London: Routledge, 1989), 48.
29. Craig, *Civilization and Enlightenment*, 60–65; Morris-Suzuki, *History of Japanese Economic Thought*, 49–50. On the continuing transnational

development of economic thought in the twentieth century, see Garon, "Savings-Promotion as Economic Knowledge"; and Timothy Mitchell, *Rule of Experts: Egypt, Techno-Politics, Modernity* (Berkeley: University of California Press, 2002), chap. 3.

30. Saitō Tsuyoshi, *Meiji no kotoba—Higashi kara nishi e no kakehashi* (Tokyo: Kōdansha, 1977), 181–83, 192–96, 220–25, translations listed on 195–220. Howland examines the history of Meiji-era translations in *Translating the West*, 158–64, 171–73. See also Yanabu Akira, *"Shakai—The Translation of a People Who Had No Society,"* trans. Thomas Gaubatz, in *Translation in Modern Japan*, ed. Indra Levy (New York: Routledge, 2010), 51–61.

31. Liu, *Clash of Empires*, 13–14, 33–34. Liu at times uses heterolinguistic sign and super-sign interchangeably.

32. Examples of the slip between word and concept can be found in Itty Abraham, "Segurança/Security in Brazil and the United States," and Driss Maghraoui, "'Ilmaniyya, Laïcité, Sécularisme/Secularism in Morocco," both in *Words in Motion: Toward a Global Lexicon*, ed. Carol Gluck and Anna Lowenhaupt Tsing (Durham, N.C.: Duke University Press, 2009), 31 and 115.

33. Liu, *Clash of Empires*, 124–29.

34. Andrew Sartori's criticism of postcolonial scholarship's focus on the "epistemic violence" wrought by foreign concepts also speaks to this point. See his *Bengal in Global Concept History: Culturalism in the Age of Capital* (Chicago: University of Chicago Press, 2008), 19.

35. On the impact of steamships on communication, see Daniel R. Headrick, *The Tools of Empire: Technology and European Imperialism in the Nineteenth Century* (New York: Oxford University Press, 1981), 30–39.

36. As Omnia El Shakry shows through the example of Egypt, the process extended beyond the work of colonial administrators. The incorporation of "population" into governance in Egypt, through the institutionalization of statistical, medical, geographical, and sociological, began in the mid-nineteenth century and culminated in the interwar period. Omnia El Shakry, *The Great Social Laboratory: Subjects of Knowledge in Colonial and Post-Colonial Egypt* (Stanford, Calif.: Stanford University Press, 2008), chap. 5.

37. Partha Chatterjee, *Nationalist Thought and the Colonial World: A Derivative Discourse* (Minneapolis: University of Minnesota Press, 1986), 41–42; Mark Anderson, *Japan and the Specter of Imperialism* (New York: Palgrave Macmillan, 2009), 52.

38. Werner and Zimmermann, "Beyond Comparison," 37–39.

39. On these points, see also Hill, *National History and the World of Nations*, 13–14.

40. Dudden, *Japan's Colonization of Korea*, 46, 101.

41. Roosevelt quoted in Frank Ninkovich, "Theodore Roosevelt: Civilization as Ideology," *Diplomatic History* 10, no. 3 (1986): 238; Dudden, *Japan's Colonization of Korea*, 15, 62–63.

42. Bowden, *Empire of Civilization*, 34–36.
43. Anderson, *Japan and the Specter of Imperialism*, 86–95.
44. On this point, see also Hill, *National History and the World of Nations*, 39. Another example is the apply-anywhere universalization of liberal political economy versus the relativizing tendencies of List's theory of "national economy."
45. On the normative dimensions of nationalist thought, see Chatterjee, *Nationalist Thought and the Colonial World*, 10–11. A recognition of the normative force of universalized concepts such as nation is missing from Erez Manela's impressive *Wilsonian Moment*, which tends to treat anticolonial nationalists' "appropriation" of Wilson's arguments for self-determination as instrumental and even opportunistic. See Erez Manela, *The Wilsonian Moment: Self-Determination and the International Origins of Anticolonial Nationalism* (Oxford: Oxford University Press, 2007), 61–62.
46. The final sentence of the essay indeed traces a reluctant passage from a generalizing to a relativizing use of the concept: "For the relevant future, there will be no universal civilization, but instead a world of different civilizations, each of which will have to learn to coexist with the others." Samuel P. Huntington, "The Clash of Civilizations?" *Foreign Affairs* 72, no. 3 (1993): 49.
47. Samuel Moyn shows the hostility of state-oriented national liberation movements to ideas of human rights in chapter 3 of *The Last Utopia: Human Rights in History* (Cambridge, Mass.: Belknap Press, 2010). On a recent, fitful clash between generalizing and relativizing universalisms at the transnational, national, and subnational levels, see Gesine Krüger, "Moving Bones: Unsettled History in South Africa and the Return of Sarah Baartman," in *Unsettling History: Archiving and Narrating in Historiography*, ed. Sebastian Jobs and Alf Lüdtke (New York: Campus Verlag, 2010), 233–50.
48. Werner and Zimmermann stress the importance of adjusting the objects, categories, and schemes of research through continuous "pragmatic induction" ("Beyond Comparison," 46–48). Gary Wilder's *The French Imperial Nation-State: Negritude and Colonial Humanism Between the Two World Wars* (Chicago: University of Chicago Press, 2005), esp. 5–6, 25–29, provides an impressive example of defining scale according to specific topics.

7

Globalizing the Intellectual History of the Idea of the "Muslim World"

CEMIL AYDIN

In the scholarly writings on the global history of the last two hundred years, we see special attention given to universal and global values, such as the ideas of sovereignty, nationalism, national rights, international law, and human rights. Various agencies of the United Nations and different international associations function on the assumption that certain ideals, legal concepts, principles, and values have both global appeal and legitimacy. This recognition of the globality of certain norms raises the question of the origins of these values, which takes us to the debate about Eurocentrism. Most globally recognized values can be traced to European intellectual history. A better account of the history of globalization and international history revised this question about Eurocentrism by emphasizing the agency of non-Western intellectuals and historical actors who were universalizing the normative values associated with "the West" at the same time as they were challenging Western imperial hegemony. Studies of the intellectual history of reformists, nationalists, and intellectuals in Asia and Africa are now indicating a kind of non-Western seizure of European universalism, a sort of subaltern fulfillment of the Eurocentric values that led to modern internationalism, and associated norms such as national self-determination, cultural rights, racial equality, and even human rights. In this new historiography, my earlier book on Pan-Islamic and Pan-Asian critiques of the West complemented the arguments of a book on Wilsonianism published around the same time.[1] In both books, seemingly anti-Western and anticolonial intellectuals from Egypt and India to China and Japan were engaging Eurocentric notions of equality, liberty, human rights, and national self-determination, utilizing them for their political struggles and globalizing them. Their intellectual revolt against the West, these two books argued, was not a sign of a clash of civilizations or a rejection of modernity. For example, Pan-Islamic and Pan-Asian intellectuals' critique of and challenge to the imperial world order shared many values they thought that European public opinion also embraced.

This emphasis on the agency and leadership of non-Western actors as part of the origin of universal and global norms was better than the simple model of the emulation, mimicry, and appropriation of liberal and universal Western values by the non-Western world.[2] The new global intellectual history model has its own weaknesses, however. While it gives primacy of historical agency to subaltern and non-Western figures in realizing and actualizing the universal potential of global values, it ends up conceding that these values originated in the small geographical area of western Europe. Thus, Ataturk, Sun Yat-Sen, and even Gandhi became avatars of Eurocentrism, even though their agency and ideas may have shaped modern international history. Did some norms and ideals originate outside the European intellectual tradition and become universal? How can we account for the legacies and impact of the intellectual traditions of the Muslim, Buddhist, and Hindu communities on modern global history? Did non-Western actors and intellectuals have a role beyond actualizing a potential that already existed in Eurocentric values or beyond reinterpreting ideas originating in Europe?

In this chapter, I revisit the period from the 1880s to the 1920s that was retrospectively characterized as the high age of both global Westernization and Muslim intellectual modernism and Pan-Islamic nationalism, to discuss global ideas and values, such as the caliphate, that did not originate in Europe. Why did the appeal and legitimacy of the Ottoman caliphate increase among Muslims outside the imperial Ottoman territories, such as Central Asia and South Asia, during an era known as the period of the rise of nationalism and the spread of Western values? The response to this question could not be the persistence of traditional values in a modernizing world, as there was something very modern about the popularity of the Ottoman caliphate, even among Shia Muslims who were not theologically invested in this notion of religious and political leadership. In addition to a focus on the global political context that helped redefine the meaning of the Ottoman caliphate, I examine the modern hermeneutic engagements with the major texts of Islamic intellectual tradition, which offered new interpretations of these texts in dialogue with other global intellectual currents. In addition, I look at the necessary connection between global intellectual history and international history by examining the importance of the destiny and grand strategy of the Ottoman Empire for Muslim modernist intellectual circles in Eurasia and Africa at that time. My case study concerns the identity of the "Muslim world," a novel transnational identity whose evolution exemplifies the inseparable connection between intellectual and international history. I present a global intellectual history of the idea of the Muslim world and discuss its political ramifications and utilization during the high age of imperialism and anticolonialism. In this context, I focus on how this notion of "the Muslim world" interacted with policies with regard to and by the Ottoman Empire and how it initiated important new hermeneutical engagements with the religious texts in the Islamic tradition pertaining to ideal political leadership, reform, and rationality. This discussion will, I hope, help us understand the politics of the contemporary usages of Muslim identity and reflect on why the colonial-era notions of the Muslim world's identity and Muslim solidarity survived the process of decolonization and Cold War throughout the twentieth century.

Conceptions of Muslim Identity and the Ottoman Empire Before the Nineteenth Century

There are several common misconceptions about the ideal of Muslim unity, the notion of *ummah* (the Muslim community), and the Ottoman Empire, as well as other empires ruled by other Muslim dynasties.

Muslim international society, or the global Muslim community, never had an inward-looking closed system. The "Muslim world," a term referring to all Muslims in the world, simply did not exist before the mid-nineteenth century. There have always been many empires covering the areas populated by Muslims as both majority and minority populations. None of the empires ruled by Muslim dynasties, such as the Safavid, Mughal, or Ottoman, can be called theocratic caliphates. Even though the Islamic intellectual tradition and Muslim religious beliefs were important to the imperial elites, their vision of empire and their politics could never be reduced to the Islamic tradition. For the Ottoman or Mughal bureaucrats of the sixteenth century, Genghis Khan and Alexander the Great were as important as the story of the early caliphs.[3] Empires in the post–Mongol Empire period had substantial non-Muslim populations and functioned according to eclectic yet cosmopolitan notions of legitimacy, kingship, and justice.[4] The idea of being Muslim, belonging to the *ummah*, or living in Dar-ul-Islam was never abstract and utopian. Instead, these identities and notions of belonging were always mediated by imperial ties and local realities.

Ottoman sultans began using the title of caliph several decades after their conquest of Egypt in 1517. But this was only one of their titles. The many other titles for the sultans reflected the eclectic roots of the Ottoman notions of kingship and their ties to various imperial traditions. Examples are caesar, khan, padishah, and sahib qiran (lord of the auspicious conjunction). As important as the title of the caliph was control of the two holy cities of Islam, Mecca and Medina, as well as Jerusalem. Muslim pilgrims to Mecca accordingly recognized the protection and upkeep of that city by the Ottoman rulers. The importance of the title of caliph changed according to the historical context, and there was no linear continuity in the self-perception of Ottoman imperial identity. For example, when the Ottoman rulers competed with the Portuguese in the Indian Ocean in the second half of the sixteenth century, they made greater use of the title caliph, and their Muslim allies referred to the caliphate. But this conflict with the Portuguese was about free trade in the Indian Ocean for Muslim merchants (which the Portuguese were trying to prevent), and once the Portuguese retreated, the Ottoman Empire lost its significance in the Indian Ocean.[5] In addition, when the Mughal empire gained control of Muslim South Asia, the Ottoman Empire lost its influence there.[6]

Although it later was identified with the Muslim world or caliphate, the Ottoman Empire was not a "Muslim empire" motivated by religious texts and visions.[7] Of course, the Muslim identity of the Ottoman elite and the values of its Muslim subjects were important to their daily lives, culture, architecture, and ceremonies. But we should not confound this with contemporary notions of a secular Europe versus a Muslim empire, or even a Christian Europe versus an Islamic empire. The Ottoman Empire had a diverse population, about half of which was not Muslim. Moreover, the Ottoman Empire always had a close relationship with other European empires, as exemplified by its alliance with France against the Hapsburgs. As early as the second half of the eighteenth century, Ottoman diplomats visiting Europe regarded peace between the Muslim-ruled Ottoman Empire and the European empires ruled by Christian dynasties as a value in itself beyond the benefit of protecting the Ottoman Empire from the threat of an alliance among European empires.[8] For example, to increase the empire's tax revenue, Ahmet Resmi Efendi (1700–1783) began to see the necessity of a new diplomatic-imperial world order based on mutually beneficial trade relations and cooperation, not on the medieval logic of imperial land expansion. He even considered the military expansion policies of Süleyman the Magnificent during the sixteenth century as a waste of resources. In their reflection on late-eighteenth-century imperial models, the Ottoman elites seemed confident about imagining a new world order with shared values and norms and without any need to sacrifice their Muslim or Christian traditions. It is in this spirit that the Ottoman Empire formed a coalition with the Russian and British Empires against the French Republic between 1799 and 1802. As part of the Second Coalition Wars, the Ottoman and Russian navies cooperated to wrest control of the Ionian islands from France. When the sultan of the Indian principality of Mysore asked the Ottoman sultan's help against the British Empire, the Ottoman sultan's response made clear that the French Empire was the enemy, because of its violation of international law, and that, if necessary, he could mediate between Mysore and the British Empire.

Thus, the Ottoman ruling elite agreed with the basic vision of imperial cooperation and dynastic legitimacy embodied in the Congress of Vienna. Between the 1780s and 1840s, the Ottoman elite revised and reinvented the empire through various reforms. In the 1839 Tanzimat Proclamation, they challenged the Eurocentric international order to clarify its principles of inclusion, suggesting that their multiethnic and multireligious empire, which included most of eastern Europe, should be a part of the European state system, even though it was ruled by a Muslim dynasty. The Ottoman elite favored diplomacy based on civilizational principles, not on Christian solidarity. In his *Treatise on the Circumstances of Europe*, the leading Ottoman reformist bureaucrat, Sadik Rıfat Paşa, even used the French word *civilisation*, without translation, to explain the political, economic, and social secrets of European power and superiority.[9] Both Lord Palmerston and Prince Metternich supported the Ottoman Empire's bid for membership in the Vienna System. The Greek revolt of the 1820s initially did not seem like a challenge to this new imperial vision (empires constantly had local revolts for various reasons), even though the 1830 London Protocol (recognizing the sovereignty of Greece), which linked specific populations to a given territory for the first time in the nineteenth century, deviated from the rules of the Vienna System.[10] The Ottoman elites may have been disappointed that the principles of the Vienna System—peace, security, and the territorial integrity of other civilized empires—were broken by the Great Powers' support of Greek independence, but the bureaucrats thought this was due to their bad image as an uncivilized empire, not because of their Muslim sultan. A year after Greek independence came the French invasion of the Ottoman province of Algeria, and before long, some of the Algerian educated elites began to refer to the Greek example when asking for more autonomy or freedom from French imperial rule.[11]

The Crimean War Versus the Indian Rebellion

The Muslim leaders of the Ottoman Empire believed they would not encounter any religious, cultural, or racial obstacles to being as civilized as the Europeans, so long as they completed a set of reforms that would allow them to reach a higher level on the universal ladder of progress. From 1839 to the 1860s, the Ottoman reformist elites found that their civilized image and their close cooperation with the leading power of European international society, Great Britain, worked to their advantage in international affairs. Their alliance with the European powers against Russia during the Crimean War (1853–1856) became the biggest achievement of Ottoman diplomacy.[12] Just two decades after the Greek rebellion, when the European powers had sided with the Greeks, the Ottoman government was in alliance with Britain and France against Russia. Ottoman generals fought alongside British and French generals in amazingly similar military uniforms. (The only difference was the Ottoman fez, which was originally adopted in 1820s to symbolize the empire's European-inspired reforms.) The Ottomans' membership in the club of European states provided a sense that the reformist diplomacy of "civilization" actually worked and that the Ottoman state had gained a legitimate right to international existence as a recognized member of the Concert of Europe at the Treaty of Paris, signed at the end of the Crimean War in 1856.[13]

On the other side of this coin, the Ottoman Muslim leaders did not support the Great Indian Revolt, led by Muslims, against the British forces in 1857. Indian mutineers reportedly planned to send a delegation to Istanbul asking the Ottomans for support against the British. The Ottoman Empire, however, supported its British allies and even congratulated them on their final victory.[14] The British Empire not only received permission for their troops to pass through Egypt and the Red Sea area, which were under Ottoman rule, but also secured a proclamation from the Ottoman sultan urging the Indian Muslims not to fight against the British forces. The Ottoman government donated money for the relief funds for orphans, widows, and wounded soldiers on the side of the British Empire. As other European empires recognized the Ottoman sultan's civilized rule over its Christian populations, the Ottomans likewise recognized the British, Russian, Dutch, and French Empires' rule over various Muslim populations. At that time, Pan-Islamism was not on the agenda of any intellectual. As a reflection of this imperial logic, the Ottoman administrators in Mecca described the pilgrims from Dutch or British colonies as Dutch or British Muslims.[15]

The Prestige of the Ottoman Caliphate
and the Idea of the Muslim World

Given the Tanzimat vision of the Ottoman elite, the increasing importance of the Ottoman sultan's title as caliph after the 1870s should not
be seen as a continuation of a centuries' long relationship between
the Ottoman Empire and the Muslim communities beyond the Ottoman borders. Indeed, the Ottoman Empire of the nineteenth century
had a very different grand strategy and imperial identity, based on
liberal civilizationism and a desire both to be part of the Eurocentric
world order and to include the non-Muslim subjects of the empire
in the administrative structure. But during the nineteenth century,
despite the Ottomans' lack of support for various Muslim resistance
movements against Western colonialism, and their commitment to a
vision of civilizing reforms, the Ottoman sultan's title as caliph of
Muslims became more popular in the colonized Muslim societies.
This was due to two main reasons, neither of which was theological.
The first was the emergence of a new Muslim world identity, and the
second was the image of the Ottoman sultan, who also carried the
title of caliph, as the head of a civilized Muslim empire with full and
equal diplomatic relations with the European powers. In other words,
it was partly the Ottoman Empire's membership in the club of European civilized empires that increased its prestige among the Muslim
societies in Asia.

It was this membership that prompted the leaders of Aceh on
the eastern edge of the Indian Ocean to ask for the Ottoman government's support against attacks by the Dutch.[16] This was more a
request for diplomatic support, asking the Ottomans to declare their
protection of Aceh under the caliph and thus the Dutch Empire to
stop its attacks. This increasing sympathy for the Ottoman Empire,
always tied to the new notion of the caliphate as the symbol of the
Muslim world's demands for reform and justice, did not necessarily
contradict other imperial identities. In one of the earliest texts written in support of the Ottoman caliphate and reforms, the Indian Muslim intellectual Cheragh Ali (from the princely state of Hyderabad)
combined his admiration for the Ottoman Empire with his loyalty

to the British Empire, described as the greatest Muslim empire in the world. For him, the Ottoman caliph symbolized the compatibility between modern civilized values and the Muslim faith and proved that Muslims were not inferior to Christians in their capacity for progress.[17]

The increasing identification with the Ottoman Empire on the part of Muslims beyond its borders, including Shia Muslims, mirrored the relationship between the European empires and the Ottoman Empire, on the one hand, and the colonized Muslim societies, on the other. When the Ottoman Empire came to be seen as the symbolic leader of the colonized Muslims in Asia, the European empires tried to exclude it from European international society, reasoning that because it was a Muslim dynasty, the secessionist demands of its Christian subjects would make it less than civilized. In discourses on the Eastern Question, European public opinion and the elites in the Russian, British, and French Empires argued about the future separation and independence of the Christian subjects of the Ottoman Empire, claiming that Christians should not be ruled by semicivilized Muslims. This bid to liberate the Christian subjects of a "Muslim empire" came at the same time that more and more Muslim societies were being subjected to the rule of European empires with Christian rulers, a paradox that was emphasized and used especially by the Indian Muslim supporters of the Ottoman caliphate. While those debating the Eastern Question depicted the Ottoman reforms as futile and ineffective and argued that the Ottoman Muslims could not create a civilized empire, the Muslim supporters of the Ottoman Empire insisted on the opposite: that the Ottoman caliph was a reformist and civilized leader and the Ottomans' treatment of their Christian subjects had always been better than the British, French, and Russian Empires' treatment of their Muslim subjects.[18] Whereas European public opinion saw the Ottoman Empire as the "sick" man of Europe, Muslims in India and Southeast Asia saw it as the civilized leader of the global Muslim community, representing their dignity and equality in a globalizing imperial world order. The European public asked for humanitarian intervention in the Ottoman Empire's internal affairs to liberate Christian Bulgarians, Romanians, and Serbians, but the Muslims in India and Southeast Asia wanted the Ottomans' humanitarian intervention to help them against their Christian colonizers. European observers began to describe this Muslim sympathy for the Ottoman Empire as Pan-Islamism, and an increasing number of Muslim observers began to describe the European hostility toward any notion of Muslim solidarity and their colonial rule as a "modern crusade" of imperialism. In this context, from the 1880s onward, a transnational debate on the meaning of Muslim solidarity and the ideals of Pan-Islamism emerged. While European circles described it as a reactionary movement against the Western civilizing mission at the instigation of the Ottoman rulers, Muslim reformist leaders both denied the existence of a Pan-Islamic conspiracy and recommended a broad Muslim solidarity to overcome the subjugation of the Muslim world by the "immoral" European imperial order. The fears of the British, Dutch, Russian, and French Empires regarding a possible rise of Muslim solidarity and revolt against their rule was countered by anticolonial Muslim hopes that this might be feasible and necessary.

The Idea of the Muslim World

The notion of the Muslim world, which became the basis of the ideal of Pan-Islamism, gained widespread global currency and usage during the 1880s, in dialogue among Muslim reformers, anxious European observers of Muslim populations discontent with the expanding colonial rule, and anticolonial figures. Whereas the European use of the term "Pan-Islamism" had negative connotations of antimodernism (fanatical Muslims against the European empires' civilizing mission and progressive reforms), the Muslim usage of the term *ittihadi Islam,* or *Muslimin* (Unity of Muslims), often included notions of reformism and progressivism coupled with anticolonial solidarity and the Ottoman Empire's mission to civilize backward Muslim areas. As a result of the interaction among diverse interests ranging from evangelical Christians and Orientalists to anticolonial nationalists, pro-Ottoman Muslim reformers in India and Central Asia, and colonial officers, a Muslim world identity emerged as commonsense knowledge, a geopolitical reality, and a civilizational-religious identity that everybody agreed on.[19] This shared identity was related to the view of Islam as an actor of history as well as the idea of the Muslim world as an almost racial category in the emerging global public sphere.

The Pan-Islamic discourse on civilization from the 1880s to the 1930s had three features, which still shape much of contemporary transnational Muslim thought.

First was a new discourse on Islamic civilization, with a shared history and the corresponding idea of a Muslim world as an almost racial unit. Some of the initial arguments for the essential racial and civilizational otherness came from hostile observers. Missionaries were the first to create a map showing Muslim majority areas in red or green and also identifying the Christian populations in these lands. Later, missionaries started a journal entitled the *Muslim World*.[20] But between the 1880s and the 1930s, tens of journals were named the *Muslim World*, in which Muslim modernists defended Islam's civilized nature insofar as it amounted to their geopolitical identity.[21]

Ernest Renan's 1883 lecture, "Islam and Science," gave a more racial view of the history of this separate Muslim civilization, arguing that it was bound to decline owing to its fanaticism and Semitic character.[22] Around the same time, Gladstone's anti-Muslim and anti-Ottoman remarks (well noted by transnational Muslim networks) prompted a worldwide response by Muslim intellectuals defending Muslims' civilized nature and capacity for progress.[23] A transnational Muslim intellectual network insisted that Islamic civilization had inherited the Greek legacy, combined it with rational and humanist Islamic values, and, through its golden age, contributed to the emergence of the modern West. This Euro-Islamo-centric view of world history implied that "service to the rise of the modern West" would become a criterion of civilizational worthiness and dignity.[24] Since European Orientalist notions of the inherently uncivilized nature of Muslims had racial implications, even reputedly irreligious and positivist Ottoman intellectuals like Ahmed Riza felt compelled to write apologetic pieces defending Islam against Orientalist positions.[25] In the debate on social Darwinism, Muslim intellectuals conceded that Muslims were underdeveloped and backward, but they denied that this was permanent inferiority. Intellectual elites could intervene with various forms of social engineering and calls for a reawakening to "end the decline" of their racial or religious communities. In that sense, the entire Muslim modernist project, as exemplified by Muhammad 'Abduh and Rashid Rida, relied on the attempt to rethink the "decline of Islam" through an engagement with the dominant European social science theories. In fact, Islamic modernism harshly criticized the contemporary Muslim decline, blaming it on Sufism or popular Muslim practices, which ironically made their arguments similar to Wahhabi calls to return to early Islam.[26] Their desire to revive the pristine values of early Islam, its rationalism, and its work ethic was often shaped by Darwinian concerns about Muslims' survival in the competitive and insecure age of high imperialism.

The second important shared content of Pan-Islamic discourses was a vision of an Islam-West conflict initially positing that any reaction to European colonial empires must be due to Muslims' innate desire to reject the Christian Western empires. Colonial observers and imperial strategists believed that Muslims were prone to react violently against Western empires. Accordingly, Germans had a plan to provoke a Pan-Islamic reaction against its rivals. Later, Italy, the Ottoman Empire, and Japan also developed Pan-Islamic policies based on this assumption. The Muslim reformers initially rejected this notion of an eternal conflict between Islam and the Christian West but soon developed a civilizational approach tying modern imperialism to historical narratives of Christian attacks on Muslims. In their view, modern colonialism was a new crusade. In the long run, these debates helped create a specific civilizational historical consciousness that did indeed put a conflict between Islam and the West at its center. Although medieval Muslim historians did write about the Crusades, a conflict between the Muslim world and the Christian West was never the main narrative of their historical accounts. (Ibn Batuta and Evliya Çelebi, premodern world travelers, did not have such a narrative.) In light of the new interest in rewriting Islamic history, mostly in regard to Eurocentric world history, Muslim reformists turned to the story of Salahuddin al-Ayyubi as one of the heroes of the Islamic world defeating an earlier European imperial/Crusader invasion. For example, the Ottoman intellectual Namik Kemal wrote a play about the life of Salahuddin during the 1870s.

If the Muslims could defeat the Crusaders, they could defeat the modern crusade of imperialism as well. It is in this narrative that the

Ottoman rule of eastern Europe was glorified as an instance of civilizational greatness, even though the same narrative of the Ottoman Empire's victories against its rivals in Europe may have conflicted with Ottoman claims to belong to the European club of empires. It was the same view of historical conflict that revived an interest in the story of Muslim Spain, which was used to bolster the argument of Islam's contribution to Western civilization through the example of Averroes and other Muslim philosophers, while implying another instance of Islam-West conflict.

All the theories concerning the clash of civilizations, which reinforced the conflict between Islam and Christianity that was based on historical narratives, relied on the literature of geopolitics and international affairs produced and read in European and American universities and reproduced in the Western media. Thus it is not surprising that the major Pan-Islamic and Pan-Asian texts concerning the conflict between Islam and the West, or between the white and yellow races, were produced by Muslim or Asian thinkers whose academic training was in Europe or America. Halil Halid's book *Crescent Versus the Cross* is based on his master's thesis at Cambridge University, and Kodera Kenkichi's one-thousand-page *Treatise on Pan-Asianism* is based on his dissertation at George Washington University (then Columbian University).[27] Similarly, Lothrop Stoddard, a white supremacist with a doctorate from Harvard, was closely read and followed by Pan-Islamic and Pan-Asian thinkers precisely because of Stoddard's realist writings on civilizational and racial conflicts in international affairs.[28] Although the Arabic translation of Lothrop Stoddard's book *The World of Islam* contains long dissenting commentaries by the leading Pan-Islamist Shakib Arslan on issues of detail, he agrees with the book's basic framework of interpreting world affairs as a conflict between the Muslim world and the West.[29]

The third shared theme of transnational Pan-Islamic discourse was an anticolonial internationalism that embraced the non-Muslim societies of Asia and Africa as well as cosmopolitan and inclusive ideologies from all over the world. During this period, together with the Hegelian discourse of East-West conflict around the notion of Islam versus the Christian West, there still was a dominant strand of internationalism. The nationalist Muslim support of Japan's modern achievements and

Chinese nationalism are good examples of this anti-Western internationalism.[30] Similarly, many non-Muslim Asians were supportive of
Pan-Islamic discourses and did not think of this as a conservative religious movement. The shared experience of engaging European ideas
of Orient and Occident brought together the predominantly Muslim
Middle East and the non-Muslim Far East around the idea of a common Asian-Eastern identity, which led to an alternative internationalism. The Theosophist link to Pan-Islamic organizations was another
sign of their internationalism. Figures like Alexander Russell Web
became interested in Pan-Islamism through his studies of Buddhism
and Theosophy (his Islamic funeral ceremony was led by a female Theosophist),[31] and the *Journal of Theosophy* wrote a very positive account
of Pan-Islamists.[32]

The growing Asian identity of Muslim intellectuals had grave consequences for the Ottoman Empire because along with the development of a pro-Western Christian identity of its Greek and Armenian
citizens, the divergence between Muslim and Christian subjects of
the empire grew wider. According to medieval Muslim categoriza-
tions of people, Muslims were closer to Christian British colonial
officers than to Shinto Japanese. But Egyptian Muslim intellectuals
of the early twentieth century had more sympathy for Japan than
for Britain. Mahatma Gandhi joined, and was welcomed, by the Pan-
Islamic Khilafat movement in India. For a very long time, the Ottoman government tiptoed around this issue. At the World's Parliament
of Religions, held in Chicago, the majority of delegates defending the
Ottoman-Muslim capacity for reform, civilized life, and progress still
were Christians and included an Armenian, a Greek, and an Orthodox Christian Syrian Arab.[33]

Saving the Ottoman Empire or Doing Justice
to the Muslim World

The political demands associated with the idea of a Muslim World
exhibited all the complexities of identity politics, religious hermeneutics, and imperial rivalries. For the broader Muslim public sphere, Pan-
Islamism was a symbol of the demand for equality and dignity to be

recovered from the injustice and humiliation of Western imperialism. Both the demands for political autonomy and the search for justice were closely tied to the notion of regaining dignity by establishing racial and civilizational equality with the Christian West.

The Ottoman Empire, however, was more interested in its sovereignty and legitimacy as an empire that included non-Muslim populations. What especially frustrated the reformist Ottoman elite was that although they were not allowed to use their Muslim credentials in international affairs, European empires would often intervene in Ottoman domestic affairs or use force under the pretext of protecting the rights and privileges of the Ottoman Empire's Christian subjects. And while Ottomans were told that they could not rule over Christian subjects, more and more Muslims were coming under the rule of Christian empires.

A Pan-Islamic identity on a global scale was as much an opportunity as a burden and a problem for the Ottoman Empire. Ideally, being the model for the rest of the Muslim societies gave prestige to the Ottoman elite. But it also brought further suspicion and hostility in the eyes of their European imperial counterparts, as well as additional responsibilities. Moreover, the Ottoman government could not officially give up its claim to the loyalty of its Christian populations, and a Pan-Islamic identity would contradict such a claim.

Meanwhile, from the 1880s to the 1920s, the prestige of the Ottoman caliphate reached a global peak, beyond the intentions and policies of the Ottoman government. A new, racialized notion of the Muslim world increased the caliphate's religious significance, despite the powerful arguments against the theological validity of the Ottoman claim to the Sunni caliphate since the publication of William Blunt's *Future of Islam* in 1883.[34] The pro-Ottoman camp decisively won this intellectual argument to the extent that by World War I, the legitimacy of the Ottoman caliphate was rarely questioned.[35]

The pro–Ottoman Muslim intellectuals' battle with British Prime Minister William Gladstone illustrates the complexity of their intellectual argument. Gladstone's hostile remarks about Muslims and Turks, such as calling them an "anti-human specimen of humanity," reflected both a larger European sentiment about "infidel Muslims" and a more refined European Orientalist discourse on Muslim inferiority.[36] The tensions between the "rights" of minorities and the legitimacy of an empire in international law can best be seen in Gladstone's accusation that the Ottoman Muslim rulers were committing atrocities against the empire's Christian populations in the Balkans. Here, the evangelical Gladstone appeared as a champion of human rights (in the form of rights for Christians minorities in Bulgaria), and the Ottoman rulers appeared to defend the rights of imperial sovereignty and international law. Indian Muslim intellectuals consistently emphasized that in reality, since 1839, Christian subjects of the Ottoman Empire had always had more rights and privileges than the Muslim subjects of the British and French Empires.[37] For them, anti-Ottoman discourses in Europe could only be about Christian biases against Muslims. Meanwhile, Indian Muslims did try to advance their own rights in British India by demonstrating that Christians in the Ottoman Empire had more rights than Muslims did in the British Empire.

In the context of the Ottoman response to European intervention in its imperial sovereignty, international law became a favorite subject of Ottoman law schools and Muslim intellectuals, as it was seen as a means of defending their position.[38] Ottoman international lawyers actively defended their notions of sovereignty in international law.[39] While Gladstone was declaring the Ottoman Empire to be illiberal and inhuman, Irish nationalists were calling Gladstone the "Anglo-Saxon Grand Turk,"[40] suggesting that the British Empire's Christianity-based anti-Ottoman and anti-Muslim rhetoric should not be seen as a critique of an illiberal empire by a liberal empire. And when the issue was the rights of Armenians, Muslim defenders of the Ottoman Empire faced a contradiction in their values and their identity similar to that of their British imperial opponents. Against the pro-Armenian Christian agitation in Europe and America during the late 1890s, both Abdullah Quilliam and Alexander Russell Web (as well as all the Indian Muslim intellectuals) rushed to the defense of the Ottoman Empire's actions. Quilliam pointed out that the Ottoman Empire was like nineteen Irelands and that the British should appreciate the empire's right to control the Armenian separatists.[41] He further noted that the white Christian British supporters of the Armenians had remained silent about the lynching of blacks by whites in the United States.

The End of the Ottoman Empire and the Caliphate

By 1914, the Ottoman Empire had become synonymous with the Muslim world, to the extent that Arnold Toynbee, as a British intelligence analyst during World War I responsible for writing reports on the Ottoman Empire, often wrote about the awakening and revolt of the Muslim world, assuming that, for the British Empire, the Muslim threat and the Ottoman threat were one and the same. In the same office, Abdullah Yusuf Ali, a prominent Indian Muslim, was trying to define a Muslim world identity loyal to the British Empire.[42] The influence of Pan-Islamic ideas, especially the view of international relations as a modern crusade by the West against the Muslim world under the pretext of civilization, became crucial to securing the Ottomans' public support for entering World War I on Germany's side.[43] In the aftermath of Italy's invasion of Libya in 1911 and the Balkan Wars of 1912/1913, the Ottoman Muslim elite became convinced that this was a new modern crusade against the last Muslim empire, which was confirmed in their eyes by the expulsion of Muslims from the Balkans by Christian armies. To the Ottoman Muslim elite, population politics was the future direction of international affairs, a conclusion that helped shape the ethnic-cleansing policy toward the Armenians in 1915.[44]

Many Ottoman pundits reasoned that they had to use intra-European rivalry to take revenge against the Christian alliance of the British, French, and Russian Empires. This was a drastic change from the nineteenth-century Ottoman foreign policy of cooperating with the leading Western powers while implementing reforms to fulfill the West's standards of civilization. In some ways, the Ottomans' insistence on securing a formal alliance with Germany as a precondition for entering the Great War was a continuation of their desire to be part of Europe, even on the losing side, rather than being excluded from European diplomacy and thus treated like European colonies in Africa and Asia. But beyond this diplomatic calculation, popular notions of Pan-Islamic solidarity provided Ottoman policymakers with the vision that when entering the war, they could use the contradictions and weak points in the legitimacy of the imperial world order by encouraging Muslim disobedience and, if possible, open revolt.

All the European empires took seriously this threat, epitomized by the Ottoman caliph's declaration of *jihad* against them. But Ottoman agents could not provoke any mass revolt of Muslims against Western colonialism, despite the strategic benefits of Pan-Islamic propaganda for the Ottoman and German Empires. The British, French, and Russian Empires countered with their own propaganda, symbolized by the successful British plan to gain Arab nationalist support against the Ottoman Empire with promises of an Arab caliphate. More important, however, the propaganda battles between the Ottoman-German alliance and the British-French-Russian alliance, in which both sides emphasized that they were fighting for civilization and freedom, deepened the legitimacy crisis of imperial order in Asia.

After the Ottoman Empire lost the war, the rise of the Bolshevik and Wilsonian internationalism at the end of World War I affected the destiny of Pan-Islamic internationalism. There now were two viable "Western" alternatives to the declining Eurocentric world order. Initially, the Bolsheviks tried to benefit from the accumulated anti-Western sentiments of Asian societies and the tide of Pan-Islamic activism, by organizing the 1920 Eastern People's Congresses in Baku, where leading Pan-Islamic personalities like Enver Paşa appeared and argued for self-determination for the Muslim world.[45] The new Bolshevik government in Russia supported the anticolonial nationalist movements in the Muslim world. Yet the Bolsheviks could not accept the idea of an alternative Eastern civilization central to Pan-Islamic discourse, and gradually the socialists distanced themselves from the Pan-Islamic movement, fearing that instead of using them, they could be used by this rival internationalism.[46] On the other side, the initial positive Pan-Islamic interest in the Bolshevik revolution, which depicted the new Russia as a sign of the awakening dynamic East against the West, also gradually turned into animosity and competition, although many former Pan-Islamists continued to cooperate with the Bolshevik government until the 1930s.[47]

After the Ottomans' defeat in World War I, the Muslim leaders of the Ottoman state saw Wilsonianism as a means to gain independence and secure a new national state in areas where Muslims were a majority. For them, Wilsonianism was an idealistic vision about the inevitability of population politics, turning away from imperial cosmopolitanism.

Accordingly, some of the most articulate advocates of Pan-Islamism in the Ottoman state, such as Celal Nuri İleri, founded the Wilsonian Principles Society in Istanbul and asked for American intervention and a mandate for a national Turkey against the potential imperial division of Ottoman lands.[48] But the demands of the Ottoman Muslim leadership to have the Ottoman state recognized as the national home of its Muslim majority was rejected by the Paris Peace Conference, again on the basis of the civilizational inferiority of the Turkish Muslims. Soon afterward, the victors of World War I endorsed the Greek invasion of Anatolia in May 1919, a step that shattered any remaining hopes for the coexistence of Muslims and Greeks in Anatolia by forcing Greek residents to choose between their loyalty to Istanbul and the invading Greek armies. With the Paris Peace Conference's endorsement of demands by Greek, Armenian, and Kurdish nationalists and its rejection of Ottoman Turkey's Wilsonian demands, the Turkish national movement became the focus of a new post–World War I–era Pan-Islamism, best embodied in India's Khilafat movement.

Established and led by Indian Muslims, the Khilafat movement symbolized a paradoxical merger of the ideals of Islamic solidarity, anticolonial nationalism, and Wilsonian notions of legitimacy. While collecting enormous material donations for the Turkish war for independence, the Khilafat movement leaders asked the British government, the colonial rulers of India, to recognize the right to self-determination of the Muslim majority in Turkey. Even though the name of the movement was Khilafat, implying that its purpose was to liberate the seat of the Muslim caliphate in Istanbul from Allied occupation, it was sending its aid to the national government in Ankara, not the palace of the caliph sultan in British-occupied Istanbul.

Ultimately, the Turkish national movement achieved its goals through a series of military victories, partly owing to moral and material support from the Pan-Islamic movement. The Lausanne Treaty negotiations, which concluded a peace treaty between the Turkish national government and the Allied powers, manifested the several decades of experience of the Ottoman Muslim diplomats and lawyers in dealing with the issue of Christian minority rights and population politics. The Turkish delegation at Lausanne persisted in minimizing the Christian minorities to an insignificant number, and they won absolute rights of sovereignty in domestic affairs. The news of Turkey's receiving most of its demands at Lausanne was seen as a victory by Muslims against the modern crusade of Christian imperialism. This also was the high moment of the Khilafat movement, and perhaps the historical peak in the popularity of an Ottoman Sunni caliph over Muslim populations all over the world, to the extent that even Twelver Shi'a and Ismaili Muslims, who did not believe in the caliphate, sympathized with and supported the Ottoman caliphate as the symbolic leader of the Muslim world.

At this crucial moment, however, the terms of the Lausanne treaty already were changing the meaning of a politically influential caliphate outside the national and sovereign territories of the new Turkish republic. With the end of the Ottoman Empire, the idea of a caliphate began losing its meaning. Turkish diplomats had to sign documents ensuring that they had no political and economic claims over former Ottoman territories. Even though post-Lausanne Turkey became a majority Muslim sovereign state with an exchange of their Turkish and Greek populations, the institution of the caliphate and its imperial implications posed challenges to the new national government in Ankara. How could a new republic with a population of only eight million Muslims host an institution that was also respected by eighty million Indian Muslims? What would and could the Ankara government do if the Indian Muslims asked the caliph in Istanbul to help them with their requests for freedom or autonomy from their British colonial rulers? It was in this context that the elite of the new Turkish republic decided to abolish the caliphate in March 1924 and disavow Turkey's Pan-Islamic claims to leadership in the Muslim world, thus indicating its own preference for a Wilsonian direction in the interwar international order.[49] The Republic of Turkey symbolized Muslim dignity and liberation in one country, which could inspire other Muslim populations, but it would not offer any diplomatic support. The legitimacy of the Wilsonian language of self-determination, coupled with the abolition of the caliphate, meant that there was no way of asking for a collective deal for justice and dignity for the Muslim world, although many Muslims continued to embrace the intellectual legacy of Pan-Islamic thought regarding identity and historical memory. In all the later independence struggles by Muslim populations, Pan-Islamic ideas of solidarity and historical consciousness were invoked not only by nationalist groups but also by the colonial regimes that tried to suppress this nationalism. For example, as late as the early 1960s, the French government depicted Algerian nationalism as a Pan-Islamic reactionary revolt against Western civilization. Yet there was still no legitimate international venue or legal framework to express Pan-Islamic (or Pan-Asian and Pan-African) demands for dignity, equality, and justice on behalf of a collective unit called the Muslim world.

One of the ironies of the abolition of the caliphate in the Turkish parliament in March 1924 was the repetition of William Blunt's anti-Ottoman caliphate arguments by some speakers at the Turkish parliament, namely, that the Ottoman caliphate was not legitimate, according to the early texts of Sunni Islam, despite the previous four decades during which the Muslim elites had vehemently refuted these Orientalist claims. Only after the abolition of the caliphate, in the midst of very strong protestations from different corners of the Muslim world, did the Egyptian scholar Ali Abdul Raziq publish his controversial thesis about the principles of government in Islam in 1925, partly defending the absence of a caliph with the contention that political theory was never supposed to be part of the Muslim religious creed. Various attempts to recreate a new caliphate failed, although different networks sustaining transnational Muslim thought continued.[50]

Conclusion

This reflection on the origins of the idea of a Muslim world reminds us why a non-Eurocentric intellectual history of global norms can be reduced to neither a clash of Western versus Islamic ideals nor a teleological triumph of universal Western ideas with the agency of non-Western intellectuals. During the last two hundred years, the global community has embraced as universal such norms as nationalism, sovereignty, and even human rights, but not as a result of the Europeanization of diverse intellectual traditions in different parts of the world. The globalization of norms did include the agency and contributions of non-Western intellectual communities. Moreover, competing and sometimes seemingly anti-Western universalisms contributed to the globalization of contemporary norms. Pan-Islamism (as well as Pan-Asian and Pan-African universalisms) are examples of these supranational universalisms.

During this long process, some universalizable norms, like cosmopolitan empires and minority rights, were abandoned at the expense of other global norms, like national sovereignty. Pan-Islamic thought contained powerful and universalist ideals such as the demands for dignity and justice for religious, civilizational, and racial groups (however imagined these communities would be), although these demands were trimmed down or suppressed during the twentieth-century contingencies of norm globalization. More important, there were significant hermeneutical engagements with the non-Western intellectual and religious traditions within the broader Pan-Islamic, Pan-Asianist, and Pan-African thought, a hermeneutical process that was shaped by global intellectual forces but could never be reduced to Eurocentric influences. The globalization of the intellectual life in diverse public spheres of the world did not signal the end of non-European intellectual traditions. Though seemingly not globalized, the products of intra-Muslim world conversations, the new pan-national and transnational identities, and the hermeneutic relations with the sacred texts shaped the emergence of the modern world and thus require a more careful and eclectic view of global intellectual history.

A new, non-Eurocentric global intellectual history can be written only in dialogue with the new international history. In our case study of Pan-Islamic thought and the idea of the Muslim world, we have seen that intellectual trends were closely related to the power struggles among various empires and were tied to the destiny of the Ottoman Empire. The complex relations between the Ottomans' grand strategy and the Muslim world's identity make it clear that the transition from a world of empires to a new world of multiple nation-states (from the Vienna System to the Paris System) was not a story of the triumph of liberal global values of nationalism over illiberal imperial notions of sovereignty and dynastic rights. We must acknowledge the significant but forgotten role of the identity of the Muslim world and idealism regarding the Ottoman caliphate from the 1870s to the 1920s. There have always been empires in world history, some more successful than others, and these empires grew stronger or became weaker and then ended or were transformed into a republic. What is noteworthy about the last fifty years of the Ottoman Empire is that it became the symbol, embodiment, and focus of global Muslim aspirations for dignity and justice. The Ottoman Empire ended as a Muslim empire, with a popular caliphate as its head, even though the early-nineteenth-century Ottoman elite had envisioned a different, civilizationist, and multireligious empire. A similar story can be written about the Japanese Empire's or Chinese Empire's relationship with the global identity of Asians, the yellow race, and Pan-Asianist thought, or the Ethiopian Empire's relationship with the idea of the black race and Pan-Africanism. There were some peculiar aspects of the Ottoman Empire, which are topics of both global intellectual history and Islamic intellectual history. For example, the debate on the validity of the Ottoman caliphate and the surprising rise in the popularity of the Ottoman caliph cannot be explained with a narrative of the convergence of global norms, although it does require global intellectual history to explain it. Although the Ottoman caliphate was abolished in 1924 by the new Turkish republic, the ideational content of the caliphate movement of the preceding five decades left a long-lasting legacy for twentieth-century intellectual and international history.

Despite the rather unexpected transition from the world of the Ottoman Empire, as the last Muslim empire, to an era of national self-determination, the contents of Pan-Islamic civilizational discourses and their historical narratives did not disappear. International history needs intellectual history to better understand the persistence of transnational identities and their ideational content. The notion that the humiliated and colonized Muslim world is in need of justice and redemption continued unabated after decolonization. From the Lausanne treaty of 1923 to the liberation of Algeria in 1963, colonized Muslim societies have had many moments of nationalist redemption. But broader narratives of Muslim history and identity merged with the foundational texts of modern nationalism and, through textbooks and other means of transmitting cultural history, shaped the contemporary historical memory of the identity of the Muslim world. Even the narratives of nationalist redemption were based on the idea of Muslims gaining equality with the unreliable-sinister-imperialistic West. Perhaps the continuing legacy and historical memory of this Pan-Islamic intellectual content should be seen as unfulfilled yet global values that in turn are still shaping contemporary transnational political movements and intellectual trends in various Muslim societies.

Notes

1. Cemil Aydin, *The Politics of Anti-Westernism in Asia: Visions of World Order in Pan-Islamic and Pan-Asian Thought* (New York: Columbia University Press, 2007); Erez Manela, *The Wilsonian Moment: Self-Determination and the International Origins of Anticolonial Nationalism.* (New York: Oxford University Press, 2007).

2. For examples of earlier scholarship that emphasizes the Westernization of the non-Western world through a diffusion model, see Bernard Lewis, *The Emergence of Modern Turkey*, 3rd ed. (New York: Oxford University Press, 2002). See also Marius B. Jansen, "Changing Japanese Attitudes Toward Modernization," in *Changing Japanese Attitudes Toward Modernization*, ed. Marius B. Jansen (Rutland, Vt.: Tuttle, 1982), 43–97.

3. For an example of an Ottoman bureaucrat who merged Byzantine, Islamic, and Mogul legacies in his imperial visions, see Cornell Fleischer, *Bureaucrat and Intellectual in the Ottoman Empire: The Historian Mustafa Ali, 1541–1600* (Princeton, N.J.: Princeton University Press, 1986).

4. For the cosmopolitan elites of the Mogul dynasty, see Sanjay Subrahmanyam and Muzaffar Alam, "The Making of a Munshi," *Comparative Studies of South Asia, Africa and the Middle East* 24, no. 2 (2004): 61–72.

5. Giancarlo Casale, *The Ottoman Age of Exploration* (New York: Oxford University Press, 2010).

6. For a sixteenth-century comparison of the Ottoman Empire and Muslim dynasties in South Asia that emphasizes differences, see Sidi Ali Reis, *The Travels and Adventures of the Turkish Admiral Sidi Ali Reis* (London: Luzac, 1899).

7. For the eclectic and inclusive worldview of the Ottoman imperial elites, see Cemal Kafadar, "A Rome of One's Own: Reflections on Cultural Geography and Identity in the Lands of Rum," in *Muqarnas: An Annual on the Visual Culture of the Islamic World*, vol. 24, ed. Gulru Necipoglu and Sibel Bozdogan (Leiden: Brill, 2007).

8. For the universalist reflections of an eighteenth-century Ottoman intellectual and bureaucrat with regard to the Ottoman Empire and the emerging new world, see the discussion of the writings of Ahmed Resmi Efendi (1700–1783) in Virginia Aksan, "Ottoman Political Writings, 1768–1808," *International Journal of Middle East Studies* 25, no. 1 (1993): 57–59.

9. Sadik Rıfat Paşa, *Müntehabat-i Asar* (Istanbul: Takvimhane-i Amire, 1858), 1–12.

10. Eric Weitz, "From the Vienna to the Paris System: International Politics and the Entangled Histories of Human Rights, Forced Deportations, and Civilizing Missions," *American Historical Review* 113, no. 5 (2008): 1313–43.

11. Jennifer Pitts, "Liberalism and Empire in a Nineteenth Century Algerian Mirror," *Modern Intellectual History* 6, no. 2 (2009): 287–313.

12. Candan Badem, *The Ottoman Crimean War, 1853–1856* (Leiden: Brill, 2010).

13. Hedley Bull, *The Anarchical Society: A Study of Order in World Politics*, 3rd ed. (New York: Columbia University Press, 2002), 32.

14. For the Ottoman response to the Great Indian Revolt of 1857, see Azmi Özcan, "1857 Büyük Hind Ayaklanması ve Osmanlı Devleti," *İ. Ü. Islam Tetkikleri Dergisi* (Istanbul) 9 (1995): 269–80. Similarly, the Ottoman government did not support the Muslim resistance to the Russian Empire in the Caucasus, except during the Crimean War. See Moshe Gammer, *Muslim Resistance to the Tsar: Shamil and the Conquest of Chechnia and Daghestan* (London: Cass, 1994).

15. Selim Deringil, "'They Live in a State of Nomadism and Savagery': The Late Ottoman Empire and the Post-Colonial Debate," *Comparative Studies in Society and History* 45, no. 2 (2003): 311–42.

16. On the Atjeh Aceh rulers' demand for aid from the Ottoman Empire, see Anthony Reid, "Nineteenth Century Pan-Islam in Indonesia and Malaysia," *Journal of Asian Studies* 26, no. 2 (1967): 275–76. Reid's article demonstrates the role played by pilgrims, students, scholars, and merchants who connected Indonesia with Mecca, Cairo, and Istanbul and revived the notion of Islamic solidarity during the 1860s and 1870s. For the broader context of the Indonesian-Ottoman links during the colonial era, see Engseng Ho, *Graves of Tarim: Genealogy and Mobility in the Indian Ocean* (Berkeley: University of California Press, 2006).

17. Moulavi Cheragh Ali, *The Proposed Political, Legal and Social Reforms in the Ottoman Empire and Other Mohammadan States* (Bombay: Education Society's Press, Byculla, 1883).

18. For the Central Asian and South Asian admirers of the Ottoman Empire, see Adeeb Khalid, "Pan-Islamism in Practice: The Rhetoric of Muslim Unity and Its Uses," in *Late Ottoman Society: The Intellectual Legacy*, ed. Elisabeth Özdalga (London: Routledge/Curzon, 2005), 203–26. See also Adeeb Khalid, "Central Asia Between the Ottoman and the Soviet Worlds," *Kritika* 12, no. 2 (2011): 451–76.

19. Samuel Zwemer, a leading Christian missionary focusing on the Muslim societies, exemplifies this popularization of the books on the "Muslim world" with his prolific writing career. For some of his early books from 1909, see Samuel Zwemer, *Islam, a Challenge to Faith: Studies on the Mohammedan Religion and the Needs and Opportunities of the Mohammedan World from the Standpoint of Christian Missions* (New York: Laymen's Missionary Movement, 1909).

20. For the early Christian missionary movements' interest in conceptualizing a united Muslim world, see their major journal *The Muslim World*, first published by the Hartford Seminary Foundation in 1911. It continues to be published under the same name by the Hartford Seminary, but it no longer is a missionary magazine. Around the same time, Pan-Islamists published their own journals with similar titles. See *Alemi-i Islam* (*The Muslim World*), edited by Abdurreşid Ibrahim and published in Istanbul, 1911/1912.

21. We still have English, German, and French journals with the same title, as well as the Japanese journal *Kaikyō sekai*. See Syed Amir Ali, *The Life and Teachings of Mohammed: The Spirit of Islam* (London: W. H. Allen, 1891); Hindli Abdulmecid, *Ingiltere ve Alem-i Islam* (*England and the World of Islam*) (Istanbul: Matbaai Amire, 1910); Abdurreşid Ibrahim, *Alem-i Islam ve Japonya'da Intişarı Islamiyet* (*The World of Islam and Spread of Islam in Japan*) (Istanbul: Ahmet Saik Bey Matbaasi, 1911).

22. For the English translation of Ernest Renan's 1883 lecture on Islam and science, see *The Poetry of the Celtic Races and Other Studies* (London: Walter Scott, 1896), 84–108.

23. For a British contemporary response to Gladstone, see H. A. Munro Butler-Johnstone, *Bulgarian Horrors, and the Question of the East: A Letter Addressed to the Right Honorable W. E. Gladstone, M.P.* (London: William Ridgway, 1876).

24. For Namik Kemal's response to Renan's speech, see Namik Kemal, *Renan Müdafaanamesi: Islamiyet ve Maarif* (Ankara: Milli Kültür Yayınları, 1962). For Afghani's response, see Jamal al-Afghani, "Answer of Jamal ad-Din to Renan," in *An Islamic Response to Imperialism*, ed. Nikkie Keddie (Berkeley: University of California Press, 1968), 181–87. For the response by Ataullah Bayezidof, see his *Islam ve Medeniyet* (Ankara: TDV Yayınları, 1993). For an account of Afghani's relationship with Renan in Paris, see Elie Kedourie, *Afghani and Abduh* (London: Cass, 1966), 41–46.

25. Ahmed Riza, *La faillite morale de la politique occidentale en Orient* (Tunis: Éditions Bouslama, 1979); Ahmed Riza and Ismayl Urbain, *Tolérance de l'islam* (Saint-Ouen: Centre Abaad, 1992).

26. For the modernism of Salafi thought during the late nineteenth century, see David Dean Commins, *Islamic Reform: Politics and Social Change in Late Ottoman Syria* (New York: Oxford University Press, 1990).

27. A Pan-Islamist Ottoman who published extensively in England on issues of the Muslim World, Halil Halid studied and taught at Cambridge University. See Syed Tanvir Wasti, "Halil Halid: Anti-Imperialist Muslim Intellectual," *Middle Eastern Studies* 29, no. 3 (1993): 559–79. For Halil Halid's autobiography, see See Halil Halid, *The Diary of a Turk* (London: A. C. Black, 1903). Similarly, the first comprehensive book on Pan-Asianism was written by a Japanese graduate of the Columbian College of Law in Washington, D.C., around the turn of the twentieth century: Kodera Kenkichi, *Dai ajiashugi ron* (Tokyo: Hōbunkan, 1916).

28. Lothrop Stoddard, *The New World of Islam* (New York: Scribner, 1921).

29. For its Arabic translation, see Lûthrub Stûdard, *Hadir al-Alam al-Islami*, trans. 'Ajjâj Nuwayhid and ed. al-Amîr Shakîb Arslân (Cairo: Matbaa-i Salafiyah, 1924). For the Ottoman translation of the same work, *Yeni Alem-i Islam*, trans. Ali Riza Seyfi (Istanbul: Ali Şükrü Matbaasi, 1922).

30. Renée Worringer, "'Sick Man of Europe' or 'Japan of the Near East'?: Constructing Ottoman Modernity in the Hamidian and Young Turk Eras," *International Journal of Middle Eastern Studies* 36, no. 2 (2004): 207–23. Also see Cemil Aydin, "A Global Anti-Western Moment? The Russo-Japanese War, Decolonization and Asian Modernity," in *Competing Visions of World Order: Global Moments and Movements, 1880s to 1930s*, ed. Sebastian Conrad and Dominic Sachsenmaier (New York: Palgrave Macmillan, 2007), 213–36.

31. Umar Abdallah, *A Muslim in Victorian America: The Life of Alexander Russell Web* (New York: Oxford University Press, 2006).

32. Mushir Hosain Kidwai's book *Pan-Islamism* mentions that in its November 1907 issue, the magazine *Theosophist* had a positive account of the establishment of the London Pan-Islamic Society.

33. Muslim representation at the Chicago World's Parliament of Religions in 1893 was relatively small, mainly composed of Ottoman envoy İsmail Hakkı Bey and Alexander Russell Web. However, there were many non-Muslim delegates who gave speeches about the civilized life of Muslims and the Ottomans, including Esmeralda Cervantes, Herant Kiretchijian, Teresa Viele, and Christopher Jibara.

34. William Scawen Blunt, *The Future of Islam* (London: Kegan Paul, 1882).

35. For many texts on the validity of the caliphate and trajectory of this debate, see İsmail Kara, ed., *Hilafet Risaleleri* (Istanbul: Klasik Yayınları, 2002), 1:65–67.

36. W. E. Gladstone, *Bulgarian Horrors and the Question of the East* (London: John Murray, 1876).

37. In various Indian Muslim defenses of the Ottoman Empire, the Ottoman Empire's appointment of Greek and Armenian bureaucrats to high-level positions is often compared with limitations for Muslims and Hindus for social mobility in British Empire. To make this point, Cheragh Ali lists almost one hundred Christian officers working for the Ottoman Empire at that time. See Moulavi Cheragh Ali, *The Proposed Political, Legal and Social Reforms in the Ottoman Empire and Other Mohammadan States* (Bombay: Education Society's Press, 1883), 40–43.

38. Almost all the major international law books of the late nineteenth century were translated and used in the Ottoman Empire. There also were original works written by Ottoman Muslim intellectuals. For example, Celal Nuri, *Kendi Noktai Nazarimizdan Hukuk-i Düvel* (*International Law from Our Point of View*) (Istanbul: Osmanlı Şirketi Matbaasi, 1911).

39. Arnulf Becker Lorca, "Universal International Law: Nineteenth-Century Histories of Imposition and Appropriation," *Harvard International Law Journal* 51, no. 2 (2010): 475–552.

40. Deringil, "'They Live in a State of Nomadism and Savagery,'" 42. Deringil quotes this term from Karl Blind, "Young Turkey," *Fortnightly Review* (1896).

41. Ron Geaves, *Islam in Victorian Britain: The Life and Times of Abdullah Quilliam* (Leicester: Islamic Foundation 2009). For an example of Quilliam's defense of the Ottoman Empire, see William Henry Quilliam, *The Troubles in the Balkans. The Turkish Side of the Question: Verbatim Report of the Speech Delivered by the Sheikh-ul-Islam of the British Isles (W. H. Quilliam) on the 22nd October, 1903, at the Town Hall, Liverpool* (Liverpool: Crescent Printing, 1904).

42. M. A. Sherf, *Searching for Solace: A Biography of Abdullah Yusuf Ali, Interpreter of the Quran* (Kuala Lumpur: Islamic Book Trust, 1994).

43. Mustafa Aksakal, "Defending the Nation: The German-Ottoman Alliance of 1914 and the Ottoman Decision for War" (Ph.D. diss., Princeton University, 2003).

44. Donald Bloxham, *The Great Game of Genocide: Imperialism, Nationalism and the Destruction of the Ottoman Armenians* (Oxford: Oxford University Press 2005).

45. John Riddell, ed., *To See the Dawn: Baku, 1920–First Congress of the Peoples of the East* (New York: Pathfinder, 1993).

46. For the separation between Communism and Pan-Islamism, see Tan Malaka, "Communism and Pan-Islamism," in *What Next: Marxist Discussion Journal* 21 (2001), also available at http://www.whatnextjournal.co.uk/Pages/Back/Wnext21/Panislam.html (accessed March 2012).

47. For an interesting example of sympathy for Bolshevism among Pan-Islamic activists, see Mushir Hosain Kidwai, *Pan-Islamism and Bolshevism* (London: Luzac, 1937).

48. Mine (Sümer) Erol, "Wilson Prensipleri Cemiyeti'nin Amerika Cumhurbaşkanı Wilson'a Gönderdiği Muhtıra," *Ankara Üniversitesi Dil ve Tarih Coğrafya Fakültesi Tarih Araştırmaları Dergisi* 3, nos. 4–5 (1966): 237–45.

49. For examples of the post–World War I Pan-Islamic movement and its ideas, see Mushir Hosain Kidwai, *The Future of the Muslim Empire: Turkey* (London: Central Islamic Society, 1919); Mushir Hosain Kidwai, *The Sword Against Islam or a Defence of Islam's Standard-Bearers* (London: Central Islamic Society, 1919); and Gail Minault, *The Khilafat Movement: Religious Symbolism and Political Mobilization in India* (New York: Columbia University Press, 1982).

50. For a recent study of the importance of the Ottoman caliphate for the world's Muslims before and after its abolition in 1924, see Mona Hassan, "Loss of Caliphate: The Trauma and Aftermath of 1258 and 1924" (Ph.D. diss., Princeton University, 2009).

8

On the Nonglobalization of Ideas

SAMUEL MOYN

S uddenly, Haiti's revolution has become a touchstone of contemporary thought, where a growing number of historians and theorists alike have alighted to right the wrong of narrative exclusion and to show that "Western" history has depended on subaltern actors to develop some of its own most cherished notions.[1] The events in question in what was then called Saint-Domingue—thanks to which slavery was ended during the French Revolution in an uprising that terrified some and inspired others forever after—deserve attention after a long period of neglect. Much is at stake in how those events are interpreted, especially how concepts are said to have informed the political explosion.

In the past, Haiti may have changed the world, including American history. Its main role today, however, seems to be to inspire a new answer to how ideas can become global. Haiti, indeed, seems to be a window— or mirror—for a self-proclaimed globalizing age to seek the roots of large-scale conceptual transmission. Perhaps most prominently, Susan Buck-Morss tried to substantiate a parallel long ago constructed by David Brion Davis, by suggesting that G. W. F. Hegel's master–slave dialectic depended on reading accounts of the Haitian uprising.[2] But in this chapter, I begin with Haiti's role in the new historiography of "human rights."

Laurent Dubois offered in this literature what has proved a remarkably fertile claim that Caribbean blacks redeemed white principles, thereby "universalizing" the notion of rights. "If we live in a world in which democracy is meant to exclude no one," he wrote, "it is in no small part because of the actions of those slaves in Saint-Domingue who insisted that human rights were theirs too."[3] He then added in his impressive study of insurrection in Guadeloupe: "Developments in the Antilles outran the political imagination of the metropole in the imagination—and universalization—of rights."[4] Whatever this claim may have meant in Dubois's own work, it has been taken by later historians, like Robin Blackburn and Lynn Hunt, to imply what I call a model of "truncation and fulfillment" in global intellectual history, a model that, in the Haitian case, takes the form of universalist truncation and subaltern fulfillment.

Even though it is framed in terms of rights, what makes this model worthy of attention is that it is a general one for conceptual spread across large spaces. On close inspection, though, the model turns out to be unpersuasive. Hunt's approach has an explicit "logic of rights," which runs from contemporary claims of citizenship by Jews and women through the Caribbean events. According to Hunt, once universal entitlements are declared, the pressure rises for remedying their original truncation. Although white Christian men may want to keep these entitlements for themselves, they are forced by the universalism of their own claim to extend them:

> Human rights have an inner logic. As soon as a highly conceivable group came up for discussion [of entitlements], those in the same kind of category but located lower on the conceivability scale . . . would inevitably appear on the agenda. . . . In the workings of this logic, the supposedly metaphysical nature of [rights] proved to be a very positive asset.[5]

Because formal universalism applies to everyone (for I assume it is the formal universalism of rights talk that matters), anyone can claim that he or she is excluded from its coverage. As they are humans too, Jews, women, and blacks can insist they are entitled to rights, thus universalizing the concept.

But how exactly does this logic of universalistic concepts work? It makes sense to consider this question from the complementary perspectives of conceptual content and historical agency. Starting with content, one might infer that the model of truncation and fulfillment posits that *only universal principles* are ones that can obey an inner "logic" that allows them to function externally as they do in and across the world. The presumption is that particularistic concepts are not limited or hypocritical in the same way. Following Dubois, Hunt insists that it is the very formal abstraction of truncated universals that allows them to travel—and to be seized from below—so unexpectedly. By contrast, particularistic concepts do not promise broad or even universal coverage in a similar manner and therefore do not invite the same moves.

It might be, of course, that nonuniversalistic concepts also globalize, but if they do, it is not according to the same logic. They presumably are more like commodities that spread according to a more random, and perhaps also less inspiring, set of mechanisms. It turns out that people like coffee, or Romantic symphonies, and disperse them from their point of origin and offer new variations of them around the world. These stories are now of considerable interest to people, as the success of much imitated books on the global percolations of various goods from cod to chocolate attests. But nobody claims that there is a *logic* of coffee or symphonies according to which they are somehow not what they really are until imported and made true to themselves. I find coffee fulfilling, but I do not fulfill it. In the current model, however, it is almost as if universals, and especially rights, have a destiny that depends on globalization to realize.

Now turn from content to agency. One interesting and potentially attractive feature of the model of truncation and fulfillment in global intellectual history is that it seems to offer a scheme in which apparently antagonistic elites and subalterns need each other. It is the (metropolitan) elites who announce universal principles, even if they keep them to themselves, and it is the (colonial) subalterns who become the fulfillers. As Blackburn emphasizes, the concepts do not work fully on their own: if the French Revolution "challenge[d] slavery," it "was not because of the French Assembly's resounding 'Declaration of the Rights of Man and Citizen' in 1789, since neither the Assembly nor its successor, the Convention, moved on their own initiative to confront slavery."[6] In other words, it took black action for white principles to rise above hypocrisy. Moreover, subaltern fulfillment is not simple mimicry but elevates the principles above their originally bounded announcement in order to make them true for the first time. If it makes any sense, Dubois's claim about the "universalization" of rights must mean this. Otherwise, what could it mean to universalize already universal principles? Clearly, they were universal in form from the beginning. But if they were "universalized" by unsuspected actors, it is presumably because they were not really universal until their genuine coverage was taken to its proper (or at least some further) extent. In this way, as such examples show, the model does intend to make room for human agency.

All the same, the role of these agents is that of *realizing the concept's already built-in potential* before subaltern agency arrives. In the model of truncation and fulfillment, the historian supposes that the universals like rights are meant to have a greater relevance than they actually do initially, so that if they travel across the globe, it is according to a potential they had from the beginning. Thus, their globalization may fulfill them and depend completely on subaltern actors, but in doing so it realizes only what they already were. If they were not originally universal, they were at least *universalizable*. Hunt's metaphor of "cascades"—the mechanism by which she says the logic of rights operates—is a good illustration of this commitment.[7] The naturalistic metaphor makes it sound as if the concept were struggling to realize its potential, that humans are its servants, or even its beneficiaries. Put in another way, in the model of truncation and fulfillment, the globalization of a concept is, in significant part, autoglobalization.

All things considered, the model is a strikingly idealist one, and not least in its presentation of confused actors whose ostensible antagonism actually works to advance unintended designs, and in its considerable allocation of agency to the built-in destiny of a concept in itself. Like the old *Weltgeist*, rights may need to work in mysterious ways, but their globalization is already implicit in their announcement.

There is considerable evidence that this model is not simply a wish-fulfilling construction. After all, Hunt is right that in the revolutionary era, universalistic concepts had "cascade" effects as unintended actors claimed them. In one of the first efforts to construct a global intellectual history, others have tried to show that in the nineteenth century, liberal and democratic promises of emancipation worked in a similar way.[8]

But the Haitian example has a few obvious problems even on its own terms. It is not the only interpretation of the events available. In an embarrassing discovery for the model of truncation and fulfillment, Jeremy Popkin showed that between 1791 and 1793 there is no evidence of Haitian slaves invoking "the rights of man" or high principle at all in their maneuvering for concessions.[9] As Malick Ghachem demonstrated, the uprising was based on legal entitlements of France's Old Regime rather than a seizure from below of a new revolutionary universalism waiting to be realized.[10]

Furthermore, the model unseats an older, Marxist interpretation of the events propounded by C. L. R. James. A Trotskyist, James's view of *droits de l'homme* seems to have been as the "wordy" promises of "eloquent phrasemakers" who, driven by the true economic motor of history to "perorate," are in the end willing to give up the aristocracy of the skin only at the point of the insurgent's gun.[11] Reviewing Blackburn's recent book, Greg Grandin commented: "Blackburn does more than defend James's argument that Haitians universalised European ideals of liberty, fraternity and equality. He extends it across all of the Americas." But clearly, James would never have affirmed a logic of rights. Indeed, his attitude toward formal abstraction could not have been more different, and therefore he would have striven for something other than the model of universalist truncation and subaltern fulfillment.[12]

What could such an alternative look like? Sticking to the concept of rights, let us move to another era, to seek the complexity that the exciting story of the Haitian insurrection may now make difficult to achieve, in part because it was so exceptional.

Contrary to the often repeated convention that in the era of the Universal Declaration of Human Rights (1948) the new idea "enjoyed enormous global attention," it turns out that the United Nations provided the sole forum in which the phrase in its international bearing (and essentially new in the English language) had any relevance.[13] There was no self-styled "human rights movement" anywhere in the world. The moment after World War II, in other words, presents the puzzle of a concept eventually destined to be a worldwide giant beginning its life by seeming to be strangled in its crib.[14] Long into the postwar era, if "human rights" meant what they now mean to anyone—principles beyond the nation-state to chasten, and the basis for nongovernmental transnational activism to name and shame—for some reason, they failed to appeal to many people in this sense.

The history of international human rights as a galvanizing idea was, in the beginning and for a very long time, a history of *nonglobalization*, especially compared with their circulation and resonance now. The example, then, challenges the model of truncated universals and subaltern fulfillment: Why did it not occur? It is not that the cascade *failed*, as in the French revolutionary bid of women to claim citizenship. As in the Haitian claims to freedom, Olympe de Gouges and other women during the 1790s look as though they tried to "fulfill" revolutionary universalism. In contrast, after World War II, almost no one experimented with the same subversive appropriation of universal human rights norms across large global spaces. The post–World War II era offers a scenario in which the cascade that one might count on instead *failed to occur*, like a river that refuses to flow even though the dam has been destroyed.

After World War II, there were good reasons that international human rights were not widely claimed. In my view, the most significant one is that the new concept came to the world along with an older concept that for a while did much better: the self-determination of peoples. In the Atlantic Charter of 1941, the document often taken as the origin of human rights, the Allies promised collective self-determination. But for British Prime Minister Winston Churchill, this was a vision of the liberation of Adolf Hitler's empire, but not his empire, let alone empire as such. Eventually Churchill convinced U.S. President Franklin Delano Roosevelt, despite the latter's dislike of formal empire, to share his interpretation. The concept of human rights, absent in the Atlantic Charter, surged after the war, just when the Allies were stepping back from self-determination. This replacement of one concept for another meant that some parts of the world saw in "human rights" not the enthralling global vision of contemporary historiography but something more like a consolation prize. Not surprisingly, the Atlantic Charter had enormous resonance across the world, including among African Americans identifying with the global anticolonialist cause. The Universal Declaration fell on comparatively deaf ears in contrast to this earlier striking "cascade."[15] (After 1950, indeed, self-determination became the first human right, even though the entire doctrine languished in the United Nations for decades.)

One way to approach the implications of these 1940s events for the model of truncation and fulfillment is to look at the same two dimensions as before: content and agency. If the nonglobalization of human rights is something the first model cannot explain on its own terms, then one must ask why—and whether it is a symptom of a larger theoretical mistake. It might even undercut the entire scheme. In offering a moment in which a logic of rights did not operate, suggesting that formal universalism need not by itself spark its potential from below, the case of the decolonizing or soon-to-be-decolonized world after 1945 might even point toward a different model of the globalization of concepts.

The first element of complexity absent from the model of truncation and fulfillment seems to be that there is often, probably always, *more than one formal universalism* available to spread. As Sheldon Pollock showed, universalism goes back a long way, with different versions of cosmopolitanism competing with one another across human history.[16] After World War II, it was collective self-determination that, though it fell under Western eyes as human rights rose, succeeded in globalizing. Now it is possible to tell a story of truncation and fulfillment about self-determination, too, as Erez Manela did in a much noticed book.[17] But my intent is not to retain the model for a different concept. In this particular historical moment, and perhaps in all such moments, it is impossible to isolate the globalization of one concept from the *nonglobalization of another*.

If fulfilling truncation is the right model at all, then perhaps the first questions are, Which truncation? Which fulfillment? In this era, the equally universalistic concept of self-determination, along with Marxism, did much better than human rights and was globalized instead. The victory of self-determination politics resulted in the greatest dissemination of sovereignty as a concept and a practice in world history, and it created the very situation the human rights movement later set itself the task of qualifying or overcoming. (For its part, Marxism did so well in reaching global spaces that if forced to think of it in terms of the truncation and fulfillment of universalisms, one would have to acknowledge that its own critique of formalism and abstraction made it impossible to understand its own global travels and reinvention.) From the perspective of content, then, my example shows that it is never enough to think that the universalism—even the false or betrayed universalism—of a particular concept is a sufficient reason for its spread. By itself, truncation may not count for much.

Now consider agency again. From this vantage point, the obvious and considerable flaws in an idealistic model of the autoglobalization of concepts seem plain. Perhaps the history of universalistic (or even all) concepts depends on how rival human actors choose to deploy them, for good or for ill, and requires frameworks in which concepts have local and time-bound implications that may make them appealing in specific and concrete historical situations. Even if universalistic concepts function in a different way, their plurality in the abstract and specific historical meaning in concrete times and places means that their fate always depends first on *which ones* subaltern actors choose to deploy.

At times, Christianity—no less formally universal than human rights—has proved the appealing ideology of to "fulfill." At other times, Marxism—no more formally universal than human rights are— has served. What, then, explains the spread of the concepts if nothing about their formal universalism by itself does? Presumably, the only persuasive explanation is the action of subaltern appropriation that selects and reinvents. Although surely it is true that the contents of alternative versions of universalism differ in crucial ways, it is also the case that subaltern selection and reinvention depend on a range of nonconceptual factors the historian cannot ignore.

Simply to pursue the example used so far, some of the important, if often implicit, questions to be answered about the meaning of rival concepts in specific historical moments are as follows: First, what are the prior associations of the concepts, and the formations of the actors who engage them? The history of twentieth-century anticolonialism suggests that the option to push for formal independence developed slowly amid the wreckage of false or failed promises of colonial reform. Although human rights were new, rights in imperial spaces were not. On one hand, they were easy to dismiss as inadequate, given their prior invocation as a gift of civilization. On the other hand, they also were open to appropriation before the 1940s, even if—in their old and new forms in the empire—they ultimately did not succeed in creating a robust enough option to stave off the bid for formal independence.[18] The 1940s were a moment combining visionary experimentalism and genuine indecision, but no plausible account could leave out the prior history of the circulation of rival universalisms that led to various subaltern interpretations and appropriations.

Second, what are the different universalistic concepts' associations with specific local and global forces? After all, different ones may seem more or less productive depending on the moment, for reasons that their universalism alone does not explain. Toussaint L'Ouverture invoked revolutionary citizenship (not "human rights" in their contemporary sense) not as an agent of the universal fulfilling itself across the globe but as a strategic actor with alternative choices in an imperial space. In the mid-twentieth century, very different subaltern internationalisms like Pan-Africanism meant a lot. Today, however, after a crisis of other languages of empowerment, many turn (or are compelled to turn) to diverse forms of Christian evangelicalism that are suddenly appealing to them—along with international human rights.[19] If one factor in those affiliations is ideological, another may be instrumental. The general story, then, must be about the subaltern judgment of the specifics of power and possibility that alternative concepts offer.

Finally, it would be a mistake to ignore the already constituted political space that actors inherit and can reshape but that is rarely, and perhaps never, the globe *simpliciter*. This is especially true for colonial history, in which subalterns were in a dynamic relationship with imperial masters, but rarely with the globe generally.

In related comments on Haiti and beyond, Frederick Cooper emphasizes the *political boundaries* of the spaces in which concepts can travel. Although he invokes Haiti and rights, too, he actually points in a different direction than truncation and fulfillment, or at least registers the critical importance of fulfillment within a preconstituted political space. "Could concepts of rights, human dignity, and participation be confined to national units?" Cooper asks:

> The Haitian Revolution in the French empire, the combination of slave revolts and antislavery mobilization in the British empire, and the tensions between creole elites and peasants and slaves in the era of revolution in Spanish America all point to the possibility that politics in metropoles could not be neatly segregated from colonies.[20]

If Toussaint and the French Revolution were in the same political space, or if (in another of Cooper's favorite examples) early negritude intellectuals like Léopold Sédar Senghor at the end of World War II were most enthusiastic about a reimagined Union française in which the imperial space might serve rather than still obstruct emancipation and equality, it is because that space mattered as a medium for the arrogation of concepts. To Senghor, at this moment, rights within a reformed political structure seemed to promise more than either rights within a prospective autonomous state or a still mostly meaningless body of global human rights. Senghor, indeed, never referred to the latter so far as I can tell, despite his often very pronounced universalism: if he took the imperial space seriously for a while, he simultaneously ignored the United Nations and its "universal human rights."

In other words, both Haitian and post–World War II cases underline the importance of political spaces, not the appeal of rights concepts by itself, in the strategic choices of subaltern actors. It is for this very reason that Cooper explicitly contrasts the logic of imperial spaces with one of "globalization." Unlike Cooper, I do not rule out conceptual dissemination at the level of the globe, or at least approximating it more closely than any other spatial category available; but it is clear that the globe itself is not a purely geographical space but a constituted political and cultural space.[21]

These three dimensions helping determine the spread of a concept— its prior trajectory, the field of power and strategic choice, and available spaces of creative intervention—suggest that there is no obvious way to find in the *content* of some concept a decisive reason for the affiliation of historical actors. Agency is much more theirs, based on a reading of what the concept means (including the sorts of alliances it allows) in specific historical situations. In the complex post–World War II moment, the history of affiliation with rights seems to be much more a matter of the political form or structure—state, region, empire, international organization, and world community and all in both their actual and imaginable forms—in which they can be invoked with a difference. In a larger view, similarly complex moments have led to the choices for an alternative doctrine to rights (Christianity, Marxism, or whatever else).

If so, there is not only no immanent "logic" to rights but also no logic of any particular concept. They are tools and weapons for unexpected and better and worse uses. Of course, in this model, conceptual mediation and spread are inseparable from practical mobilization (including potential violence). Concepts inform such mobilization, but not in the way that "spirit," in G. W. F. Hegel's philosophy of history, is supposed to make passion blindly serve its cause. Instead of the cunning of reason, in other words, global intellectual history needs to be based on the cunning of action.

— ⚬⚬⚬ —

The risk of insisting on overdetermined conjunctures, and free agency within them, is that it ignores that conjunctures are always made of powerful forces and that agency is always constituted by those forces, not free in some ineffable sense or strategic on the basis of the unshaped preferences of mythical "rational actors." From one point of view, my proposal can skirt the dilemma of structure and agency, since no version of its resolution could permit a vision of global intellectual history in which concepts autoglobalize through the passive intermediation of human beings. The multiple pathways of any approach to social structure and its evolution—especially on a large geographical scale—prevent stories of truncation and fulfillment from being very compelling. Yet it is important to acknowledge that the critique of truncation and fulfillment, despite the latter's prominence in contemporary accounts of rights and other globalizing themes (like economics and law), is not itself a theory of global intellectual history. Instead, it is compatible with many approaches to that emerging genre.[22]

William Sewell's state-of-the-art engagement with historical theory shows the dilemmas to which a commitment to nuance can lead.

Instead of a coercive theory of structure, Sewell emphasizes that structure is never just a constraint; it is a resource too. In his terms, structure is always "dual," exerting causation and providing opportunity. In accounting for events, there is never just one structure. Drawing on and criticizing Marshall Sahlins, Sewell suggests that events do not happen spontaneously but are based on the conjuncture of structures. The plurality and collisions of these structures, occurring in endless new patterns, are what exerts whatever "structural determination" there is from case to case. As if such complications were not enough, Sewell also sticks to the "cultural turn" that has defined so much of humanities research in the past generation. Meaning is "thick" and requires interpretation to reconstruct the imaginative worlds of actors.[23]

One sobering thought after reading Sewell is that the requirements of a currently plausible social theory make it extremely difficult to render large spatial (as well as *longue durée*) phenomena intelligible, precisely because accounts must deal with the duality and plurality of structures as well as with the way that cultural meaning inflects them. For the purposes of global intellectual history, my suggestion is that an acknowledgment of dual and plural structures permeated with cultural meaning also makes obvious that it is this complexity, rather than ineffable or unconstituted agency, that must be the starting point for understanding how individual actors choose to use concepts in some specific, conjunctural, and culturally laden moment.

Nonetheless, an approach like mine, emphasizing competing alternatives and situational appropriations, may seem to omit or sideline the way in which a "universal concept" like rights in general or human rights later "emerges in the modern epoch [and] transcends the boundaries of linguistic and cultural specificity to achieve global plausibility as a means of construing the world." This is, at any rate, the way that Andrew Sartori describes culture, the specimen theme he studies in what is the most conceptually sophisticated attempt in recent historiography to write a global intellectual history.[24] His description of it seems applicable to the problem of the globalization of rights and human rights, the example I have been considering here.

Sartori wants to force historians to confront the fact that certain universal concepts can be disseminated in versions that—whatever the problems and difficulties of their mediation and "translation" across linguistic and other barriers—are recognizably similar. Even in the case of a European concept, as Sartori observes, one must acknowledge its spread and not fear treating its secondary users as derivative, for its appropriation itself is always as inventive as its earlier coinage.[25] Out of a desire to avoid idealistic treatments of conceptual spread (as well as reductive materialistic approaches), Sartori suggests that the project of global intellectual history at its most ambitious must both describe and explain this breakthrough in modern times to global transmissibility, which only the fact that "some fundamental structures of social practice span the real and enormous differences that separate diverse and regional lifeworlds" could explain.[26]

For Sartori, those structures are provided by the modern breakthrough to capitalism as well as by its evolving characteristics. Following Karl Marx and certain of his heirs, from Georg Lukács through Moishe Postone, Sartori claims that capitalism explains how universal concepts can afford the illusions of subjective autonomy (whether individual or collective) that interlock with the objective determination of social life. Thus it is no accident, since capitalism is modern, that only modernity is the forum for "the emergence of new, specifically modern concepts whose plausibility and power are at once real, persistent over time [and] globalizing in reach."[27]

Sartori's intent to offer a model for global intellectual history beyond the details of his own case study is so provocative that it requires anyone interested in the future of the enterprise to engage it directly. And distressingly, given my preceding argument, Sartori's approach might reveal that the model of truncation and fulfillment is preferable to the model of situational appropriation. After all, Sartori himself is committed to the relevance of modern universalistic concepts as well as to his own "logic" of their spread. As I showed, while rarely explicit in their theoretical commitments, those proposing truncation and fulfillment tend to apply it to specifically modern promises of emancipation, either rights by themselves or a package including dignity and citizenship. Similarly, this special regard for universalistic concepts is related in Sartori's book to the fact that they play a unique ideological role in the modern, capitalistic circumstances that allow for their spread. In other words, their globalization very much obeys, for Sartori too, a "logic." True, Sartori prefers to reclaim the universalizing spread of concepts like liberal rights and collectivist self-determination as ideological effects leading merely to the "liberation" of class relations. His account, nonetheless, is still one of necessarily modern universalisms and their globalizing cascades.

To be sure, Sartori breaks with the idealism of the model of truncation and fulfillment, on the grounds that the explanation for the cascades through which spreading occurs must be found in social practices whose basis is at least partly or, in the final instance, material. Similarly, there is little doubt that Sartori would avoid the notion of fulfillment, but not because he is averse to acknowledging transmission from the West to the rest. He is not impressed by the implicit sense of Western superiority that such a model offers, but he is also not concerned that acknowledging Western origins is somehow a strike against the originality of others. For Sartori, capitalism is a general sociohistorical phenomenon that, even if it appeared (along with various concepts) in one place first, is modern but not "Western." In any event, conceptual spread is an occasion for subaltern originality rather than simple derivation. Above all, Sartori's globalization of concepts is an ideological effect of materially rooted domination, rather than a triumphant moment of idealistic "reconciliation."

Sartori's presentation of universalistic concepts and their globalizing logic may escape my criticisms of truncation and fulfillment. I nevertheless worry that his model—with its intent to do justice to both the modernity and the spread of key concepts, in order to ally global intellectual history with a critical social theory—makes it difficult to understand the details of *competition* that my example of "human rights" in the postwar world is intended to demonstrate. It is true that Sartori's narrative of the dissemination of culturalism to Bengal and beyond is premised on a succession from individualist liberalism to collectivist emancipation (including indigenism) that fits my story of the competition of personal "human rights" and collective self-determination very snugly.[28] Yet the details of that competition, especially the invention of "human rights" as a consolation prize and the situational preference for self-determination, appear to depend on factors that neither truncation and fulfillment nor "capitalist modernity" can easily explain. If Sartori's response is that capitalism creates a framework for competing key concepts, then his social theory has stopped short of the resolution of key conflicts, leaving room for agents to maneuver on the ground and contingent accidents. In any case, like the early resolution of the competition in favor of self-determination, the postponed but eventual ascendance of human rights—against the background of the crisis of the developmentalist state around the world—is similarly hard to separate from the contingent details of global politics, including the appropriations of subalterns.[29]

In fairness, Sartori is clear that his framework does not preclude the particularities of local and temporary circumstances, which he illustrates in his own case study, even if his agenda of recapturing the modernity and generality of globalizing conceptual transmission takes pride of place.[30] But it is unclear the extent to which he is willing to incorporate not so much cultural difference as historical contingency in his model. If I have understood him correctly, Sartori might say that instead of dropping the modernizing and universalizing features of the model of truncation and fulfillment in favor of a picture of situated interpretation and appropriation, we should save those features for a new theory that respects or even incorporates the focus on context and agency that I have stressed. There remains the problem, however, of finding the right compromise between the "logic" of concepts and the contingencies of their spread. Resolving that problem seems difficult, but after Sartori's book, it is perhaps unavoidable.

I am perfectly happy with that resolution, since it is compatible with the lesson that I have stressed: if there is to be a global concept history, it must put comparison and competition of potentially global concepts at its heart. Another crucial proviso is that comparisons are frequently made, and competition resolved, by situated actors in precise historical moments—and no logic of truncation and fulfillment controls either the actors or the moments. Above all, concepts do not spread one by one. They are not only bound up with larger political and cultural processes but also selected out of larger actual and possible sets of alternative concepts. This means that for every concept that does globalize, others do not do so. For this reason, the nonglobalization of ideas—even in modernity when remarkable episodes of transmission do indeed occur—is a critical and necessary part of any plausible global intellectual history.

Notes

1. For exclusion, see Michel-Rolph Trouillot, *Silencing the Past: Power and the Production of History* (Boston: Beacon Press, 1989).

2. David Brion Davis, *The Problem of Slavery in an Age of Revolution, 1770–1823* (New York: Oxford University Press, 1975), esp. epilogue, "Toussaint L'Ouverture and the Phenomenology of Mind"; Susan Buck-Morss, "Hegel and Haiti," *Critical Inquiry* 26, no. 4 (2000): 821–65; Susan Buck-Morss, *Hegel, Haiti, and Universal History* (Pittsburgh: University of Pittsburgh Press, 2009). For the effects of Haiti on America, see Edward Rugemer, *The Problem of Emancipation: The Caribbean Roots of the American Civil War* (Baton Rouge: Louisiana State University Press, 2008); and Ashli White, *Encountering Revolution: Haiti and the Making of the Early Republic* (Baltimore: Johns Hopkins University Press, 2010).

3. Laurent Dubois, *Avengers of the New World: The Story of the Haitian Revolution* (Cambridge, Mass.: Harvard University Press, 2004), 3.

4. Laurent Dubois, *A Colony of Citizens: Revolution and Slave Emancipation in the French Caribbean, 1787–1804* (Chapel Hill: University of North Carolina Press, 2004), 2.

5. Lynn Hunt, *Inventing Human Rights: A History* (New York: Norton, 2007), 150.

6. Robin Blackburn, *American Crucible: Slavery, Emancipation, and Human Rights* (New York: Verso, 2011), 174. Given the intention and subtitle of his book, it is surprising that Blackburn devotes almost no space to the proposition that "human rights" were on the mind of insurgent blacks in that era or, indeed, later.

7. For a more contemporary use of the metaphor, consider Kathryn Sikkink, *The Justice Cascade: How Human Rights Prosecutions Are Changing World Politics* (New York: Norton, 2011), as if justice were not created or enacted but flowed through the world in somewhat the same way that communism was once viewed as spreading like dominoes falling. Compare Samuel Moyn, "Of Deserts and Promised Lands," *Nation*, March 19, 2012.

8. C. A. Bayly and Eugene Biagini, eds., *Giuseppe Mazzini and the Globalisation of Democratic Nationalism, 1830–1920* (Oxford: Oxford University Press, 2008).

9. Jeremy D. Popkin, *You Are All Free: The Haitian Revolution and the Abolition of Slavery* (Cambridge: Cambridge University Press, 2010), esp. 17n.

10. For the case that in an act of "strategic ethics," slaves appealed to conventional "old regime" law rather than natural or universal principles,

see Malick W. Ghachem, *The Old Regime and the Haitian Revolution* (Cambridge: Cambridge University Press, 2012).

11. C. L. R. James, *The Black Jacobins: Toussaint L'Ouverture and the San Domingo Revolution*, new ed. (New York: Vintage Books, 1963), 24, 116, 139. James thought that what mattered to Toussaint was that the "cascade" of citizenship did not happen by itself. Instead, it had to be forced through violence, and what these radicals insisted on was mainly their right to be masters of their fate. The same was true in twentieth-century history.

12. Greg Grandin, "The American Crucible," *Guardian,* July 8, 2011. It is interesting that even though he is one of the world's senior Marxist historians today, Blackburn pays almost no attention to the long-standing Marxist critique of rights or formalistic abstraction in general. Compare Robin Blackburn, "Reclaiming Human Rights," *New Left Review* 69 (May/June 2011): 126–38.

13. Paul Kennedy, *The Parliament of Man: The Past, Present, and Future of the United Nations* (New York: Vintage Books, 2006), 179.

14. See Samuel Moyn, *The Last Utopia: Human Rights in History* (Cambridge, Mass.: Belknap / Harvard University Press, 2010), esp. chap. 3; as well as Samuel Moyn "Imperialism, Self-Determination, and the Rise of Human Rights," in *The Human Rights Revolution: An International History*, ed. Akira Iriye et al. (New York: Oxford University Press, 2012).

15. For the Atlantic Charter as the origin, see, for example, Elizabeth Borgwardt, *A New Deal for the World: America's Vision for Human Rights* (Cambridge, Mass.: Harvard University Press, 2006); and Elizabeth Borgwardt, "'When You State a Moral Principle, You Are Stuck with It': The 1941 Atlantic Charter as a Human Rights Instrument," *Virginia Journal of International Law* 46, no. 3 (2006): 501–62. On the interpretation of the Atlantic Charter by the Allies as the war continued, see Wm. Roger Louis, *Imperialism at Bay: The United States and the Decolonization of the British Empire, 1941–1945* (New York: Oxford University Press, 1978).

16. "There has been," Pollock concludes in his comparative study of the rival universalisms of the premodern Latin and Sanskrit language zones, "not just one cosmopolitanism in history but several." Sheldon Pollock, *The Language of the Gods in the World of Men: Sanskrit, Culture, and Power in Premodern India* (Berkeley: University of California Press, 2006), 280.

17. Erez Manela, *The Wilsonian Moment: Self-Determination and the International Origins of Anticolonial Nationalism* (New York: Oxford University Press, 2007).

18. See, for example, Jane Burbank and Frederick Cooper, "Empire, droits, et citoyenneté, de 212 à 1946," *Annales E.S.C.* 63, no. 3 (2008): 495–531; Bonny Ibhawoh, *Imperialism and Human Rights: Colonial Discourses of Rights and Liberties in African History* (Albany: State University of New York Press, 2007).

19. To reflect on black Africans and "rights" today, consider the following contending presentations: Harri Englund, *Prisoners of Freedom: Human Rights and the African Poor* (Berkeley: University of California Press, 2006); Makau wa Mutua, "Human Rights in Africa: The Limited Promise of Liberalism," *African Studies Review* 51, no. 1 (2008): 17–39; and Lucie White and Jeremy Perelman, eds., *Stones of Hope: How African Activists Reclaim Human Rights to Challenge Global Poverty* (Stanford, Calif.: Stanford University Press, 2010).

20. Frederick Cooper, *Colonialism in Question: Theory, Knowledge, History* (Berkeley: University of California Press, 2006), 28–29.

21. Ibid., chap. 4.

22. For several years, political scientists have been addressing these topics under the heading of "norm diffusion." See, for example, Amitav Acharya, "How Ideas Spread: Whose Norms Matter? Norm Localization and Institutional Change in Asian Regionalism," *International Organization* 58, no. 2 (2004): 239–75; and for the theorizing as applied to criminal accountability protocols, see Sikkink, *Justice Cascade*.

23. See William H. Sewell Jr., *Logics of History: Social Theory and Social Transformation* (Chicago: University of Chicago Press, 2005).

24. Andrew Sartori, *Bengal in Global Concept History: Culturalism in the Age of Capital* (Chicago: University of Chicago Press, 2008), 47.

25. Ibid., 19, and the literature on translation cited on p. 241, n. 76.

26. Ibid., 18; compare p. 48 for a similar formulation.

27. Ibid., 63.

28. Liberalism and culturalism, though generally emerging and working in historical succession, were, Sartori says, "both . . . conceptions of subjective autonomy [that] proceed from the historically specific structures of capitalist society [and] must both be understood in terms of an antinomy internal to the logic of capitalist social forms." Ibid., 51. Thus, Sartori's story is one about competition rather than the mere sequence of conceptual schemes.

29. It is perhaps interesting here that although the breakthrough of human rights around the world coincides with his periodization of "neoliberalism," David Harvey refuses to reduce the former to the latter. See David Harvey, *A Brief History of Neoliberalism* (New York: Oxford University Press, 2005), esp. 177–80.

30. See, for example, Sartori, *Bengal in Global Concept History*, 20:

> While I do insist on a radical epochal break from the forms of nonmodern social relations that characterized premodern South Asia, I do so to emphasize the historical specificity of global social structures into which these older institutions have come, in an inevitably transformed manner, to be embedded, and not to negate the concrete continuities of particular social practices.

9

"Casting the Badge of Inferiority Beneath Black Peoples' Feet"

Archiving and Reading the African Past, Present, and Future in World History

MAMADOU DIOUF AND JINNY PRAIS

A t the turn of the twentieth century, African and black writers were active participants in the international debates and controversies concerning modernity, its attributes, and its expressions.[1] Intellectuals such as W. E. B. DuBois, William Henry Ferris, and J. E. Casely Hayford were among the first generation of thinkers to seek a more inclusive understanding of universal narratives of the human past and experience. Deploying new universalizing narratives derived from Enlightenment and imperial discourses, they sought to establish connections among a diverse and widely dispersed black community and, at the same time, delineate a space for Africa in world history as a way to validate specific political claims and to proclaim a past and future role for all black peoples in human history. In their quest to relocate Africa in world history and reaffirm Africa's presence on the world stage, many black thinkers attributed to Africa the role of guide and savior and produced a form of intellectual history that effectively recomposed universal history.

At present, however, the quest to locate Africa in universal narratives has been less pronounced among scholars of African and African American studies. Until now, scholars writing in the post–World War II period have not been involved in the debate on global intellectual history in the same way as Asian/Indian historians like Ranajit Guha and Dipesh Chakrabarty and global intellectual scholars like Jack Goody have. The professionalization of African studies has ended the quest for a global presence and understanding of the African trajectory in world history. This tendency has been reinforced by the emergence of two narratives of nationalism—African nationalism and civil rights in the United States—that have led to the creation of African American and African studies and their simultaneous dissociation. This trend remains dominant particularly in history, which stresses archival research, the acquisition of African languages, field research, and rural communities in the search for an African authentic "library" despite the inclusion of Africa in broader fields such as Atlantic, Africana, and African diaspora studies, and world history.

Today, the most fruitful areas for discussions of a global intellectual history that include Africans and people of African descent are Atlantic and black Atlantic studies. African intellectuals in the Atlantic world laid claim to sources of political authority and cultural advancement by soliciting Atlantic religious, cultural, and institutional resources and by taking their inspiration from law and human sciences. Their documents and ideas, largely influenced by the Bible, religious scriptures, and evangelical discourses, provided a historical framework and promoted new historical narratives to serve communities that were no longer local and exclusively African. Yet despite ample evidence of an African presence in the Atlantic, the dominant conceptualizations of the Atlantic world, including studies of the black Atlantic,[2] have largely ignored and/or dismissed the role of Africa and Africans.[3]

Historian John Thornton offers the most controversial and challenging approach to Africa in the Atlantic world by reintroducing Africa as a key entity and Africans as critical actors. The area of Thornton's history is the West African coast and the islands off the coast—Cape Verde, São Tomé, and Príncipe—the Congo kingdom, and Angola. According to him, the communities that took part in the Atlantic world such as those of Africans or Eurafricans,[4] Luso-Africans,[5] Afro-Victorians,[6] and Originaires/Inhabitants[7] are African Atlantic peoples, imagined and represented as "people of the sea" by the "people of the land." Hence, the African Atlantic is conceived as part of the Atlantic community with its Atlantic traders, thinkers, and kingdoms.

This topography of the black Atlantic can be expanded to encompass the historical relationship between African and African American intellectuals and activists in the early twentieth century. Many of these intellectuals were connected to one another through political and intellectual alliances formed in the European and North American metropoles. Here they encountered numerous opportunities for intellectual exchange at the various congresses such as the Pan-African conferences (1900, 1919, 1945) and the First Universal Race Congress (1911) in western Europe. The presence of participants like DuBois and Casely Hayford at these congresses, in addition to the travels of individuals such as J. E. K. Aggrey and Edward Wilmot Blyden between West Africa and New York, nurtured and strengthened the international connection and dialogue among black intellectuals and launched black global intellectual history.[8]

Black intellectuals traveled in the same black circuit that encompassed the Atlantic world. African Americans such as DuBois and Ferris were familiar with the work of African intellectuals living in Africa and in Europe, including Gold Coast (present-day Ghana) lawyer, writer, and political activist Casely Hayford. For example, Casely Hayford and DuBois, along with other black intellectuals, including Edward W. Blyden, Alexander Crummell, and Martin Delany, were present at the first Pan-African Congress in London in 1900. Their direct communication and collaboration did not stop there, however. In 1903, Casely Hayford sent DuBois a congratulatory letter for the publication of *The Souls of Black Folk*. In 1909, DuBois asked Casely Hayford, among such other well-known people as Blyden, Franz Boas, and Giuseppe Sergi, to serve on the editorial board of the *Encyclopedia Africana*.[9] Notably, William Henry Ferris included Casely Hayford as one of the "Distinguished Foreign Negroes" in his book *The African Abroad*.[10]

Accordingly, by examining the writings of three global intellectual historians, W. E. B. DuBois, William Henry Ferris, and J. E. Casely Hayford, this chapter seeks to expand Thorton's topography of the black Atlantic in ways that allow us to recover this late-nineteenth- and early-twentieth-century conversation among black intellectuals. It asks: How do we retrieve this library as part of framing the field of global intellectual history? Of primary interest are these writers' adaptations of and engagements with universal narratives of history and the political motivations and strategies that fueled them. These acts gave them a better understanding of the patterns of universal history and enabled them to posit plural modes for imagining the black presence in the narrative of past and also future human history. Their insistence on including Africa in world history was essential to their own political and social survival, as it enabled them to reclaim their identity as human in the aftermath of the Atlantic slave trade and imperialism in Africa. Black thinkers constituted an economy of knowledge that was constantly reshaped and contested internally. They used this knowledge to engage with Western intellectual constructions of human evolution, culture, and citizenship from which they were excluded. The inclusion of the black economy of knowledge in a discussion of global intellectual history will undoubtedly force scholars to rethink this field and, heeding the lessons of black scholars in the early twentieth century, to recognize the Western framing of universal history as only one trajectory of many.

Africa at the Turn of the Twentieth Century

For African and diasporic people throughout the Atlantic, Africa was vital to their antiracism and their anticolonial crusades.[11] In the nineteenth century, Africa was a physical space that gave African Americans an opportunity to demarcate an alternative geography in which to build their lives, and it thus played a key role in their ideological and rhetorical combat against slavery in the United States. The dominant African American view of Africa during this period was strongly influenced by an evangelical Christian vision of the continent as a land of heathens needing conversion and as a space in which they themselves could find freedom from racial oppression.[12] Consequently, African Americans' debate on Africa revolved around the question of African American emigration back to, or the colonization of, Africa, with Fredrick Douglass loudly declaring his opposition to emigration in favor of integration into American society, and Delany, Henry H. Garnet,[13] and Crummell strongly advocating the relocation of African Americans to West Africa or Central America and the Caribbean.[14]

In this early discussion of Africa, the continent was not a resource for validating African American claims to political inclusion in the United States. Rather, Africa was a physical territory in which African Americans could exercise religious, economic, and political agency. Africa had not yet become the foundation for black claims to inclusion in a universal narrative of human history.[15] It was not until the late nineteenth century, with the rise of ethnology, that information about ancient African societies and cultures began to circulate through the dissemination of anthropological research in the public domain. This information sparked intense discussion and debate in popular magazines among white American and European academics. African Americans used this information to their own advantage to carve out a historical space and unveil their trajectory in world history. By explaining the world of cultures and races, black scholars reframed the intellectual history of the world as well as the instruments and sources of its production. Through this process, they established a library and a knowledge economy that registered the essential traits of cultural evolution and proposed a solution to the question of the human horizon for black people.

This process began with the work of African American writers Jesse Max Barber, Delany, Ferris, and DuBois. The writing of Ferris and DuBois, in particular, benefited substantially from the shift in thinking about Africa in the Western world that began at the end of the nineteenth century with the work of Leo Frobenius and Franz Boas. Their ideas, while still marginal until the early twentieth century, intersected with and informed the work of DuBois and Ferris and eventually gained traction and legitimacy in the popular press and academy during the years leading up to and immediately following World War I. The view that race and culture were mutually constitutive, despite Boas's efforts to disentangle these two concepts, remained the dominant understanding of race during the prewar years. In science, popular literature, and art, the depiction of Africans as "savage" and "primitive" continued unabated, although the critique of Western civilization that developed after the war helped increase the credibility and distribution of more positive theories and images associated with

Africa.[16] The war weakened the dominant proimperialist vision of the West as the only representation of civilization and thus created space for other expressions of civilization to be recognized and valued. At the same time, Africa, once labeled the "dark continent," became a resource for artists, intellectuals, students, and statesmen in the West as they sought to repair what was perceived to be an ailing civilization overtaken by imperial greed, industrialization, and war.[17]

Scholars such as Frobenius, Boas, Bronislaw Malinowski, and Maurice Delafosse, who worked in the new sciences of the late nineteenth and early twentieth centuries, imagined African societies and cultures as endowed with reason and sophisticated aesthetic sensibilities.[18] Their research provided evidence of African civilization—political and social organizations, states and legal institutions, and systems of justice—and insisted that African civilizations had existed long before African contact with Europeans. The combination of academic and artistic productions in which Africa was rethought (not always in a positive light) helped create a more positive attitude toward Africa in Europe and North America. For black intellectuals, it offered an archive of evidence about African societies, cultures, and histories from which they could assemble a usable past and put forward a new vision of Africa to the world.

Black thinkers used this evidence and the new perspectives on Africa to critique and revise many of the Enlightenment principles and narratives, particularly the works of G. W. F. Hegel, that were used to support the European "civilizing mission" in Africa.[19] Hegel's philosophical interventions had profound implications for black peoples' inclusion in modernity and history, as well as for their access to freedom and citizenship. In the works of Hegel and that of other Enlightenment thinkers, Africa and Africans came to occupy the unenviable position of the radical "other," which in evolutionary terms represented the early stages of the history of humankind. This articulation of the unilineal version of the evolution of "Man," which was further developed and integrated into Hegel's theory of universal history, or "World History,"[20] obscured Europe's geographical and cultural specificity by merging it with the concept of civilization itself and identifying the European as Man. As the epitome of civilization and the alleged harbinger of a predictable future solidly grounded on science and technology, Europe took a leading role in making sense of the history of the world, a project largely motivated by imperial expansion. This entailed the simultaneous integration and exclusion of non-Western cultures and communities from the flow of history. As the West incorporated the non-Western world, it rendered it incapable of contributing to the movement of history's grand teleological narrative. Despite evidence to the contrary, most Europeans conceived of Africans as having left no signs, architecture, or monuments in the landscape and no script and written records. Accordingly, they constructed Africa's past as an absence, a continent and people without history or progress. Within the purview of Hegel's "providentialistic philosophical plan"[21]—the necessary course of history—and after considering that African societies possessed neither the modern state political culture and institutions nor the indispensable knowledge and technologies to transform nature, he wrote, "What we properly understand by Africa, is the Unhistorical, Underdeveloped Spirit, still involved in the conditions of mere nature, and which had to be presented here only as on the threshold of the world's History."[22] In this narrative, which played a critical role in Europe's "civilizing mission" in Africa, Africa is established as devoid of historical agency, neither a subject nor an object of history before its encounter with Europe.

Black intellectuals[23] deployed a strategic historical vision that undermined the unitary, normative authority of the Hegelian theory, which based history on political accomplishments. They adopted the "prominent strands of the Counter-Enlightenment . . . and the ensuing romantic movement"[24] that alleged "different periods demonstrate different tastes and preferences in ethics and aesthetics" and that no single group was in "a position to rank them or objectively choose between them."[25] Black thinkers advocated a cyclical approach that posited a continuous cycle of the rise and fall of human civilizations. Suggesting that "time moved in cycles," many black writers argued that all civilizations, including the once powerful African civilizations, were subject to periods of advancement and decline and that Africa would rise again.[26] They drew on the research of Count Volney, Abbé Grégoire, and Thomas Bowdich, which suggested that ancient Egypt was a black civilization originating from the lower Nile valley region and Ethiopia—the Egypt of the black men.[27] They also constructed their own archive, which documented the antiquity and pioneering role of Africa and Africans in the political, cultural, economic, and religious patterns of a cyclical understanding of universal history.[28] For some scholars, highlighting the civilizing mission of black Egyptians in early antiquity served as a powerful device to bring about a new geography and history of the continent and of human civilization. This evidence helped them recompose a global historical narrative and posit a black presence in human history, both in the past, at the beginnings of civilization (ancient Egypt and Ethiopia), and in the future.[29]

This task, as these black intellectuals defined it, was not to construct a history entirely outside the Western world, but to establish their histories and cultural manifestations within the Western universal framework. In their search for a universal history redesigned by the black contributions, these thinkers considered the history of African, African American, and Afro-Caribbean communities always to be parcels of larger Atlantic and world histories. They worked within the intellectual and political culture of the West. Their production of black history and identity was primarily located in an Atlantic and diasporic context inasmuch as one could argue that "black is a country"[30] in the Western world. By inscribing their historical and philosophical interventions on race rather than space, ethnicity, or nation, they circumscribed a physical space that dramatically revised Hegel's geography of the black continent and compiled worldly intellectual and cultural resources to support their claims.

The Restoration of Africa in World History

Ferris, DuBois, and Casely Hayford each were deeply engaged in restoring Africa to world history. Collectively, they made common cause to "bolster both Negro American and emergent African nationalist esteem" and to constitute a group that historian George Shepperson describes as the "Negro history movement."[31] They developed their ideas in relation to one another as members of a black global intellectual community. Common to each was the quest for political rights—for black Americans, political rights in the United States, and, for Africans, political rights in the European empires—and the contestation of the exclusionary theories and practices of citizenship based on racial identity in the United States and in colonial Africa. Each appealed to African history, particularly the African contribution to world history and the progress of humanity as the primary mode for securing these rights. Through their countering of the universal narrative of history and insistence on the location of Africa within it, they provided evidence of their humanity and their contribution to its history and its future development. This, in turn, invigorated their claim to be recognized as men deserving of political and social rights.

William Henry Ferris did not present a coherent academic history of Africa or the "African abroad." Instead, his two-volume monograph, *The African Abroad, or, His Evolution in Western Civilization, Tracing His Development Under Caucasian Milieu*, published in 1913, is an attempt to chronicle the history and accomplishments of black people in the Americas by archiving the global conversation about Africa and race. Ferris, a graduate of Yale (1891) and Harvard (1900), was a marginal member of the "Talented Tenth." He moved even further away from the black middle class in 1919 when he became the associate editor of Marcus Garvey's *Negro World*.[32] His intellectual and political work has largely been overlooked by scholars of African American history, however, with the exception of Kevin Gaines's *Uplifting the Race*, which contains a chapter on Ferris. Wilson Moses also refers to Ferris in several of his books.[33] Both Gaines and Moses describe Ferris's book as a ramble and series of "philosophical meanderings," and *The African Abroad* was not well received at the time of its publication.[34] Its main problem, according to many reviewers, was its alleged excessive praise of Anglo-Saxons.[35] Other problems, such as the confusing nature of the book, did not enhance its reception. Several chapters also include lengthy excerpts from book chapters, pamphlets, speeches, and newspaper articles, accompanied by long monographs.

The African Abroad might best be described as an archive of materials that document an international discussion of Africa and Africans' role in the history of humanity. Using the limited resources on Africa available in English, Ferris proposed several chapters on the history of the continent using the latest anthropological research.[36] Critical to this project was the contemporary debate on Africa and its history in the North American press. Especially important were two articles that appeared in the May 1906 issue of *Century Magazine*. Both articles— also reprinted in the June 1906 issue of the *Colored American Magazine*—framed the larger debate about Africa that was taking shape in the United States and Europe in the early part of the century. The first article, by Charles Francis Adams, used ethnographic data from his experience living in Omdurman, Sudan, to argue that Africans were inherently and inevitably savage peoples, an argument he supported with evidence of what he perceived to be the primitive and savage nature of the Sudanese living in Omdurman. He concluded that the project of reconstruction in the United States was doomed, that the Negro in America could be neither assimilated nor expelled. The editor of the *Century Magazine* disagreed with Adams's conclusion and argued that his view of the Sudanese was flawed. In referring to Boas's recent article, "What the Negro Has Done in Africa," published in *The Ethical Record* in March 1904, the editor maintained that Africans were highly advanced peoples, basing much of his discussion on Boas's research on the social and political organizations of "African tribes and extended kingdoms," the primary illustration being the Lunda Empire in central Africa.

Further defending the view that Africans were civilized, Ferris reprinted Pixley Ka Isaka Seme's speech, "Regeneration of Africa," which won him the Curtis medal oration first prize at Columbia University in 1906. He argued that Seme's accomplishment as a Zulu man from South Africa proved that Africans were not inhibited by their race but could achieve success at the highest level in Western society. Next Ferris reprinted an article, "The Zulus as Fighters," that appeared in the *Cable Dispatch* on May 31, 1906. In his own commentary, Ferris noted recent praise offered to King Menelek of Abyssinia in the *Independent* and the tremendous progress of the black republic of Liberia. He included an article from the *New York Independent* (October 6, 1906) on African Americans and Africans in Liberia, who were described as contented and industrious people, "in spite of all that has been said of the inherent laziness of the Negro."[37] In another chapter, "Africa at the Dawn of History—The Negro in Pre-Historic Times," after discussing Africans' full capability of participating in scientific and technological progress, Ferris continued to build his case in favor of Africans' contribution to human history. He based his argument on the work of Boas, W. C. Taylor, C. S. Henry, Sergi, W. Z. Ripley, Grégoire, and Volney.[38] Ferris opened the chapter with a discussion of Sergi's and Ripley's findings that the "civilizing" race had originated in Africa and Asia and that Africans and Asians were the "founders of the world's civilization, that they gave the world the foundations of art, science, astronomy, mathematics, and religion."[39]

As he did in other chapters, Ferris included lengthy selections from these scholars' work as well as reviews and analyses of their findings in popular magazines and newspapers. The first of these is a review by A. J. Jones on Ripley's *The Races of Europe: A Sociological Study* (1899), in which he argued that the true origin of the European races was in Africa and Asia. Jones adapted this evidence to illustrate the fundamentally flawed nature of the imperial project and the mission to civilize. To further support his argument in favor of Africa's contribution to human history, Ferris reprinted sections from Volney's research on ancient Thebes and Taylor's work on ancient Ethiopia. Volney's work suggested that the Africans of ancient Thebes made a lasting and significant contribution to humanity in the realms of religion, philosophy, and astronomy, while Taylor's work attested to the advanced civilization of ancient Ethiopia. Ferris also included selections from the writings of the French Roman Catholic priest and advocate of racial equality, Abbé Grégoire, on the African's affinity for art and trade and love of freedom. Additional support in the form of a pamphlet by Boas, *The Anthropological Position of the Negro*, also was reproduced. In this pamphlet, Boas's main purpose was to contest the research findings of R. B. Bean (published in *Century Magazine*), suggesting that black people's brains were, on average, smaller than those of white people. Bean used these findings to conclude that black people were racially inferior to white people. Boas argued with the logic of Bean's conclusion and provided his own findings on the complexity of African social, economic, and political organizations, stating, "There is no scientific proof, that will stand honest criticism, which would prove the inferiority of the Negro race."[40] Ferris used this evidence to conclude,

Thus we see that many ancient and modern authorities testify that the blacks in Africa have made some contributions to civilization. Then, again, in the month of June 1908, the papers were telling how seven tons of architectural and sculptural matters from Africa were shipped to the curator of the University of Pennsylvania, thus proving that the blacks in Egypt, centuries ago, did have a civilization. So the race of black men has done something in the past.[41]

Other chapters include detailed discussions of the research findings on Egypt, Ethiopia, and African empires. In the chapter "Africa, the Dark Continent," Ferris sets out to dispel the dominant understanding of Africa as primitive and savage. His main source of ammunition was Boas's scholarship providing evidence of African accomplishments in agriculture, the art of smelting iron—"when the ancestors of the Aryans were using stone implements, and were introducing bronze weapons"—and legal procedure and state formation.[42]

Throughout, Ferris sought to prove that Africans were part of human history and that Africans, like all human beings, sought two things in their lives: bread and freedom. Upholding the Hegelian idea of freedom as the highest human striving, he pointed to the Haitian revolution as evidence of black people's natural quest for freedom. Black people in the Americas had a prophetic role to play in the development of humanity. The "African abroad," whom he identified as a "Negro-Saxon," had, through a process of assimilation, effectively absorbed the lessons of Anglo-Saxon civilization. Ferris described them as the group from which world historical figures—conceptualized in ways similar to Hegel's understanding of a "World-historical individual"—capable of transforming human history would emerge. The historical experience of the Negro-Saxon had brought people of African descent to the Americas and into contact with what he described as the highest and most advanced civilization of the Anglo-Saxon people. Because of their location in the West, he contended, Negro-Saxons were well positioned and equipped to advance human civilization to a higher level of sophistication.

Dominating Ferris's engagement with a global narrative of history was the Hegelian evolutionary worldview, which he revised so that it included African peoples and cultures. Ferris believed that

Africans in the West, Negro-Saxons, would play a critical role in history. In making this argument, he wrote that the Anglo-Saxon race represented the most advanced of civilizations. He did not, however, attribute Anglo-Saxon achievements to a natural or inherent superiority to other cultures, as many of Ferris's critics have assumed, but to the Anglo-Saxon historical experience. The Anglo-Saxon people, he argued, had benefited from other, including African, civilizations. Times were changing, and the moment was ripe for a new race of people to exploit the cultural advancements of the Anglo-Saxon race and thus propel humanity to a higher level. This action, he believed, could be undertaken only by Western-influenced and -educated Africans and people of African descent living in the Americas and Europe, that is, Negro-Saxons, who, he proclaimed, were destined to move beyond the Anglo-Saxon race to produce a more advanced civilization. His valorization of the Anglo-Saxon race had little to do with a love of the white man, as his critics have complained, but, rather, with a love of humanity. Ferris had carved out a space for Africans and people of African descent to use in the development of human history, here and now. Not only were Africans present at the very beginning of human civilization, the "Africans abroad," in the Americas and in Europe, but they also were to play a prophetic role in stimulating the growth and development of humanity once more. In this way, Ferris framed his narrative within the Hegelian understanding of the linear progress of history, though he moved beyond history as limited to political affairs to emphasize history as the product of encounters, interactions, and transactions among human communities.

Similarly, J. E. Casely Hayford, a Gold Coast lawyer and the founder of the National Congress of British of West Africa (1919), believed that Western-educated Africans had a prophetic role to play in the future of humanity, although Casely Hayford's engagement with a global narrative of history was influenced more by Counter-Enlightenment thought, particularly the cyclical view of history. As he professed in *Ethiopia Unbound*, Africa, the source of humankind and the site of the world's greatest civilizations, would lead humanity once again. Casely Hayford sought to counter the Hegelian exclusion of Africa from world history in two steps. First, he emphasized the importance of African civilizations; second, he adopted the Gibbonesque theory of the rise and fall of civilizations. The first approach is captured in his speeches and writings on Gold Coast native institutions and history.[43] The second is taken up in Casely Hayford's 1911 novel, *Ethiopia Unbound*, in which he argued that an Africa once home to great civilizations would inevitably "rise again." He explained that all modern societies, including the British, borrowed from other societies in their development and that these acts of borrowing enabled societies to advance. Africa would regain its former stature by borrowing and building on lessons learned from Western and non-Western societies.[44] Furthermore, he suggested, African societies possessed unique spiritual knowledge that, when combined with Western civilization, could greatly advance humanity. Africa, as the oldest and youngest (in terms of industrialization) continent, was ideally situated to lead the world into the future. Africans, Hayford stated, had learned the formula for true progress: respectful study and comparison of all human society's "methods," and the wisdom to blend and carry these lessons into something better. Through the valorization of shared knowledge and blended cultural forms, he authorized an African modernity that could not be reduced to a Western form.

The ideas expressed in *Ethiopia Unbound* were not new. Black intellectuals from around the world were discussing the global race problem and generating a range of explanations and solutions.[45] Among the first was Edward Blyden, a native of St. Thomas who emigrated to Liberia with the assistance of the American Colonization Society. Blyden was a pioneering figure in the Negro history movement. His *African Life and Customs* (1908) brought a sociological perspective and holistic approach to the study of African societies. It argued for a deep appreciation and recognition of the inherent logic and necessity of African customs and traditions, in both the past and the present. His work, therefore, represents a slightly different view from that of African Americans associated with the Negro history movement. He was less concerned with documenting Africans' contribution to human civilization. Rather, he sought to define the "African personality" and establish Africa's right to be judged like any other race for creating the social, economic, religious, legal, political, and familial patterns that best suited their environment.[46] His argument was an expression of cultural relativism associated with Boas and popularized by the students Boas trained at Columbia University in the 1920s and 1930s. Blyden had a tremendous impact on Casely Hayford's ideas, which is reflected in *Ethiopia Unbound* and also in his earlier study of African institutions.[47] While his intellectual influence on DuBois and Ferris is less evident, Blyden was in regular communication with African Americans, and he was considered a leading authority in the study of Africa and prominent African nationalist.

This was a time when a number of black intellectuals were looking to one another to discover how to assert a distinctive cultural identity that would win them recognition as participants in the advancement of human civilization and world progress. Different groups fitted themselves into the Western-dominated international community in various ways, although most during this period entered the conversation by forming their own clubs, founding magazines, and attending international and imperial conferences as men of learning dressed in three-piece suits. In these ways, they professed their right to lead their own "civilizing" missions of their countries or race of origin and sometimes in competition with one another. It was the development of a transatlantic network of ideas that propelled many black thinkers to engage with the universal narrative of history.

In 1911, the same year *Ethiopia Unbound* was published, DuBois attended the First Race Congress, which met at the University of London and where he discussed the possibility of "a future world which would be peaceful, without race prejudice," and a new internationalism that might someday include all of humankind.[48] DuBois's political and intellectual work on the continent began with the publication of his monograph *The Negro* in 1915, which he described as a short general statement on the history of the Negro peoples. *The Negro*, inspired by a lecture by Boas that he attended at Atlanta University in 1903, drew on the latest research in the social sciences to provide a brief history of the continent.[49] Along with Ferris and Carter Woodson, DuBois seized the image of Africa developed in the work of Boas and Frobenius to demonstrate a black contribution to civilization and to legitimate their own claim for citizenship in the context of the United States. The research they produced was a "more complex ethnographic engagement with black culture" and introduced a wealth of information about Africa and African societies.[50]

These works gave African and African American thinkers the building blocks from which they could write political and intellectual history and make their claims to citizenship. DuBois produced two revisions of *The Negro*—*Black Folk, Then and Now; An Essay in the History and Sociology of the Negro Race* in 1939, and *The World and Africa: An Inquiry into the Part Which Africa Has Played in World History* in 1946.[51] Africa's exclusion from history, DuBois argued in 1946, was not for lack of evidence but was an intentional omission performed largely in the service of European imperial expansion and accumulation of wealth. It was an imperial project designed to justify the enslavement, colonization, and exploitation of the continent and its peoples. The ethnographic data on Africa, particularly the work produced during the interwar years, enabled him to revise *The Negro* and to present in *The World and Africa* less a comprehensive history of "the Negroid peoples" and more "a statement of their role in human history from pre-historic to modern times."[52] Because it actively sought to return Africa to world history and human destiny, *The World and Africa* was a political intervention that used the new studies of the interwar period to contest a philosophy of history born from a desire to authorize European imperialism and its "mission to civilize."[53]

For Ferris and DuBois, the motive for their engagement with world history was political. Through the reproduction of archival material in his book, Ferris documented a moment in global intellectual history in which men like Boas and Frobenius talked about the origins of humanity and the meaning of race and the relations among race, culture, and civilization. Ferris's concept of the Negro-Saxon—based on his understanding of the Anglo-Saxon accomplishments as the highest ideal the world had ever seen, an ideal from which Africans Abroad had benefited[54]—was critical to his political agenda, despite the poor reception the concept received in the black press. Ferris's primary aim was, first, to demonstrate that Africans had contributed to the beginning of human civilization and, second, to suggest that the African Abroad would continue to contribute to the progress and future of humanity. His concept of the Negro-Saxon enabled him to include Western-influenced black thinkers writing outside the United States (e.g., Casely Hayford) in his narrative about the past and future of humanity. Different from many black American intellectuals at this time, most notably DuBois, Ferris moved his discussion of the Negro-Saxon beyond the provincial narrative of the black American rescue of Africa and Africans from the dustbin of history. For DuBois, the turn to African history was largely motivated by his concern with the possibilities of citizenship in the United States.[55] Less interested in documenting the work and ideas of African intellectuals (as was Ferris's emphasis in his archive of intellectual history), DuBois actively sought a path for black American involvement in the future of Africa. In 1919, he traveled to Versailles, where he argued as a representative of the NAACP for the internationalization of the former German colonies. Like many African Americans at this time, DuBois hoped to see black Americans playing a key role in the development of Africa.[56]

Conclusion

In this chapter, we looked at global intellectual history, in particular how black intellectuals have and will figure in this area of study based on an analysis of Africa's first black historians. In our investigation of this early history, we examined the ways that early black thinkers from Africa and North America grappled with their political exclusions from empires and nations by turning to world history and locating Africa in it as a means to counter and repair the universal narrative of history that had excluded them. If the field is to incorporate black intellectual global history, it must include Africa and its diaspora and recognize the epistemological tradition that has already structured the parameters of this discussion.

The lessons we can draw from black intellectuals' interventions and operations address key issues of global intellectual history. First, the territory in which these intellectuals worked and formulated their ideas was global precisely because of their physical dispersal throughout the Atlantic. The global nature of their situations allowed them to reexamine the designs, methods, languages, and theories of global intellectual history through their own international networks, which had one function: reconstituting the dismembered world of the black people (Africa and its diasporas) through a continuous conversation about African history and culture. Second, through the methods they deployed—in this case, their adaptations of universalizing narratives to include Africa and people of African descent—black intellectuals built an archive and proposed multiple ways of reading and explicating the location and contribution of African people in the past, present, and future in the history of humanity. These two moves were crucial to raising new questions and establishing new parameters regarding the resources, methods, and objects of global history to address the intellectual and ethical issues of their exclusion from universal narratives of history and modernity. They used intellectual European categories and epistemological and ethical values to reclaim their agency as a single community of Africans and people of African descent. This enabled them to rectify the misinterpretation of their history and to uncover more decisively the European misinterpretation of its history. Their example will allow historians of global intellectual history to examine the ways that a group of historical actors, while operating in the physical and discursive intellectual territories of the global, revised and contested evolutionary theories of history and found a place for themselves in the history of humanity.

Notes

1. The title of this chapter is from William Henry Ferris, *The African Abroad or His Evolution in Western Civilization: Tracing his Development Under Caucasian Milieu* (New Haven, Conn.: Tuttle, Moorehouse and Taylor, 1913), 446. From this point forward, we use the term "black" to represent Africans and people of African descent living outside the continent.
2. The best example is Paul Gilroy's work on the black Atlantic, which posits a single Atlantic world and community and excludes Africa from the black Atlantic as a geographical and cultural space. See Paul Gilroy, *The Black Atlantic: Modernity and Double Consciousness* (Cambridge, Mass.: Harvard University Press, 1993); and Paul Gilroy, *Against Race: Imagining Political Culture Beyond the Color Line* (Cambridge: Harvard University Press, 2000).
3. For some examples of this trend in Atlantic studies, see Roxanne Wheeler, *The Complexion of Race: Categories of Difference in Eighteenth-Century British Culture* (Philadelphia: University of Pennsylvania Press, 2000); Marcus Rediker, *Between the Devil and the Deep Blue Sea: Merchant Seamen, Pirates, and the Anglo-American Maritime World, 1700-1750* (Cambridge: Cambridge University Press, 1987); Felicity Nussbaum, *Torrid Zones: Maternity, Sexuality, and Empire in Eighteenth-Century English Narratives* (Baltimore:

Johns Hopkins University Press, 1995); P. J. Marshall and G. Williams, *The Great Map of Mankind: Perceptions of New Worlds in the Age of Enlightenment* (Cambridge: Cambridge University Press, 1982); Nicholas Canny and Anthony Pagden, eds., *Colonial Identity in the Atlantic World, 1500–1800* (Princeton, N.J.: Princeton University Press, 1987); Pierre Chaunu, *Conquête et exploitation des nouveaux mondes* (Paris: Presses universitaires, 1969); and Pierre Chaunu, *Séville et l'Amérique aux XVIᵉ et XVIIIᵉ siècles* (Paris: Flammarion, 1977).

4. George Brooks, *Eurafricans in Western Africa: Commerce, Social Status, Gender, and Religious Observance from the Sixteenth to the Eighteenth Century* (Athens: Ohio University Press, 2003).

5. Peter Mark, *"Portuguese Style" and Luso-African Identity: Precolonial Senegambia, Sixteenth-Nineteenth Centuries* (Bloomington: Indiana University Press, 2002).

6. Simon Gikandi, "Introduction to Africa, Diaspora and the Discourse of Modernity," Black Atlantic Issue, *Research in African Literatures*, 27, no. 4 (1996); John Lonsdale, "Jomo Kenyatta, God and the Modern World," in *African Modernities*, ed. Jan-Georg Deutsch, Peter Probst, and Heike Schmidt (Portsmouth, N.H.: Heinemann, 2002), 135–57.

7. Mamadou Diouf, "The French Colonial Policy Assimilation and the Civility of the Originaires of the Four Communes (Senegal): A Nineteenth Century Globalization Project," in *Globalization and Identity: Dialectics of Flow and Closure*, ed. Brigit Meyer and Peter Geshiere (Oxford: Blackwell, 1999), 71–96.

8. Aggrey traveled to the United States as part of the Phelps-Stokes education tour in the 1920s.

9. David Levering Lewis, *W. E. B. DuBois, 1868–1919: Biography of a Race* (New York: Holt, 1993), 248, 292, 279–80.

10. Ferris, *African Abroad*, 135.

11. Clare Corbould, *Becoming African Americans: Black Pubic Life in Harlem, 1919–1939* (Cambridge, Mass.: Harvard University Press, 2009), 10.

12. Dennis Hickey and Kenneth C. Wylie, *An Enchanting Darkness: The American Vision of Africa in the Twentieth Century* (East Lansing: Michigan State University Press, 1993), 240.

13. Garnet was the founder of the African Civilization Society (1858) and the author of *The Past and Present Condition, and the Destiny, of the Colored Race: A Discourse Delivered at the Fifteenth Anniversary of the Female Benevolent Society of Troy, N.Y., Feb. 14, 1848* (Troy, 1848) in which he noted "that by almost common consent the modern world seems determined to pilfer Africa of her glory," referring to the two patriarchs of history, "Moses for sacred history" and "Herodotus for profane," who "lead one back to Egypt in Africa and Africa in Egypt." See John Ernest, *Liberation Historiography: African American Writers and the Challenge of History, 1794–1861* (Chapel Hill: University of North Carolina Press, 2003), 70.

14. Hollis Lynch, "Pan-Negro Nationalism in the New World, Before 1862," in *The Search for a Homeland in Black Brotherhood, Afro-Americans and Africa*, ed. Okon Edet Uya (Lexington, Mass.: Heath, 1971), 59–60.

15. Ibid., 7.

16. Charles Darwin, *On the Origin of the Species by Means of Natural Selection, or the Preservation of Favoured Races in the Struggle for Life* (1859); Charles Darwin, *The Descent of Man and Selection in Relation to Sex* (1871); Count Joseph Arthur de Gobineau, *Essai sur l'inégalite des races* (1853).

17. James Clifford describes this artistic, musical, literary, intellectual, and scientific interest in Africa as collectively representing "negrophilia" in the West, which he defines as a "multivalent aesthetic and cultural phenomenon" in which Africa was reimagined through visual and plastic arts, as well as in popular material and mass culture. He associates negrophilia with the fields of anthropology and ethnology. James Clifford, "Negrophilia," in *A New History of French Literature*, ed. Denis Hollier and Howard Bloch (Cambridge, Mass.: Harvard University Press, 1989), 901–8. See also Petrine Archer-Straw, *Negrophilia: Avant-Garde Paris and Black Culture in the 1920s* (London: Thames & Hudson, 2000).

18. Especially the works of Leo Frobenius, Maurice Delafosse, Carl Meinhof, and Arnold van Gennep, and the Mission Dakar-Djibouti and the Frobenius expeditions.

19. Of course, they recognized the various and sometimes opposing interpretations and expressions of Enlightenment thought.

20. G. W. F. Hegel's concept of "World History" and his narrative of a unilinear evolution of human history is the dominant view of universal history of the Enlightenment. One of the best expositions and sharpest critiques of Hegel's perspective can be found in Ranajit Guha, *History at the Limit of World History* (New York: Columbia University Press, 2002). The book is also a critique of "the forms of modern history writing . . . practices are necessarily intertwined with the rationality of the state and always implicated in the practices of domination." See Partha Chatterjee, editor's introduction to *The Small Voice of History*, by Ranajit Guha and ed. Partha Chatterjee (Ranikhet Cantt: Permanent Black, 2009), 16. Another powerful internal critique of history and Eurocentrism we would like to mention is Jack Goody, *The Theft of History* (Cambridge: Cambridge University Press, 2006). Of course, the Hegelian view was contested by Counter-Enlightenment thinkers such as J. G. Hamann and Johann Gottlieb Herder, both of whom insisted on the unique quality of each civilization and time and rejected the concept of absolute and universal value, as well as by later thinkers such as Friedrich Nietzsche and Oswald Spengler, who proposed a cyclical approach to history.

21. Gianni Vattimo, *Dialogue with Nietzsche*, trans. Wiliam McCuaig (New York: Columbia University Press, 2008), 31.

22. G. W. F. Hegel, *Lectures on the Philosophy of History, 1830–1831*, trans. J. Sibree (New York: Dover, 1956), 99.

23. For example, Eric Porter mentions the analytical influence of "Hegelian dialectics" and "Herderian nationalism" on W. E. B. DuBois's four books and numerous articles devoted to African history and the place of Africa in world history. These four books were *The Negro* (1915); *Africa: Its Geography, People and Products* (1930); *Africa—Its Place in Modern History* (1930); and *Black Folk, Now and Then* (1939). The most important of the articles published during this period is "The African Roots of the Great War" (1915). See Eric Porter, *The Problem of the Future of the World: W. E. B. DuBois and the Race Concept in the Midcentury* (Durham, N.C.: Duke University Press, 2010), 104.

24. Maria Baghramian, *Relativism* (New York: Routledge, 2004), 38. On the "Counter-Enlightenment" intellectuals, see Isaiah Berlin, *Three Critics of Enlightenment: Vico, Hamann, Herder*, ed. Henry Hardy (Princeton, N.J.: Princeton University Press, 2000).

25. Baghramian, *Relativism*, 39.

26. Kevin Gaines, *Uplifting the Race: Black Leadership, Politics, and Culture in the Twentieth Century* (Chapel Hill: University of North Carolina Press, 1996).

27. Their research was overshadowed by the work of the French classical scholar, philologist, orientalist, and decipherer of the Egyptian hieroglyphs, Jean-François Champollion.

28. This development began as early as 1794 when "early African historical writers" had to contend with and against the developing tradition of white American historical thought, as well as the pointed erasure of Africa as a site of history in enlightenment thought. This line of intellectual history inquiry took a remarkable turn in 1879 with Delany's *Principia of Ethnology* and continued in the work of Ferris and DuBois. In *The African Abroad*, Ferris revisited and recirculated the work of Volney and Grégoire and augmented their arguments with the research findings from leading ethnologists, historians, and sociologists of the late nineteenth and early twentieth centuries. DuBois engaged this literature in *The Negro*.

29. Corbould, *Becoming African Americans*, 59.

30. Nikhil Pal Singh, *Black Is a Country: Race and the Unfinished Struggle for Democracy* (Cambridge, Mass.: Harvard University Press, 2004).

31. George Shepperson, "Notes on Negro American Influences on the Emergence of African Nationalism," *Journal of African History* 1, no. 2 (1960): 308.

32. His marginal status might have had little to do with his politics, at least initially. Ferris admired DuBois and was a member of the Niagara movement. He devoted an entire chapter to DuBois in *The African Abroad*. Despite his efforts to fit in, he remained an outcast. Lewis, *W.E.B. DuBois*, 466; Gaines, *Uplifting the Race*, 117.

33. Wilson Moses, *Creative Conflict in African American Thought* (Cambridge: Cambridge University Press, 2004); Wilson Moses, *Black Messiahs and Uncle Toms: Social and Literary Manipulations of Religion* (University Park: Pennsylvania State University Press, 1982); and Wilson Moses, *The Golden Age of Black Nationalism, 1850–1925* (New York: Oxford University Press, 1978).

34. Gaines, *Uplifting the Race*; Moses, *Golden Age*, 311.

35. Many book reviews support this view. As one reviewer, F. H., writing for the *Journal of the Royal African Society*, explained, [Ferris] was quick to seize on the application of these modern ethnological data and to draw conclusions favorable to the black man.

36. DuBois, much more so than Ferris, benefited from this research, as he had more resources to pull from, in part because of his training in German, which allowed him to draw from the work of Leo Frobenius written in German. Perhaps because of this, his work was met with less criticism from the academic community. Reviews of *The Negro* include J. A. Bigham, review of *The Negro*, by W. E. B. DuBois, *Journal of Negro History* 1, no. 2 (1916): 217–18.

37. Ferris, *African Abroad*, 461–62.

38. Giuseppe Sergi, *The Mediterranean Race: A Study of the Origin of European Peoples* (London: Walter Scott, 1909).

39. Ferris, *African Abroad*, 444.

40. Ibid., 460.

41. Ibid., 446.

42. Ibid., 429.

43. J. E. Casely Hayford, *Gold Coast Native Institutions* (1903; repr., London: Frank Cass, 1970).

44. For example, Casely Hayford was deeply impressed with Japan and looked to it as a model for how Africa could assimilate knowledge from other cultures without becoming a "bare imitator." He was inspired by Japan's ability to remain distinctively eastern while wearing Western clothing and engaging with Western cultures. Casely Hayford, *Ethiopia Unbound: Studies in Race Emancipation* (London: Cass, 1969), 170–72.

45. African Americans, including DuBois, Booker T. Washington, and, especially, Blyden had influenced Casely Hayford. Casely Hayford found Blyden more compelling than DuBois. Casely Hayford, *Ethiopia Unbound*, 163.

46. Tracy Keith Flemming, "Negro: Travel and the Pan-African Imagination During the Nineteenth Century" (Ph.D. diss., University of Michigan, 2010), 55–56.

47. Casely Hayford, *Gold Coast Native Institutions*.

48. W. E. B. DuBois, *The World and Africa* (New York: Viking Press, 1947), 4.

49. W. E. B. DuBois, *Black Folk Then and Now* (New York: Oxford University Press, 2007).

50. Clifford, "Negrophilia," 904.

51. *The Negro* (1939), the first sequel to the book *Black Folk, Then and Now*, is considered by Sidney Mintz as "surely the first serious global overview of African (especially African American) history ever published." Sidney Mintz, *Three Ancient Colonies: Caribbean Themes and Variations* (Cambridge, Mass.: Harvard University Press, 2009), 4.

52. W. E. B. DuBois, *The World and Africa: An Inquiry into the Part Which Africa Has Played in World History* (New York: International Publishers, 1965), viii.

53. Such an abstract process is "brought about by the logic of *Aufhebung*, that is, "the act of superseding" whereby "denial and preservation, i.e., affirmation, are bound together." Guha, *History at the Limit*, 2.

54. Ferris, *African Abroad*, 405.

55. See Corbould, *Becoming African Americans*, chaps. 2, 3.

56. James Weldon Johnson, *Along This Way: The Autobiography of James Weldon Johnson* (1933; repr., New York: Penguin Books, 2008).

10

Putting Global Intellectual History in Its Place

JANAKI BAKHLE

I n this chapter I use India's most controversial anti-colonial national-ist—Vinayak Damodar Savarkar (1883–1966)—to consider the con-tours of a new global intellectual history. Savarkar is the classic example of the early-twentieth-century revolutionary Indian nationalist who went to London to study law only to become seen by the metropolitan police as outside the law. Fairly early on, during his days in college, Savarkar came to be associated with the wing of Indian nationalism that colonial officials termed the "extremists." His companions during the five years he spent in London were a motley group of like-minded revo-lutionary Indian students, all of whom idolized Irish nationalists (in par-ticular the Fenians), Russian bomb makers, and Italian thinkers. Within six months of his arrival, he translated Giuseppe Mazzini's biography into Marathi, and by the end of the year he had started a secret, revolu-tionary society called the "Free India," which clearly was modeled after Mazzini's "Young Italy." Mazzini (1805–1872) was one of his heroes, and given the centrality of the devotion to *patria* and the shared sense of duty that permeates Savarkar's early writings in Marathi, it is indisput-able that Mazzini had a formidable influence on Savarkar.

In 1910, on the charge of waging war against the king and making seditious speeches in India four years earlier, Savarkar was arrested and brought back to India for trial. The notoriety surrounding his trial made him a "terrorist" of world fame, capturing the interest of both the international press and figures such as Maxim Gorky. Savarkar was sentenced to two life terms in the notorious Andaman Cellular jail. After he was brought back to India in 1922, he wrote an extended essay in English entitled "Essentials of Hindutva," which soon became the de facto manifesto for right-wing extremist and militant Hindu nationalism. He was placed under house arrest until 1937, after which he became the president of the Hindu political party, the Hindu Mahasabha. By this time, his rhetoric had taken a particularly strident and virulent tone, denouncing the Indian National Congress, the main voice of Indian nationalism, for taking too soft a line on Muslims. As a result, Savarkar stayed first under British, and then Indian, surveillance, and although he was never formally charged, he was believed to have been implicated in the assassination of Gandhi on January 30, 1948.

If Gandhi is considered the father of the nation-family, Savarkar would be its ostracized, reviled, and hated black sheep, referred to on occasion as "the principal philosopher of terrorism."[1] Savarkar's influence on modern India has rivaled Gandhi's, as evidenced in the rise and growth of the Bharatiya Janata Party, the Hindu nationalist party, and the rather prominent role in modern Indian political life of the ideology known as Hindutva, whose name was taken from the title of Savarkar's infamous text and the core concept of which has come to be known as "Hindu fundamentalism," however misleading the term. For the very reasons that Savarkar sits awkwardly in a history of Indian nationalist history—a stark and unpleasant contrast to Gandhi, to say the least—his life provides an opportunity to rethink the regional, national, imperial, and international circuits that require our attention if we are to find new ways to write global intellectual history.

"Is there a global intellectual history?" is the central question for this chapter. The question presumes that key concepts or ideas travel around the world and that tracking and analyzing their itinerary is the dominant mode of writing a global intellectual history.[2] Before addressing this question, I first will situate Savarkar in three strands of interlinked historical scholarship: modern Indian history, early modern South Asian literary history, and Marathi literary and political history. When discussing them, I will use one or more representative works in order to lay out the field before turning to Savarkar and his political and literary career. I will conclude by suggesting that Benedict Anderson's recent work on the poet/anarchist José Rizal offers us one way of thinking about a new global intellectual history that is neither deterministic nor closed off from a range of hermeneutic approaches that are required to capture the full complexity of the global frame.

———— ∞ ————

The modern discipline of history writing in India began as a response to almost two centuries of British colonial occupation (1757–1947) and its epistemic and representational domination. In a sense, modern Indian (intellectual) history began as an anticolonial rebuttal and grew into a nationalist counterattack. From the mid-eighteenth to the mid-twentieth century, the large group made up of religious reformers, social reformers, political thinkers, and philosophers whom we might think of as public intellectuals wrote in new registers as the presence of the East India Company slowly spread its tentacles over much of India, setting the stage for the powerful and pervasive British Raj. Broadly speaking, all the intellectuals were nationalists of one kind or another.[3] Accordingly, official history in India has always been nationalist history, but even most other historiographical traditions, both that created by critics of nationalism like the members of the Subaltern Studies Collective and the work that emerged from the American modernization framework of the global history of ideas like Stanley Wolpert, Stephen Hay, and Ainslee Embree, have also been decisively determined by a nationalist frame and set of preoccupations.[4]

Indian nationalist history typically includes both those scholars who counted as intellectuals and those ideas that could properly be considered part of the history of the Indian national triumph. After the stunning success of Mohandas K. Gandhi, the long hand of the nation appears to have reached back into the entire period of colonial rule and classified some Indian nationalists as worthy of study and others, on the incorrect side of the nation, as worthy of condemnation. Barring a few notable exceptions, the almost obsessive (and variably critical, historical, and analytic) scholarship that has been trained on

Gandhi, Jawaharlal Nehru, or Rabindranath Tagore is conspicuously absent in the case of right-wing nationalists such as Vinayak Damodar Savarkar, who has been studied and analyzed as the historical figure either who gives us the starting point from which we can draw a straight line to the contemporary Hindu right wing or who has been praised by partisan apologists and eulogizers.[5] For the most part, Savarkar is written about in primarily ideological terms, as someone to be either denounced or admired. But his writings in Marathi are rarely read, and the literature on him written in Marathi is seldom analyzed except by Marathi lay writers. Such scholarly neglect has produced a somewhat unbalanced historiographical account of nationalist politics and modern intellectual history. It also has meant that when they are not altogether ignored, significant political figures and genealogies of political and intellectual thought are fundamentally misunderstood.

The national frame itself therefore requires considerable adjustment. But if we move beyond the political frame of Indian nationalist history and locate Savarkar in the larger international political milieu of anarchism, the problems do not go away. Even if we took as axiomatic or a starting point for this chapter that an idea or concept travels around the world, tracking the global itinerary of a putatively international idea—for example, revolutionary nationalism, liberalism, and secularism—would have its own difficulties.

"Anarchism" as an idea, for instance, traveled (or, if a more determinist formulation is preferred, was taken) around the globe from, roughly speaking, the middle of the nineteenth century through the early decades of the twentieth. It was invoked by revolutionary nationalists in Italy, India, Ireland, the Philippines, and Russia, among others. But anarchism's historical development in India as a political movement did not add up to very much, never ascending to the level of a movement. If it acquired any real purchase at all, it did so outside India, by Indian exiles such as Lala Hardayal.[6] Within India itself, all other movements in the early to mid-twentieth century were rendered subservient to the growing influence and dominance of the mainstream nationalist body, the Indian National Congress. Moving farther east, to the Philippines, as Benedict Anderson's recent work demonstrates, the canonical anarchist José Rizal was perplexed when his novels *El Filibusterismo* and *Noli me tangere* were seen as incendiary, even though they are regarded today as anarchist masterpieces. Perhaps the only location in which the integration of the idea and history came together into something we might call a movement was Russia.[7] Despite such major differences, the term "anarchism" was used widely by colonial officials to describe and proscribe all forms of anticolonial nationalism, from Ireland to Egypt to India and the Philippines.[8] Colonial officials provided much of the language for understanding anticolonial nationalists at the same time that many of the ideas that traveled in the modern period did so because they were responses to imperial rule. This language itself had a uniformity, even across different national styles and experiences, that was recognizable from locations as various as Pune, Madras, or Shanghai. Marx, or Macaulay, was locally received through predominantly anti-imperial lenses. Thus the importance of Lenin, for example, to anticolonial thinkers and nationalists, and the centrality of Mazzini or Garibaldi to nationalists like Savarkar.

In writing an intellectual and social history of Hindu political fundamentalism, we can begin with the premise that there was an international circuitry of exchange demonstrated by recognizable similarities between Italian nationalism of the Mazzinian variety and the development of the ideas of extremist nationalists in India.[9] But in order to move forward, we would need to tackle the standard understanding of Indian extremism as one that was merely fed by Mazzini.[10] Newer iterations of the argument attribute some agency to individual readers and translators, and in place of the first, the argument would now read like this: Savarkar read Mazzini and translated his ideas into a Marathi (native, local) idiom, but Mazzini's influence could not be underestimated in the development of revolutionary nationalism.[11] Even in this newer formulation, however, the large premise remains the same: ideas originate in Europe, and their globalization can be equated with their indigenization in a local milieu. In such a historical understanding of Savarkar, local history merely adds color to a universal premise but does not alter it in any way, nor does it explain how the ideas arrived in India. In asking whether there is a global intellectual history, we must therefore confront a hidden assumption about both the origin of all authentically global ideas and the direction in which they travel.

The aim of this chapter is not to suggest a simple reversal of the flow of information and concepts but to pose the question of the expansion of frames in order to move past a straightforward unidirectionality of influence and travel of ideas. That Mazzini read the Bhagavad Gita (in translation) does not mean that its ethics directly influenced his *On the Duties of Man* and *Manifesto for Young Italy*. It does mean, however, that such a question (might this reading have played a critical historical role?) continues to be difficult to pose within the conventional frames of history.[12] Mazzini was undoubtedly central to Savarkar's own development as a thinker, but we should not begin our analysis by simply presuming the nature and character of intellectual influence. More interesting, perhaps, is to compare Mazzini and Savarkar, noting the ways in which they were similar (if far from identical) intellectual figures. Both Mazzini and Savarkar saw themselves as literary figures and succeeded more in the realm of writing than in politics. Neither was a systematic thinker. Both were cosmopolitan nationalists, stipulating that the nation should be based more on a common political project than on ethnicity, religion, culture, or language. But whereas Mazzini saw the potential possibilities of the pan-Slavic, Italian, and Hungarian movements, united in the individual determination of each unit for its own nation, Savarkar opposed the pan-Islamic Indian Khilafat movement because it was predicated on opposition to the territorial integrity of India and began instead with a religious understanding of territory that seemed to him to undermine Indian political unity.

Mazzini's national citizens were an association of people who would be governed by their will, which in turn was tempered by moral law. The moral law in question was not named as such but was clearly religious in character. Savarkar had no moral theory at all. Mazzini himself was a deeply devout and religious man; Savarkar's relationship to orthodox Hinduism was fraught at best. Unlike Immanuel Kant, with whom his notion of the will as being tempered by an individually determined morality is sometimes compared, Mazzini was neither agnostic nor willing to hide his religious devotion.[13] Savarkar thrived on making outrageous claims about Hinduism. Mazzini's interlocutors included some of the most prominent intellectual figures of his time such as Pierre-Joseph Proudhon, Karl Marx, John Stuart Mill, and John Morley (the liberal secretary of state for India). Yet the same

John Morley was among the many liberal colonial officials to wonder whether Savarkar and his London group were simply fanatics.[14] Mazzini and Savarkar were theorists of a middle-class nationalism, but whereas Mazzini's anti-Marxism was overtly apparent, Savarkar was simply not interested in Marxism, nor was, for the record, Gandhi. Mazzini wrote in the language of progressivism, in favor of women's education, and was incensed that he was seen as reactionary or conservative. Savarkar was irate and frustrated all his life that he had been misunderstood as a reactive conservative. An early champion of the abolition of caste, he despised the empty rituals of orthodox Brahmin Hinduism, spoke approvingly of miscegenation and interregional marriage, wrote enthusiastically in favor of science and modernity, and approved of women's education. According to such logic, the real conservative Hindu nationalist should be Gandhi, who spoke in the language of faith and religion, approved of the caste system in principle, and had no time for science and progress. Yet history decreed the opposite.

My point beyond sketching similarities and differences is not just to highlight the histories of both these important individuals but also to show that anarchism, or any other great world idea, took very different forms in different parts of the world. It is also to pose as a problem the question of how we understand what it is that such intellectuals wanted to do and who they thought they were, rather than straitjacketing their messy historical trajectories into unidirectional determinist or insular culturalist frames. Savarkar (and Gandhi, B. R. Ambedkar, Nehru, Jyotirao Phule) drew inspiration from a canon of influences that extended beyond the standard texts of English or European intellectual history. They developed their own theories and teleologies, which were expressly part of universal history that simultaneously incorporated a local agenda with the desire to participate in a larger conversation. They were hardly derivative thinkers, to use Partha Chatterjee's frame, but they had no problems using sources and ideas from outside their own traditions to both legitimate and expand their own ideas. They operated neither under the anxiety of influence nor in a world in which they felt the need to be wholly original, indigenous, or consistent. They were simultaneously global and Indian, with no sense of either contradiction or determination.

To locate Savarkar in the world of global intellectual history would therefore require reading him conjuncturally while also expanding the frame of internationalism. Beyond analyzing texts and authors in local and international circuits, however, we would also need to recognize that Savarkar and his actions circulated in the subterranean intellectual circles of other nationalisms. The interrelations and connections between Egyptian nationalists and Indian extremists were strong enough to make Savarkar's early historical book on the 1857 rebellion the chief source of Indian history for the Egyptian nationalist paper *Al-liwa*. Following the assassination of Sir Curzon-Wyllie by one of Savarkar's associates, Madanlal Dhingra, what traveled was the image of an Indian nationalist martyr in Egypt. Indeed, Dhingra became a far more nationalist hero in Egypt than he did in moderate Indian nationalist politics.[15] Ibrahim Nassif al-Wardani, who was well acquainted with the Dhingra case, later shot the prime minister, Boutros Ghali, leading some British officials to focus on his connection to Indian extremism.[16] Wardani, Dhingra, and Savarkar all were subsequently viewed as religious fanatics (along with Mazzini and partly because of his putative influence), even though the colonial authorities had to concede that they could not find evidence of religious hatred, let alone a defense of religion in their actions.[17] It is in these lateral rather than horizontal global circuits that we might locate with some precision the genealogical history of how and why a reference to Mazzini would immediately signal to a colonial policeman a global threat and presence of "fanaticism" and, curiously enough, "anarchism."

In confronting the relationship between a figure like Savarkar and the questions surrounding a new global intellectual history, we must further ask how to keep a sense of balance between the recognition that colonial occupation and international intellectual influences were central to the development of Indian political thought and the need to remain attentive to the importance of locality and proximate as well as indigenous intellectual forces to the shaping of any of the key figures of Indian intellectual history. Reading Savarkar's full Marathi corpus, perhaps like reading Mazzini's voluminous Italian writings, presents a very different picture of a man whom we have so far characterized as "nationalist," "anarchist," or "fundamentalist." Indeed, Savarkar was less interested in history as a form of writing than I have so far presumed, and in many respects, he was far more a literary than a political figure. Even in his prose, history was simply equated with ideology, in that history was an ideological instrument used as bluntly as possible. In much of Savarkar's historical writing, whether his first work on the 1857 rebellion as a nationalist rebellion or his last work, *Saha soneri pane*, or the six "glorious epochs" in Indian history as he perceived them, the standard elements of historical writing— basic commitments to accuracy, facts, and historical causation and sequence—seem unimportant at best and often absent altogether. They are replaced with passion and polemic. There is simply no reason for us, given what we do know about Savarkar's education in both India and England, to believe that he did not know his dates or that he was simply stretching a historical fact or working with another chronology. How, then, do we explain his fundamental disinterest in history? Might we perhaps need to look elsewhere for a more authentic understanding of his basic theory of history?

Most of all, Savarkar fashioned himself as a poet. His first publications were poems, the genre to which he turned repeatedly in moments of crisis and that also was the core literary motif of his most incendiary essay, "Essentials of Hindutva."[18] His poetry was as ideological as his prose, addressing the political problems of his time, such as child widowhood, the plague, the emasculation of the Hindus, and the need for an Indic civilizational malaise to be enlivened with a hearty dose of modern medicine. Yet his poetry is also rooted in his sense of regional literary tradition, the importance of Sanskrit meter, and the recognition that the genre of the *mahakavya* took as their subject matter both mythological themes and political biographies.[19] Savarkar seems to see himself as following in a tradition in which—as Lawrence McCrea argued in his essay on Bilhana's *Vikramankadevacharita*—the real king makers were poets, not historians, and poetry "does not simply publicize or preserve the memory of heroism of royal virtue—rather it creates them." Savarkar may be more accurately understood as not having fashioned himself as just another poet but as a mixture of Mazzini and Bilhana—as the exemplary, all-powerful bard who could marshal a classical idiom with a local tradition to bring into being a modern nation-state.[20]

Savarkar's poetry varies in its quality. Some of it is good, some pompous, and some lyrical, and all of it is difficult and convoluted.

This is not unusual, for his poetic voice matures and finds its stride. His desire to write *kavya* is clear, but the subject of the panegyric whose virtues he extolled is not the king of earlier times but the nascent nation, allegorized as a mother, sister, or widow. Narayan Rao has argued that poetry as a medium is not authentic unless it is recited, spoken, and fundamentally aural.[21] But Savarkar wrote his poems to be read and be published in magazines by a new readership that recognized old meters.[22] He knew enough to use context-specific compounds and sounds, to turn on style for effect, and to recognize that *rasa* (emotive content) and meter could not compete with each other and that the emotive aspect of his poetry was more important than the simple use of rhyming.[23] He used both regional Marathi and Sanskrit classical meters such as *Shardulavikridit* and *Mandakranta*, and the verses, with some exceptions, scan correctly. As Philip Engblom noted, the kinship between Marathi and Sanskrit was strong enough that such adaptations of Marathi poetry to Sanskrit norms were not far-fetched.[24] Marathi also has enough Sanskritic texture, with its combination of *purusha* and *mridu* sounds, to have enabled Savarkar to write in a peculiar hybrid style that sought to preserve the sense of a single literary tradition for Sanskrit and Marathi. At the same time, Savarkar occasionally used the dischordant *mya* when referring to the first-person singular in his poems instead of *amhi*, or *aasacha* instead of *asaycha*, perhaps as a means of letting the reader know his facility with an older and more rustic Marathi, or the poetry of Samartha Ramdas. He might also have been trying to invert the usual relationship between classical and vernacular forms.

The poetry therefore can be said to minimally reference Savarkar's personal trajectory. He was born in rustic Maharashtra in a small town called Bhagur and was educated first in Nasik and then in the city of Pune. His own personal trajectory took him from one of the smallest towns in western India to progressively larger and more cosmopolitan milieus, from Pune to the heart of empire in London. Despite his international travel, local roots and histories remained powerful for him, in his literary upbringing and in the development of a historical consciousness. Both the colonial author Grant Duff in his *History of the Marathas* (1826) and V. K. Rajwade, the eminent historian of Maharashtra, wrote about the region's claim to its own national history from about the seventeenth century until the final defeat of the Marathas in 1818 by the British East India Company. As a result, Maharashtra's history cannot be easily assimilated into the broader Indian nationalist frame, even though it was linked to it. The memory of the Maratha chieftain, Shivaji Bhonsle (1690–1708), and his recurrent battles with Aurangzeb, the last great Mughal emperor, makes up a significant portion of the region's self-identification, as Prachi Deshpande showed.[25] The militant poet-sage, Samartha Ramdas, who was Shivaji's political and spiritual adviser, in effect became the patron saint of a modern Marathi community that memorialized him in several literary and poetic works. If we are to guess at the contents of Savarkar's library, we would certainly need to acknowledge, in addition to Mazzini and the modern Marathi poets, the influence of premodern poets such as Ramdas and Moropant, whose aryas were well known in literary circles.

As an example, let us look at one of Savarkar's longer, more interesting poems, on the subject of child widowhood introduced to us through the plague. In the early twentieth century in western India, the plague had devastating effects on the rural countryside and towns, revealing the immense cultural divide between English colonial attempts to curb and contain it and the manner in which those attempts were seen by everyday Maharashtrians. Savarkar uses a natural disaster made worse by colonial policy to lead us to the traditional and older scandal of child widowhood, in which he excoriates widowers for being able to live on and prosper at least as much as he goes after a fossilized shastric law.

The poem itself has 102 verses, in the arya meter. I offer here a rough translation focusing solely on the themes he used. Savarkar changes voices constantly, from his own as the poet to that of the plague, a householder, the ghost of the dead wife, a young wife, and the young widow to whom the entire poem is dedicated. He moves to an intimate space, that of a home and household in which the wife has died, the husband is bereft, and the son is disconsolate and terrified that his father will leave as well. Here the tone could well be autobiographical, as Savarkar lost his mother to the plague and eventually his father, too. His mother was a young woman when she died, and Savarkar moves to an examination of the love between husband and wife, but the couple is childlike. The description of love play is that between children, not sexual in the usual sense of the word, but familiar as if these were girls and boys younger than Savarkar was when he wrote the poem.

He switches voices again, to the ghost of the young wife who died and then back to Savarkar. Should we read this use of the female voice, written by a male poet, as evidence that he would have known or read Satavahana Hala's *Sattasai*? He begins with the palace—*prasada*—that is built for the plague with the mortar of oppression and the humiliation of the earth. The first line scans perfectly, and the second requires a little juggling. But in the first line, he lets his reader know that he knows the rules of Sanskritic meter.[26] The plague muses to itself (it is a masculine voice) about the beauties of the land—*aryavarta*—unlike any others. Its eyes are filled with this land's beguiling beauty, indexed by the Sanskritic "la" alliteration: *bhulala, khulala, vadala.*[27]

The plague travels, sees all of India, caresses (with a terrible hand) Bombay (Mumbai), then goes to Pune, Nasik, makes sacred pilgrimages, bathes in the Godavari, and goes to Puri.[28] Savarkar's own voice asks rhetorically, What else can I say? In one fell swoop he (the plague) circumnavigated the country, without tiring. The plague destroyed cities, and none of the mantras and chants that could be chanted had any effect.[29] Again and again, Savarkar emphasizes the fallacy of believing in Sanskrit chants and prayers.

Beginning in verse 29, Savarkar is relentless in making sure no heartstring, no emotional avenue, no intellectual avenue is left unexplored to let us know the horrors of child widowhood.[30] The critical voice of this poem is that of an early feminist engaged in raising social consciousness about the miserable plight of the child widow. In subsequent verses, Savarkar leaves no road untrod, exoriates all the sacred cows of orthodox Hinduism: the Vedas, the lawgivers, the priests. His pen fiercely denounces society, particularly merry widowers who remarry young girls even when they are in their dotage. In that sense, the poem is an antihegemonic text that by recourse to a classical idiom marshals an ideological critique of a nation that has not yet come into being.[31] For women, the plague piles insult on injury. Not only does it create child widows who lead miserable lives, but it also kills mothers, sisters, and wives thereby coming close to eradicating the entire female race. What does he advocate? And to whom does he turn?

Savarkar appeals to the leader of orthodox Hindus, the *Shankaracharya*, to support widow remarriage, to found schools for widows that can be run by older widows so that a new society can benefit from generations of educated young women.

Why is this one poem important, other than that it won an award and marked him at an early age as an upcoming poet in western India? Partly because the long hand of presentism has disallowed real historical inquiry about key figures like him, and partly because the history of nationalism has disallowed a more regionally specific understanding of how figures like him feature in the region. But more important, his poetry was the most intellectually demanding of all his writings and accordingly must be taken extremely seriously. Why did Savarkar choose to write in a Sanskritic idiom that was deliberately convoluted yet more attentive to tradition than his historical prose? The tentative answer to this question cannot be found in the literature on the modern period. It therefore must engage and acknowledge the connections between the kind of writing that Savarkar presents and the precolonial global world that Sheldon Pollock describes as the world of the Persian and Sanskrit cosmopolis.[32] That world, Pollock writes,

> may be said to know three international culture languages: Sanskrit, the major Indo-Aryan language of premodernity, with a literary history of two and a half millennia; Persian, whose own history began anew at the start of the second millennium; and from the eighteenth century on, English. Added to these are a small number of Middle Indo-Aryan script languages of the first millennium: the Prakrits (above all Maharashtri and Saraseni), Pali, and Apabhramsha; the New Indo-Aryan languages of the second millennium, including Bangla, Gujarati, Hindi, Sindhi, Sinhala, and Urdu; and four major Dravidian languages of South India first attested at different points in the first millennium: Tamil, Kannada, Telugu, and Malayalam.[33]

Savarkar's knowledge and use of Sanskrit, Maharashtri, Apabhramsha, and modern Marathi locates him as part of a literary culture that has been international in a non-European direction for two millennia through the overlapping Sanskrit and Persian cosmopolis.

In a widely cited essay, "The Death of Sanskrit," Pollock laments the loss, by the late nineteenth century, of Sanskrit as the language and medium in which original thought and conception could be articulated. Identifying four text moments across a large swath of time and region in precolonial India, Pollock argues that by 1800, the capacity of "Sanskrit thought to make history had vanished."[34] Furthermore, as he put it, "The great experiments in moral and aesthetic imagination . . . ha[d] entirely disappeared, and instead, creativity was confined within the narrow limits of hymnic verse."[35] The ability to innovate in one of the world's oldest and greatest literary languages was lost. Pollock's argument, which balances, on the one hand, the appreciation and acknowledgment of exceptional literary work written across the centuries and regions and, on the other hand, the death of such creativity, leads to an interesting historical situation: genius must recur across time and region in order to play its own pallbearer. The final scene ends in two acts: one with penultimate finality in the colonial period, and the last with ultimate and disastrous consequences for Sanskrit in the nationalist and postcolonial period. For Pollock, this ends Sanskrit creativity.

A little more than a hundred years earlier, Vishnushastri Chiplunkar (1850–1882), the writer and publisher of "Nibandhamala" (1874), asked Pollock's question about Marathi. With the most unabashed and staunchly nationalist ideological vantage point, very different from what Pollock would use a century later, Chiplunkar agitated in an early essay over the possibility that Marathi was in imminent danger of falling into disuse as an organic and live language. Chiplunkar's clear intent was writing to raise consciousness in a colonial time, in which the quickness and facility of English threatened to take over the slower and more sedimented seriousness, depth, and beauty of Marathi.[36] The language of political sovereignty that had taken the Maratha empire to Attock and Delhi, and the language of poets like Tukaram, Ramdas, Mukteshwar, Waman Pandit, and Moropant, was, in his time, in real danger of being replaced by those who thought it too beggarly to be used as anything other than a translation language and who believed it incapable of being used for innovative thought. Chiplunkar mentioned the robustness of Marathi in a political context as well, distinguishing between the language of rule and the language of colonial occupation. Muslim rule, as he called it, required the learning of both Arabic and Persian, which had entered Marathi but without destroying it and paradoxically had strengthened it. This was not the case with English. Chiplunkar's explanation for this is quasi-spatial. Persian and Marathi interacted but did not appropriate each other's spaces, even though it was clear that Persian had become part of Marathi. This was not the case with English, however, which maintained no separations and had become a virtual craze. In turning their heads to follow the spread of English, the Marathi intelligentsia had lost their heads altogether. This infatuation with English was made even worse for Chiplunkar, because at its best Marathi was now considered useless even as a translational language, but insofar as it would be used for that purpose, it would serve the servile purpose of spreading English even more widely. For that reason, Marathi did not need to be relegated to a past in which English was the future, but to be remembered as a language that could do it all, including Sanskrit.

According to Chiplunkar's logic, then, Marathi was always "global," even though it had regional connections and traditions that were just as important. More than a hundred years later, Sheldon Pollock made the same argument, from an antinationalist point of view, about Sanskrit and Persian cosmopolitanism strengthening rather than obliterating vernacular languages.[37] Savarkar's agreement with and exemplification of Chiplunkar's argument, albeit maintaining that Sanskrit was privileged over other languages, was nowhere more evident than in his poetic corpus, which indexes a particular moment in Indian history in which the worlds of the folk and classical, the premodern Sanskrit cosmopolis, and the deep regional poetic tradition come together with a clearly anticolonial and nationalist agenda. Elsewhere I have argued that it was precisely Savarkar's slipperiness that made it possible for his infamous text, "Essentials of Hindutva," to be read across a political spectrum, then and now. The larger project to which his poetry, prose, and polemics were devoted was the purification of Marathi, the Hinduization of geography, and the nationalizing of Indian history. Pollock writes that "kavya . . . is itself often an argument about how language is to be used, indeed, about how life is to be used."[38] If that is the case, then Savarkar clearly let us know what he knew, how he was going to use language, and, indeed, how he was going to use his life.

The curious aspect of Savarkar's poetry is that while it is recognizably Marathi, it is also so Sanskritized as to be incomprehensible to an average Marathi reader, even to those familiar with poetry. It is neither Marathi nor Sanskrit but both, neither classical nor folk but deliberately mixed, a form of writing that seems to have been intended to interpolate equally both a native Marathi speaker and a Sanskritist. In harking back to a previous generation of Marathi poets, Savarkar ignores the modern divide between the linguistic communities of Sanskrit and Marathi, insisting instead on bringing them together in a national and self-critical moment. It is a poetry that both Sanskritists and Marathi scholars deride, for it does not reify either canon overtly, even though it pays its respects to both of them. It breaks as many rules as possible while letting the rule keepers know that the poet knows the rules. Savarkar worships Ramdas, imitates Moropant in a secular register, and pays attention to Chiplunkar, with whose politics he sympathizes while thumbing his nose at Orientalists, Indologists, and conventional Sanskritists who then and now read his hybrid Sanskrit as inaccurate Sanskrit and bad politics to boot. In response, Savarkar aggressively lays claim to Sanskrit and all the languages adduced by Sheldon Pollock in the earlier quotation of the Indo-Aryan millennium as belonging to him and to do with what he pleases. It is undoubtedly an arrogant, autodidactic, hubristic, protonationalist move, but Savarkar makes it as a poet with full knowledge of the tradition of which he is a part and whose rules he can bend to his craft.

How, then, does one write an intellectual history of a figure like Savarkar? It is clear that while conventional categories are useful in a piecemeal understanding, all four frames are inadequate. The Marathi regional frame is inadequate to understanding him because he was far more than just a Marathi poet. The national frame is inadequate because it completely ignores the regional density of literary history and nationalists who do not match the Gandhian standard. The modern nationalist frame is inadequate because it takes no account of the continuity between an older Sanskrit cosmopolis and Savarkar's experimentation. Finally, the early modern frame is inadequate because it discounts Savarkar's later hybrid Sanskritic experiments as inelegant and incorrect.

Before seeking to find a way to bring all these frames into some kind of alignment with one another, I will turn to Benedict Anderson's recent book *Under Three Flags* on the Filipino poet José Rizal. This is an international and global history in many threes, about nationalism under three banners depicted on the cover: the anarchist flag, Cuban flag, and Filipino flag. There are three Filipino patriots to whom Anderson pays close attention: Isabelo de los Reyes, Mariano Ponce, and José Rizal, although the last member of this group interests him more than the others. The tripartite worlds of Bismarck, Global Anarchism as a phenomenon, and the declining Spanish Empire make up the larger historical backdrop for the development of these ideas and their circulation. Anderson sets his frame around symbolism, literary figures, and Spanish and American imperialism, but he does not give the frame a single explanatory role. Empire (not colonial occupation) globalized the world of the late nineteenth century in unprecedented ways. The Philippines attract Anderson because "in the 1890s, though on the outer periphery of the world-system it briefly played a world role which has since eluded it."[39] His subject, José Rizal, lived in a globalized world interconnected through the community of letters, with anarchism as the traveling concept. According to Anderson's definition, even though international anarchism was "the main vehicle of global opposition to industrial capitalism, autocracy, latifundism, and imperialism,"[40] he is careful to offer more questions than answers, eventually suggesting that despite their global spread, ideas are distinctly of their own time and owned by no particular place or group.

In a work that is both personal and experimental, Anderson does not depart from some of his earlier concerns but writes more to open interpretive ground than to ground a single global argument. And he does so with stunning erudition. His comfort level with literature in French, Spanish, Dutch, and English (in addition to what he calls the last pure language, Latin) allows a familiar, but more subtle, attack on globalism and American imperialism. *Under Three Flags* incorporates a vast network across Europe, in and out of which his selected nationalists/anarchists moved. Familiar tropes reemerge in this work, such as the quintessentially modern birth of the novel form in Asia and the production of a national community through recourse to folklore and oral transmissions. "Enlightenment" *comes* to the Philippines through the "unbackward" language of "backward" Spain, a formulation that depicts Isabelo de los Reyes, living in colonial Manila, as he published a Spanish-language text called *El folk-lore filipino*. Isabelo is shown fashioning himself as one who brought "into the mental darkness of the colonial regime . . . the light of modern Europe."[41] Germany is privileged over Spain, but the language in which this hierarchy is established is Spanish!

In the same year that *El folk-lore filipino* was published, José Rizal also published his anarchist and incendiary first novel, entitled *Noli me tangere*. Anderson emphasizes the cosmopolitanism of Filipinos, leading him to pose the central question about how we might understand the international circulation of ideas. Filipinos

> wrote to Austrians in German, to Japanese in English, to each other in French, or Spanish, or Tagalog. . . . [S]ome of them knew a bit of Russian, Greek, Italian, Japanese, and Chinese. A wire might be sent around the world in minutes, but real communication required the *true, hard, internationalism of the polyglot*.[42]

At the close of the book, the reader is left with a series of unanswered but productive questions.

The connections between anticolonial (Spanish) nationalism in the Philippines and Cuba are explored primarily through his intense focus on José Rizal: what he did and did not read, where he might have read it, how his writings might have been interpreted, where his works were circulated, and where they were misunderstood. Anderson follows Rizal around the world, reads his books, opens his suitcases, and is struck by the presence of certain authors in his library (Chateaubriand, Voltaire, Zola, Cervantes, Balzac, and Swift, among others) but also by the absence of political writing (Hegel, Fichte, Marx, Tocqueville, Comte, Saint Simon, Fourier, Bentham, Mill, Bakunin, and Kropotkin), despite having spent ten years in metropolitan centers such as Madrid, Paris, London, and Berlin.[43] The importance of international radical movements is, of course, central to the development of homegrown nationalism, but Anderson takes local literary production on its own terms even as the literature reveals an instrumental relationship and deployment of the "science" of anthropology or the development of folklore. What seems most compelling about Anderson's new work is that his early version of the determinate spread of nationalism is now more complicated. The interesting circuitry of exchange of ideas is not about overdetermination, let alone or easy or straightforward influence, and Anderson repeatedly abjures the simple or single answer.

As I tried to understand Savarkar's relationship to similar circuitries of global and local ideas and influences, I took my cue from Anderson's refusal to privilege similarity over difference, answers over questions, and generality over particularity. Savarkar's "anarchism" can certainly be affiliated with the international "political project of spectacular assassinations . . . committed by despairing and hopeful anarchists"[44] and compared with Rizal's despair and pathos expressed in a letter in 1892 at the age of thirty-one with instructions that it be opened posthumously:

> I also want to show those who deny patriotism that we know how to die for *our duty* and for our convictions. What does death matter if one dies for what one loves, for one's country and those beings whom one reveres? . . . I have always loved my poor country and I am sure I shall love her to the last moment . . . my future, my life, my joys, I have sacrificed all for love of her.[45]

Some common tropes seem inescapable: the fetishization of martyrdom, the overwhelming sense of duty to a feminized country, the sublimation of all erotic desire into this abstraction. But there are local affiliations, too, as I have pointed out, not least Savarkar's debt to and location within a long-standing Marathi literary tradition. Savarkar's anarchism cannot be easily explained in relationship to, or be reconciled with, the persona of the beleaguered Brahmin as the exemplar of heteronomy in an overwhelmingly conservative Hindu milieu—which is how Savarkar fashioned himself in his autobiographical works, and the image that his Marathi and Hindi biographers recreated repeatedly. Without recourse to folklore but with a vague and inchoate autodidacticism apropos of Sanskrit treatises, Savarkar, in "Essentials of Hindutva," wrote against Gandhi by putting in place the idea of territorial India as an antique land populated with a mythohistorical people. Neither Rizal nor Savarkar used the term "anarchist" as a means of self-identification. But colonial policemen used the term, and now historians do. The term calls attention both to global forces and meanings and to deep and fundamental contradictions, even when the question of influence seems undeniable.

—⚭—

I have noted the precolonial and early colonial (pre- and early modern) global configurations chiefly to point out that there was always a global circuitry of ideas but also that the centrality of Enlightenment categories to Indian intellectual history cannot be separated from colonialism. Colonialism was as much a contingent historical force as it was a provocation for both nationalist resistance and claims of civilizational autonomy or superiority in opposition to the idea of European origins of all ideas. It was colonial rule and the epistemological assumptions of colonial/imperial/global history that cemented the force of the categories that have long since been under dispute (tradition/modernity, European enlightenment/colonial enlightenment, origin/reception) by world historians. None of these categories can by themselves do all the work they need to for a global intellectual history. "The study of history," Partha Chatterjee wrote in an earlier structuralist frame of mind, "must concern itself with the ceaseless process by which structures are transformed into events and events into structures. Historical discourse is constituted on that constantly shifting, tension-ridden, inherently polemical terrain of knowledge." This is not an easy task, and Chatterjee prescribes for us the bitter herb that all historians must chew. Historians need to accept as a theory of history "the uneven development of contradictions, a varying order of antagonism," and here's the rub: "a large zone of theoretical indeterminacy." At the very least, this would require acknowledging the fundamental character of colonial domination at the same time putting in play the particularistic histories that can be seen for all the figures adduced in this chapter, including not just Savarkar and Mazzini but Rizal and others, too. As Anderson's *Under Three Flags* shows us, there is a first salutary lesson to be learned. If we are to proceed at all with a global intellectual history, the hermeneutic frame first must be expanded and then resolutely, and permanently, left open. It is one thing to acknowledge, as

Sudipta Kaviraj did, that the ghost of Europe hovers over us all; it is quite another to argue that the specter of Europe should (or ever did) set the terms of the arguments, or worse, that it has already done so and we just do not recognize it.

Notes

I am grateful to Samuel Moyn and Andrew Sartori for giving me the opportunity to present an earlier version of this chapter at their workshop on global intellectual history. Much of this chapter was worked out in conversation with the workshop participants. For a characteristically brutal reading of both my prose and ideas, I am indebted to Nicholas Dirks. I would also like to thank Partha Chatterjee, Mamadou Diouf, Satya Mohanty, Rosalind O'Hanlon, Sheldon Pollock, Narayan Rao, Rahul Sarwate, Somdev Vasudeva, and Akbar Zaidi for helping me think through some of the problems in writing about a figure as difficult as Vinayak Damodar Savarkar. All the errors remain mine alone. For ease of publication, I have not placed diacritical or accent marks for the Marathi passages quoted and have offered as well only a rough transliteration in English of the Marathi poem to which I refer. The full text of the poem is readily available in the published version of Savarkar's collected works.

1. Rajendra Vora, "Maharashtra Dharma and the Nationalism Movement in Maharashtra," in *Writers, Editors, and Reformers: Social and Political Transformations of Maharashtra, 1830–1930*, ed. N. K. Wagle (New Delhi: Manohar, 1999), 26.

2. For an analysis of how a key concept, namely, culture, travels in the determinist frame of global capitalism, see Andrew Sartori, *Bengal in Global Concept History: Culturalism in the Age of Capital* (Chicago: University of Chicago Press, 2008). In this genre, Sartori's work is easily the best example. My purpose in this chapter, however, is to suggest some limitations with such a determinist frame.

3. The list here is long, and I cite the names of only a few scholars whose work falls into the large category of Indian intellectual history: Stephen Hay, Ainslee Embree, Edward Shils, Ranajit Guha, Thomas Metcalf, Eric Stokes, Sudipta Kaviraj, Partha Chatterjee, Dipesh Chakrabarty, Amales Tripathi, Stanley Wolpert, Veena Naregal, Francesca Orsini, Prachi Deshpande, G. P. Deshpande, M. S. S Pandian, V. Geetha, and Gopal Guru.

4. For a few examples, see Stanley Wolpert's two works of intellectual history: *Tilak and Gokhale: Revolution and Reform in the Making of Modern India* (Berkeley: University of California Press, 1961); and *Morley and India: 1906–1910* (Berkeley: University of California Press, 1967); as well

as Ainslee T. Embree, *Charles Grant and British Rule in India* (New York: Columbia University Press, 1962); and Stephen N. Hay, *Asian Ideas of East and West: Tagore and His Critics in Japan, China, and India* (Cambridge, Mass.: Harvard University Press, 1970). There was and remains a long tradition of writing about India that emerged out of an imperial history framework, as, for example, in some of the revisionist work on nationalism in the early Cambridge school. As one example, see John Gallager, Gordon Johnson, and Anil Seal, eds., *Locality, Province and Nation: Essays on Indian Politics, 1870–1940* (Cambridge: Cambridge University Press, 1973).

5. One notable example is John Pincince's dissertation, "On the Verge of Hindutva: V. D. Savarkar, Revolutionary, Convict, Ideologue, c. 1905–1924" (Ph.D. diss., University of Hawai'i, 2007).

6. Maia Ramnath, *Decolonizing Anarchism: An Antiauthoritarian History of India's Liberation Struggle* (Oakland, Calif.: AK Press, 2011).

7. I am grateful to Thomas Hansen for his discussion with me about global anarchism.

8. See the letter from the Viceroy of India, Earl of Minto to Secretary of State John Morley, November 19, 1909, Mss Eur D 573/22, folio 93, London, British Library, Oriental and India Office Collection.

9. Stefano Recchia and Nadia Urbinati, introduction to *A Cosmopolitanism of Nations: Giuseppe Mazzini's Writings on Democracy, Nation Building, and International Relations*, ed. Stefano Recchia and Nadia Urbinati (Princeton, N.J.: Princeton University Press, 2008). For an analysis of the rearticulation of Mazzini's politics in a specifically Marathi idiom, see also E. Fasana, "Deshabhakta: The Leaders of the Italian Independence Movement in the Eyes of Marathi Nationalists," in *Writers, Editors, and Reformers: Social and Political Transformations of Maharashtra, 1830–1930*, ed. N. K. Wagle (New Delhi: Manohar, 1999), 49–55.

10. Gita Srivastava, *Mazzini and His Impact on the Indian Nationalist Movement* (Allahabad: Chugh Publications, 1982).

11. Ibid.

12. C. A. Bayly, "India, The Bhagavad Gita and the World," *Modern Intellectual History* 7, no. 2 (2010): 275–95. On the Bhagavad Gita, see the recent forum in *Modern Intellectual History* in which the contributors analyze its use and circulation in both Indian and international circles. In colonial India in the late nineteenth and early twentieth century, the Gita was picked up as the exemplary text of Hinduism in India in large part because of its versatility. That is, it could equally be marshaled in support of one's politics whether as a liberal, radical, militant, or pacifist nationalist. Yet as Chris Bayly argued, outside India the Gita emerged as a global text in large part because the ground had been cleared for it by the failure of Christian evangelicalism and a loss of faith in apostolic infallibility in the West.

13. I am taking this summary from a conversation with Stefano Recchia and from the introduction to Recchia and Urbinati, eds., *Cosmopolitanism of Nations.*

14. See the letter from Secretary to State John Morley to the Viceroy of India, the Earl of Minto, May 27, 1909, Mss Eur D/573/4, folio 116, London, British Library, Oriental and India Office Collection. Morley was alert to the idea that colonial rule was untenable and that resistance to it would take violent form:

> I have a painful feeling of the want of all sense of proportion in my political friends who never recognize the immense advance we have now made in the progressive direction. . . . You are no Ultra-Alarmist, nor more am I, but it is really senseless for these politicians to argue as if India were Yorkshire, or even as if it were Ireland. Such a want of imagination, and still worse such flat ignorance of the facts of the case—bombs and plots—and the greatest and deepest fact of all, that we are governing a population who don't love us, and who will less and less patiently acquiesce in our rule. (Morley to Minto, July 2, 1909, Mss Eur D/573/4, folio 134, London, British Library, Oriental and India Office Collection)

Indeed, in the correspondence between these two officials there is a good bit of confusion about how to label the group, as they are variously called murderers, extremists, anarchists, seditionists, and fanatics.

15. See Noor-Aiman Iftikhar Khan, "The Enemy of My Enemy: Indian Influences on Egyptian Nationalism, 1907–1930" (Ph.D. diss., University of Chicago, 2006), 74–78.

16. Ibid., 81.

17. Ibid., 86.

18. See Janaki Bakhle, "Country First? Vinayak Damodar Savarkar (1883–1966) and the Writing of 'Essentials of Hindutva,'" *Public Culture* 22, no. 1 (2010): 149–86.

19. I refer here to the argument made by Lawrence McCrea, "Poetry Beyond Good and Evil: Bilhana and the Tradition of Patron-Centered Court Epic," *Journal of Indian Philosophy* 38, no. 5 (2010): 503–18. Philip Engblom noted as well that such writing is a continuation of the pandit tradition in western India. See Philip Engblom, "Vishnu Moreshwar Mahajani and Nineteenth-Century Antecedents to Keshavsut," in *Writers, Editors, and Reformers: Social and Political Transformations of Maharashtra, 1830–1930*, ed. N. K. Wagle (New Delhi: Manohar, 1999), 143. Engblom details some of the early poetic experiments in the modern period by poets such as Mahadev Moreshwar Kunte, among others.

20. I follow the line of argument made by Fasana, "Deshabhakta," 45.

21. A personal comment to me at the Cornell Workshop on the Folk and the Classical, May 2011.

22. For an analysis of the encounter between the larger world of English literature and poetry and Marathi literature and poetry that resulted in the development of modern Marathi poetry, see Philip Engblom, "Keshavsut and Early Modernist Strategies for Indigenizing the Sonnet in Marathi," *Journal of South Asian Literature* 23, no. 1 (1988): 42–66. Engblom is sensitive to the different strands of Marathi poetry, to poets who either resisted English influence by sticking resolutely to older Shastric and Sanskritic norms or assimilated and emulated it by trying in effect to write English poetry in Marathi, by working with a more natural idiom rather than the convoluted and difficult medium of Sanskrit. Between 1870 and 1920, a few exceptional poets who marked modern Marathi poetry were Keshavsut (Krishnaji Keshav Damle, 1866–1905), whose famous poem "Tutari" is claimed to have trumpeted the birth of modern Marathi poetry chiefly in its use of the sonnet form. Tryambak Bapuji Thombre (1890–1918), known as Balkavi, was the best exponent of the romantic modern poetry while, Bha. Ra. Tambe, or Bhaskar Ramachandra Tambe (1874–1941), wrote poetry for the emerging middle class.

23. I am grateful to Somdev Vasudeva for reading this poem with me and helping me with many of its Sanskrit features. I owe this insight to him.

24. Engblom, "Vishnu Moreshwar Mahajani and Nineteenth-Century Antecedents to Keshavsut," 145.

25. Prachi Deshpande, *Creative Pasts: Historical Memory and Identity in Western India, 1700–1960* (New York: Columbia University Press, 2006), esp. chap. 2, "Representing Maratha Power."

26. The poem was submitted by Savarkar for a competition held by the Bombay Hindu Union Club. He wrote it in 1909, and the full Marathi text can be found in *Samagra Savarkar Vangmaya*, 8 vols. (Bombay: Savarkar Smarak Publications, 2000), 8:42.

   Paaya paravashata jya, dushkalachya shilahi zho rachila
   Avanati-krutant-keli-prasada plague kalas tya khachila (1)

27.   Nandanavanasam mohak srishticha saarbhut ha desh
   Ho drishti dhanya pahuni, dharuni asa plague hridayi uddesh (2)
   Aryavarti aala, mumbaila thevile mag padala
   Zhala ant sukhacha ye ut anantvakatra-vipadala (3)
   Jee aikili tyahuni shatapat adhikachi suruchita dhanya
   Pahuni bhulala khulala vadala; mohak na bhu ashi anya (4)

28.   Kela nishchaya aisa, kuravaluni Mumbai bhayan kari
   Ho dhig na nij jine te, yastav baghnya pune prayan kari (6)
   Godasnanastav kari shrimattrayambak puris gamanala
   Ala panchvateela tethuniya ramraya namanala (7)

29. Bahu kay vado? Kele aikya abdat deshparyatna
    Pavanahuni javan, nachi damla ha ki vichitra vidhighatna (8)
    Plague kashacha ala? Krutkarmachachi bhog avatarala
    Karmayatta phalachya upabhogaveen kon bhav tarla? (9)
    Keli bhayan nagare, nagarasam dat sarva vana vasate
    Damale namale gamale hatsattvachi mantra tantra sunvasa te (10)

30. Jata nath streecha tee gai-huni gay manave
    Sutka ablanchi tya karnya ghesi na ka yama nave? (31)
    Bandhu na, bandhav na, na matapitar jya abhagite (32)
    Tya majhi dukhachi prabhuji! Pochti na ka nabha geete?
    Mee alpavayi bala, majha saubhagyanidhi aha jalala
    Vaidhavyacha durdhar bhayankar giri ha prachand kosalala (33)
    Kay karu? Zau kuthe? Ho majhe aptsoyre sare
    Tara anath bala, chal baghta svastha baisuni ka re? (34)
    Dete ka koni ' ablechya hya madeey hakela?
    Bola ho, bola ho, dheeracha shabda ek tari bola (35)

31. I am indebted for this insight to Satya Mohanty and the other participants at the Cornell workshop, including Narayan Rao, Leela Prasad, and Lawrence McCrea.

32. Sheldon Pollock, "The Sanskrit Cosmopolis, 300–1300: Transculturation, Vernacularization, and the Question of Ideology," in *Ideology and Status of Sanskrit: Contributions to the History of the Sanskrit Language*, ed. J. E. M. Houben (Leiden: Brill, 1996). Here Sheldon Pollock, who insists on an earlier literary cosmopolitanism, challenges the modernist emphasis solely on a world that is global because of capitalism. The literary cosmopolis of Sanskrit is a case in point.

33. Sheldon Pollock, introduction to *Literary Cultures in History: Reconstructions from South Asia*, ed. Sheldon Pollock (Berkeley: University of California Press, 2003), 23.

34. Sheldon Pollock, "The Death of Sanskrit," *Comparative Studies in Society and History* 43 (2001): 394.

35. Ibid., 398.

36. V. S. Chiplunkar, "Marathi Bhashechi Sampratchi Sthiti," 4–5, in *Nibandhamala*, 2 vols. (Pune: Varda Books, 1993), 1:1. For a historical analysis of Chiplunkar's work, see Deshpande, *Creative Pasts*, 100–105.

37. Pollock, "Introduction," 25.

38. Pollock, "Death of Sanskrit," 394.

39. Benedict Anderson, *Under Three Flags: Anarchism and the Anti-Colonial Imagination* (New York: Verso, 2005), 4. Many of the ideas in the sections on Benedict Anderson come from a vibrant discussion about his work in my class on revolutionary nationalism around the world in spring 2009. I am grateful to my students Monica Saini, Sylvia Abdullah, Mujeeb Mashal,

Samiha Rahman, Tamar Newman, Tim Curley, Louis Miller, Gus von Hagen, and Ben Honrighausen for their stimulating discussion, and I would like to acknowledge their role in my formulations.

40. Anderson, *Under Three Flags*, 54.
41. Ibid., 13, 23.
42. Ibid, 5 (italics added).
43. Ibid, 105.
44. Ibid, 41.
45. Ibid, 134 (Anderson's translation).

11

Making and Taking Worlds

DUNCAN BELL

If there is but one world, it embraces a multiplicity of contrasting aspects; if there are many worlds, the collection of them all is one. The one world may be taken as many, or the many worlds taken as one; whether one or many depends on the way of taking.

—Nelson Goodman, *Ways of Worldmaking*

Exerting an almost shamanic aura, the adjective "global" routinely serves as a legitimating device for a vast array of contemporary practices and projects. A spatial reorientation is well under way across the human sciences, reshaping various fields and spawning innovative research agendas. In the disciplinary matrix of history, this is exemplified by the striking expansion of "global" history, while in political thought—my own main disciplinary home—it has led to an emerging discourse of "comparative political theory."[1] Global intellectual history is a product of these interlacing trends. Have we reached a potential "threshold moment" in the study of the human imagination?[2]

In the first chapter of this volume, Samuel Moyn and Andrew Sartori sketch a conceptual map of the various ways in which global intellectual history could be conceived. Despite the substantial differences between them, most of the iterations share a structural similarity: a failure to adequately conceptualize "the global." While frequently invoked in contemporary historiography, the idea is rarely interrogated. What is the question to which "global" is the answer? One way of thinking about this is to reflect on its possible antonyms, two of which are woven through existing discussions. The first contrasts the global with the particular, or the local. The main target here is methodological nationalism, the view that the boundaries of a particular political community set both the terms and the limits of inquiry. From this perspective, global intellectual history is an antidote to a debilitating form of scholarly parochialism, insisting that ideas are not constrained or constituted by political borders but are instead produced and consumed within cross-cutting, geographically dispersed fields of discourse. This criticism is well taken but limited. While there are indeed many interpretive questions that cannot be asked or answered adequately in a national (or statist) frame, there are others for which it may well be apposite. It all depends on the question being posed. Exhibiting the same logic of foreclosure, methodological globalism mirrors the limitations of methodological nationalism, fixing the parameters of the answer before the investigation begins. Second, the challenge lands only a glancing blow on the field, for many intellectual historians already operate in an intraregional or transcontinental mode.[3] Much European intellectual history, for example, focuses on a spatially extended, multilingual republic of letters. Moreover, while the histories of circulation and reception that dominate Sartori and Moyn's survey cover fascinating topics, few can claim to be truly global in scope, and they follow in the footsteps of long-established (if sometimes marginalized) scholarly traditions.

The second, perhaps more common, antonym of the global is "Western." The idea here seems to be that global intellectual history is configured as a challenge to the pernicious reduction of intellectual history to the intellectual history of the West. Aiming to open the debate to a multitude of voices from previously disregarded locales, it represents an act of resistance against scholarly practices that reinscribe destructive North-South dynamics in the heart of the modern university. Once again, this is a welcome challenge, but here it is necessary to distinguish between disciplinary sociology and methodology. It is true that as practiced in European and American universities, intellectual history and political theory are dominated by "Western" intellectual concerns and movements. Incorporating other voices in pedagogy and research would reap considerable political-intellectual benefits and would have significant implications for syllabus construction, hiring decisions, and publishing practices. From this perspective, reconfiguring intellectual history is ultimately a self-dissolving enterprise: global intellectual history would be rendered obsolete at the moment of its success. The result would be a new disciplinary constellation, a (suitably modified) "intellectual history." But even if the project to reshape the field in this manner were accomplished, it would not necessarily make the resulting scholarship "global" in any conceptually interesting sense. Studying the intellectual history of India or North Africa, the circulation of ideas in Ottoman or Ming Chinese imperial spaces, or the political theory of Sufi Islamic scholars or Latin American liberation theologians, is no more "global" than studying the intellectual history of Germany, the United States, or northern Europe; the philosophical cultures of the British or Spanish imperial metropoles; or social democratic ideologies in Scandinavia. The "global," then, often seems to be a geopolitical placeholder, a term signifying not (or not only) Western.[4]

Consider two cases: the transmission of European social and political ideologies into, first, British-occupied North America during the mid-eighteenth century and, second, British-occupied India a century later. Both were shaped by the dynamics of empire, albeit in different ways. Both involved ideas traveling across great distance and complex acts of translation, adaptation, and resistance. Are both fitting subjects for global intellectual history? If so, then the nomenclature adds little: this kind of work has long been practiced by scholars, including such luminaries as Bernard Bailyn, J. G. A. Pocock, and Eric Stokes.[5] It is new wine in old bottles. But if only the second is an instance of global intellectual history, it is not clear what differentiates it from the nonglobal alternative. What work is the adjective doing? It cannot be that one case involves movement over greater distances than the other or that one demands a switch in language (the transatlantic migration could be French or Spanish in origin). Is it that the former is intra-Western and the other moves beyond "the West"? This kind of critique remains trapped in the spatial categories that it professes to transcend; it presupposes what it should explore. I would argue that neither case is profitably characterized as a "global" practice. Arif Dirlik suggests that much of what is labeled "world history" is better viewed as transnational or translocal history.[6] The same could be said about the bulk of the work surveyed by Moyn and Sartori.

What, then, of the global? In this chapter I suggest a tentative answer by sketching two main lines of argument. First, that the human sciences—including intellectual history—can be conceived of as the study of practices of world making. Second, that global intellectual history can be characterized as a mode of social inquiry that focuses on articulations of "globality." This argument is a version of what Moyn and Sartori label an "actor's category" approach, but it is not synonymous with studying a "consciousness of the globe" or representations of the planet.[7] Viewing global intellectual history as a species of world making does not assume or prescribe any particular spatial scale. Rather, it concentrates on enunciations of universality, on attempts to cognitively encompass a given world (of whatever physical scale).[8] According to this perspective, then, "global" is not a geographical designation or a synonym for "non-Western" but instead denotes the perceptual scope of an argument or other act of imagination.

Making and Taking Worlds

The conceptual apparatus that I use in this chapter is inspired by the work of the American philosopher Nelson Goodman. I skim the surface of Goodman's oeuvre, utilizing some of his key ideas as a starting point for thinking about the character of the human sciences.[9] I claim that much of the scholarly work pursued in often discrete academic disciplines and on seemingly divergent subjects is united by a concern with identifying and analyzing practices of world making, on how humans symbolically construct worlds. It is worth noting, though, that this argument could be elaborated using different intellectual resources. A parallel case could be made by employing the fertile conceptual repertoire of the phenomenological tradition. Foucault's *epistemes*, Bourdieu's *doxa*, Castoriadis's *imaginaire social*: these, too, could underpin related accounts. Linguistic contextualism, advocated most influentially by Quentin Skinner, is likewise a fellow traveler. Despite their very different epistemological and ontological commitments, these intellectual projects converge at important points. The "themes and attitudes" shared by such scholars, writes Ian Hacking, "are not so different," for they all "involve iconoclastic questioning of varnished reality, of what the general run of people take for real."[10] While they differ in their accounts of agency—the degree to which individuals are constituted and constrained by the world(s) in which they are embedded—they all seek to unveil the ways in which social life is imagined and stabilized, maintained and reproduced.

Goodman identified "the multiplicity of worlds, the speciousness of 'the given,' the creative power of the understanding, the variety and formative function of symbols" as central motifs in his philosophical project, buttressing a "skeptical, analytic, constuctionalist" intellectual orientation.[11] As Hacking glosses the term, constructionalists (or "constructivists") "aim at exhibiting how, or proving that, various important entities, concepts, worlds, or whatever are constructed out of other materials."[12] Elsewhere Hacking identifies two related strands of this project: "historical ontology" and "historical meta-epistemology." The former studies the emergence, diffusion, and effects of a wide variety of "things," including institutions, technologies, and modes of classification, while the latter subset traces the fabrication and functions of "organizing concepts" concerned with "knowledge, belief, opinion, objectivity, detachment, argument, reason, rationality, evidence, even facts and truths."[13] These are some of the raw materials of "worlds." Goodman's main target was philosophical realism—the view that there exists a singular reality independent of our descriptions of it—which he regarded as a philosophical dead end. Instead, he developed a nominalist position that he labeled "irrealism," neither affirming nor denying the existence of a basic reality.[14] Reality, he concluded, "like realism in a picture, is largely a matter of habit."[15] What was important was the way in which humans fabricated symbolic systems, how they constructed and reconstructed worlds, drawing on the existing resources available to them, worlds carved from the materials of other worlds. For Goodman, the cognitive operations of classification—composition, decomposition, weighing, ordering, deleting, supplementing, deforming, and so on—structure the worlds in which we live and across which we move. "For there is, I maintain, no such thing as the real world, no unique, ready-made, absolute reality apart from and independent of all versions and visions. Rather, there are many right world-versions, some of them irreconcilable with others; and thus there are many worlds if any."[16]

Much follows from this "radical relativism under rigorous restraints."[17] Among other things, the epistemic boundaries between art and science (as well as other supposedly discrete domains of knowledge) blur into one another, while "truth" is detached from correspondence to a preexisting reality (though it is not dispensed with completely).[18] The cornucopia of human interests, symbols, and purposes moves center stage:

> Goodman denied anything beyond the actual and [dismissed] the idea of a world that could be described in one crucial and basic (i.e., scientific) manner. Instead, language provided us with many sets of interwoven and related terms by means of which we might organize our experience for different purposes. But we did this because of practical demands. No one constellation of descriptions of the world—no one vocabulary—could be said to be more true than the others; different descriptions might prove more or less efficacious depending on our changing aims and practices.[19]

For Goodman, construction goes all the way down: there is nothing outside the symbol-system. This is most apparent in his famous discussion of how humans make the stars. Since no star entities existed prior to our conceptualizations of them, we literally fabricate stars and constellations. According to this account, facts are carved out through the construction of theories and conceptual systems.[20] But how, critics ask, is it possible for humans to make something that existed before life on earth?

> Plainly, by making a space and time that contains those stars. By means of science, that world (and many another) was made with great difficulty and is, like the several worlds of phenomena that also contain stars, a more or less right or real world. We can make the sun stand still, not in the manner of Joshua but in the manner of Bruno. We make a star as we make a constellation, by putting its parts together and marking off its boundaries.[21]

All humans partake in world making, although many do so only insofar as they help reproduce existing worlds. (Perhaps this is better seen as a world-stabilizing function.) There are limitations to Good-man's account. While he offers a powerful analysis of the ways in which human classification works—of the various cognitive tasks, routines, and strategies employed in (re)creating worlds—he does not explore how specific worlds came to be made in the first place or how some displace others. He also does not pay much attention to the power relations that stabilize some collective worlds, embedding them in institutions and reproducing them for the benefit of some people over others. As such, his work has sometimes been criticized for leaving out the politics.[22] Yet as these critics recognize, his general epistemological and ontological framework applies in principle to all symbolic systems, and thus to all of human culture, past, present, and future. Highlighting how this works while remaining sensitive to how power relations distribute world-making opportunities and capacities is a central task for those working in the human sciences.

While Goodman does not typically feature in discussions of intellectual history, his work has resonated in several areas of the human sciences, chiefly in philosophical aesthetics and the study of visual culture. His work has also been used by psychologists (notably Jerome Brunner) and anthropologists (including Clifford Geertz and Mary Douglas).[23] Offering a rather vague gloss, Geertz reads Goodmanian "world constructing" as denoting practices of "meaning making, meaning seeking, meaning preserving, meaning using" and thus (presumably) as central to interpretative social science.[24] For Joanna Overing, Goodman's work proved helpful in comprehending the ritual chant language of the religious leaders (*ruwang*) of the Piaroa people in the Orinoco basin of Venezuela, as their "hallucinogenic and shamanic reasoning" was rendered (more) intelligible when conceptualized as an instance of world making:

> His approach not only allows a deeper communication between philosophy and anthropology, but even more importantly, it can lead to a conversation between anthropologists and "the other" in which the latter can be treated as an adult. Goodman's acceptance of the multiplicity of experiences and knowledges, his recognition that each may be irreducible to the next, and his insistence that fact is

tied to world-versions, and that the cognitive is inextricably tied to the emotive, should all appeal to the anthropological sensibility.[25]

Worlds are "taken" in a double sense. The first is the one indicated by Goodman in the epigraph opening this chapter. Here it means that worlds are construed or conceptualized with a particular interest or purpose in mind. But they can also be taken by force, made and remade in the image and at the behest of others. Imperialism, according to this account, is a technology for the taking and (re)making of worlds. Jonathan Lear has explored how people face the annihilation of a way of life.[26] He focuses on the fate of the people of the Crow Nation of (what is now) the western United States, who, like so many other First Peoples, were forced to give up their nomadic life for a reservation. His analysis probes the possible meaning of the words of Plenty Coups, last chief of the Crow: "When the buffalo went away the hearts of my people fell to the ground, and they could not lift them up again. After this nothing happened."[27] Lear's answer—whose details need not detain us—focuses on what it is like for a world to be destroyed, for it to lose not only its physical infrastructure and living traditions but its very concepts. In such a situation, the self-understandings of the culture and the basic rhythms of its existence are rendered unintelligible, incomprehensible, to its members. This is a world in which meaning has been erased. Most instances of world taking are not as complete as this, but they nevertheless involve displacement, rupture, and disorientation. The *degree* to which worlds are transformed when taken is an empirical one, open to historical investigation and disputation. Think, for example, of the long-standing dispute over the extent to which British imperialism either aimed to, or succeeded in, fundamentally transforming Indian worlds.[28] Scholars themselves are world makers, narrating descriptions and crafting stories that can sometimes (re)orient the beliefs and attitudes of others.

Intellectual historians have typically concentrated on interpreting texts. Another productive topic to investigate is how world makers themselves are made. The anthropologist Hugh Gusterson, for example, studied the construction of the worlds of nuclear weapons scientists, people who work on technologies capable of annihilating our species.[29] The modern human sciences also offer a productive site for investigating the construction of world makers. Exploring what we might term "technologies of the scholarly self" would look at the kinds of activities that individuals undertake to become scholars of a particular stripe: game theorists, postcolonial critics, Marxists, Straussians, and so forth. One entry point is through studying the construction of varied intellectual "personae." Ian Hunter argues that thinking is constituted by "ensembles of cognitive and ethical arts maintained in particular institutional settings."[30] Scholarly performance, in this view, is an assemblage of "logico-rhetorical methods, cognitive techniques, and ethical exercises" that draw on "a repertory of *techne* and practices—timetables, architectures and spatial organizations, practices of meditation and self-scrutiny, skeptical exercises of various kinds, and a whole variety of discursive rhetorics—whose mode of existence is that of the historically instituted arts of the self." Through pedagogical and training routines, individuals of a specific kind are created and maintained. Scholarly practices thus express, even require, "an array of acts of inner self-transformation, of work on the self by the self, aimed at forming personae suited to an open-ended variety of ethical aspirations, "psychological" deportments, cognitive dispositions, public duties, and private desires."[31] This is a form of "spirituality." To become a scholar of a particular type—or to become a nuclear weapons engineer, for that matter—requires various acts of self-discipline, monitoring, habituation, and cognitive transformation.

Thus far I have argued that the human sciences—or at least parts of them, including intellectual history—can be perspicuously redescribed as disciplines focused on the study of world-making practices. (This is, of course, itself an attempt at world making.) There are several reasons for doing so. Perhaps the most significant is to help dissolve disciplinary boundaries, to highlight the potential similarities across different domains and scales of human activity. This includes a challenge to the arbitrary boundaries often drawn between intellectual history and other forms of history writing, or between history and other human sciences.[32] All of them concentrate on the way in which human actions, beliefs, and intentions fabricate the very worlds in which we live and between which we move. Intellectual historians are world makers, then, conjuring up forgotten worlds and, at their most successful, helping audiences see things afresh, make connections and juxtapositions that alter fields of vision.

Histories of the Global

In the remainder of this chapter I discuss three different topics that exemplify my claims about the character of world making. The first outlines how shifting conceptions of time and space transformed perceptions of political feasibility in nineteenth-century Britain and the United States. The second extends my earlier discussion of the world-making functions of theoretical discourse in the human sciences. Finally, I examine how images of the planet itself can figure in making worlds. These examples reflect my own research interests; they do no more than highlight some of the many ways in which scholars can explore world-making practices. Moreover, they draw on materials from *within* the Euro-Atlantic intellectual milieu, for, as I contend, global intellectual history is capable of being pursued wherever certain kinds of ambitious world-making projects are found.

The nineteenth century witnessed a revolution in conceptions of time and space that in turn fundamentally altered practices of world making. Emphasizing the accelerating expansion of global capitalism, David Harvey observed that 1848 should be regarded as the key moment in this epochal transition.[33] Yet this misses the point that during the nineteenth century, there were two distinct episodes of time-space compression, one in the 1830s and 1840s and the other in the 1860s and 1870s. Both followed the introduction of new transport and communications technologies. In the first instance, the spread of railways revolutionized the geographical imagination of Europe, shattering previous understandings of distance, speed, and national geography. It also popularized a vocabulary for capturing this shift: "the annihilation of space through time" was a widespread phrase from the 1840s onward. Commenting on the opening of a rail link between Paris and Rouen in 1843, the poet Heinrich Heine proclaimed that the "elementary concepts of time and space have begun to vacillate. Space is killed by the railways, and we are left with time alone." This was, he contended, a "providential event."[34] But it was only during the closing four decades of the century that the intellectual elites of the Atlantic world saw the globe itself shrink; space and time were "annihilated" on a planetary scale. The shift was catalyzed above all by the introduction of the electrical telegraph. From the 1860s onward, new communications technologies radically altered the way in which individuals perceived the physical world and its sociopolitical possibilities, spawning fantasies about eliminating geographical distance that prefigure late-twentieth-century narratives of globalization. Writing at the turn of the twentieth century, H. G. Wells declared that "modern mechanism" had created "an absolute release from the fixed conditions about which human affairs circled."[35]

Hubristic interpretations of technological change restructured intellectual horizons—remaking the kinds of (political) worlds that agents considered both plausible and desirable. This cognitive shift inaugurated a new imaginative regime of global governance. It was the condition of possibility for the emergence of widespread debates, beginning in the 1870s, over the unification of the British colonial empire—the attempt to create a planet-straddling Anglo-racial polity encompassing Britain, Canada, Australia, New Zealand, and South Africa.[36] From the turn of the century, this intersected with an embryonic discourse about the possibilities for an Anglo-American (re)union. These projects for Anglo-racial dominance resonated throughout the twentieth century.[37] While arguments for colonial union had circulated throughout the eighteenth and nineteenth centuries, they were typically dismissed as utopian dreams, blind to the impossibility of governance over vast geographical spaces. For Edmund Burke, natural boundaries were fixed for eternity: "*Opposuit natura*—I cannot remove the barriers of the creation."[38] In the early 1860s, John Stuart Mill reiterated the argument: "Countries separated by half the globe do not present the natural conditions for being under one government, or even members of one federation."[39] Yet in the closing decades of the nineteenth century, this argument lost its force: the barriers were removed, and the natural conditions transfigured. Technological developments, so it was claimed, had defeated nature itself.

Advocates of a globe-spanning British community argued that conventional understandings of the relationship between geography and political temporality were obsolete. For W. E. Forster, a leading liberal politician and imperial federalist, technology heralded the ability to create a gigantic, ominicompetent, British polity:

> The inventions of science have overcome the great difficulties of time and space which were thought to make separation almost a necessity, and we now feel that we can look forward, not to the isolated independence of England's children, but to their being united to one another with the mother country, in a permanent family union.[40]

J. R. Seeley, the leading ideologue of imperial unity, proclaimed that he was living in an age "when inventions have drawn the whole globe close together," and as such, it was possible to "realise the old Utopia" of a unified Greater Britain.[41] This community was often conceptualized as a transoceanic British nation-state—a racial-political whole bound by a strong sense of identity and belonging—and it implied a novel articulation of a spatially diffuse "translocal" public sphere.[42] But this was not only a moment of radical possibility, for the shrinking of the world heralded danger. The "same inventions which make vast political unions possible," Seeley warned, "tend to make states which are on the old scale of magnitude unsafe, insignificant, second-rate."[43] As distance dissolved, time accelerated, and the European powers and then America embarked on a frenzy of imperial conquest, the world seemed to become a more hazardous place. It was this freighted spatial imaginary that underpinned the emergence of geopolitical discourse at the turn of the century, linking Frederick Jackson Turner's frontier thesis with Halford Mackinder's fear of global congestion. As Mackinder warned in "The Geographical Pivot of History," the four-hundred-year "Columbian period" of Western expansion had come to an end; the world was now "closed."[44] Compression, acceleration, annihilation, closure: these were the spatio-temporal coordinates of Euro-American modernity.

While this discourse was racially delimited—centering on the creation of an Anglo-dominated world—it was explicitly universalist in its implications. It sought to make the world anew. Indeed, aspects of the fin-de-siècle discourse on Anglo unification can be seen as an articulation of utopian desire.[45] The utopianism resided in the belief that if the United States and Greater Britain were properly aligned, the

"Anglo-Saxon race" would help bring peace, order, and justice to the earth. Andrew Carnegie maintained that the "new nation would dominate the world and banish from the earth its greatest stain—the murder of men by men." Cecil Rhodes contended that "if we had not lost America, or even if now we could arrange with the present members of the United States Assembly and our House of Commons, the peace of the world is secured for all eternity!" He predicted that if the British Empire and the United States were (re)combined, "universal peace" would be secured within a century. W. T. Stead, a pioneering radical journalist, was adamant that "war would by degree die out from the face of the earth."[46] In Reinhart Koselleck's terms, this was a species of "temporalized" utopianism.[47]

Another opportunity for studying sophisticated practices of world making is the production of "theory" itself. Theoretical models construct worlds, and those worlds sometimes have performative effects in reshaping human practices.[48] Ian Hunter applied his historicization of "thinking" to both early modern philosophy and "Theory" in the postwar American humanities academy. For Hunter, "Theory" is not best defined by a canon of thinkers or a shared conceptual language but by a deportment, a set of dispositions—"sustained by a certain inner discipline"—and, above all, by skepticism about empirical experience and various a priori formalisms. This is illustrated nicely by Bruno Latour's sardonic observation that in the United States,

> entire PhD programs are still running to make sure that good American kids are learning the hard way that facts are made up, that there is no such thing as natural, unmediated, unbiased access to the truth, that we are always prisoners of language, that we always speak from a particular standpoint, and so on.[49]

This is world making in action. The reshaping of scholarly disciplines produced a new range of personae in the late twentieth century, and the "degree to which this philosophical ascesis goes to work on the field of empirical disciplines—transforming them into structures of transcendental possibility, problematizing their claustral character in relation to being, promising to cultivate a new kind of openness—is itself a matter for historical investigation."[50] To the horror of Frederic

Jameson, among others, Hunter concludes his act of historicization by arguing that "Theory" in the contemporary university is the unwitting heir of early modern German Protestant metaphysics.[51]

Many of the most important developments in the postwar social sciences—the age of what we might call "big social science"[52]—are transversal phenomena, crisscrossing and helping (re)constitute various disciplines and fields.[53] Moreover, theoretical constructs, even of the most abstruse kind, are not "cameras" passively recording an external reality but "engines" actively engaged in world making.[54] They can have significant performative effects. Two brief examples illustrate the point: modernization theory and neoliberalism. Synthesizing a variety of different scholarly discourses, modernization theory was one of the polestars of social science during the 1960s and 1970s, its proponents seeking to identify the developmental trajectories along which "traditional" societies should travel to reach the promised land of modernity. They stood as heirs to the generations of European thinkers who had constructed accounts of the normative superiority of the "civilized," who had made worlds whose basic ontological unit was race. Modernization ideas shaped attitudes toward what used to be called the "Third World," as well as political-military strategy in Vietnam and beyond, and it continues to play a subterranean role in contemporary debates about "development."[55] Focusing on a number of different knowledge complexes, including the famed Department of Social Relations at Harvard, MIT's Center for International Studies, and the Social Science Research Council's Committee on Comparative Politics, scholars have tracked the development of modernization theory, its ideological functions, and the multiple interconnections between academic research and government.[56] Much more work remains to be done on big social science as an engine for the production of worlds.

Neoliberalism has been poorly served by intellectual historians.[57] Developed in the late 1940s, through, among other things, the Free Market Project of the University of Chicago Law School (1946) and the Mont Pelerin Society, neoliberalism rose to prominence in the 1970s and has shaped much of the global economic architecture and practices of state governance since.[58] Neoliberalism is a world-making project in at least two senses. First, the kind of world that it conceptualizes and helped disseminate is one of radical atomism, of (all) humans modeled as rational utility maximizers, and of communities as mere aggregates of deracinated individual choosers. Here *homo economicus* is a universal specimen, stripped of culture, place, and history.[59] While articulating a reductive, dehumanizing social ontology, neoliberalism also instantiates its own epistemological regime, one in which positivist science (institutionalized in neoclassical economics) could provide fruitful theoretical models and, above all, predictive capacity regarding the social world.[60] But it is world making in another sense, in that it is an explicit political project supported by powerful social actors. From its heartlands in the Anglo-American core, neoliberalism has been globalized, often by those trained in the leading U.S. universities, perhaps most (in)famously Augusto Pinochet's "Chicago Boys."[61] Today we all live with the disastrous consequences of this flourishing world-making project.

My final example is representations of the planet itself. The analysis of the many ways in which people have conceived of the totality of the planet offers insights into a host of issues in political thought and intellectual history. Speculative representations of the globe can be traced back to the dawn of Western intellectual history, and they have played a formative role in underpinning assorted spiritual, cosmological, and political projects, from ancient empire building to the contemporary environmental movement. The globe, after all, is apprehended only through its representation, and "representations have agency in shaping understanding and further action in the world."[62] Such studies need not exhibit the modernist bias identified by Moyn and Sartori. Indeed, according to Denis Cosgrove, the preeminent scholar of European representations of the globe, the major imaginative revolution took place in the sixteenth century, as explorers and empire builders mapped and discovered regions previously unknown to them.[63] Yet owing to the development of innovative technologies, a new range of visual practices came to the fore in the last two hundred years. The globe played a formative role in various aspects of nineteenth-century culture, and from then into our own time, images of the planet have served "as the icon for the interrelated processes of connection, communication and control that characterize modernity."[64] Such planetary imaginings fed into imperialist ideologies in assorted ways.[65] The twentieth century was a time of planetary dreaming, the iconology of the earth penetrating ever more deeply into social consciousness. Flight—the dream of humanity for thousands of years—unleashed visions of transcendence and fantasies of a technocratic future.[66] It was fundamental to the geopolitics of the age, a reference point for envisaging global power in its manifold forms:[67]

> Rhetorics of world empire, geopolitics, the airman's vision, universal brotherhood, one world, whole earth, and globalism shaped planetary social discourse in the twentieth century as the inheritance of the Enlightenment and modernity, while as a new millennium opens, the poetics and politics of the globe emphasize fracture, difference, and locality, individuating human dignity and rights of embodied men and women.[68]

The globe gave way to the cosmos. A time of intense utopian speculation, the middle of the twentieth century saw the emergence of an "astrofuturist" discourse, straddling hard science and speculative fiction in which humanity escapes the bounds of the earth and sets out for the stars—a new frontier to colonize and control.[69] The apotheosis of such dreaming could be found in the geopolitical competition between the United States and the Soviet Union to land on the moon. The ensuing space race produced millions of images, a combination of the sublime and the banal, the most celebrated of which was "Earthrise," captured by Apollo 8 astronaut Bill Anders in 1968. It is now the most reproduced image in history.[70] This was a defining cultural moment: the photographs exerted a mesmeric power, their impact rippling out through culture, high and low, helping fuel competing dreams and desires. The space race produced, William Connolly writes, a "new perspective on the world enabled by speed. We have still not plumbed the limit of its effects."[71] The dominant mood was one of optimism.

The dream of one-worldism was captured in words by the American poet Archibald MacLeish, in the most famous literary meditation on the Earthrise photographs:

> The medieval notion of the earth put man at the center of everything. The nuclear notion of the earth put him nowhere—beyond

the range of reason even—lost in absurdity and war. This latest notion may have other consequences. Formed as it was in the minds of heroic voyagers who were also men, it may remake our image of mankind. No longer that preposterous figure at the center, no longer that degraded and degrading victim off at the margins of reality and blind with blood, man may at last become himself. To see the earth as it truly is, small and blue and beautiful in that eternal silence where it floats, is to see ourselves as riders on the earth together, brothers on that bright loveliness in the eternal cold—brothers who know now they are truly brothers.[72]

Benjamin Lazier outlined some of the philosophical, cultural, and political repercussions of the new imagery of earth, highlighting how, in the "Earthrise era," we witness the vertiginous clash of competing globalisms, of alternative visions of the relationship of humanity, nature, space and place. "Within the span of a decade, something had changed—evident both in philosophical reflection and in Western culture writ large. The "Earthrise era had begun. In some ways, it is also our own." Images of the globe are pervasive, the consequences profound:

> There now holds sway a world picture in which the condition of "earthliness" is conjured by way of a view from the most unearthly of places—the void; in which the horizons of earthbound experience compete with horizons that are planetary, or capital-E Earthly, in scope; and in which the vision of the naked Earth is also the view of a globe in disguise, the greatest of organisms a man-made planet. Thinking globally is probably now less our choice than our lot.[73]

Although many commentators welcomed the new era, others feared its repercussions. Focusing in particular on the writings of Hannah Arendt, Martin Heidegger, and Hans Blumenberg, Lazier traces the emergence of profound anxieties about the technological conquest of space and its implications for the human condition. Viewing it as the symptom of a deeper malaise, Arendt and Heidegger feared that human capacities for being at home in the world were threatened by the encroachment of technology and that the visual impact of the impersonality of the world-as-planet would reinforce this long-standing process.[74] Indeed for Arendt, space travel was nothing less than a "rebellion against human existence."[75]

Anxieties about extraplanetary travel also found other intellectual outlets. The visionary British writer J. G. Ballard, for example, saw the quest to conquer space as having the potential to unsettle human consciousness in perplexing ways. Just look, he instructed, at what happened to so many of the returning astronauts, their inward journeys into mysticism, addiction, reclusiveness. His short stories are populated by the abandoned infrastructure of space exploration—"the launching towers rose into the sky like the rusting ciphers of some forgotten algebra"—and by dead astronauts circling the earth for eternity, an admonition to humanity etched in the sky.[76] Mixing surrealism, pop art motifs, psychoanalysis, and incisive examination of the modern mediascape, at one point Ballard suggests that humanity is not yet capable of transcending its habitat, that in attempting to do so we betray our evolutionary limitations, even our destiny: "Could it be that travelling into outer space, even thinking and watching it on television, was a forced evolutionary step with unforeseen consequences, the eating of a very special forbidden fruit?"[77] In tune with the phenomenological pessimism of Heidegger and Arendt, this is space less as a heroic frontier than as a fatal temptation, the spectral shadow of Cold War triumphalism and utopian fantasies about the world-transformative power of technology.

Blumenberg, however, demurred from this dark rendering of modernity. He felt that the magnificent revelation of a world suspended in space would help reconcile us to the earth, to cherish it. The sight produced "a felt experience of a planet *so eccentric, so exceptional,* that it became the only thing worth attending to in the first place."[78] In an ironic reversal, and much to the dismay of the astrofuturists, the cosmos gave way to the earth. "The space programme, which was meant to show mankind that its home was its cradle, ended up showing that its cradle was its only home. It was the defining moment of the twentieth century."[79] Its effects continue to reverberate, its imagery helping reconstitute the world picture. "The sedimentation of Whole Earth and its progeny into the mental architecture of the West means that for the foreseeable future, environment will be inflected by planet, cityscape by globe, and skyline by space—not the "space of experience" but the void."[80] In one form or another, globalization is a very old phenomenon, but much of its current imaginative vocabulary and iconic power is a product of recent decades. As Denis Cosgrove notes, "Whether pictured as a networked sphere of accelerating circulation or as an abused and over-exploited body, it is from images of the spherical earth that ideas of globalization draw their expressive and political force."[81] Among other things, they opened the way to the proliferation of "global" as an adjective and to the imaginative geography of globalization itself, the very things that stand behind the ambition to create the field of global intellectual history.

Conclusion

Discussing the prospects for a global history of political thought, David Armitage observes that "quite what such a [history] will look like, or even what its subject-matter will be, is still far from clear. What is certain is that the possibilities for such a global history—or even for multiple histories under this rubric—remain enticingly open-ended."[82] Global intellectual history faces a similarly open-ended future. The "global" turn in historical research, and more generally across the human sciences, presents both a range of exciting opportunities and a set of theoretical and methodological conundrums. In this chapter, I have reflected on a couple of these, arguing that many of the different intellectual practices traveling under the sign of the "global" are probably better characterized in other ways—as transnational, translocal, or regional. If we are to use the label "global" at all, I have outlined an argument—in skeletal rather than comprehensive form—suggesting that it is best reserved for a class of world-making practices that articulate forms of universality.

Notes

I would like to thank the following people for reading the draft of this chapter and/or for illuminating discussions about the topic: David Armitage, Ze'ev Emmerich, Ian Hunter, Sarah Fine, Joel Isaac, Duncan Kelly, Benjamin Lazier, Samuel Moyn, and Andrew Sartori. All the usual disclaimers apply.

1. See, for example, Fred Dallmayr, *Comparative Political Theory: An Introduction* (Basingstoke: Palgrave, 2010); Andrew F. March, "What Is Comparative Political Theory?" *Review of Politics* 71, no. 4 (2009): 531–65; Christopher Goto-Jones, "Comparative Political Thought: Beyond the Non-Western" in *Ethics and World Politics*, ed. Duncan Bell (Oxford: Oxford University Press, 2010), 219–38.

2. Samuel Moyn and Andrew Sartori, "Approaches to Global Intellectual History" (chap. 1, this volume).

3. See also David Armitage, "The International Turn in Intellectual History," in *Rethinking Modern European Intellectual History for the Twenty-First Century*, ed. Darrin McMahon and Samuel Moyn (Oxford: Oxford University Press, forthcoming). American intellectual history is a partial exception to this norm, although a number of important works do embrace transnational perspectives. See, for example, James Kloppenberg, *Uncertain Victory: Social Democracy and Progressivism in European and American Thought, 1870–1920* (Oxford: Oxford University Press, 1988); Marc Stears, *Progressives, Pluralists, and the Problems of the State: Ideologies of Reform in the United States and Britain, 1906–26* (Oxford: Oxford University Press, 2002); Daniel T. Rodgers, *Atlantic Crossings: Social Politics in a Progressive Age* (Cambridge, Mass.: Harvard University Press, 1998).

4. The "West" is, of course, a highly problematic concept, but this helps reinforce my argument. The category should be an object of analysis—the focus of genealogies—not a spatial frame for demarcating it.

5. Bernard Bailyn, *The Ideological Origins of the American Revolution* (Cambridge, Mass.: Harvard University Press, 1967); J. G. A. Pocock, *The Machiavellian Moment: Florentine Political Thought and the Atlantic Republican Tradition* (Princeton, N.J.: Princeton University Press, 1975); Eric Stokes, *The English Utilitarians and India* (Oxford: Clarendon, 1959).

6. Arif Dirlik, "Performing the World: Reality and Representation in the Making of World Histor(ies)," *Journal of World History* 16, no. 4 (2005): 406.

7. Moyn and Sartori, "Approaches to Global Intellectual History" (chap. 1, this volume).

8. The *Oxford English Dictionary* provides several definitions of "global," including "(a) Relating to or encompassing the whole of anything or any group of things, categories, etc.; comprehensive, universal, total, overall. (b) Of, relating to, or involving the whole world, worldwide; (also in later use) of or relating to the world considered in a planetary context." I take the global in GIH to refer principally to (a), with (b) an important subset.

9. Lydia Liu, *The Clash of Empires: The Invention of China in Modern World Making* (Cambridge, Mass.: Harvard University Press, 2004), is a fascinating account of the role of semiotics in making worlds, but it does not draw on Nelson Goodman's work.

10. Ian Hacking, *The Social Construction of What?* (Cambridge, Mass.: Harvard University Press, 1999), 48–49.
11. Nelson Goodman, *Ways of Worldmaking* (New York: Hackett, 1978), 1.
12. Hacking, *Social Construction of What?* 47.
13. Ian Hacking, *Historical Ontology* (Cambridge, Mass.: Harvard University Press, 2002), 9, 8.
14. Irrealism is "not realism, not anti-realism, but an intellectual indifference to such questions, which is in itself a metaphysical stance." Hacking, *Social Construction of What?* 61.
15. Goodman, *Ways of Worldmaking*, 3, 20.
16. Nelson Goodman, "Realism, Relativism, and Reality," *New Literary History* 14, no. 2 (1983): 269.
17. Goodman, *Ways of Worldmaking*, x.
18. According to Nelson Goodman, "On Starmaking," in *Starmaking: Realism, Anti-Realism, and Irrealism*, ed. Peter McCormick (Cambridge, Mass.: MIT Press, 1996), 144:

    I maintain that many world versions—some conflicting with each other, some so disparate that conflict or compatibility between them is interminable—are equally right. Nevertheless, right versions are different from wrong versions; relativism is restrained by considerations of rightness. Rightness, however, is neither constituted nor tested by correspondence with a world independent of all versions.

19. Bruce Kuklick, *A History of Philosophy in America, 1720–2000* (Oxford: Oxford University Press, 2003), 250–51. For technical details, see Daniel Cohnitz and Marcus Rossberg, *Nelson Goodman* (London: Acumen, 2006), esp. chaps. 1, 7, 8. For critiques of Goodman from staunchly realist perspectives, see Paul Boghossian, *Fear of Knowledge: Against Relativism and Constructivism* (Oxford: Oxford University Press, 2006), 32–35; John Searle, *The Construction of Social Reality* (London: Penguin, 1995): "Contrary to Goodman, we do not make 'worlds'; we make *descriptions* that the actual world may fit or fail to fit" (166).
20. See McCormick, ed., *Starmaking*; Damian Cox, "Goodman and Putnam on the Making of Worlds," *Erkenntnis* 58, no. 1 (2003): 33–46; Robert Schwarz, "I'm Going to Make You a Star," *Midwest Studies in Philosophy* 11, no. 1 (1986): 429.
21. Goodman, "On Starmaking," 145.
22. Mary Douglas and David Hull, introduction to *How Classification Works: Nelson Goodman Among the Social Sciences*, ed. Mary Douglas and David Hull (Edinburgh: Edinburgh University Press, 1992), 11; Hacking, *Social Construction of What?* 47; W. T. J. Mitchell, "Realism, Irrealism, and Ideology: A Critique of Nelson Goodman," *Journal of Aesthetic Education* 25, no. 1 (1991): 23–35. But compare Catherine Elgin, "What Goodman Leaves

Out," *Journal of Aesthetic Education* 25, no. 1 (1991): 89–96, replying to Mitchell.

23. Jerome Bruner, "Self-Making and World-Making," *Journal of Aesthetic Education* 25, no. 1 (1991): 67–78; Mary Douglas, "Rightness of Categories," in *How Classification Works: Nelson Goodman Among the Social Sciences*, ed. Mary Douglas and David Hull (Edinburgh: Edinburgh University Press, 1992), 239–72; Clifford Geertz, "The World in Pieces: Culture and Politics at the End of the Century," in *Available Light: Anthropological Reflections on Philosophical Topics* (Princeton, N.J.: Princeton University Press, 2000), 211; Clifford Geertz, "Notes on the Balinese Cockfight," in *The Interpretation of Cultures* (New York: Vintage Books, 1973), 447–48, 451; Clifford Geertz, "Local Knowledge: Fact and Law in Comparative Perspective," in *Local Knowledge: Further Essays in Interpretative Anthropology* (London: Fontana, 1983), 180–81, 184.

24. Geertz, "World in Pieces," 211.

25. Joanna Overing, "The Shaman as a Maker of Worlds: Nelson Goodman in the Amazon," *Man* 25, no. 4 (1990): 618.

26. Jonathan Lear, *Radical Hope: Ethics in the Face of Cultural Devastation* (Cambridge, Mass.: Harvard University Press, 2006). See also Cora Diamond, "Losing Your Concepts," *Ethics* 98, no. 2 (1988): 255–77.

27. Lear, *Radical Hope*, 2.

28. William R. Pinch, "Same Difference in India and Europe," *History and Theory* 38, no. 3 (1999): 389–407.

29. Hugh Gusterson, *Nuclear Rites: A Weapons Laboratory at the End of the Cold War* (Berkeley: University of California Press, 1998). See also Carol Cohn, "Sex and Death in the Rational World of Defense Intellectuals," *Signs* 12, no. 4 (1987): 867–718; Sharon Ghamari-Tabrizi, *The Worlds of Herman Kahn: The Intuitive Science of Thermonuclear War* (Cambridge, Mass.: Harvard University Press, 2005).

30. Ian Hunter, "The Persona of the Philosopher and the History of Modern Philosophy," *Modern Intellectual History* 4, no. 3 (2007): 574.

31. Ibid., 574; Ian Hunter, "Talking About My Generation," *Critical Inquiry* 34, no. 3 (2008): 586.

32. In *"The Logic of the History of Ideas—Then and Now," Intellectual History Review* 21, no. 1 (2011): 105, Mark Bevir makes a very strong version of the argument:

> Intellectual history is not just a sub-field of history. Intellectual history is the basis of all the human sciences. Properly to understand social life just is to refer to the intentionality of the relevant actors. Properly to explain intentionality just is to place it in the relevant historical context. Thus, all the human sciences necessarily depend on intellectual history.

33. David Harvey, *The Condition of Postmodernity* (Oxford: Blackwell, 1989), 241, 252, 261, 264.

34. Quoted in Wolfgang Schivelbusch, *The Railway Journey* (Berkeley: University of California Press, 1986), 37. On the dating of "time and space," see Michael Freeman, *Railways and the Victorian Imagination* (New Haven, Conn.: Yale University Press, 1999), 21, 150–171.

35. H. G. Wells, *Anticipations of the Reaction of Mechanical and Scientific Progress upon Human Life and Thought* (1902; repr., Mineola, N.Y.: Dover, 1999), 38, 44. In general, see Stephen Kern, *The Culture of Time and Space, 1880–1918* (Cambridge, Mass.: Harvard University Press, 1984).

36. Duncan Bell, *The Idea of Greater Britain: Empire and the Future of World Order, 1860–1900* (Princeton, N.J.: Princeton University Press, 2007).

37. Duncan Bell, "The Project for a New Anglo Century: Race, Space and Global Order," in *Anglo-America and Its Discontents: Civilizational Politics Beyond East and West*, ed. Peter Katzenstein (London: Routledge, 2012), 33–56.

38. Edmund Burke, "Speech on Conciliation with America" (March 22, 1775), in *The Writings and Speeches of Edmund Burke*, ed. W. Elofson with John Woods (Oxford: Oxford University Press, 1996), 3:152.

39. John Stuart Mill, *Considerations on Representative Government* (1861), in *Utilitarianism, Liberty, and Representative Government*, ed. A. D. Lindsay (London, 1910), 379.

40. W. E. Forster, comments made in *Imperial Federation* (London, 1884), 27.

41. J. R. Seeley, *The Expansion of England: Two Courses of Lectures* (London: Macmillan, 1883), 288, 74.

42. See Duncan Bell, "Imagined Spaces: Nation, State, and Territory in the British Colonial Empire, 1860–1914," in *The Primacy of Foreign Policy in British History, 1660–2000*, ed. William Mulligan and Brendan Simms (Basingstoke: Palgrave, 2011), 197–214.

43. Seeley, *Expansion of England*, 75.

44. Halford Mackinder, "The Geographical Pivot of History," *Geographical Journal* 23, no. 4 (1904): 421–37. See also Gerry Kearns, "Fin de Siècle Geopolitics: Mackinder, Hobson and Theories of Global Closure," in *Political Geography of the Twentieth Century: A Global Analysis*, ed. Peter Taylor (London: Belhaven, 1993), 9–25.

45. Duncan Bell, "Dreaming the Future: Anglo-America as Utopia, 1880–1914," in *The American Experiment and the Idea of Democracy in British Culture, 1776–1914*, ed. Ella Dzelzainis and Ruth Livesey (Aldershot: Ashgate, forthcoming).

46. W. T. Stead, ed., *The Last Will and Testament of Cecil J. Rhodes* (London: Review of Reviews, 1902), 73, 66; W. T. Stead, *The Americanization of the World: Or the Trend of the Twentieth Century* (New York: Horace Markley, 1902), 435.

47. Reinhart Koselleck, "The Temporalization of Utopia," in *The Practice of Conceptual History: Timing History, Spacing Concepts*, trans. Todd Presener et al. (Stanford, Calif.: Stanford University Press, 2002), 84–100.

48. The following paragraphs draw on Duncan Bell, "Writing the World: Disciplinary History and Beyond," *International Affairs* 85, no. 1 (2009): 3–22.

49. Bruno Latour, "Why Has Critique Run Out of Steam? From Matters of Fact to Matters of Concern," *Critical Inquiry* 30, no. 3 (2004): 227.

50. Ian Hunter, "The History of Theory," *Critical Inquiry* 33, no. 1 (2006): 78, 112. Also on the history of "French Theory," see François Cusset, *French Theory: How Foucault, Derrida, Deleuze and Co. Transformed the Intellectual Life of the United States*, trans. Jeff Fort (Minneapolis: University of Minnesota Press, 2008).

51. See the exchange between Hunter and Jameson in *Critical Inquiry*, 34 , no. 3 (2008): 563–82.

52. Compare Peter Galison and Bruce Hevly, eds., *Big Science: The Growth of Large-Scale Research* (Stanford, Calif.: Stanford University Press, 1992).

53. See, for example, Joel Isaac, *Working Knowledge: The Human Sciences from Talcott Parsons to Thomas Kuhn* (Cambridge, Mass.: Harvard University Press, 2012). See also Joel Isaac, "Tangled Loops: Theory, History, and the Human Sciences in Modern America," *Modern Intellectual History* 6, no. 2 (2009): 397–424.

54. Donald MacKenzie, *An Engine, Not a Camera: How Financial Models Shape Markets* (Cambridge, Mass.: MIT Press, 2006).

55. See, for example, the essays on "Modernizing Missions: Approaches to 'Developing' the Non-Western World After 1945," *Journal of Modern European History* 8, no. 1 (2010).

56. David Engerman, *Modernization from the Other Shore: American Intellectuals and the Romance of Russian Development* (Cambridge: Cambridge University Press, 2003); Nils Gilman, *Mandarins of the Future: Modernization Theory in Cold War America* (Baltimore: Johns Hopkins University Press, 2003); Michael Latham, *Modernization as Ideology: American Social Science and "Nation Building" in the Kennedy Era* (Chapel Hill: University of North Carolina Press, 2000).

57. With some exceptions: Philip Mirowski and Dieter Plehwe, eds., *The Road from Mont Pelerin: The Making of the Neoliberal Thought Collective* (Cambridge, Mass.: Harvard University Press, 2010); Ben Jackson, "At the Origins of Neo-liberalism: The Free Economy and the Strong State, 1930–47," *Historical Journal* 53, no. 1 (2010): 129–51; Michel Foucault, *The Birth of Biopolitics: Lectures from the Collège de France, 1978–79*, trans. Graham Burchell (Basingstoke: Palgrave, 2008).

58. For an account of how neoliberalism was supplanted in the 1980s by (equally pernicious) network-centric models of governance, see Mark Bevir, *Democratic Governance* (Princeton, N.J.: Princeton University Press, 2011).

59. For an excellent critique of rational choice models, see Michael Taylor, *Rationality and the Ideology of Disconnection* (Cambridge: Cambridge University Press, 2006).

60. The most influential elaboration of this epistemology is Milton Friedman, "The Methodology of Positive Economics," in *Essays in Positive Economics* (Chicago: University of Chicago Press, 1953), 3–43.

61. Juan Gabriel Valdés, *Pinochet's Economists: The Chicago School of Economics in Chile* (Cambridge: Cambridge University Press, 1995); Karin Fischer, "The Influence of Neoliberals in Chile Before, During, and After Pinochet," in *The Road from Mont Pelerin: The Making of the Neoliberal Thought Collective,* ed. Philip Mirowski and Dieter Plehwe (Cambridge, Mass.: Harvard University Press, 2010), 305–47.

62. Denis Cosgrove, *Apollo's Eye: A Cartographic Genealogy of the Earth in the Western Imagination* (Baltimore: John Hopkins University Press, 2001), x; see also Denis Cosgrove, *Geography and Vision: Seeing, Imagining and Representing the World* (London: I. B. Tauris, 2008).

63. Cosgrove, *Apollo's Eye*, chaps. 4–6. See also Jens Bartelson, *Visions of World Community* (Cambridge: Cambridge University Press, 2009), esp. chaps. 1–3.

64. Cosgrove, *Apollo's Eye*, 206, 225.

65. For Egyptian perspectives on the peculiarities of Western ways of world making, see Timothy Mitchell, "The World as Exhibition," *Comparative Studies in Society and History* 31, no. 2 (1989): 217–36.

66. Robert Wohl, *A Passion for Wings: Aviation and the Western Imagination, 1908–1918* (New Haven, Conn.: Yale University Press, 1996); Robert Wohl, *The Spectacle of Flight: Aviation and the Western Imagination, 1920–1950* (New Haven, Conn.: Yale University Press, 2007); Denis Cosgrove and William L. Fox, *Photography and Flight* (London: Reaktion, 2010).

67. Jenifer L. Van Vleck, "'The Logic of the Air': Aviation and the Globalism of the 'American Century,'" *New Global Studies* 1, no. 1 (2007): 1–37.

68. Cosgrove, *Apollo's Eye*, 235. On the trend for intellectual dissolution in late-twentieth-century U.S. cultural life, see Daniel T. Rodgers, *Age of Fracture* (Cambridge, Mass.: Harvard University Press, 2010).

69. De Witt Douglas Kilgore, *Astrofuturism: Science, Race, and Visions of Utopia in Space* (Philadelphia: University of Pennsylvania Press, 2003). This encompasses figures such as Wernher von Braun, Carl Sagan, Robert Heinlein, and Arthur C. Clarke.

70. Robert Poole, *Earthrise: How Man First Saw the Earth* (New Haven, Conn.: Yale University Press, 2008).

71. William Connolly, "Speed, Concentric Cultures and Cosmopolitanism," *Political Theory* 28, no. 5 (2000): 612.

72. Archibald MacLeish, "Riders on the Earth Together, Brothers in Eternal Cold" (1968), in *Riders on the Earth: Essays and Reflections* (Boston: Houghton Mifflin, 1978), 42. On its genesis and reception, see Poole, *Earthrise*, 8, 32–33, 35.

73. Benjamin Lazier, "Earthrise; or, the Globalization of the World Picture," *American Historical Review* 116, no. 3 (2011), 605, 609: "As a stand-in for the idea of the Whole Earth itself, it has acquired an iconic power that helps to organize a myriad of political, moral, scientific, and commercial imaginations as well." For another phenomenological account, see Joshua J. Yates, "Mapping the Good World: The New Cosmopolitans and Our Changing World Picture," *Hedgehog Review* 11, no. 3 (2009): 7–27.

74. Lazier, "Earthrise," esp. 609–14.

75. Hannah Arendt, "Man's Conquest of Space," *American Scholar* 32, no. 2 (1963): 527–40. See also the preface to Hannah Arendt, *The Human Condition*, 2nd ed. (Chicago: University of Chicago Press, 1998): "The Earth is the very quintessence of the human condition" (2).

76. J. G. Ballard, "The Dead Astronaut" (1968), in *The Complete Short Stories* (London: Flamingo, 2001), 760.

77. J. G. Ballard, "Myths of the Near Future," in *Memories of the Space Age* (London: Arkham, 1988), 173. Compare Umberto Rossi, "A Little Something About Dead Astronauts," *Science-Fiction Studies* 36, no. 1 (2009): 101–20.

78. Lazier, "Earthrise," 623, italics in original.

79. Poole, *Earthrise*, 199.

80. Lazier, "Earthrise," 627.

81. Cosgrove, *Apollo's Eye*, ix.

82. David Armitage, "Globalizing Bentham," *History of Political Thought* 32, no. 1 (2011): 64.

Part III

Concluding Reflections

12

How Global Do We Want
Our Intellectual History to Be?

FREDERICK COOPER

Samuel Moyn and Andrew Sartori have sufficient confidence in their way of doing global intellectual history to ask a known skeptic on the analytical usefulness of the concept of globalization to comment on their project.[1] I hope not to disappoint, in the sense of both underscoring the value of their effort to broaden the scope of intellectual history as commonly practiced and questioning the value added by the notion of "global." Their introduction and the design of their collection focus on the most difficult question: What does it mean for historians interested in intellectual life to go global? They are explicit about the diverse, even conflicting, meanings that such an endeavor could entail.

At one end of the spectrum is what we might call the "soft" version of the global: to get away from national, continental, and perhaps even temporal and cultural boundedness. Intellectual history has most often meant studying western European and North American subjects. While there are rich traditions of studying Chinese or Islamic "civilizations," such studies are often confined to East Asian or Middle Eastern studies. Intellectual history is usually the study of written—usually printed—texts, thereby excluding oral transmission by people who are trying to understand and explain their life worlds and who might well deserve the title of intellectual as much as do writers based in Paris or New York.[2] Europeans who wrote canonical texts on other peoples frequently drew on conversations with indigenous people who were intellectuals—thoughtful analyzers of social situations—in their own right, and in her chapter, Vanessa Smith points to the ambiguity of these important but asymmetrical relationships.

The case for intellectual historians to be more inclusive in the range of persons, texts, and interactions they consider is strong, and this volume does much to demonstrate how much can be learned from a more "global" approach. The key questions are how far the range should extend and the extent to which we can do more than throw more cases from more parts of the world into the intellectual stew. Moyn and Sartori and the contributors to this book take on the task of exploring the actual connections across space and, to a certain extent, across time.

But when we use the word "global," do we really mean "global," or do we mean "long-distance connections"? If we want to explore interconnected intellectual movements and traditions, why don't we call our endeavor "interconnected history" or "*histoire croisée*," as some French historians like to put it? What's at stake here may be a certain fussiness about literal meanings, but beyond that is the issue of what sorts of questions we want to encourage our students to ask. By stressing connections, we are calling attention to limits, to the specific pathways or circuits that people and ideas follow. The adjective "global" and the nouns "globalization" and "globality" all derive from a root that suggests that the unit we want to focus on is the entire planet.

That brings us to the other end of the spectrum, the "hard" version of the global.[3] Moyn and Sartori explicitly address this version. According to that conception, global intellectual history should center on ideas that truly encircle the world or that formulate propositions about the world as a whole. Moyn and Sartori frankly admit that the hard version of global intellectual history is "modernist," that it presumes a technology of communications extensive and dense enough to make global interconnection feasible. Sartori developed an illuminating study of Bengali intellectuals who think about liberalism and political economy generally in universalistic terms, in engagement with British thinkers, and he explains the resonance of their arguments by asserting that the development of commodity exchange forced intellectuals to come to grips with their insertion into worldwide structures of exchange, however complex the way that such structures affected economic life in any one space.

From this perspective, intellectual history was able to become global only after some point in the nineteenth century. What makes Sartori's argument plausible is that he can show his Bengali intellectuals—in books, tracts, and articles as well as in the way that lawyers frame issues in court cases—actually engaging with concepts of political economy employed elsewhere. But Sartori wants to explain something specific, what Bengali intellectuals say and write—by evoking something general: global commodification, as analyzed from a present-day, Marxist-inflected perspective. He recognizes that the conceptual apparatus of Bengali intellectuals reflects different influences and their own historical trajectories, and he argues that their engagement with liberalism and political economy produced complex reactions, including a defense of cultural particularity. But in his argument, the *causal* basis of the resonance that their intellectual position acquired can be understood only in relation to something worldwide: the extension of the commodity form.

This argument becomes more complicated if we see capitalism not just as commodification but also as relations of production, specifically in patterns of "primitive accumulation," the alienation of producers from the means of production and the consequent emergence of a class with nothing to sell but its labor power. This phenomenon is necessarily specific and cannot be reduced to a universal logic of capital, since it is the process by which capitalist relations of production are created. It depended (at least in Marx's analysis) on coercion, the naturalization of certain forms of property relations, the development of a framework of rule of law, and the ability of elites and the state to contain social tensions.[4] Can we generalize about the connection between globalist thinking and global capitalism when the actual experience of economic relations varies and when the representations of those relations in any given situation do not axiomatically follow from their supposedly intrinsic logic?[5] Perhaps Sartori's world is not as "global" as he would have it. And are there other ways in which thinkers and writers formulated notions of wide connectivity, maybe even wider, maybe older than those brought about by the broad but uneven spread of capitalist relations?

Sartori and Moyn are careful to set out multiple options for intellectual history and suggest the insights and occlusions that might result from each, but Duncan Bell goes further in contending that whatever we want to call those histories that stress the variety and interconnections of intellectual trends around the world, the notion of "global intellectual history" should be reserved for "world making," for those endeavors that fully envision a framework that embraces all of humanity.[6] His conception provides a coherent mission statement for *global* intellectual history, but does it represent a fruitful approach to *intellectual history*? I am skeptical. Much more interesting is to look at intellectuals as they are, working with multiple frameworks and reacting to arguments adjacent or opposed to their own. To isolate global intellectual history from intellectual histories of a regional, national, religious, or ethnic dimension—studying only unbounded connections but not the greater array of those that are border crossing but finite—is to define a field in artificial terms. Global intellectual history might give itself no other subject than global intellectual history.[7]

In between hard and soft versions of global intellectual history lie possibilities for expansive thinking. Sheldon Pollock's contribution is a case in point. His Sanskrit cosmopolitanism does not take in the entire world, nor does it apply to the majority of people living in the same space as the intellectuals with whom he is concerned, but he makes a strong case for an intellectual circuit of large proportions spreading across all of South Asia and, in a less integrated fashion, into Southeast Asia, crossing boundaries of political units and vernacular languages.[8] His argument has the virtue of escaping the modernist trap while following a methodology that applies across time, sensitive to both the limits of an intellectual circuit and its extent and the mechanisms by which it was produced.

Shouldn't we be thinking in similar terms about what came to be called Europe?[9] Why should the project of global intellectual history not make much of the spread of the Latin language under the Roman Empire, when poetry and history could be written across a vast space north, east, and south of the Mediterranean? This process led to the development of an intellectual culture in monasteries from Anatolia to Iberia, and it eventually produced a shared discourse of theology, philosophy, and literature that was spread by missionaries to many parts of the world.

The only other chapter in this volume that looks very far back in time is that by Siep Stuurman, who compares the treatment of the relationships between nomads and settlers by three writers who had no direct connection to one another: Herodotus, Sima Qian, and Ibn Khaldun. His chapter looks at intellectuals in different places and times trying to think through the significance of the "common humanity" they perceived across lines of cultural difference and political affinity, as well as confronting common problems that transcended particular intellectual and political frameworks.

Pollock's and Stuurman's chapters, along with the editors' introduction, go the furthest to offer an alternative to the overly fashionable concept of incommensurability.[10] Moyn and Sartori openly admit the difficulty of understanding how writing, ideas, and visions travel. Following Lydia Liu in noting the complexities of translation—emphasizing the inequality of power as much as the characteristics of the languages themselves—they point out that nevertheless translation continues. Most important, as Pollock's example of the formation of a Sanskrit-based elite culture in the empires of South Asia makes clear, the very units whose core constructs might be seen as incommensurable with others are themselves the products of interactions over time, of translations and mistranslations, imperious impositions, appropriations and reformulations. The histories of polities and peoples, in Africa and Asia as much as in Europe, are filled with earlier connections, earlier conversations, and earlier mutual influences, as well as earlier extensions of imperial power, with all the political and cultural asymmetry that this implies. In other words, commensurability has been with us for a long time, and the units in which intellectuals operated, in South Asia or elsewhere, should not be seen, as Pollock puts it, as a "history of emergence of primeval and natural communities."

What this book as a whole focuses on most intensely is a subset—an important subset, to be sure—of the complex and diverse engagement of African and Asian intellectuals with the cultural force of Europe. Janaki Bakhle, Jinny Prais and Mamadou Diouf, Cemil Aydin, and Christopher Hill all examine the long-distance connections of Indian, African, Ottoman, and Japanese intellectuals trying to come to grips with European colonization, by drawing on resources from creative reinterpretations of European sources, intellectual connections across the Atlantic, and a rethinking of connections among Muslims in different parts of the world.[11]

The people who are the subjects of these chapters are obsessed with Europe. Even J. E. Casely Hayford and W. E. B. DuBois felt they had to cite white people—Leo Froebenius and Franz Boas—to legitimate their defense of the black race. Young Ottomans saw themselves in relation to European constitutionalism, whereas British elites did not evaluate their position in relation to Ottoman ways of governing.

These chapters help us see that asymmetry in intellectual relationships is not the same as dichotomy and not the same as incommensurability. Instead, they are about intellectual engagement, about seeing what Africa has to say to the West as well as what the West has to say to Africa, about intellectuals confronting the threatening extension of European power by examining the different ways in which Europeans conceived of issues, arguing in terms that Europeans could understand and without giving up the belief that the Ottoman Empire should remain Ottoman and that African peoples should retain their integrity and independence. Hill describes this perspective particularly well in regard to how Japanese thinkers abstracted European concepts and gave them a "different breadth of application." He wants scholars to concentrate on the "historically specific process of universalization characterized by physical circulation, mediation, reproduction, and abstraction, in which many critical steps took place outside Europe."

It would be unfortunate if extending intellectual history in space meant, in practice, limiting it in time. We cannot fully gauge what is "new" in modes of thought and patterns of interaction if we presume, rather than analyze, the "old." Nor can we gauge the impact of European thinkers on framing problems of human commonality and forms of social and political life around the globe without looking at the expansion—and the limits of expansion—of other intellectual currents in space and time.

Take Cemil Aydin's notion of a "Muslim world." He makes a perfectly reasonable case that this is a nineteenth-century construct, a direct response to the challenges to the Ottoman Empire of the extension of European power. We can readily accept that Aydin's Muslim world is different from the *ummah* of earlier Muslim formulations, but our understanding of his Muslim world would be enriched by exploring its connections with and differences from other conceptions of Islamic affinities, how they spread in earlier times, and the limits of their inclusiveness.

Why should would-be global intellectual historians not put first and foremost the spread of Arabic learning, which by 711, less than eighty years after Muhammad's death—had reached the Iberian peninsula, produced a flowering of learning, and made Cordoba into a major center of intellectual life? We could say the same about the spread of Islamic learning to the East and explore the significance of Islamic learning in Persia and India, or, later, how Arabic and Persian scholarship and artistic traditions were spread in the thirteenth and fourteenth centuries by the great conquerors who came out of Mongolia and who, despite their own originally shamanistic religious tradition and nomadic, warrior ways, sponsored the development of centers of learning and the arts in places like Samarkand in the Eurasian steppes? Shouldn't we be following Zvi Ben-Dor Benite to look at the implanting of Arabic-language learning and Islamic communities in China, at great distance—culturally as well as geographically—from the place where Islamic scholarship began?[12] And shouldn't we acknowledge that the very European culture whose extension is associated with "globalization" owes much to the transmission, via centers of Islamic learning, of Hellenistic culture to western Europe? When we do so, we might note that translation issues are not specific to the forced imposition of Western intellectual norms but that the establishment of cultural traditions in what we call western Europe entailed translations from Greek into Arabic into Latin and then into vernacular languages.

The chapters in this book by Janaki Bakhle, Mamadou Diouf and Jinny Prais, Andrew Sartori, Cemil Aydin, Vanessa Smith, and Christopher Hill all focus on problems of empire. They show that coming to grips intellectually with the extension of state power across space, and combating it politically, also entailed connections across space.

In his chapter, Samuel Moyn makes the important point that some arguments resonate "in imperial spaces" but not at a global level. He is thinking about concepts of "rights": the argument that slavery in the colonies was a "stain on the British flag" is an example of a political discourse taking place in the framework of an empire. We can cite many more examples. In the sixteenth century, Bartolomé de las Casas vehemently criticized Spaniards' actions in regard to Native Americans, and he took seriously what he considered their civilizational attainments. His framework was the idea of "Catholic monarchy" that was fundamental to the ideology of imperial rule and whose principles he believed Spaniards were violating. From another angle, one might ask about Garcilaso de la Vega, the son of a conquistador and an Incan princess, who proudly proclaimed his *mestizo* origins and became the chronicler of the Incan Empire. Here were intellectuals operating in the space of empire, confronting people across that space with the power of their analyses, and influencing people in other empires (e.g., las Casas's works were translated into English).

Without being as explicit as Moyn, most of the chapters in this book confront the movement of ideas in empire space and in interempire space. Empires are big but finite, and thinking about their role in the movement of ideas and knowledge around the world is one way to avoid the problems of a too hasty leap to the "global." Empires imposed their linguistic hierarchies and, at times, fostered linguistic divisions among the people they governed: Africans rightly lament the enduring fissures wrought by the fragmentation of continental space (with its own linkages and fissures) into francophone, anglophone, and lusophone territories. Empires created networks of communication, which people in different parts of them both used and sought to transcend, so that both people and ideas crisscrossed and moved within empires.

Our concern with the social conditions for the development, diffusion, and reconfiguration of knowledge should not obscure the creativity that is part of intellectual life—the originality and profundity of reflections on the commonalities and differences in the human condition illustrated by Stuurman in the Greek, Chinese, and Islamic empires. Other examples of people working creatively in long-distance but bounded intellectual frameworks that are shaped but not determined by imperial cultural projects are Vukile Khumalo's study of late-nineteenth-century mission-educated Zulus who developed a culture of letter writing among themselves and sent petitions to Queen Victoria, or the work of other Africanists exploring people who used their mastery of a European language to put in writing the

oral traditions handed down over generations by their own intellectual ancestors.[13] Such people lived in many circuits—pan-African or
Islamic, cross empire as well as intraempire, mission based as well
as focused on professional networks of lawyers or journalists. The
chapters in this book touch on but do not fully elucidate the contested and uncertain discursive structures in a world of intersect-
ing empires, labeled (in ways that both illuminate and obscure their
dominant elements) British, French, Portuguese, Belgian, German,
Ottoman, Russian, and Japanese.

Did the world, over time, become more interconnected and hence
more amenable to analysis through the concept of the "global"?[14]
Empires produced both connections and fragmentation. Religious,
political, and other cross-empire networks—whatever forms of communication they used—also encouraged divisions in how people
thought as well as the linkages among them. That the technical means
of long-distance communication became more rapid and effective
over time is obvious, but more than the linear growth of connection,
what stands out, in the nineteenth century and today, is the uneven-
ness of those connections. Intellectual history does not need to be
attached to the view that we have been moving toward a world of ever
increasing flows. We may be writing about intellectuals who live in
Jakarta, Accra, Calcutta, São Paulo, and Los Angeles, not just London
and New York, but we need to ask whether we are still writing about
a few thousand people, linked with one another across great distances
but perhaps poorly connected to millions who live a few miles from
each of those centers and who do not speak the language of "global"
intellectual communication.[15] Whether we are thinking about imperial
spaces or the spaces of different cosmopolitanisms and cultural diasporas, the exploration of mechanisms of connection and their limitations opens up a wider and deeper field of inquiry than does the quest
for globality.

In the end, the question of whether the terms in which certain intellectuals operate is truly "universal" or truly "global" is not the most
revealing one historically. The more important problem is to figure
out what intellectuals' frameworks were, with their openings and clo-
sures, linkages, and dead ends. Unless we give more than a nod to the
plurality of universalisms, to the time depth of connections, and to the

ways in which different frameworks combine and conflict, we will be extending our twenty-first-century parochialism.

If we can avoid the linkage of "global" and "modern," we might have a better understanding of the limits of contemporary claims to the unbounded circulation of ideas. Even today, in the era of the cell phone, the Internet, and revolutions organized by Twitter, communications technology does as much to fragment as to tie peoples together. Accordingly, we should be asking who talks to whom and what they say, not presuming that even the most widespread and effective technology spreads a web of interaction or shared ways of thinking.

In short, the concepts of "global" and "modern" are two-edged swords when it comes to understanding the world. They are supposed to help us think. They also are straitjackets that, however much we seek them as antidotes to Eurocentric, teleological, nation-centered histories, push us into other sorts of confinements. The path to an intellectual history that takes in most of the world will lead us to a less-than-global intellectual history.

Notes

1. Frederick Cooper, "What Is the Concept of Globalization Good For? An African Historian's Perspective," *African Affairs* 100, no. 399 (2001): 189–213, reprinted in Frederick Cooper, *Colonialism in Question: Theory, Knowledge, History* (Berkeley: University of California Press, 2005).

2. For a more inclusive view of who is an intellectual, see Steven Feierman, *Peasant Intellectuals: Anthropology and History in Tanzania* (Madison: University of Wisconsin Press, 1990). Taking off from Valentin Mudimbe's argument that views of Africa have been shaped by the dominance of the "colonial library," Ousmane Kane argues for expanding the range, especially by including what he refers to as the "Islamic library" in Africa. Ousmane Kane, *Non-Europhone Intellectuals* (Dakar: CODESRIA, 2012), available at http://www.codesria.org/spip.php?article1651&lang=en (accessed August 17, 2012). See also Valentin Mudimbe, *The Invention of Africa: Gnosis, Philosophy, and the Order of Knowledge* (Bloomington: Indiana University Press, 1988); and Thandika Mkandawire, ed., *African Intellectuals: Rethinking Politics, Language, Gender and Development* (Dakar: CODESRIA/Zed, 2005).

3. The confusion between soft and hard definitions colors some historians' attempts to carve out a field of "global history" in a general sense. En route

in April 2011 to the Third European Congress on World and Global History in London, I was asked by a British customs official the purpose of my visit. When I replied "to attend a conference on global history," he asked, "What is the difference between global history and history?" I had no answer, but he let me in anyway. The working definitions at the conference ranged from anything that included two or more places to processes that covered the entire surface of the planet.

4. For a recent addition to the corpus of writing on the necessary role of the state—an imperial state, in fact—in making possible the development of industrial capitalism in Great Britain, see Prasannan Parthasarathi, *Why Europe Grew Rich and Asia Did Not: Global Economic Divergence, 1600–1850* (Cambridge: Cambridge University Press, 2011).

5. In addition to Andrew Sartori's chapter in this volume, see his *Bengal in Global Concept History: Culturalism in the Age of Capital* (Chicago: University of Chicago Press, 2008).

6. Duncan Bell's elaboration of an "Angloglobalization" takes on a current in British thinking in the late nineteenth and early twentieth century that postulated a Greater Britain spread around the world, but its "global" perspective was in fact a very white vision of empire and could not encompass even the majority of people living under the British flag. See also Daniel Gorman, *Imperial Citizenship: Empire and the Question of Belonging* (Manchester: Manchester University Press, 2010).

7. Samuel Moyn makes a similar point in chapter 8, calling for concepts that may be globalizing to be analyzed in relation to "larger actual and possible sets of alternative concepts" (201).

8. Sugata Bose and Kris Manjapra also make a case for multiple cosmopolitanisms in different historical periods. Sugata Bose and Kris Manjapra, eds., *Cosmopolitan Thought Zones: South Asia and the Global Circulation of Ideas* (Houndsmills: Palgrave Macmillan, 2010). In the introduction, Manjapra argues against contrasting a "singular dominant abstract universalism versus multiple minor culturally rooted particularisms" (3).

9. In chapter 3, Sheldon Pollock cites Hellenization, Indianization, Romanization, Sinicization, Christianization, Islamization, and Russification as "ways in the past of being translocal, of participating—and knowing one was participating—in political and cultural networks that transcended the immediate community" (59).

10. Dipesh Chakrabarty, *Provincializing Europe: Postcolonial Thought and Historical Difference* (Princeton, N.J.: Princeton University Press, 2000), 254. As Pollock points out, we need to analyze the construction of vernaculars as much as that of imperial languages. For another critique of the notion of incommensurability, see Seyla Benhabib, *The Claims of Culture: Equality and Diversity in the Global Era* (Princeton, N.J.: Princeton University Press, 2002), 30.

11. Vanessa Smith makes the connection in the opposite direction, bringing out the ambivalence of European explorers in relation to the "native intellectuals" they encountered overseas.

12. Zvi Ben-Dor Benite, *The Dao of Muhammad: A Cultural History of Muslims in Late Imperial China* (Cambridge, Mass.: Harvard University Asia Center, 2005).

13. Vukile Khumalo, "Epistolary Networks and the Politics of Cultural Production in KwaZulu-Natal, 1860 to 1910" (Ph.D. diss., University of Michigan, 2004).

14. To a large extent, globalization arguments replicate those about modernization, not least in the confusion, deliberate or otherwise, of normative and descriptive elements. As advocates of opening the world to the free flow of capital, technology, and cultural products—notably after the collapse of the Soviet Union—sought to make their case, they had a powerful argument that globalization was an ongoing, ineluctable force. Modernization theorists in the 1950s and 1960s said much the same thing. Modernization theory was subject to withering criticism, much of which applies to the globalization concept as well.

15. Mkandawire makes the point that African intellectuals need "to reconnect to their societies" (*African Intellectuals*, 7). For a rather extreme example of an anthropology of flows that fails to examine the mechanisms and limits by which ideas and cultural patterns travel and insists on their being new without any curiosity about the past, see Arjun Appadurai, *Modernity at Large: Cultural Dimensions of Globalization* (Minneapolis: University of Minnesota Press, 1996).

13

Global Intellectual History

Meanings and Methods

SUDIPTA KAVIRAJ

T wo types of scholarly practice usually pass under the sign of intellectual history, although their cognitive purposes, methodological techniques, and intellectual direction are distinct. This has been a difficulty in the coherence of the discipline. Some historians want to understand how large intellectual ideas or trends cause the events that make history. Their object of epistemic interest is social history, in which they wish to assess the significance of the causal efficacy of ideals and intellectual processes. For a second group of scholars, the objects of analysis are the intellectual systems or processes themselves. The history they study is the history of their making, and "history" in the broader sense forms its context. Global intellectual history is a new discipline in which we can discern the same range of interpretation of its subject and purposes.

All the chapters in this volume accept a common nomenclature of "global intellectual history," albeit without a strict consensus on what this form of intellectual history is. Yet the fact of this collaboration signals at least a vague collective sense that this intellectual history is sensible, definable, and worthwhile. The contributors also believe that the future of intellectual history as a discipline lies in this direction. Accordingly, my remarks in this chapter are confined to the two questions of meaning and method: the different and plausible ways in which various writers construe the nature of the discipline and the methodological implications of each of those constructions.

In an enterprise of this kind, the questions of meaning and method are intertwined. What is "global intellectual history"? How is it best practiced? Evidently, any answer to the second question must depend on how we answer the first. All the chapters here ask this question directly or by implication, as does Christopher Hill (chap. 6), preferring to narrow the same question to "What is global in global intellectual history?" Two types of divisions are evident along two distinct axes. The first difference is between premodern and modern examples of globality. Except for the chapters by Siep Stuurman (chap. 2) and Sheldon Pollock (chap. 3), all the others fall, in some sense, into the temporal field of the *modern*.

Furthermore, there is a discernible clustering of the explorations toward the time that, in each of these societies, can be called the birth of the modern. This time can vary from one society to another: in the eighteenth century in Japan, the nineteenth century in India, and the mid-twentieth century in the African Atlantic. But it is significant that many of the chapters in this book focus on this peculiarly important time, because underlying that is a common belief (which could be inflected very differently) that something happened in the nature of thinking in these societies at these times that makes it imperative to write the history of new thinking in a new way, demanding a more global field of vision.

A second distinction also runs through these chapters: in some cases the globality of approach or address is a result of the analysts' *optional* intentionality, and in others, the authors believe that the nature of the intellectual field can be approached only globally, going beyond the usual "national" template on the study of social thought.

Imputative Globality (or Was There a "Global" Before the Modern?)

Stuurman acknowledges in chapter 2 in his wide-ranging survey of three thinkers drawn from distant, ancient reflective cultures that there was no underlying connective process, which the thinkers did not see, that historians are trying to uncover. For this kind of uncovering, what is uncovered must have existed previously, even though it may have been cognitively inaccessible. An intriguing suggestion underlies Stuurman's comparison of Herodotus, Sima Qian, and Ibn Khaldun that is somewhat similar to the functionalist anthropological argument that internally situated social actors may not be able to see a pattern that an outside observer can, simply because he is outside the structures of patterned intentionality implicit in social behavior.

Anthropological analyses of behavior provide the best examples of such explanations (in the strong sense of the term). An external anthropological observer might find that a group entertained religious beliefs that forced them to burn, in religious worship, a large amount of grain at the end of a an agricultural season. While the social agents might truthfully say that they are acting on the basis of their religious belief that the grain should be offered to the deity in thanksgiving, the anthropologist might point out that this results in the destruction of a potential surplus resource that might lead to a class differentiation in the compactly egalitarian society. The analytical question raised in this case is obviously, and classically, whether an explanation of an action can be something that is not present in the agents' intention. Nonetheless, the truth of the first, narrowly intentional, explanation need not disqualify the explanatory force of the second.

Stuurman suggests that all three of his protagonists were historical theorists of ancient cultures that had to deal with vast nomadic hinterlands. Although they could not have known about one another's reflections, the problem they addressed was *structurally* similar. It is worth considering what this shows in methodological terms: Is there a deep structure here, "deep" in the sense that historical actors and interpreters cannot grasp its existence but that after centuries, historians can? Or is this an anachronistic conceit?

In trying to understand premodern thought, it is important to remember that "worlds" in a suitably relativistic sense existed before our times of insistent and explicit globality. As Pollock insists in chapter 3, all cultures must engage in a process of intellectual "worlding": producing and working with a conception of the maximal stretch of what we know exists, because this is a condition of some essential operations of human thinking. At times, we see cultures with a clear conception that "the world" is more extensive than their relevant community, existing as a gray penumbra outside their own world.

All three of Stuurman's civilizations shared this feature, of a boundary between the civilized and the nomadic across which there was serious exchange. Clearly, there is a "world" conceived here underlying these separate theoretical reflections. Thus we can search for a prehistory of the global, a picture of the world in which writers live inside a nearby and known region, which exists, however, in a relationship of permanent tension and exchange with a far away and less known region. These cultures reflect on what to do with "the unlike" that disturbs the moral and cognitive tranquillity of the known world but nonetheless must be acknowledged and dealt with.

This is a highly rewarding field of comparative, but not connected, intellectual history. The connection is supplied by the modern analyst; it does not exist inside the intentional fields of the history that is being explored, which helps us see the difference between comparative and connected in history writing. Despite much casual interchangeable use of these terms, "comparative history" is quite different from "connected history," which also calls for an intrinsic instead of an extrinsic comparativism. Cases like al-Biruni's study of India can complicate this picture. His analysis begins with a "worlding" of a universe around Islam, but he is forced by the evidence of growing knowledge to admit that what exists outside this frontier is not a nomadic world but a world of a complex but entirely different construction.

From Imputative to Intrinsic Globality

Pollock's chapter, and his work more generally, illustrates a second historical configuration, which may be termed "global" without embarrassment or equivocation. Pollock's examples—Hellenization, Romanization, and Islam—are, in part, similar to Stuurman's but, in part, quite different. All of Stuurman's texts come from inside civilizations founded on some discovered principle of universal applicability, which created a world divided between the part of it in which such principles were realized and the world beyond. The three reflections consider what to do with this boundary: to close it off or to allow it to remain open so that the universalistic principles of their civilizing culture can expand and colonize the outside, which contains the equal danger of being imperiled by forces coming from across that cultural horizon and defeating it.

In contrast, in his chapter, Pollock defines the premodern global differently, avoiding the use of extrinsic connectivity imputed by historians. Above all, he is interested in a different reading of the idea that "the frontier is the engine of history," even though his frontiers are not always spatial. Mughal rulers who were militarily pushed out of Central Asia toward that world's margins, entered another Indo-Islamic world and, in a relatively short historical period, produced a worlding of the social and the political that left a deep impact on the historical constitution of South Asian society. A central thrust of Pollock's writing has been to work a theoretical shift from a nearly causeless spread of religion carried by Sanskrit texts to a harder, historicized picture of what really happened in the *longue durée* in the Sanskrit world and in the shift of attention to the relation of power and social authority, the persistent alliance that power seeks with poetry. This raises a methodological-theoretical question that is similar to Andrew Sartori's view in the modern context. Despite the difference in their historical periods, both Pollock and Sartori are skeptical of the unassisted diffusion of ideas, whether religious, poetic, or cultural. For them, cultural forms spread because of a causal force: in Pollock's case, political power's search for a more poetic aura of authority and, in Sartori's case, the insistent, intangible, but ubiquitous force of expanding networks of capitalist economic interdependence. Culture must be carried by some larger structural agency.

Their cases have different emphases. Pollock's methodological case is intriguing and complex. Once its sacerdotal links were broken, Sanskrit spread with astonishing rapidity across a vast space in South and Southeast Asia, yet as he notes, the causal agency is unclear. This is not a case of an identifiable centralized political power like Rome, which carried a cultural template into new spaces. The "poetry of polity" spread by something like cultural emulation rather than by the coercive power of a single imperial polity. Perhaps like other imperial cosmopolitan spaces, Sanskrit space also, as Pollock shows, demonstrates a feature of all such spatial constellations. Because the principles or styles must be generalized across such huge territories, they necessarily have to be economical and abstract, so consequently they soon require local figurations. Sanskrit *kāvya* thus developed distinctive stylistic variations of regional *ritis*. Still more fascinating is Pollock's demonstration of the peculiar historical dynamic between the cosmopolitan and the vernacular. Abstract Sanskrit poetic forms develop a strange transactional relation with the locally thick life of vernacular literatures.[1] At least initially, the emergence of the vernacular did not require a repudiation of the cosmopolitan. Rather, the vernacular was required precisely in order to inhabit the upper-level cosmopolitan field and to retain a strong aesthetic contact with the life worlds of the regions it encompassed. This shows an interesting feature in the changing historical meanings of the cosmopolitan. Premodern cosmopolitanism was usually predicated on the mastery of two or several cultures. In modern times, cosmopolitanism is often misinterpreted as a universalization of a single dominant culture.[2]

Clearly, there are notable implicit theoretical differences between the first and the second methodological models of approaching premodern global history. The first model offers two kinds of globality. The first is the globality of a single but expansive culture forming the context for the reflections of the three thinkers about what lay inside and what lay beyond, and not intrinsic globality of the historical example itself. The intellectual analysis was not specifically of questions about why these cultures and not others became global, but about how they saw and interpreted their globality by focusing on "the frontier" as a problem. This question is comparativist and was brought into the investigation by historians; it was not present in the intellectual intentions of the authors themselves. Thus, if we work with a strongly interpretivist definition of intellectual history, basically trying to understand what the authors "in their own languages" could in principle have thought (to use the expression introduced by Quentin Skinner), this is not strictly the task of intellectual history.

In contrast, the second model, Pollock's model of the premodern, centers on what I call "intrinsic globality": it is the careful and rigorous scholarly pursuit of an intellectual culture that invents a universalistic principle and spreads across an enormous area. This kind of intellectual history does not bring anything into the subject of cognitive pursuit from outside its time. Instead, it is strictly time intrinsic, but it contains two accompanying observations. The first is the tendency for this global formation to float on top of lower-level cultural constellations of the vernaculars, which, to use a political term, makes this cosmopolitan culture a federal rather than a centralized structure. More recent research into the cosmopolitan overlaps between the Sanskrit and the Persian languages in Mughal India shows that the premodern cosmopolitan also produces, at its margins, fascinating new cultures of transaction. On top of the immense global formations of Sanskrit and Persian, Indian culture saw new overlaps and the historic production of bicultural public spheres forcing modern historians to devise even wider angles of vision to capture these facts.[3]

Peculiarities of the Modern Global

A majority of the chapters in *Global Intellectual History* implicitly posit a strong historical connection between the modern and the global, but this apparently simple assertion also has many possibilities. This connection can be interpreted in several distinctive ways, some reflected in the chapters themselves. Many of the contributors are somewhat vague about the intensity and implications of their claims, and such indeterminacy of meaning gives them the freedom to play with a range of techniques in their historiographical practice.

Authors in this volume generally agree that material and technological conditions emerge in the modern world that make it possible for the first time for the universalist conceptions of dominant cultures to acquire a real global scope. In that sense, modern Western civilization has an interesting dual relation with earlier instances of universalist cultures like the Sanskrit cosmopolis, global Christendom, and the Islamic religious community.

In chapter 7, Cemil Aydin's study of the Islamic world provides an interesting case bridging the two meanings of "global." If anything global in the premodern world can be compared in its imaginative ambition of universality and its actual spatial spread, it is the world of Islam. Islamic expansion is perhaps the most impressive form of premodern globality. In terms of scale, the Islamic cosmopolis, which was a second-order structure that comprised the Persianate universe as a subset, besides the Arabic, North African, Andalusian, and later Southeast Asian components, covered a large part of the world. It was one world, with strong techniques of self-recognition and interpretation, that is, specific means of "worlding" peculiar to itself. Thus its globalized structures had two sides, a powerful and distinctive intellectual impulse based on an explicitly universalistic religion, and an associated military-political organization that carried it materially forward into new space.

Aydin argues persuasively, however, that before the advent of modernity, the Islamic world community meant little substantive or even imaginatively agentive. Politically significant were the imperial formations of the Ottoman, Persian, and Mughal powers, but nothing beyond and encompassing them. The distinctly modern discovery of an Islamic community worldwide reveals two aspects of new global formations of thinking on social matters. Aydin shows that before the emergence of modern cognitive apparatuses, there was no concept of a global Islamic *ummah*. Probably the material scale of self-recognition of Islamic groups was not possible earlier, and in addition, there was no condition to conceive of a collective *agency*, in however minimal a sense.

In contrast, however, Aydin demonstrates the significant role of non-Western intellectuals in producing a conception of global norms. It is striking that some of the signal normative ideas of modern politics—sovereignty, nationalism, and international laws based on human rights—unproblematically traced to a Western provenance by traditional scholarship, actually evolved in a more complex pattern, which fits Samuel Moyn's model of truncated universalism.[4] Norms were enunciated in a universalist form but absentmindedly restricted to exclusively Western settings.[5] Values and norms like these were generalized more by a "non-Western seizure of European universalism, a sort of subaltern fulfillment of . . . Eurocentric values" (Aydin, chap. 7, this volume). Aydin states that the Islamic world responded to new conditions of conceiving universality by subtly altering the meaning of the institution of the caliphate as the leader of a worldwide Muslim community. Particularly interesting is his claim that "the global community has embraced as universal such norms as nationalism, sovereignty, and even human rights, but not as a result of the Europeanization of diverse intellectual traditions in different parts of the world." This was as a transactive production of common norms in which competing anti-Western intellectual trends participated, but Aydin should have added that at every stage in the academic presentation of this history, this subaltern presence and contestation was erased in the retelling, so that the historical re-presentation of this process is far more European than the process itself. It follows that "a new, non-Eurocentric global history" can be written only in dialogue with a new international history (Aydin, chap. 7, this volume).

Aydin's account substantially complicates the received understanding of global thought in modern conditions by challenging a narrative of Western origins and subsequent diffusion of modernist ideals and by suggesting a substitute story of greater plausibility and complexity. However, his narrative is about pure thought—in one sense. The presentation, the offer, and the disputations occur entirely in the sphere of thinking and intellectual production. Except for a rather general reference to "conditions of modernity," these large transformative movements of ideas do not seem to require casual impulses outside themselves. Several of the chapters in *Global Intellectual History* stress interesting methodological complications in our understanding of global thought by raising questions about the precise character and causal weight of those conditions themselves.

Globality and Transformation of Concepts

Janaki Bakhle's exploration in chapter 10 of the thinking of a strange figure of Indian nationalism, V. D. Savarkar, confirms several of these observations and also demonstrates some startling continuities from the premodern to modern. Savarkar's thought is a prime example of the trajectory of modular universalism—the rise of an idea/ideal in the West and its spread to different corners of the world—but a "particularizing universal" idea (in Christopher Hill's phrase) that requires fitting its abstract nature to the conditions of relevant regional history. Bakhle shows that terms like "anarchism" become meaningless through transposition in the political discourses of multiple users from political theorists to police informants, to denote anyone considered a potential threat to civic order.

The paradox is especially striking in Savarkar's case, as he is the great exemplar in Indian thought of the comprehensive adoption of the Western European model of the nation-state, based on an intense affective foundation of cultural homogeneity. But this does not stop all kinds of observers and commentators from designating him as an "anarchist," a definitional adversary of states. Political language certainly "spreads" from Western centers, but what happens to their semantics is strange — circulating toward a descent into meaninglessness. Bakhle's reading of Savarkar captures a second significant feature of the global movement of ideas/ideals. As Hill, too, argues in chapter 6, abstract ideals like nationalism must be mediated to audiences inhabiting specific cultural milieus, often of powerful vernacular regional cultures. Mediation is a condition of the expansion. The absorption of Western ideas of the nation, or of romantic love, depended on their finding a vehicle in preexisting poetic intelligibility. Savarkar may have read Mazzini, but his own ideas were hardly an obedient translation of Italian political discourse, and in any case, his readers would not have heard of Mazzini or his influence on Savarkar. This also shows the longevity of the peculiar structure of two-tiered cosmopolitanism that Pollock points out. A long-term geometry of cosmopolitan thought-structures seems to persist, bridging the premodern and the modern. Although most of the chapters in *Global Intellectual History* are not literary, Bakhle's brief emphasis on the poetry is helpful in understanding the paradoxes of originality. Poetry commands an originary presence of a peculiar kind, and lyricism has undeniable newness that is immediately apparent to its audience, obliterating borrowed intellectual origins. Poetry's great power is that it makes us forget everything except the presentation of the ideas in a lyrical form.

This might also explain a persistent difficulty with readings in intellectual history. When a traditional global intellectual history is presented, it often becomes a story of an entirely one-sided network of "influence" with the implication that "new" ideas are implanted into the minds of conventional non-Western intellectuals who begin to think these unprecedented thoughts. It is a history of truly imperialist ideas that travel to far corners of the world and conquer their imagination. This is often helped by an ignorance of the vernaculars, so that in English or French translations, they are listening to only echoes of their own voices. Local audiences do not read the ideas; they read the poetry that is absurd to attribute to solemn social theorists, and they celebrate the birth of something entirely "new." It is essential to remember that the movement of ideas leads to something like a "translation process" in which the receptive language has thick connotative features that are never quite turned off when foreign ideas are received, and therefore this process cannot be understood except through a truly linguistically and culturally double-sided history.

Intermediation/Intermediaries and the Problem of Unequal Description

Another problem in already existing intellectual histories with a global scope can be illustrated by an example drawn from painting. When painters of battles or of court scenes depicted large bodies of people on huge canvases, they practiced a skilled art of grading individuality. Accordingly, in court scenes, the nobles and aristocrats in the front rows are painted as individuals whose features are carefully rendered, and the others gradually fade into a necessary but faceless presence. Their presence is essential, however, because they show the others as "leaders," noticeable in the midst of a crowd of others condemned to facelessness.

The influence model is defective not simply because of its one-sidedness and the sketchiness of its knowledge about the destination of European ideas. Its Eurocentrism is enhanced by its perfunctory knowledge about where these ideas go and what they are made to do in these different intellectual ecologies. This kind of intellectual history loses its interest in Western ideas the moment they leave European shores on long uncertain journeys. This shows that there can be grades of globality in global history. Influence-history is certainly a recognizable form of global history, but there are serious flaws in the way that globality is conceived. To produce a real global history, historians must shift their focus to the processes of intermediation and to the real life of intermediaries.

Again, there is a "world" in this history, but its various parts are unequally described. It is still a world of entirely European making. The recent history of the British Empire in India has brought attention to this group of people, without whom the large edifices of colonial knowledge would have been impossible.[6] Although the picture that obliterates the structures of power in asymmetric exchanges in colonial knowledge is misleading, it captures the fact that colonialism inaugurates a new epoch of both coercive and emulative transactions on an unprecedented scale. Conventionally, these spaces of cognitive and intellectual exchange were described unevenly. Intellectual production by black intellectuals and the creation of "a black Atlantic" have been opened up to serious investigation only relatively recently.

These studies, including chapter 9 in this volume by Mamadou Diouf and Jinny Prais, confirm the fecundity of the "truncated universals" approach to the history of modern ideas. Black intellectuals initially take ideas of Enlightenment universals literally, which enables them to produce a different geography of connections among various nodes of black intellectual production. Using a second strand of that universalism, they seek to resituate blacks inside world history, and every addition also leads to a recomposition of the geometry of global history (Diouf and Prais, chap. 9, this volume). New approaches also spell a remaking of the fundamental topography of "the black Atlantic," and Diouf and Prais suggest opening the study of a new cognitive object, a black economy of knowledge, which had an effervescent history from the start of the twentieth century. The same impulse to bring forward undescribed parts of that geography is now pushing scholars to explore the intellectual history of the African past in Arabic traditions.[7]

As Diouf and Prais point out, an entry into the intellectual history of Africa and of black peoples has several startling features. It shows a strangely fragmented, tragic global geography. The fatal scatter of black people between Africa and the Americas makes the spatiality of this history—the dismembered world of black experience—different from others, in which at least the spatial integrity of a common heritage of language and experience were not violently mutilated (Diouf and Prais, chap. 9, this volume). Diouf and Prais show how black intellectuals had to innovate from within dominant Western traditions whose advocates often deliberately tried to suffocate their expression, using secrecy, irony, absconding, but nonetheless turning the truncated declaration of universality itself into a weapon against the hypocrisy of nineteenth-century liberalism. This was the triumph of the story of subaltern seizure and the fulfillment of universal ideals (Moyn, chap. 8, this volume).

Parallel to the faded or darkened world of black intellectuals is the case of the other kind of interlocutors, the "native informants," learned men from Polynesia, such as those presented in Vanessa Smith's recuperative history in chapter 4, who made possible the structure of colonial knowledge. Smith highlights an additional dimension of obliteration from memory. As long as the only sources of intellectual history are written texts, they will unavoidably overlook those people who did not themselves write but made others' writing possible. As European knowledge systems, with their methodological rules and their writing conventions, soaked up information about distant parts of the world, they created "centers of circulation" (in Bruno Latour's phrase) in which intermediaries who could access repositories of oral knowledge played a crucial role in providing the preconditions of later events.

Without them, Smith (chap. 4, this volume) emphasizes, this new acquisition of European knowledge could not get off the ground. Her retelling of the amazing, though tragic, story of Joseph Banks's intellectual exchange with Tupaia highlights several features of an astonishing sequence of events of the voyage of discovery and the subsequent narration of this story. Smith traces the remarkable rise of Banks's respect as he slowly comes to appreciate Tupaia's ability to mediate between two cognitive systems. Banks comes to acknowledge the Raiatean as senior not just in age but also in knowledge, an exceptional attitude for a European in that age.

Between the two men, a relation grows that is both reciprocal and interlocutory and therefore dialogical in the true sense, and Banks admires Tupaia's decision to travel with the expedition, a decision driven by his curiosity. Even though it may not have been driven by the methods of modern science, it obviously was no less intense (Smith, chap. 4, this volume). Banks, after all, traveled to the Pacific for a short period and brought his new knowledge into the familiar and secure world of the British capital surrounding the Royal Society. Tupaia, by contrast, left a world in which he had a dominant role but brought it with him as a fund of knowledge. His conduct was much stranger and more inscrutable than that of the Indian scholars who supplied critical information to the British about the Hindu and Muslim social world of South Asia.

Tupaia emerges from the story as a more genuine cultural comparativist than the "scientific" Europeans who treated indigenous knowledge as both true and false at the same time, providing the merely factual ballast out of which Europeans could produce a true picture, even though at first they knew nothing about what it really contained. Actual dialogues in new epistemic fields were transformed in the retelling of stories about the Europeans' discovery of the world, in which the world and its inhabitants had nothing to do except to exist passively as objects of the Western cognitive initiative. It is this entirely skewed conception of internally asymmetric globality, in which its constituent parts are described unequally, that a number of the chapters in this volume (notably, those by Diouf and Prais, Smith, Aydin, and Hill) try to rectify.

The Temporal Ends of the Globality of the Modern

The chapters by Christopher Hill (chap. 6) and Duncan Bell (chap. 11) both center on the question, "What makes intellectual history truly global?" and both are skeptical of the view that globality can appear in a premodern context. In fact, the chapters here that deal with this theoretical question can be grouped into two sections: Aydin, Hill, and Bell clearly believe that true globality is impossible before the arrival of the modern, but they do not explain why this is the case. Moyn and Sartori, however, do and sketch out some of the methodological implications of the different versions of globality. Hill's demonstration of how concepts become global is strictly tied to a story of global modernity, and it makes some interesting comparisons with Sartori's approach.

To the question, "What makes the global?" Hill's answer in chapter 6 is that modern conditions producing various forms of connection, both colonial and noncolonial, provide the necessary causal circumstances. But he makes the unconventional claim that "as concepts moved around the world, they experienced multiple mediations" that "attenuated the concepts' connections to their originators and to the European historical examples from which they were derived," a picture that confirms the process described by Bakhle. By using the example of the Japanese absorption of the idea of "civilization-enlightenment," Hill shows how the demands generated by modern practices induce conceptual change, in the form of both neologisms, which would have been unintelligible in the traditional grammar of concepts, and semantic shifts in conventional terms.[8] Although it is not exactly the same as the truncation model of universal ideas, Hill illustrates a historical version of universality: the concept of civilization by which Japanese society was to be reordered was regarded as "true anywhere, anytime." This reveals an interesting capacity in the historical-universalist idea of progress to force earlier and widely divergent historical and cultural trajectories to arrive at the same final destination.

According to this theory, the preexisting diversity of human history was to be gathered into a single, universal, final stage. Clearly, this universalist conception of progress had powerful imaginative reverberations in all cultures, not just Japan's. The central insight in Hill's narrative is his assertion that the farther a universal ideal travels, the more it will forget its origins and become usable for other and entirely local historical purposes, assisted by the often overlooked but important fact that users in other cultures do not always access ideals from high texts, but from vulgates. The sources might even become irrelevant after a time, when the idea acquires a life of its own. To take a contemporary Indian example, the idea of representative democracy, especially the technical idea of universal suffrage, came to perform a fundamentally transformative operation on traditional caste society, and in this generation, many of the major leaders of this transformation would not know much about where this universal came from and would not be bothered by their ignorance.[9]

Thus, in Hill's intriguing account, "universalization" is used in a shifted meaning, crucially different in its connotation from the standard version of the idea. Scholars exploring the travel and translation of ideas would find Hill's distinction between "universality" and "universalization" helpful in the various contexts of globality. Universality is the quality of a concept that is regarded by its original user as applicable "anywhere, anytime," but universalization is a process familiar to students of non-Western thought. In some contexts, universals in the first sense actually go through a process more like the second. Even concepts that were not meant to be universal are often taken from their original context and applied to contexts that historically have been very different. In each iteration, the concept expands its scope of geographical use, and it also becomes diverse in its actual connotative charge and its intellectual functions, in what precisely it does for people who are using it in their contexts.

The first sense of universality has drawn fierce criticism from critical and postcolonial theory. The second use of "universalization," however, captures an important feature of the circulation of ideas and ideals. "For historians," Hill observes, "the ultimate measure of the universality of an idea must be its incorporation into social practice in places far from its origin, including not only behavior in the world of ideas but also modes of governance and, potentially, resistance" (chap. 6, this volume). A detailed scholarly exploration of these new histories of meaning requires, as Hill states, a change in methods.

Two Methodological Perspectives

The two chapters by Moyn and Sartori address this question more directly, as both recognize that opening up the global field in space and in social depth to include subaltern figures previously ignored raises serious questions of method. Is this new history to be new simply in its embrace of other cultures? Or does this extension also require a new way of writing these histories?

There is a general sense in the entire volume that scope and method have an intimate connection, and most of the chapters reflect on methodological issues relevant to their particular body of material. In chapter 8, Moyn suggests a powerful theoretical model through recent writings about the Haitian revolution. The interpretative deployment of the Haitian uprising adds a twist to an older conventional narrative of the universalization of Enlightenment values. It was a common part of the older narrative to view revolutionary waves to have begun at the center of the radical universe (Paris in 1848) and to have radiated to the world's peripheries, which were conveniently organized in concentric circles from eastern Europe to the Near East to the far ends of the globe. Revolutionary waves spread in ripples or cascades, but understandably the central ideas became fainter and more misinterpreted as they spread to the darkened parts of the world, and universal ideals of liberty and equality evoked lisping imitations from the colonies. Enlightenment ideas were contaminated as well by the grossness of dark vernaculars.[10] This picture of both emulation and inadequacy was central to the period of liberal imperialism, as it endorsed the theory of European intellectual tutelage of colonial societies.[11]

In recent years, in both historical discussions of Haiti and the history of the idea of human rights, a strange inversion was effected on this high narrative of diffusionism.[12] This is clear in a realistic history of the idea of rights, a history that is not content simply to rummage inside textual meanings but is interested also in measuring those ideals, precisely because they are ideals, against relevant practice.[13] Abstract declarations of the rational equality of all human beings, or the universal eligibility for moral autonomy, were seriously reduced by implicit exceptions so well understood that they needed no explicit mention. Women, colonial peoples, colored inhabitants of Western societies, and blacks in America all were either excluded from this declamatory equality or existed on steep rights slopes that fell away from the center.

Another example of a similar claim distorted by similar slopes of difficulty was the idea of the "open" public sphere, which was open to the circle of white, male, propertied, educated citizens but was steeply sloped for other prospective entrants.[14] Moyn describes this as a model of truncated universals, "a general one for conceptual spread across large spaces." This model has several historical advantages. It notes a purely *formal* feature in the exceptionless universalistic enunciation of these ideas. A second interesting feature of this model is the role played by subaltern agency: it is the subaltern groups that must trust the literal universalistic offer and demand its real fulfillment. In a remarkable inversion of the conventional influence model, which names European culture as the universal instructor of the world, this model shows liberal or socialist universalism as intrinsically truncated. But through a kind of cunning of reason, subaltern groups' belief and agency open up a global field in which, through a complex mixture of absorption, emulation, misunderstanding, and catachresis, these ideals move toward occasional realization.

Moyn's chapter also points to a serious difficulty with this model in its idealist theory of "autoglobalization." This complex of ideals does not require any contextual causal field that starts the process of its demand for realization. The *formal* character of the idea itself obviates that requirement: the universal interpellation built into the form itself is a sufficient cause or, rather, a sufficient substitute for a cause in the usual sense. On this basis, Moyn introduces two significant qualifications into this method. Universalizing concepts available to a particular group at any time may be several, and there can be an implicit competition among them. The competition can be of two types. Moyn's example is of the simultaneous availability of different ideals of political life—the collective right of sovereignty and the human rights of ordinary individuals. In the early decades of the United Nations, self-determination was picked up far more widely than human rights. In some cases, the adoption of one universalistic idea required the rejection of another, as in the liberal and socialist conceptions of rights regimes, so that each necessarily obstructed the adoption of the other. The collapse of the imagination around conventional socialism in the 1980s might be one background reason for the emergence of the new utopia of human rights on a world scale.

The second of Moyn's methodological requirements endorses Hill's remark that some global ideas are "particularizing universals," so that they are capable of spreading from their points of origin yet require at each site of reception a translation into the vernacular. Although Hill's chapter does not directly address the methodological debate about autoglobalization and the demand for a causal field, it accords with Moyn's insistence that the act of subaltern seizure and interpretation is crucial, as the historical constitution of the place in which ideas are received inflects their meaning for agents who wish to act on that history through them. Moyn's methodological analysis produces an interesting combination of admitting the normative power of ethical-political ideals purely out of their deontic force but also showing a field of competition. In any case, there is usually some background of intended action behind the choice of these ideas.

In chapter 5, Sartori offers a forceful and comprehensive methodological challenge to the entire project of global intellectual history. Ideas in modern times travel between historically asymmetric societies. Without denying that in terms of scale, globality did appear in history before the advent of the modern, Sartori presents two fundamental arguments for scholars in this discipline. His argument is recognizably Marxist, although his methodological emphasis in this chapter, and his interpretative practice in modern Bengali intellectual history, carefully disentangles it from reductionism.[15] In a general sense, Sartori and Pollock raise a historicist concern that is at the heart of any intellectual history with explanatory ambitions.[16] Of course, it is possible to practice with great subtlety a form of intellectual history, particularly in the familiar terrains of social and political theory, in which the primary question is of textual hermeneutics, to understand with clarity and performable precision what exactly the questions behind a thinker's texts were, what the nature of the "language" of his thought was, and exactly how he answered the questions. In the most familiar and forceful presentation of the case for this version of textual reading, Quentin Skinner criticized the subtle attribution of individual textual arguments to a collective subject like a social class. Objections of the Cambridge school to a secret, illegitimate methodological collectivism in the reading of political theory blocked further speculation on this subject.

Although Sartori draws on the Marxist tradition, he does not use this implausible idea of a reflection of "class consciousness" in social theory. Instead, he draws his methodological inspiration from a very different segment of Marxist theory: its elaboration of a theory of abstraction and reification. But the question of a historical connection between social interest and social thought remains important despite these objections, because intellectual history can have many forms, and not all of them consist primarily of reading texts. Whenever study of social thought is practiced in a less individual, and less textual, form, when a strand of social thinking is studied in the context of historical change, the question of the role of social interest in rational plausibility is immediately revived.

Sartori's suggestion is powerful simply because it raises the under-lying question of the causal background of the acceptance and efficacy of ideas in a general form. Following the Marxist tradition, Sartori is not convinced that ideas attract people by their simple rational force or validity. Rather, ideas become plausible by the play of interests and constellations of historical circumstances. At least, when we find evidence of circulation of ideas between societies, not transmission between individual theorists, there is always a second methodological question to answer, regarding what propels that circulation. Sartori's argument, however, does not simply demand a circulatory causal-ity. His more specific suggestion is that in modern times, the rise of the capitalist economy produces a new kind of abstract interrelation among subjectified individuals—"real abstractions," in his terms—which creates the conditions for the rapid and irresistible circulation of those ideas. As Moyn observes, this move obviates the necessity to depend on the two common methods of intellectual history: the model of causeless circulation by virtue of the deontic force of truncated uni-versals and the model of situated appropriation. The distinctiveness of Sartori's use of Marxism is that what he expects to be generalized across the world is not a pattern of events but a logic of processes. Accordingly, he escapes the charge of either a class reduction of ideas or a replication of uniform patterns of structural development.

One secondary implication of Sartori's version of this argument is significant: it is skeptical of the recent invocation of an appellation of "early modernity" in the case of seventeenth- and eighteenth-century Indian history because for Sartori, the birth of the modern is closely connected to the rise of a capitalist political economy, which was not available in precolonial India.[17] Indeed, what historians have shown is the rise, and sometimes the immediate fall, of strands of change, which are similar to aspects of the European "modern"—strands such as the spread of a commercial economy, the rise of an instrumentalist conception of *niti*, a more accurate sense of linear historical time—that appear and collapse after a while or continue without any accom-panying reinforcing changes to move the society toward a general modern transformation. Such single strands of social change do not demand a fundamental change in conceptual structures. Historians of modernity must believe either that "enlightenment ideas" do not need a nonintellectual cause or that they do, and they must specify what that cause or causal field is.

Sartori's approach also raises problems of method. The first question is one featured in more complex forms of Marxist analyses. Marxists generally agree that capitalism was "modern but not Western in any profound way," and therefore its rapid spread from the points of contingent origin to other spaces did not raise for them a particularly hard problem of "the West versus the rest." Instead, the relation between capitalist and precapitalist was far more significant, and it was a boundary that was dynamic in both space and time. Despite a general consensus among Marxists that the rise of capitalism in the West established a capitalist world economy that brought the rest of the world's economies under its dominance, there was considerable disagreement regarding the nature of this "subsumption." One opinion was that capitalism began to influence and transform those societies through its trade and colonial contacts themselves and gradually and substantively subsumed those economies. Others remained skeptical of this power of distance causation and insisted that "the logic of capitalism" could have serious results only when these economies' production itself was undergoing capitalist transformation, when capitalism became a matter of experience rather than an object of elite desire. Thus the "logic of capitalism" wavers between an internal and an external causal field.

Two features of Sartori's arguments may bring similar objections. First, he tends to speak rather generally and, consequently, vaguely of the power of "capital," rather than of capitalist economic structures. This expansive locution raises the question of whether it is a reference to the narrowly economic logic of capitalist production or to associated, fundamental modern transformations. True, this expansive language avoids the usual pitfalls of reductionist explanation, but it can suffer from the opposite problem of insufficient clarity in causal attribution. Some strands of Marxist thinking, such as that of Georg Lukács, went further along these lines to claim that modernity introduced several interconnected processes with parallel logics of "reification," especially the bureaucratic operations of the Weberian state. This would offer an expanded version of Sartori's case that modernity inserts a new kind of "structural logic" into social worlds, which forms the background for the attraction and acceptance of concepts of modern subjectivity. There is no doubt that conditions of modernity—again vaguely invoked—attract large social groups, usually among educated elites, to concepts of a particular theoretical family, from the field of economy to the state to ethical life. Concepts from both the liberal and the socialist vocabularies, which advocated competing responses to the challenges and opportunities of modernity, have experienced this kind of generalized circulation. Sartori's position seems to be closer to the more conventional emphasis on "political economy" than the Lukácsian expanded argument.[18]

Second, even if we acknowledge that a background condition for the attractiveness of modern conceptual systems is the presence of capitalism, the meaning of its "presence" remains ambiguous. This puzzle is logically similar to that regarding the subsumption of economies into the world system, but its point is more significant. Even under formal subsumption, commodities or goods produced in economies under precapitalist conditions made a definitive journey through the different levels of the system of circulation. Here, however, circulation refers to ideas, something more intangible. For these concepts to make sense and appear attractive, what is the intensity or the level of "presence" required? Surely, intellectuals in mid-nineteenth-century Bengal did not experience capitalist economic relations in any direct sense: to anchor the conceptual demand in some form of experience would fail. Yet equally certainly, cosmopolitan intellectuals felt the enchantment of emancipatory ideals of freedom and equality sufficiently strongly to believe that either a liberal or a socialist utopia could be realized "anywhere anytime" and to write the texts and devise political practices that they did. Sartori's study of modern Bengali intellectual history is a fine-grained textual analysis of individual texts and their writers that does not suggest a straightforward causal relation with the abstract logic of capitalism or state formation.

Conclusion

A way out of these dilemmas could be to view these approaches to intellectual history not as exclusive to one another but as complementary or, in a different solution, to regard intellectual history as an internally heterogeneous discipline that allows pursuits of different levels of generality requiring appropriately different degrees of causal modulation. In a study of the rise and circulation of concepts like "the market," "the state," and "the law," the general historical processes that Sartori invokes must be given causal priority. In a study of the historical semantics of social and political principles like freedom and equality, besides these general conditions of modernity, capitalism and the idea of *Rechtstaat* are significant, but so is their truncated universalist form. In reading individual texts and grasping the "point" of theoretical utterances, these larger and grosser causalities would be less appropriate, because we shall be moving out of the level of explanation into textual hermeneutics.

Global intellectual history is an immense discipline, and it is composed of diverse reading practices. Some forms of intellectual history study comprehensive structures of theory, like liberalism or socialism; others follow histories of clusters of ideas like "rights" or "freedom"; still others ask why a theorist wrote an interrogative sentence instead of an assertoric one. Methods that clarify these tasks are bound to be different, and global intellectual history is bound to have many methodological choices. The questions that arise from Sartori's emphatic restatement of the demand for historical causality and from his skepticism about taking ideas as sufficient causes for their own circulation must continue to be addressed if the discipline of global intellectual history is to move forward. We must think about what the discipline means, that is, what it studies, which in turn will decide how it can best be studied.

There undoubtedly is a link between the globality we experience in the present and the globality we seek in history. The brute fact of the global may have increased our sensitivity to the global networks of the past. We live in a global world in which militants inspired by radical Islam can spread terror in Western cities, and democratic ideas can spread through the fugitive ubiquity of the social websites to undermine invincible autocracies. Two facts are undeniable in this world. The forces of modernity spread irresistibly across the globe—but unevenly, unequally, and differently. Modernity, therefore, is not a force that makes the world more uniform but actually what makes it more diverse. A simple implication follows from this acknowledgment for the history of ideas, because the spread of modernity is inextricably linked to the circulation of modes of thought. Circulation is a strange and complex process subject to the "cunning" of history. When ideas reach other cultures, their futures become strange and uncertain and cause surprises. In this astonishing history, even those non-Western figures who tried hard to follow the Western thinkers they admired often turned out to have come, to their own surprise, to think thoughts that were their own.

Notes

1. Although these are not abstract in the sense in which Andrew Sartori (chap. 5, this volume) glosses Marx's thesis about capitalism.
2. The new liberal cosmopolitanism grinds down particularities in favor of a merciless standardization around the figure of a rational individual with human rights in his mind and a McDonald's hamburger in his hand. It is interesting to note that there is some curious affiliation between conditions of modernity and this kind of travesty of cosmopolitan culture. The conservative Wahhabi conception of Islam—in which all Muslims of the world think and act exactly like those who favor their recidivist ideology—is a mirror image of the Western liberal utopia.
3. Such cultures present serious challenges for modern scholarship in many different ways. One of the most obvious is that contemporary intellectuals understood these transactions because they were bilingual and bicultural, but the entrenchment of habits of monolingualism in modern scholarship makes it especially hard for moderns to open them up historically.
4. There is a remarkable similarity in the arguments, even though this is not an instance of truncated universals in the strict sense. In some ways, the processes could also be likened to what Christopher Hill calls "particularized universals."
5. Like John Stuart Mill's famous assertion in *On Liberty* that representative government was normatively the best form but that historical conditions prevented it from being realized anywhere outside civilized Western Europe.
6. Most notably, C. A. Bayly's remarkable work, *Empire and Information: Intelligence Gathering and Social Communication in India, 1780–1870* (Cambridge: Cambridge University Press, 1996). I feel uneasy about this research because it might implicitly encourage a revision of the picture of imperial

rule into an entirely amiable cultural cooperation devoid of the operations of power.

7. But it is possible that new research through initiatives like the Iffriqiya colloquium, by introducing an Arabic lingual and reflective strand into this African knowledge economy, might shift both the space and the history even further.

8. In the Western context, similar developments were explored in Terence Ball, James Farr, and Russell L. Hanson, *Political Innovation and Conceptual Change* (Cambridge: Cambridge University Press, 1989).

9. This in itself is not surprising, and it confirms the arguments by Moyn and Hill about truncated universals and the declining relevance of origins.

10. "These walking lies had nothing left to say to their brothers; they only echoed. From Paris, from London, from Amsterdam we would utter the words 'Parthenon! Brotherhood!' and somewhere in Africa or Asia lips would open . . . thenon! . . . therhood!'" Jean-Paul Sartre, preface to *The Wretched of the Earth*, by Franz Fanon (Harmondsworth: Penguin, 1963), 7.

11. John Stuart Mill's analysis of India in *On Liberty* is a classic example of this line of thought.

12. Susan Buck-Morss, *Hegel, Haiti and Universal History* (Pittsburgh: University of Pittsburgh Press, 2009); Samuel Moyn, *The Last Utopia: Human Rights in History* (Cambridge, Mass: Harvard University Press, 2010). It is important to note the various advantages of conventional diffusionism. It preserved the idea of Europe as the center of the human universe; yet the "weakening" of the ideals and their realization as they spread outward also legitimized the postponement of colonial enlightenment. As Mill's reasoning showed, Indians could be ennobled by the idea of a distant achievement of rationality but that did not imply an imminent offer of political rights.

13. Moyn, *Last Utopia*.

14. Critics of Jürgen Habermas's work showed this emphatically in Craig Calhoun, ed., *Habermas and the Public Sphere* (Cambridge, Mass.: MIT Press, 1992).

15. Andrew Sartori, *Bengal in Global Concept History: Culturalism in the Age of Capital* (Chicago: University of Chicago Press, 2008).

16. This argument is shared by all historicist approaches, although Marxism introduces some special kinds of explanatory considerations and thus differs from other forms.

17. I do not want to digress into the rich and interesting discussion about "early modernity."

18. With liberal borrowings from Max Weber, as Jürgen Habermas demonstrated in *Theory of Communicative Action*, trans. Thomas McCarthy, 2 vols. (Boston: Beacon Press, 1984).

Contributors

CEMIL AYDIN is associate professor of history at the University of North Carolina–Chapel Hill. He is the author of *The Politics of Anti-Westernism in Asia: Visions of World Order in Pan-Islamic and Pan-Asian Thought* (Columbia University Press, 2007).

JANAKI BAKHLE is associate professor of history at Columbia University, where she teaches South Asian history. Her first book was *Two Men and Music: Nationalism, Colonialism and the Making of an Indian Classical Tradition* (Oxford University Press, 2005), and she is now at work on Vinayak Damodar Savarkar, known as the chief ideologue of Hindu fundamentalism.

DUNCAN BELL is a senior lecturer in the Department of Politics and International Studies at the University of Cambridge and a fellow of Christ's College. He works on assorted issues in political theory, international relations, and British and American intellectual history. He is the author of *The Idea of Greater Britain: Empire and the Future of World Order, 1860–1900* (Princeton University Press, 2007) and the editor of several collections.

FREDERICK COOPER is professor of history at New York University. His most recent book, coauthored with Jane Burbank, is

Empires in World History: Power and the Politics of Difference (Princeton University Press, 2010). Cooper is currently completing a study of citizenship in France and French Africa after World War II.

MAMADOU DIOUF is Leitner Family Professor of African Studies and History, Columbia University, where he also directs the Institute for African Studies. His most recent book, coedited with Ifeoma Nwankwo, is *Rhythms of the Afro-Atlantic World: Rituals and Remembrances* (University of Michigan Press, 2010). Diouf is currently completing a monograph on youth, citizenship, and politics in urban Senegal.

CHRISTOPHER L. HILL is adjunct associate research scholar, Weatherhead East Asian Institute, Columbia University. He focuses on the transnational history of literary genres and social thought. He is the author of *National History and the World of Nations: Capital, State, and the Rhetoric of History in Japan, France, and the United States* (Duke University Press, 2008) and is now at work on the rise of the naturalist novel and its movement around the world in the late nineteenth and early twentieth century.

SUDIPTA KAVIRAJ, professor in the Department of Middle Eastern, South Asian, and African Studies at Columbia University, is a specialist in intellectual history and Indian politics. He works on two fields of intellectual history—Indian social and political thought in the nineteenth and twentieth centuries and modern Indian literature and cultural production. His most recent book is *The Imaginary Institution of India* (Columbia University Press, 2010).

SAMUEL MOYN is professor of history at Columbia University, where he has taught since 2001. His most recent book is *The Last Utopia: Human Rights in History* (Harvard University Press, 2010).

SHELDON POLLOCK is William B. Ransford Professor of Sanskrit and Indian Studies at Columbia University. He is the general editor of the new Murty Classical Library of India (Harvard University Press), and his last book is *The Language of the Gods in the World of Men: Sanskrit, Culture, and Power in Premodern India* (University of California Press, 2006).

JINNY PRAIS, assistant director of the Institute of African Studies at Columbia University, holds a doctorate in history and women's studies from the University of Michigan. She also lectures in the Department of Middle Eastern, South Asian, and African Studies at Columbia.

ANDREW SARTORI, associate professor of history at New York University, is an intellectual historian of modern South Asia, with a special focus on Bengal. His first book was *Bengal in Global Concept History: Culturalism in the Age of Capital* (University of Chicago Press, 2008), and he is currently working on the history of liberal political-economic and political-theoretical ideas in the same period.

VANESSA SMITH is associate professor of English at the University of Sydney. Her writings straddle the eighteenth and nineteenth centuries and are primarily concerned with issues of intercultural contact. Her most recent book is *Intimate Strangers: Friendship, Exchange, and Pacific Encounters* (Cambridge University Press, 2010).

SIEP STUURMAN has taught European history at Erasmus University in Rotterdam and at Utrecht University. Author of *François Poulain de la Barre and the Invention of Modern Equality* (Harvard University Press, 2004), Stuurman's last book, *De uitvinding van de mensheid* (Bert Bakker, 2010) (*The Invention of Humanity*), was a best seller in the Netherlands and is being translated into English.

Index

CPSIA information can be obtained
at www.ICGtesting.com
Printed in the USA
LVHW111153080919
630308LV00003B/575/P